P9-CFV-999

Biba's
TASTE *of* ITALY

OTHER BOOKS BY BIBA CAGGIANO

Italy al Dente: Pasta, Risotto, Gnocchi, Polenta, Soup

From Biba's Italian Kitchen

Northern Italian Cooking

Trattoria Cooking

Modern Italian Cooking

Biba's

TASTE *of* ITALY

Recipes from the
Homes, Trattorie,
and Restaurants of
Emilia-Romagna

Biba Caggiano

WM

WILLIAM MORROW
75 YEARS OF PUBLISHING
An Imprint of HarperCollins*Publishers*

HarperCollins books may be purchased for educational, business, or sales promotional use. For information please write: Special Markets Department, HarperCollins Publishers Inc., 10 East 53rd Street, New York, NY 10022.

FIRST EDITION

Designed by Mauna Eichner

Photographs by Stuart Schwartz

Printed on acid-free paper

Library of Congress Cataloging-in-Publication Data
Caggiano, Biba.
    Biba's taste of Italy : recipes from the homes, trattorie, and restaurants of Emilia-Romagna / Biba Caggiano.
        p.   cm.
    ISBN 0-688-15815-3
    1. Cookery, Italian–Northern style.   2. Cookery–Italy–Emilia-Romagna.   I. Title
TX723.2.N65 C34 2001
641.5945'4–dc21   00–059451

01   02   03   04   05   QW   10 9 8 7 6 5 4 3 2 1

641.5945
CAG

3/01

TO MY HUSBAND, VINCENZO,

From Bologna to New York to Sacramento,

Through thick and thin, with more love than ever

CONTENTS

ACKNOWLEDGMENTS

Where does one begin giving thanks to the many people who directly or indirectly have contributed to this book? In Emilia-Romagna, I must begin with my family, friends, and acquaintances, whose collective culinary knowledge and experiences I was able to tap into, time after time, and with whom I share the unique bond of having been raised on the splendid food of Emilia-Romagna. Many loving thanks to my brother, Gianni, and his wife, Emma, a wonderful regional cook, who, with her many sisters, contributed several recipes for this book. Thanks to my sister, Carla, and her husband, Beppe. Thanks to my nieces and nephews, Daniela, Maurizio, Marcello, and Maurizia, all enthusiastic table companions, and fearless food critics. (A virtue or failing most Italians share.) Thanks to Enzo and Gilberto, longtime owners of the splendid Rodrigo restaurant in Bologna, who always share with me good food and invaluable expertise. Thanks to Ivan and Barbara Albertelli of Hostaria da Ivan in Roccabianca, Parma, for their superlative food and for their unrestrained enthusiasm for the classic food of their area. Thanks to the extremely talented Alessandra Buriani and Fabio Cavicchi of Ristorante Buriani in Pieve di Cento, for their commitment to uphold the glories of the region's food while updating and refining it.

Thanks to the cooks of the many little trattorie scattered throughout the region who still serve the type of generous food that sustained past generations: Gigina in Bologna, Da Pippo in Cesenatico, Da Amerigo in Savigno, Dolce e Salato in San Pietro in Casale, Quattro Colonne in Rimini, and so many more.

Thanks to Dott. A. Egaddi of Parma Alimentare, to Dott. Paolo Tramelli of Consorzio Prosciutto di Parma, and Dott. Igino Morini and Dott. Leo Bertozzi of Consorzio Parmigiano-Reggiano for their support. Also a special thanks to Renzo Cattabiani, the now-retired *Segretario Provinviale* of Parma's Consorzio Parmigiano-Reggiano, for the many years of friendship and assistance, and to Dr. Gianna Spezia of Servizio Turismo of Bologna for her kindness and availability to answer my many requests.

In this country, I want to thank deeply a handful of very important people:

My husband, Vincenzo, my constant travel companion and greatest supporter, who, while attending the University of Medicine in Bologna many years ago, fell totally in love with the food of Bologna and of the region.

My daughters, Carla and Paola, who love the food of Emilia-Romagna just as much as I do (especially *tortellini in brodo*).

To my agents and friends, Maureen and Eric Lasher, for their constant encouragement, and for their brilliance in steering me to great career choices.

To Harriet Bell and Pam Hoenig, both superb editors, whose guidance has been invaluable.

To my immensely gifted kitchen staff, Don Brown, John Eichhorn, T. K. Kodsuntie, Tony Sanguinetti, Cindy, Paul, Dylan, and Henry, for all their help and for having to put up with me during deadline.

My thanks also goes to the Ferrari-Carano Vineyards & Winery for their beautiful estate, which was used as a backdrop for the jacket photo.

Thanks also to Williams-Sonoma in Sacramento and William Glen for the use of their tableware and dinnerware as seen in the interior photos.

And, finally, I want to thank Emilia-Romagna, my beautiful region, for having enriched my life with so many layers of culinary and cultural experiences, and for having taught me that the daily ritual of food preparation is as much about love as it is about food.

This book is a very modest tribute to the food of my region.

LOMBARDY

VENETO

E2

E54

Zibello *Po River*

Piacenza

Busseto

Roncole Verdi • Soragna

Travio

Colorno

Po River

San Secondo

Guastalla

Mirandola

Fiorenzuola

Castell' Arquato

Fidenza

E2

Carpi

Pieve di Cento

E7 • Ferrara

Comacchio

Bobbio

Salsomaggiore

Parma

Nonantola

Altedo

Adriatic Sea

Fornovo

Felino

Reggio nell' Emilia

Modena

E2

Bologna

Langhirano

A15

Maranello

Bazzano

Lugo

Ravenna

Vignola

Monteveglio

Castel-San-Pietro

LIGURIA

Savigno

Sasso-Marconi

Imola

E2

Faenza

E6

Castel Bolognese

E1

E6

Riolo Terme

Brisighella

Forli

Cesenatico

Castrocaro Terme

Bertinoro

Cesena

Ligurian Sea

Predappio

E2

Rimini

Riccione

Sogliano al Rubicone

0 Miles 10 20 30 40

0 Kilometers 40

TUSCANY

SAN MARINO

MARCHE

© 2000 Jeffrey L. Ward

SWITZERLAND

AUSTRIA

FRANCE

Milan

LOMBARDY

VENICE

VENETO

SLOVENIA

PIEDMONT

LIGURIA

Genoa

EMILIA-ROMAGNA

Bologna

Florence

MARCHE

Adriatic Sea

Ligurian Sea

TUSCANY

UMBRIA

ITALY

Rome

Tyrrhenian Sea

Naples

SARDINIA

0 Miles 100 200

0 Kilometers 200

SICILY

Emilia-Romagna

MY EMILIA-ROMAGNA

f the cuisine of Emilia-Romagna had a symbol, it would be a large sheet of thin, golden homemade pasta, a sheet so large that it would cover and embrace the whole region. It is a region made up of mountains, lakes, great fertile plains, and glorious sea, and it has given Italy and the rest of the world a rich, luscious cuisine noted for its superlative ingredients and long tradition. Emilia-Romagna is my region. Bologna, the capital, is my native city, and this is a book about its food, today kept alive by dedicated home cooks and by the many trattorie and restaurants that still serve and strive to preserve the great traditional food of the region.

There was a time, not so long ago, when a woman's kingdom was the kitchen. Women made the food that nurtured their families. They were bakers, pasta makers, and skilled cooks. The food they prepared was the same food their mothers and grandmothers cooked, uncompromisingly regional, simple, and flavorful. They took pride in what they did and were in complete charge of their domain. Even during the Second World War, when it was almost impossible to find and afford ingredients, these women somehow managed to put food on the table. Not only did they manage but, with resourcefulness and *fantasia*, they created tasty dishes with the few humble ingredients they had at hand. My mother was one of those women.

My brother, sister, and I grew up during the Second World War. We lived in a two-hundred-year-old five-story apartment building facing one of the most beautiful cobble-stone squares of Bologna, Piazza San Domenico, named after the thirteenth-century church that stands majestically at the other end of the piazza. The piazza was our outdoor living room. It was the place where the neighborhood kids met and where the elderly sat under the large trees to escape the oppressive summer heat. Sometimes, touched by the glory of a beautiful summer day, we would forget briefly about the war that was raging all around us, about the bombs falling in the middle of the night, about the cold, dark cellar of our apartment building where our family took refuge, and we would pretend that the war had ended, that no planes were bombing our cities, and our lives had returned to normality. When the war did end in 1945, I was nine years old, my brother was eleven, and my sister was six. Italy was half-destroyed, and my father, like the majority of other Italians, was left without a job. During those hard years of coping and making do, my mother became a magician at preparing wonderful dishes out of a handful of basic ingredients. Those were years of extreme frugality, where one pot of bean soup fed us for days, and polenta was a mainstay because it was filling and inexpensive. Occasionally, eggs, flour, and a few scrawny chickens could be found and were quickly transformed into almost luxurious dishes by the magic hands of my mother. Our kitchen, which, because of its large black wood-burning oven, was the only warm room of the house, became our sanctuary. It was where we congregated, talked about our hopes, and expressed our fears. Among all the disarray and destruction, the food my mother cooked was the only stable part of our lives. It was in that large unadorned kitchen that I first stirred the sauce and the polenta. It was there that I helped my mother make the soup, and stuffed myself with roasted chestnuts. It was also there that I learned to love food, because its preparation often was the only carefree moment of our day.

My father eventually found a new job, Italy began to recover, and life became full of possibilities again. During the years of my childhood and young adulthood, the world still seemed a very large place. The trip from Milan to New York took eighteen hours by plane.

It took nine days to travel from Genoa to New York by ship. Television arrived in Italy in the early fifties, and Italy struggled toward a postwar recovery. At that time, the food of Italy was still strictly regional.

In the span of fifty years, Italy has become affluent, urban, and highly industrialized. What was once an agricultural society is now a fast-paced, rich, diversified country. Women have left the home kitchens, the factories, and the fields for the universities. They have become doctors, lawyers, and bankers. They raise their children and meet new more complex challenges. They strive for acceptance and equality and, in the process, have lost some of their culinary traditions.

Even in a food-loving region such as Emilia-Romagna, one can see culinary changes. Not too long ago, Bologna and the other major cities of Emilia-Romagna routinely served the rich, sensuous food of the region. The cooking of Bologna, with its silky hand-made pasta dishes, was legendary. Pride was evident everywhere and one didn't need to leave town in order to eat great traditional food at reasonable prices. But progress, prosperity, and a faster pace of life have changed the culinary landscape of the larger cities of the region. While some restaurants and trattorie still serve the same time-honored preparations, others, catering primarily to tourists, seem to have become complacent and serve food that is often disappointing.

But if the food of the larger cities is not what it used to be, the food of the little trattorie and restaurants scattered throughout the rich farmland, the hill towns, and small coastal towns of the region seem to be enjoying a revival. In these places, where the pace of daily life is still felt, good food is everywhere, food prepared by humble cooks who are indebted to their ancestors and relish their traditions just as their mothers and grandmothers did. Here you can still find first-quality basic ingredients from the immediate area.

Quite often the cooks in these small establishments are women. That is probably why the food they serve is homey and reassuring. This *cucina delle donne* is an extension of the food of the home. These women have magic hands. They roll out perfect pasta, knead dough for magnificent bread, prepare complex ragùs, and turn the splendid ingredients of the region into fragrant, succulent dishes. Their experience and wisdom in the kitchen is innate, because the love of food was breathed into them at an early age. These women are the keepers of the flame of the wonderful, traditional food of Emilia-Romagna.

The food of Emilia-Romagna is as diversified as the rich tapestry of its history and the individuality of its people. Because Emilia-Romagna borders on five others regions—Veneto, Lombardy, Liguria, Tuscany, and the Marche—the food has long been influenced by these regions, as well as by its geographical landscapes and local history. The differences are evident even within the region, in the smaller towns and villages, where home cooks and chefs alike will tell you proudly of their traditional dishes and point out the uniqueness of their food.

The differences in cooking styles between Emilia and Romagna are even more remarkable. The food of Emilia is traditional, not prone to experimentation, and relies heavily on local ingredients such as balsamic vinegar, Parmigiano-Reggiano, prosciutto di Parma, and many other quality pork products. This is the land of great stuffed pasta dishes such as tortellini, anolini, tortelli, lasagne alla Bolognese, and rich, complex ragùs, which are combined in blissful union with the splendid, golden homemade tagliatelle of the area. In Emilia, most pasta dishes are lightly tinged with the red of the sweet, locally produced tomato paste or *conserva di pomodoro*, the homemade preserved tomato sauce that is put up for winter cooking. These dishes are prepared with the sweet butter of the local farms, and milk, not cream, is used to lighten a sauce, while fresh herbs and spices are used sparingly (with the exception, perhaps, of nutmeg, a vital ingredient in the filling for tortellini).

The cooking of Emilia is rich and succulent. The Emiliani take a slice of pale, tender veal, coat it with bread crumbs, sauté it in butter, top it with prosciutto and Parmigiano, and simmer it in wine until the cheese is melted, then serve it sprinkled with shaved white truffles!

The lusty cooking of Romagna is more open to experimentation. Seafood is a mainstay and is used exuberantly in pasta sauces, salads, and splendid *brodetti* (seafood stews). Garlic is used in moderation, since its strong aroma would overpower the delicate flavor of the fish. Meats and fowl are predominantly cooked on open-air spits. The fresh pasta of Romagna is paired not only with a meat-sausage ragù, but also with a variety of shellfish, fresh herbs, and fresh tomatoes. *Peperoncino*, chile pepper, borrowed from central Italian regions, is used in many preparations. Olive oil is the fat of choice. The Romagnoli wait for the fresh catch of the day, then grill large *grigliate miste*, a variety of seafood, in the straightforward manner of the Adriatic coast, brushed only with extra virgin olive oil and lemon juice. Perhaps it is because of all these differences that the gastronomy of Emilia-Romagna is so captivating.

As a teenager, I spent a few weeks each year vacationing on the splendid beaches of Romagna. Rimini, Riccione, Cattolica, Milano Marittima, and Cesenatico were, for me, enchanting small coastal towns that had miles of sandy white beaches, a gentle, placid sea, and great food. I would look forward to eating dishes that my mother never cooked—large plates of homemade tagliatelle or spaghettini loaded with succulent tiny fresh clams, or plump mussels and a bit of *peperoncino* or seafood risotto prepared with a rich assortment of shellfish. There were mussels and clams served on the half-shell, and mouthwatering *brodetto,* made with an incredible variety of local fish. But what I loved most about the food of Romagna were the appetizers. Every little trattoria or restaurant displayed large platters of them—seafood salads, marinated anchovies and vegetables, local sausages and salami, marinated cheeses, and *piadina*, the local flat unleavened bread, topped with prosciutto. We ate this food in tiny, unpretentious trattorie, crowded together around wooden tables with no tablecloths. We drank local wine and laughed and lingered at the table for hours. In these small trattorie, one wouldn't dare to ask for lasagne alla Bolognese or tortellini in brodo, typical fare in Emilia. Instead, one would discover the joy of a new regional dish that used local ingredients, was simply prepared, and tasted great.

That is the food that still excites me. My quest and my passion for the mouthwatering food of Emilia-Romagna has called me back time after time. There has not been a day since I left Bologna as the young bride of an Italian American doctor in 1960 that I have not yearned for the food of my region. After twenty-five years of cooking professionally, first as a cooking teacher, then as a restaurant chef-owner, television chef, and author, I can truly say that the food of my region has been a constant source of inspiration in all I have done. Bologna, capital of Emilia-Romagna, and still home to my brother, sister, and extended family, is the first place I visit when I return to Italy. The first meal I have is Bolognese, with all the trimmings, and it keeps us at the table for hours, generally at the home of my brother or sister. Then, on succeeding days, we all go to the little trattorie that members of my family have discovered. And in these unassuming little places that I love so much, where the mother is generally in the kitchen and the father, daughters, or sons tend to the customers, I recapture the aroma and the honest flavors of local cooking and home.

However, the country is now going through a slow transition, and one would have to be blind not to see the culinary and social changes that are occurring. American products such as Timberland and Nike are everywhere. Hip Italian boutiques geared to teenagers sell American jeans and American sportswear at a furious pace. The style of wearing a baseball cap with the visor toward the back has become popular with Italian teenagers. American words are interspersed liberally with Italian. American singers are at the top of the charts, and kids flock to McDonald's like bees to honey.

A very talented chef, owner of a top restaurant in Bologna, said to me, "*Signora*, I cook good traditional food. My pasta is rolled out with the rolling pin, not the machine. My meat ragù simmers slowly for hours, just like my mother taught me. I take pride in making everything from scratch. Everything I use is fresh and I am proud of the quality of the food that I put on the table day in and day out. And do you know what my son, who is eighteen, loves to eat? Hamburgers and French fries! I simply want to cry!"

We know that in life everything changes and evolves, even food, which adapts itself to new lifestyles. There are customs and rituals in Italy built on centuries of traditions that unfortunately will soon vanish. As countries become more globally connected with each other and as affluence and a faster pace of life encroach on time-consuming preparations, some of the individuality and food of the Italian regions will be lost. And yet, when I think about the many dedicated cooks I met while researching this book, who, with unmitigated pride and hard work keep alive the great food of Emilia-Romagna, I feel optimistic about our ability to carry on the flame of the great regional foods of Italy, because, in spite of the changes and the threat of fast food, the pleasures of the table are still central to the Italian way of life.

About the Region

Emilia-Romagna is Italy's most fertile region. It is a region of capital cities, agriculturally rich plains, and illustrious names. It is the region that nurtured the talents of Guglielmo Marconi, a native of Bologna who carried out his first radio experiment in 1895 at his home in the small village of Pontecchio, and that also nurtured the musical talents of Verdi and Toscanini and the cinematic creativity of Fellini, Antonioni, and Pasolini. Emilia-Romagna is one of the wealthiest regions of Italy, with the highest per capita income.

This prolific region is situated in the northern, flattest part of Italy. Its main larger cities are Piacenza, Parma, Reggio-Emilia, Modena, Bologna, Ferrara, Ravenna, Imola, and Forlì. Several of these medieval cities follow one another every twenty-five miles or so down an almost straight line from the northwest tip to the southeast part of the region, alongside the ancient Roman road, the Via Emilia, which once was the principal route linking northern and southern Italy. Almost evenly divided between mountains and plains, Emilia-Romagna is bordered by the Apennine Mountains in the south, the Adriatic Sea on the east, and Italy's longest river, the Po, on the north.

Through the centuries, the region that is now Emilia-Romagna has absorbed waves of conquerors—Etruscan, Greek, Gaul, and Roman—who left behind their cultures and culinary secrets. Many of these influences can be seen in the medieval and Renaissance centers of many of the region's cities. Emilia-Romagna has the highest-developed, most extensive, and richest farmland in all of Italy, and it produces some of the region's best and most sought after culinary products: prosciutto di Parma, mortadella di Bologna, Parmigiano-Reggiano cheese, balsamic vinegar, superlative sausages, luscious vegetables and fruit, and incomparable homemade pasta.

Emilia-Romagna's artistic heritage is visible everywhere, from the Romanesque cathedrals to Ravenna's great mosaic's and Byzantine basilicas, from the Renaissance and patrician villas to the castles and fortresses of the lords, to the majestic monuments, towers, intimate piazzas, and frescoes that dot the landscape of its cities.

The region's vibrant economy is fueled by the active industrial sector, which includes prestigious names such as Ferrari (automobiles), Barilla (pasta), and Cantine Riunite (wine), known worldwide. Within a few generations, the region has evolved from a primarily agricultural economy to a multifaceted one with industries such engineering, food, textiles, clothing, and ceramics leading the way. The strong tourism of the region is particularly developed along the Adriatic Sea with its eighty miles of sandy beaches and with the many beautiful small resort towns that dot the coast.

Approximately four million people live in this prosperous region, known also for its hospitality and friendliness, and, above all, great food.

Bologna

Bologna has many names: *Bologna la grassa*, "the fat," because of the lusciousness of its food. *Bologna la rossa*, "the red," because of the terra-cotta hue of its buildings. And *Bologna la dotta*, "the learned," because of its nine-hundred-year-old university, the oldest in Europe. Bologna is also known as the city of porticoes because of its twenty miles of fashionable covered streets, many of them centuries old, which shelter the Bolognesi from rain, wind, and sun. The longest stretch of porticoes runs for more than two miles up the Guardia hill, ending at the top next to the Madonna di San Luca sanctuary.

The city lies in a luscious valley, surrounded by rich farmland and soft, green hills. The city center, which is dominated by the silhouettes of medieval, Renaissance, and baroque churches, monasteries, patrician palaces, and towers from different periods, is one of the best preserved in Italy. The two most important brick towers, the ones instantly identified with the city, are the Garisenda, which is 150 feet high and is sharply leaning, and the Asinelli, which at 320 feet is one of the tallest towers built in Europe in the Middle Ages. About one hundred towers were built around the thirteenth century by the patrician families of Bologna, who constructed them as a sign of prosperity and power. Today there are just fifteen visible towers. The nineteenth-century historian of the Italian Renaissance, Jacob Burckhardt, wrote, "If one considers the single buildings, there are four or five other cities preceding Bologna, but Bologna is and remains the most beautiful Italian city for the beauty of its streets as a whole." Proof of this can be seen in old maps of the city, which show medieval Bologna shaped in an almost perfect circle. From the center of town, twelve long arcaded avenues radiate identically outward, almost like long spokes of a wheel, until they reach the circular outer brick wall, with its twelve large gates. When closed, the gates protected the city from invaders.

While other cities in Italy boast greater splendor, fame, and glories, Bologna seems happy to have been left relatively alone. The few tourists who venture to Bologna are amazed to discover that the intimate small piazzas, Renaissance buildings, and churches are practically free of tourist buses. A city of half a million people, Bologna is an active commercial and industrial capital very much in tune with the demands of the twenty-first century. Nevertheless, a visitor to Bologna feels immediately at home. The human quality of Bologna is perhaps best seen in the maze of its old, narrow streets and alleys and in the splendor of its medieval open market. Its human quality is also reflected in the faces of its many old people, who are fully integrated into the life of the city and in the everyday family life of their children and grandchildren. They sit at outdoor cafés, they shop for food, they stroll arm in arm under the porticoes while holding the hands of their grandchildren, and they pray in the many splendid churches of the city.

Within the shelter of the porticoes, sitting at an outdoor café, one can experience and witness the pulse of the active city while remaining somewhat insulated and protected. It is under these arcades that some of the best shops and museums of the city are located. It is by walking under the arcades that one has access to medieval or Renaissance buildings whose large, heavy front doors open into stunning, beautiful gardens that belong to time past. And it is by strolling under the porticoes that one can view the compelling sight of the Church and Square of Santo Stefano, a cloister of seven churches tied together by a harmonic architectural design that took many centuries to achieve.

Again and again, as I walk under the arcades, often rich with centuries-old frescoes, I am mesmerized by the beauty of Bologna: The light and sun that filters through the large pilasters and splatters the porticoes with chiaroscuro effects. The terra-cotta and rosy colors of the buildings. The intricate patterns of the floors, which speak the language of a beautiful, civilized city with a great noble past. And it is within the shelter of these arcades that I am most intimately reconnected with Bologna, the city of my youth.

THE INGREDIENTS
AND BASIC SAUCES OF
EMILIA-ROMAGNA

Many years ago, one of my students told me that she had made one of the dishes I had prepared in class, but "it just didn't taste like yours." So I asked her to tell me exactly how she did it. "Well," she said, "I sautéed the onion, carrot, and celery just as you did, but because I did not have Italian sausage, I used some Polish sausage I had at hand. Then, since I could not find any dried porcini, I used white cultivated mushrooms, and I used some red wine I had at home instead of Marsala . . ."

Ethnic cooking, to be true to its roots, needs ethnic ingredients. Occasionally some basic Italian ingredients are hard to find. In those situations, we must substitute. But does that mean that if the recipe calls for Gorgonzola you can use Stilton? I think not. The particular taste that distinguishes one dish from another depends on the specific ingredients used in preparing it.

Does it mean then that we must be a slave to the recipe? Of course not. What it means is that we must substitute judiciously, with ingredients that share a common bond. It is fine to use prosciutto in place of pancetta in a sauce, chicken instead of rabbit in a stew, or cannellini beans instead of borlotti beans, Swiss chard instead of spinach. Keep in mind, however, that even such seemingly innocuous changes will alter the taste of the dish.

In the late sixties and early seventies, the availability of authentic Italian ingredients outside a few of the larger American cities was almost nonexistent. When I moved to Sacramento from New York in 1969 with my family, I felt as if I had been cut off from my culinary universe. Luckily, the only Italian store in town, Corti Brothers, was able to provide me with some basic Italian ingredients.

What a change thirty years have made. Today, many American kitchens are stocked with Italian ingredients: Olive oils from every part of Italy. Parmigiano-Reggiano and Grana Padano, Gorgonzola, Fontina, pecorino. Dried porcini mushrooms, polenta, Arborio rice, Italian tomato paste. Factory-made pasta in endless shapes and sizes. Balsamic vinegar, sun-dried tomatoes, and on and on. And on occasion, we even can get fresh porcini mushrooms and white truffles from Piedmont. What a joy for people like me, who rely on authentic Italian ingredients to produce uncompromisingly Italian dishes for my restaurant!

Because of the availability of ingredients and because of the fact that many Americans travel to Italy each year, there is a broader understanding of Italy's regions and regional ingredients, which remain the unquestionable backbone of true Italian cooking.

If food is synonymous with the culture and civilization of a country, then Emilia-Romagna has a lot to be proud of. The following are some of the basic ingredients that contribute to the unique dishes of Emilia-Romagna. These ingredients are now widely available in this country, and I urge you to go the extra mile if necessary to secure them. You will be very handsomely rewarded.

Balsamic Vinegar
Aceto Balsamico

Imagine a vinegar that was so precious that in the sixteenth century it was often part of a legacy in a will or given as a dowry. Aromatic, concentrated, nectar-like, balsamic vinegar is produced in the province of Modena, made from the boiled-down sweet juices (must) of white Trebbiano grapes, following a centuries-old tradition. The production of artisanal balsamic vinegar takes many decades. The reduced must is aged for many years in a series of barrels of diminishing sizes and different woods, each of which gives a different fragrance to the vinegar. As the vinegar ages, evaporates, and concentrates, each barrel is refilled from the next larger barrel. The process is repeated approximately once a year until the vinegar has acquired the special dense quality that defines a true *aceto balsamico*. True artisanal balsamic vinegar bears the Modena consortium seal that reads *"Aceto Balsamico Tradizionale di Modena."* The vinegar must have been made in Modena or its province and aged not less than twelve years. It should have an intense aroma, a rich brown color, and be syrupy. It should be velvety and highly aromatic, with a well-balanced sweet-and-sour taste. The older the vinegar, the more precious and expensive it is.

In Modena, a few drops of this vinegar are sprinkled over grilled and roasted meats. It is added judiciously to young tender salad leaves, and over strawberries and vanilla gelato. It enriches traditional sauces and gives a glorious burst of flavor to the classic *bollito misto*. And, at the end of a meal, it is also drizzled over chunks of aged Parmigiano-Reggiano.

Today many specialty food stores across the country carry artisan-made balsamic. If you can find a twelve-, fifteen-, or twenty-year-old balsamic, and money is no object, buy it and use it sparingly and wisely. The good thing is that, unlike an expensive bottle of very good wine, a small bottle of balsamic can be kept for a very long time. Unfortunately most of the balsamic vinegar available in this country is commercially produced, often made outside of Emilia-Romagna. This imitation balsamic, often too sweet or too vinegary, bears absolutely no resemblance to the traditional product.

Butter
Burro

The extraordinarily fertile Emilian plain is rich grazing land for cattle. These cattle give superlative milk, and the milk is turned into outstanding cream, cheeses, and sweet butter. That is why the people of the region, and particularly the Emiliani, are formidable butter lovers. Butter is vital to the cooking of Emilia-Romagna. How could one prepare succulent spinach lasagna, alla bolognese, or a great meat ragù without butter?

But, while this basic ingredient is for the people of the region as vital today as it was decades ago, many cooks, including my brother and my sister in Bologna, use it with considerably more moderation. In this book, I have tried to use butter with good common sense, without changing the taste of the original dish. If the amount used in the recipes is too much for you, reduce it a bit and compensate with extra virgin olive oil. Do not, however, fiddle with the amount of butter called for in the desserts, or their texture, consistency, and flavor will be altered.

Cotechino
Fresh Pork Sausages

Cotechino is one of the great fresh pork sausages of Emilia-Romagna, and particularly of the cities of Bologna and Modena. The word *cotechino* comes from *cotica*, meaning rind. Cotechino is made with a large amount of pork rind, meat from the shoulder and neck of the pig, as well as salt and pepper, other spices, and, occasionally, wine. An average cotechino weighs between 1 and 1½ pounds, and is 2 to 3 inches thick, and 9 to 10 inches long. Cotechino is almost always boiled. Its skin is pricked in several places with a fork, then it is placed in gently simmering water and cooked. A properly made cotechino should have a moist, creamy consistency and a mild, almost sweet taste. Cotechino is one of the indispensable elements of Mixed Boiled Meats *(bollito misto)* (page 298). It is perfect paired with mashed potatoes or stewed lentils. While the great cotechino of Emilia-Romagna is still not available here, it is possible to find some quite good American-made cotechino in Italian markets or specialty food stores.

Garlic
Aglio

In Emilia-Romagna, garlic is used with considerable restraint. Its presence is often understated—it never shouts and never draws attention to itself. It is there when needed to highlight the flavors of a roast, a stew, or a pasta sauce without overpowering them. In fact, for many dishes, a peeled whole garlic clove is cooked until lightly browned and then discarded, leaving behind only a whiff of its aroma. When cooking garlic, remember this: Use a small amount. Cook it briefly and gently, only until lightly colored. Do not let it turn dark, or it will become unpleasantly bitter.

Herbs
Erbe

When I started teaching Italian cooking in Sacramento in the early seventies, I began with the food of Emilia-Romagna. Students were amazed that I did not use herbs in every dish and that when I did use them, it was with a lot of restraint. In the cooking of Emilia-Romagna, herbs, like garlic, are used as an accent. With a few exceptions, they never dominate a dish. They simply lend support to other flavorful ingredients. The following are some of the favorite herbs of the region.

Parsley   Sweet, fragrant, flat-leaf parsley, also called Italian parsley, is preferred. It is available in most supermarkets.

Rosemary and sage   Used as a flavoring for roasted meats, game, fish, and potatoes.

Thyme, bay leaf, and juniper berries   Great with game, in marinades and stews.

Basil   Perhaps the favorite herb, used on pasta and in salads.

Mortadella

Rosy pink, thinly sliced mortadella is the first thing I crave when I return to Bologna. The slices, which softly overlap one another on the plate, have a most incredible fragrance, aroma, and taste, reflect centuries of skill and artisanship in the art of sausage making.

Years ago, when I first saw "bologna" in this country, with the name of my city on the wrapping, I was somewhat confused. I bought it and tasted it. The texture was dense, and the only thing I could taste was salt. When my husband told me that "bologna" was the American answer to the *mortadella di Bologna*, I almost began to cry.

Mortadella is one of the best of all pork products. Popular since Roman times, mortadella apparently derived its name from the mortar that was used to grind the meat into a smooth paste. Mortadella is made with a combination of lean meat, from selected hogs, and fat from the pork jowl, pounded into a creamy mixture, then mixed with salt, pepper, nutmeg, cubes of pork fat, and spices, which vary slightly from producer to producer. The mixture is then pressed into a large casing, hung on racks, and cooked slowly for hours in special steam ovens.

In Emilia-Romagna, mortadella is served alone, or with other cured meats as a lovely antipasto. (Many trattorie in Bologna greet customers with a small plate of cubed mortadella and Parmigiano-Reggiano.) Mortadella is an essential ingredient in a tortellini filling. It is an important ingredient in *polpettine* and *polpettone*, meatballs and meat loaf, and in many vegetable fillings. One of the fondest treats that my mother put in my lunch pail was a large roll of bread stuffed with nothing but sweet, fragrant mortadella. Mortadella is now being imported into America. Look for it at your Italian market or specialty food store.

Olive Oil
Olio d'Oliva

While sweet (unsalted) butter is generally the fat of choice of Emilia, olive oil is often favored in Romagna. Of the many grades and types of olive oil available now in American markets, the one that any good cook should always choose is extra virgin. To qualify as extra virgin, the oil must be produced without chemical means, by stone-crushing and cold-pressing hand-picked olives, and it must have under 1 percent of acidity, the lowest acidity of any olive oil. The characteristics, flavor, and aroma of an olive oil are strictly tied to their place of origin and to the individual producer. It is fruity and somewhat peppery in Tuscany and Umbria, light and fragrant in some parts of the Veneto, mild and unobtrusive in Liguria, fuller in body, color, and taste in Puglia and Sicily. Try a selection until you find those that appeal to your palate. I prefer oils that are not too aggressive, with a light golden color and a smooth, light, round flavor, neither too sharp nor overly peppery, because they pair well with many dishes. Extra virgin olive oil is a bit more expensive than regular olive oil, but it is worth it. To taste olive oil, choose two or three extra virgin olive oils from different regions. Put them in small clear bowls and let stand at room temperature for a while. Look at their color and body. Are they green or pale yellow? Do they have sediment? Unfiltered oils have sediment, and some people prefer them to clear oils. Smell each oil just as you would wine, to appreciate its aroma. Take a small spoonful of oil and sip it slowly, letting it linger on the tongue and palate. When you swallow it, pay attention to its taste. Sip a bit of white wine, then go on to each of the other oils. The main characteristics of whichever oil you choose, be it lightly peppered, nutty, or fruity, should be lightness and freshness, with absolutely no hint of rancidity.

Olive oil keeps well for several months. When you find an oil that you like, buy a few bottles and keep them unopened in the coolest, darkest place of your kitchen or pantry, away from light and heat until ready to use. Do not store the oil in plastic containers, which absorb/retain other flavors, and do not refrigerate it.

Pancetta

Pancetta, from the word *pancia,* belly, is unsmoked Italian bacon that is cured with salt, pepper, and other spices for a few months. It comes rolled up like a large salami, and it should have approximately the same proportions of fat and lean meat. The best pancetta has a savory, not-too-salty taste and a creamy consistency. Its importance in the kitchens of Emilia-Romagna is surpassed only by that of prosciutto and butter. One or two ounces of pancetta can enrich a pasta sauce, a soup, and a stew like nothing else. Add an ounce of diced pancetta to potatoes during the last five minutes of roasting; you won't be able to stop eating them. Regrettably, Italian pancetta is not yet imported into the United States. Check with your Italian market or specialty food store for a good American-made brand.

Parmesan Cheese

Parmigiano-Reggiano

It is truly impossible to imagine the cooking of Emilia-Romagna without Parmigiano-Reggiano cheese. Parmigiano-Reggiano is a low-fat cow's milk cheese (it is made from partially skimmed milk) that comes from the best possible milk, has a high protein content (33 percent), and is completely free of additives. Parmigiano-Reggiano is produced under strict regulations in an area designated by law, which includes the provinces of Parma, Reggio-Emilia, Modena, and Bologna in Emilia and Mantua in Lombardy. Twelve hundred dairies with artisanal cheese makers produce this superlative cheese by hand, following rigorous standards and traditions that have remained unchanged for seven centuries. The superiority of Parmigiano-Reggiano is due to these time-honored methods of making it, in spite of modern technological progress.

Parmigiano-Reggiano is, of all cheeses, the one that requires the longest aging period, from one to three years. A two-year-old mature Parmigiano has a deep fragrant, almost nutty quality. The aroma of a perfectly aged Parmigiano should be invitingly fragrant, with no hints of sharpness. Its color may range from pale yellow to yellow. Its texture in the mouth should be somewhat grainy and creamy at the same time. Its taste should be nutty and just barely salty.

Authentic Parmigiano-Reggiano will have the following trademarks of authenticity: The words *Parmigiano-Reggiano* should be etched in tiny dots all over the cheese surface; the word "export" should be branded on the rind; the year and month of production of the cheese should be clearly visible; and an oval trademark that reads "Parmigiano-Reggiano Consorzio Tutela" should be branded on the rind.

Parmigiano is an expensive cheese, but a little bit goes a long way. Buy a piece and grate the cheese as needed directly over pasta, risotto, or soup. Some stores will offer to grate the cheese for you. Don't, as it's flavor will quickly dissipate. Keep in mind that Italians don't generally use Parmigiano with seafood dishes, for its fragrant aroma would overwhelm the delicate taste of the fish.

To store Parmigiano, wrap it tightly in plastic wrap, then again in foil, and refrigerate it. It will keep well for several weeks.

Grated domestic "Parmesan" bears absolutely no relation to Parmigiano-Reggiano.

Parma Ham

Prosciutto di Parma

Prosciutto di Parma is unsmoked salted and air-cured ham made with the hog's hind thigh. The quality and fragrance of prosciutto di Parma, one of Europe's most prized hams, is derived from several factors. The special breed of pig used is fed a high-protein diet of grains and whey. Also important is the *salatura*, the centuries-old curing method of massaging sea salt into the meat. The *stagionatura*, the slow, natural air-curing and aging of the hams that takes place in the luscious hills of Langhirano in the province of Parma, are blessed by perfect climatic and ecological conditions.

The curing process for prosciutto may range from ten months to two years. During that time, the water content of the meat is slowly drawn out by the salt, while moisture is replaced by the periodical application of *sugna*, softened suet. At the end of the prescribed time, the hams are inspected by the Consortium of Prosciutto di Parma, and the eligible ones are branded with their Parma crown of guarantee.

When buying prosciutto di Parma, look first for the Parma crown on the ham. When sliced, the prosciutto should have a rich rosy color with a little marbling of fat. Perfectly cured prosciutto di Parma should have a sweet, savory taste, never salty. The texture should be firm and moist. In Emilia-Romagna, the thin layer of fat that surrounds prosciutto is never removed, for its savory flavor balances the sweetness of the lean meat.

Prosciutto is one of the most vital ingredients of the region's cuisine. It stands alone beautifully when served thinly sliced as an antipasto, or when it takes the center stage in dishes such as Tagliatelle with Beans and Prosciutto (page 127) and Veal Cutlets with Prosciutto, Parmigiano, and Marsala (page 277). It gives a deeper, more pronounced flavor to pasta stuffings and sauces. It enriches stews, braised meats, and vegetables. Its flavorful versatility is simply unmatched.

Sliced prosciutto, wrapped in plastic, can be kept for 1 to 2 days in the refrigerator, but it is at its best when used the day it is bought.

Porcini

Fresh porcini mushrooms   I never stop marveling at the color and aroma of wild Italian porcini. These succulent, woodsy mushrooms, with their unique fragrance and meaty texture, are, without doubt, a gift of nature to the Italian table. Spring and fall in Italy are porcini season. Food markets arrange them in large clusters for everyone to see. Trattorie and restaurants showcase them in large baskets set out for the patrons to admire. One of the most delicious ways of eating porcini is to grill the large meaty caps with a sprinkling of extra virgin olive oil and a little dab of chopped garlic and parsley.

Fanano, a small mountain town between Bologna and Modena, is surrounded by richly wooded forests that supply a seemingly inexhaustible bounty of fresh porcini. II Fungo d'Oro, the Golden Mushroom trattoria, takes full advantage of this blessed gift and, during mushroom season, has nothing but mushroom dishes on its menu. Fresh porcini are sometimes available in Italian markets and specialty food stores, especially in large cities. In risottos, sauces, stews, ragùs, and stuffing, substitute fresh porcini with dried porcini. For grilling, use portobello caps. When buying fresh porcini, look for medium-sized mushrooms, with firm, creamy yellow or light brown caps. (Medium-sized caps are best because they are young, with firm caps and tight pores.) Use the mushrooms as soon as you can. If you need to hold them for a day, wrap them in a clean kitchen towel and refrigerate. Clean the mushrooms by wiping them with a damp cloth or paper towels.

Dried porcini mushrooms Dried porcini mushrooms are not a substitute for fresh ones, but they do have their own merits. With their highly concentrated, woodsy flavor, they are not only delicious, but also quite versatile. Because of their concentrated, musky aroma, they are used in the kitchen in a supporting role. A handful of reconstituted dried porcini can enrich pasta sauces and stuffings for meat, fish, vegetables, risottos, soups, stews, braised meats, and much more. Dried porcini are less expensive than the fresh and can be kept conveniently for up to a year.

Look for imported Italian dried porcini in Italian markets, specialty food stores, and and even some supermarkets. They are usually sold in small cellophane bags of approximately 1 ounce. Look for a bag that contains large creamy or light brown slices of mushrooms, with a minimum of broken pieces. Always check the expiration date on the package. If unopened and stored in a cool, dark place, dried porcini keep well for a considerably long time. If you have some mushrooms left over from an opened package, seal them securely in a plastic bag, store them as instructed above, and use them within a few months. Dried mushrooms must be soaked in water before using them. The soaking water, which becomes intensely flavored with the flavor of the mushrooms, is also used in many preparations. The softened reconstituted mushrooms need to be rinsed under cold water to remove any bits of sand and dirt.

Tomatoes
Pomodori

The pastas of Emilia-Romagna are never drenched in tomato sauce. Most traditional sauces take their faint red color from small amounts of intensely flavored locally produced sweet tomato paste or equally small amounts of preserved homemade tomato sauce made from fresh tomatoes cooked with vegetables and pureed. A pat of sweet butter or a tablespoon of heavy cream is often added to a sauce during the last few minutes of cooking, lightening the color of the tomato while imparting to the sauce some richness.

Some of the recipes in this book, especially traditional ones, call for imported tomato paste in tubes. Some use Homemade Tomato Sauce (page 22), the sauce my mother used to put away for winter use, while others use canned tomatoes, which have become very

SPECIALTY MEATS FROM EMILIA-ROMAGNA

At this writing, there are some ingredients from Emilia-Romagna that are unavailable here and for which there are no substitutions. If you travel throughout the region, seek out these cured meats and try them at their source.

Culatello is the most prized and delectable ham of the region. Made in and around several small towns of the Bassa Parmense (the Parma lowland), an area along the Po River shrouded in morning fog, culatello is known to the people of the region as "Sua Maestà il Culatello," King of Hams. Shaped something like a pear, round at the bottom and narrower at the top, culatello weighs between 6 and 8 pounds. Its meat, which is sweet, moist, and pleasantly savory, is cured much like prosciutto di Parma, and takes its particular identity from the unique microclimate of the area, the fog and humidity being some of the important elements.

Salame di Felino, a splendid salami named after the town that bears its name, is made with two-thirds lean pork and one-third fattier meat, plus salt, peppercorns, and assorted other spices. The mixture is then stuffed into casings and cured for several months.

Spalla di San Secondo is a boned pork shoulder that is cured for one month in white wine with salt, pepper, and assorted spices. The meat is then enclosed in large casings and steamed.

Zampone is a large pig's foot that has been boned, scraped clean of its insides, and then stuffed with a finely chopped mixture of lean and fat pork meat, pork rind, salt, pepper, and assorted spices, not unlike the stuffing used for cotechino. Zampone is cooked by a method similar to that for cotechino. The skin of the zampone is pricked in several places with a fork or a needle, then it is placed in simmering water and cooked to a soft, creamy consistency. The best-quality zampone, which is undoubtedly Modena's most succulent sausage, has a mild, almost sweet taste, a gelatinous consistency imparted by the pork rind, and an exquisitely tender texture. In Modena, zampone is always part of a traditional *bollito misto* (page 298). Zampone, like cotechino, goes well with mashed potatoes, stewed lentils, and spinach with butter and Parmigiano-Reggiano. Unfortunately, Modena's great zampone is not available here. The zampone we do find here, while acceptable, is somewhat drier and saltier than its Modenese counterpart.

popular with the modern cooks of the region because of their convenience and quality. When buying canned tomatoes, look for imported San Marzano peeled plum tomatoes, which are packed at their ripest, when red, plump, and full of tomato flavor. Of course, fresh tomatoes are used in simple light sauces and in Romagna are often paired with seafood in delicious pasta sauces.

Tubes of imported double-concentrated tomato paste are available in Italian markets, supermarkets, and specialty food stores. Use what you need and then store what is left in the tube in the refrigerator. It will keep well for about 1 month.

Wine
Vino

For Italians, wine is food, and when used in conjunction with cooking, wine literally becomes food. In Emilia-Romagna cooking, many sauces are simply a reduction of pan juices, wine, or broth. Therefore, the quality of wine used in a sauce is quite important. Think of wine as a very important flavoring agent that will add to the overall taste of your dish. When I cook with wine, I use the same wine I want to serve with that dish. See page 389 for more on the wines of Emilia-Romagna.

THE FLAVOR FOUNDATIONS
Battuto e Soffritto

When I was growing up in Bologna, around 11 o'clock every morning you could hear a chopping sound coming from the open windows of our apartment building: chop, chop, chop. The housewives were at work preparing the *battuto* and *soffritto* for what would become their *pranzo,* lunch.

Most dishes of the region begin with several flavoring ingredients slowly browned into a savory base. The ingredients may be a mixture of onion, carrots, and celery, or of pancetta, garlic, and onion, or again of vegetables, meats, and herbs. These ingredients, when raw, are turned into a *battuto* by very finely chopping them with a *mezzaluna,* a half-moon–shaped Italian knife. The *battuto* is then slowly sautéed in butter or oil, or a combination of the two, until golden brown and soft. Once cooked, this aromatic, savory base is called a *soffritto*. A *soffritto* imparts to dishes a rich base of flavors that add depth to the dish. This technique is used throughout the book for pasta, soups, ragùs, stews, and braised meats.

AGLIONE—THE SECRET FLAVOR ENHANCER

MAKES ABOUT ½ CUP

3 large sprigs rosemary

10 medium leaves sage

1 large garlic clove, peeled

1 teaspoon juniper berries, crushed, optional,

1 teaspoon coarse salt

Freshly ground black pepper to taste

To infuse roasts, stews, and potatoes with additional flavor, the cooks of Emilia-Romagna use a mixture of garlic, chopped with coarse sea salt, rosemary, and sage. The salt is chopped together with the garlic and herbs because it provides a gritty base to which the flavorings adhere. In the countryside surrounding Bologna, Modena, Parma, and Piacenza, this mixture is called aglione. *This flavor booster can be kept in a tightly closed jar in the refrigerator for several weeks, ready to be used on the spur of the moment. Just try it on roasted chicken or pork roast, or toss it with roasted potatoes during the last ten minutes of roasting. You will be amazed by the flavor it adds. Fresh herbs are vital to* aglione. *If they are unavailable, though, you can substitute dried herbs, using restraint.*

COMBINE all the ingredients except the pepper on a chopping board and chop very fine. Place the mixture in a small bowl and stir in a bit of pepper. Refrigerate, tightly covered, until ready to use.

HOMEMADE TOMATO SAUCE

Conserva di Pomodoro

12 pounds very ripe tomatoes, preferably plum tomatoes, cut into chunks

2 large onions, cut into pieces, coarsely chopped

3 carrots, cut into small rounds

3 celery stalks, cut into small pieces

1 cup loosely packed flat-leaf parsley leaves

1½ teaspoons coarse salt, or more to taste

Small bunch of basil, stemmed (20 to 30 leaves)

¼ cup extra virgin olive oil

Six 1-pint canning jars with two-part lids

Canning tongs

Boiling-water canner

There was a time when every Italian family had a large supply of conserva di pomodoro, preserved homemade tomato sauce, in the pantry. Tightly closed jars or bottles of conserva lined the pantry shelves. The pantry, which was often in the cellar of the house or the apartment building, was the perfect place to store items that needed to be kept in a cool, dark place. My father kept his wine in the cellar, too, as well as a few prosciutti *and* salami. *My mother stored jars of vegetables marinated in oil or vinegar, and her* conserva, *which she used throughout the winter.*

The conserva-*making ritual took place in late summer or early fall, when tomatoes were abundant and cheap. My mother would go to the market and buy huge quantities of* pomodori di seconda scelta, *second-choice tomatoes, which were less expensive because they were often bruised. Over the next few days, she cooked the tomatoes with onions, carrots, celery, and parsley or basil in several large pots. The sauce was put through a food mill and then poured into glass bottles. It was a slow, messy process, but we were assured of a steady supply of tomato sauce throughout the winter months.*

Today the practice of preserving food at home has almost disappeared, because the precious commodity of time does not allow it. At least, quality canned tomatoes from southern Italy can be found in many markets. But if you have a garden that has been taken over by tomatoes, if you want to save money, if you take satisfaction in the nurturing act of preserving and cooking, then make conserva di pomodoro.

COMBINE the tomatoes, onions, carrots, celery, parsley, and salt in a large stockpot, over medium heat, and cook, stirring occasionally, until the tomatoes are beginning to fall apart and the other vegetables are soft, 45 minutes to 1 hour.

PUREE the tomato mixture in batches in a food processor fitted with the metal blade. Place a food mill fitted with the disk with the smallest holes over a large bowl and pass the tomato puree through it to remove the seeds and skins. Return the sauce to the pot and season with salt. Cook it at a gentle boil until it has a medium-thick consistency. Stir in the basil and turn off the heat.

MEANWHILE, sterilize six 1-pint canning jars in the dishwasher. Bring a small pan of water to a full boil, add the rings, lids, and a pair of canning tongs, and simmer for 30 seconds. With the tongs, transfer the jars and lids to clean kitchen towels.

FILL the hot sterilized jars with the tomato sauce, leaving about ½ inch of headspace at the top of each jar. Wipe the rims of the jars with a hot damp towel, place the lids on top, and tightly screw on the rings. Place the jars on the rack of a canner. Fill the canner with enough hot water to cover by 2 to 3 inches and bring to a gentle boil. Lower the rack into the hot water. Add more hot water if needed to cover the jars by 2 inches. Adjust the heat so that the water simmers gently and simmer for 20 to 25 minutes. Remove the jars from the water with the tongs and set them upright on a towel to cool completely.

AFTER the jars are cool, test them by pressing down on the center of each lid. If the lid stays firm and doesn't flex up or down and doesn't pop, the lid is sealed. Store the jars in a cool dark place for up to 8 months. If the lid springs back at your touch, it means the jar was not properly sealed. Place the jar (or jars) in the refrigerator and use within a week or two.

WHEN CANNING IS NOT FEASIBLE

If preserving food is not your idea of how to spend the day, make the sauce, use what you need, and freeze what is left over. But by all means try making this sauce, because its light, delicious taste will win you over.

GREEN SAUCE WITH BALSAMIC VINEGAR

Salsa Verde al Balsamico

MAKES ABOUT ¾ CUP

1 slice Italian or French bread, crust removed and cut into pieces

2 cups loosely packed flat-leaf parsley leaves

1 garlic clove, finely minced

2 anchovy fillets

2 tablespoons capers, rinsed

½ cup extra virgin olive oil, or more to taste

2 tablespoons balsamic vinegar, or more to taste

Salt to taste

Salsa verde is a delicious, versatile northern Italian sauce that is traditionally served with Mixed Boiled Meats (Bollito Misto) *(page 298). The piquant sauce takes on a different identity depending on the region and the area in which it is made. In Emilia-Romagna, it is flavored with red or white wine vinegar, or with balsamic vinegar if it is to be served with boiled meats, with lemon juice if it is to be served with fish. The ingredients that are always part of a traditional* salsa verde *are parsley, garlic, bread, capers, ancho-vies, and extra virgin olive oil. However, other ingredients such as diced bell peppers, pickled green peppers, gherkins, or small* cipolline *(onions) may be added to the sauce according to the cook's whim.*

Italo Pedroni, owner of Osteria di Rubiara *in Nonantola, a small hamlet in the countryside of Modena, makes* salsa verde *using a superlative balsamic vinegar, which he produces in his century-old family-owned* acetaia *and serves as an accompaniment to cotechino (page 12).*

PUT all the ingredients except the salt in a food processor fitted with the metal blade and pulse until the ingredients are finely chopped but not pureed. Transfer the sauce to a small bowl and season with salt. The sauce should have a medium-thick consistency, but it should be fairly fluid and should glisten with oil. If too dense, stir in a bit more oil or vinegar. Cover and refrigerate until ready to use. Bring to room temperature before serving. (The sauce can be refrigerated for 4 to 5 days.)

SALSA VERDE ALLA BOLOGNESE Substitute 2 to 3 tablespoons good-quality red wine vinegar for the balsamic vinegar.

PIQUANT GREEN SAUCE WITH SHALLOTS

Salsa Verde Piccante

MAKES ABOUT 1 CUP

Yolks of 2 hard-boiled eggs

3 cups loosely packed flat-leaf parsley leaves

1 garlic clove

2 anchovy fillets

1 tablespoon capers, rinsed

4 small pickled gherkins, drained and cut into pieces

2 small pickled green Italian peppers, cut into pieces

½ cup extra virgin olive oil, or more to taste

2 to 3 tablespoons good-quality red wine vinegar, or more to taste

⅓ red or yellow bell pepper, cored, seeded, and finely minced (about ½ cup)

1 tablespoon finely minced shallots

Salt to taste

This is one of the many variations of the classic salsa verde, *which uses hard-boiled egg yolks instead of bread (blended with the other ingredients, both yolks and bread give the sauce a velvety, creamy consistency), along with shallots, pickled gherkins, and pickled green Italian peppers, which make the sauce considerably more piquant than the traditional version. It pairs well not only with boiled meats and cotechino, but also with sliced meat loaf, preferably a day old so its flavors have mellowed, served at room temperature.*

PUT all the ingredients except the bell pepper, shallots, and salt in a food processor fitted with the metal blade and pulse until the ingredients are finely chopped but not pureed. Transfer to a bowl.

STIR in the peppers and shallots and season with salt. The sauce should have a fairly fluid consistency; if it is too dense, stir in a bit more olive oil or vinegar. Cover the bowl and refrigerate for 2 to 3 days until ready to use. Bring to room temperature before serving.

SWEET-AND-SOUR SAUCE

Salsa Agrodolce alla Parmigiana

3 tablespoons unsalted butter

2 tablespoons extra virgin olive oil

1 tablespoon very finely minced shallots

1 garlic clove, finely minced

2 cups loosely packed flat-leaf parsley leaves, finely chopped

2 tablespoons double-concentrated Italian tomato paste, diluted in 1½ cups water

Salt to taste

1 tablespoon granulated sugar

2 tablespoons good-quality red wine vinegar

On the Emilia side of the region, this sweet-and-sour sauce takes its rightful place alongside Mixed Boiled Meats (Bollito Misto) (page 298). *Serve it warm, as a delicious alternative to Green Sauce with Balsamic Vinegar (page 24).*

HEAT the butter and oil in a medium saucepan over medium heat. Add the shallots and cook, stirring, until lightly golden and soft, about 5 minutes. Add the garlic and parsley and stir for about 1 minute. Add the diluted tomato paste and salt to taste, bring to a gentle boil, and cook for 3 to 4 minutes.

STIR in the sugar and vinegar and simmer, stirring a few times, for 3 to 4 minutes longer. Taste and adjust the seasoning. Serve warm.

MAYONNAISE

Maionese

MAKES 1½ CUPS

2 large egg yolks, at room temperature

Salt

1⅓ cups olive oil or vegetable oil

1 tablespoon fresh lemon juice

efore making mayonnaise, have all the ingredients and equipment at room temperature. Add the oil very slowly, or the mayonnaise will curdle and break. Make sure the eggs you buy are very fresh and the equipment you use is very clean.

PLACE the egg yolks and a pinch of salt in a medium bowl and beat with a large wire whisk or with an electric hand mixer until pale yellow and thick. Whisking constantly, very slowly drizzle in the oil until the mayonnaise is thick and emulsified. Whisking constantly, dribble in the lemon juice. Taste and correct the seasoning. Cover tightly and refrigerate for 2 to 3 days until ready to use.

MAYONNAISE MADE WITH A FOOD PROCESSOR Place the yolks and salt in the food processor fitted with the metal blade and process for about 15 seconds. Add the lemon juice and process about 10 seconds.

Run the machine and begin adding the oil in a very thin stream, making sure to add it very slowly at first. As the oil incorporates into the yolks and they begin to thicken, you can add the oil a bit faster. Stop the machine when the oil has been all incorporated. If the mayonnaise seems to be quite thick, run the machine and add more lemon juice.

Transfer the mayonnaise to a bowl or jar, cover tightly and refrigerate. It will keep well for 2 to 3 days.

BÉCHAMEL SAUCE

Salsa Balsamella

MAKES ABOUT 1¾ CUPS

1½ cups milk, plus more if needed

3 tablespoons unsalted butter

3 tablespoons all-purpose flour

Pinch of salt

In Emilia-Romagna, balsamella, *or béchamel sauce, is used to lighten sauces and add flavor to many dishes. It is an essential element of lasagne alla Bolognese and other baked pasta dishes.*

HEAT the milk in a small saucepan over low heat.

MEANWHILE, melt the butter in a small saucepan over medium-low heat. When the butter begins to foam, beat in the flour with a wooden spoon or a whisk and cook, stirring for about 2 minutes, making sure not to let the flour brown.

REMOVE the saucepan from the heat and add the hot milk all at once, whisking energetically to prevent lumps. Put the saucepan back over low heat, add the salt, and cook, stirring constantly, until the sauce is medium-thick, about 5 minutes. If the béchamel is too thick, stir in a bit more milk; if it is too thin, cook a bit longer.

PREPARING BÉCHAMEL AHEAD

If making béchamel ahead, butter a sheet of plastic wrap and press it directly against the surface of the béchamel to prevent a skin from forming. Béchamel will thicken as it stands; if necessary, reheat gently before serving, whisking in a little more milk until smooth.

ANTIPASTI

sk anyone from Emilia-Romagna what they like to begin a meal with when dining outside the home, and the answer will probably be *affettati*. Nothing is more characteristic or more dear to the heart and soul of the people of the region than a platter of mixed locally cured meats: prosciutto, mortadella, culatello, coppa, ciccioli, and salame, to mention just a few. These superlative pork products are so entrenched in the culinary riches of Emilia-Romagna that to neglect or dismiss them would be heresy.

At a trattoria, a waiter will greet you at the table with: *"Cominciamo con un piatto di affettati?"* (Should we begin with a nice platter of cured meats?) And before you can blink an eye, the platter is placed in front of you.

I have fond memories of summer excursions with friends to the countryside for the sole purpose of eating various cured meats with *crescentine* or *gnocco fritte*, the thin, almost transparent deep-fried savory bread that is the traditional accompaniment in Emilia. In Romagna, *affettati* are paired with a basket of hot *piadina*, a flat savory grilled bread.

Literally translated, *antipasto* means "before the meal." Figuratively speaking, the role of an antipasto is to tease the palate and stimulate the appetite. Most of the restaurants and trattorie of the region know this quite well. They also know that you eat first with your eyes, then with your palate, so they entice you with a colorful display of platters of hard-to-resist *antipasti*.

Beginning a meal with a platter of cured meats or other antipasto is more popular in restaurants and in country trattorie than at home. At my family's table in Bologna, *antipasti* were served only on special occasions, and even then were simple affairs. A few slices of prosciutto, a few chunks of Parmigiano, and some cubes of mortadella, or a slice of *capon galantina* from Tamburini, the celebrated food store of Bologna, highlighted a holiday menu, an anniversary, or an important birthday. My mother, who came from a peasant background, could not understand the fuss about *antipasti.* She considered them superfluous, and the only times she indulged in them was when we vacationed on the Adriatic shore, for she loved the tiny deep-fried fish and calamari found in the local trattorie.

There's no reason to limit *antipasti* to the beginning of the meal. A stuffed artichoke, a frittata, or a mussel salad can be served as a light supper or lunch. Many other appetizers are also served as side dishes or entrées, especially now that the Italian way of eating has become more relaxed and less structured.

MIXED CURED MEATS
Affettati Misti

This antipasto can look elegant or casual: Two or three slices of perfectly aged prosciutto, very thinly sliced and artfully draped on a beautiful dish, will look exquisite. Several types of cured meats overlapping each other on a large platter, accompanied by baskets of fritters and bowls of marinated small onions and roasted peppers, on the other hand, will look very rustic. Choose your cured meats carefully for they will determine the success of the dish. Serve them the same day you buy them, and bring to room temperature before serving. Serve this in small amounts. For 6 people, I would serve about ¾ pound assorted meats—¼ pound each thinly sliced prosciutto di Parma, prosciutto cotto, and mortadella— alternatingly on a large platter and serve alone or with slices of ripe melon or whole figs; Crescentine *(Gnocco Fritte)* (page 61) or Piadina (page 64); small chunks of Parmigiano-Reggiano; or Marinated Roasted Peppers (page 311) and Fried Zucchini with Vinegar (page 315).

ARTICHOKES STUFFED WITH PROSCIUTTO AND MORTADELLA
Carciofi con Ripieno di Prosciutto e Mortadella

SERVES 6

Emilia-Romagnans have a penchant for savory stuffed dishes. We stuff pasta, meat, fish, vegetables, even desserts, and by doing so, we enhance the taste of the dish and make it positively irresistible. I cannot imagine eating an artichoke without a stuffing, since the artichokes that my mother prepared were always filled with savory ingredients. This appetizing version of stuffed artichokes comes from Tamburini, Bologna's best and best known specialty food store.

Juice of 1 lemon

6 large artichokes with stems

1 lemon, halved

3 cups loosely packed pieces
2-day old Italian bread
(crusts removed)

1 thick slice prosciutto
(about 2 ounces), cut into
small pieces

1 thick slice mortadella
(about 2 ounces), cut into
small pieces

½ cup freshly grated
Parmigiano-Reggiano

¼ cup chopped
flat-leaf parsley

Salt and freshly ground black
pepper to taste

1 garlic clove, finely minced

½ to ⅔ cup extra virgin
olive oil

1 cup dry white wine

To prepare the artichokes, fill a large bowl with cold water and add the lemon juice. Pull off and discard the tough outer leaves of the artichokes. With scissors, cut off about one-third of the remaining leaves until you reach the central cone of leaves. Cut off the green tips of the cone. Gently open each artichoke wide and remove its fuzzy inner choke with a spoon or a melon baller. As you work, rub the lemon halves over the cut surfaces of the artichokes to prevent discoloration. Cut off the stems at the base and set aside. With a small knife, trim off the outer green parts of the artichoke bottoms. Add the artichokes to the bowl of lemon water. With the knife, peel away the fibrous green outer part of the artichoke stems and add the stems to the lemon water.

PUT the bread in a food processor fitted with the metal blade and pulse until finely chopped. Transfer the bread to a bowl. Add the prosciutto and mortadella to the processor and pulse to finely chop. Add to the bowl together with the Parmigiano and parsley, season with salt and pepper, and stir well. Combine the garlic and ½ cup oil, pour over the stuffing, and stir well until the mixture is thoroughly coated and has a moist, soft consistency; add a bit more oil if needed. Taste and adjust the seasoning.

ONE at a time, hold the artichokes over the bowl of stuffing and, with your hand, press of a generous amount of the stuffing between the leaves and into the center of the artichoke, letting the excess fall back into the bowl. Place the stuffed artichokes in a heavy pot that holds them snugly and sprinkle any remaining stuffing over and around the artichokes.

ADD the artichoke stems, wine, and enough water to come halfway up the sides of the artichokes. Bring the liquid to a boil, then cover the pot, reduce the heat to medium-low, and cook, checking the artichokes from time to time and adding more water if necessary, until they are tender when pierced with a thin knife, 35 to 45 minutes. (The artichokes can be prepared several hours ahead and set aside in the liquid covered, at room temperature.)

To serve, transfer the artichokes to individual serving dishes. Set the pot over high heat and boil, stirring occasionally, until the liquid is reduced to about ½ cup. Spoon over the artichokes and serve at room temperature.

ARTICHOKES STUFFED WITH SAUSAGE Omit the prosciutto and mortadella, and add 1 link mild Italian sausage, casing removed, finely chopped and browned in olive oil, to the bread mixture.

ARTICHOKES STUFFED WITH ANCHOVIES Omit the prosciutto and mortadella and add a few anchovy fillets packed in oil or salt (rinsed if packed in salt), finely chopped, to the bread mixture.

HIS MAJESTY THE PIG

Once upon a time, the famous pigs of Emilia-Romagna roamed free and wild in the lush forests, where they grazed on acorn and chestnuts. For several centuries B.C., the pigs were hunted and eaten fresh or preserved in salt by the Etruscans, the most ancient population of central Italy, who exported cured pigs' legs to Greece. In Roman times, wild pigs were a source of sustenance for the locals and for the Roman army, which carried large supplies of salt-cured ham and salt-preserved pork on their campaigns. Centuries later, when the pigs had been domesticated and could be kept on farms or in small yards, they flourished on a new, improved diet based on corn and whey, the watery residue from the making of Parmigiano.

Because pigs were "low maintenance," even poorer families living off the land could own one (or several). Like chickens, rabbits, and ducks, the pig meant food for the table, but it was the most economic of all, for every little bit of its delicious meat would be turned into a special morsel, assuring a steady supply of food for the household during the long, harsh winter season.

While Emilia-Romagna owes its status to many great people—the town of Parma and its surrounding green undulating countryside and luscious hills were a constant source of inspiration for Giuseppe Verdi, and Stendhal wrote about those same hills in his novels—there is no doubt that the rich economy of the region owes part of its success to the unassuming pig. And there is also no doubt that without it, the cooking of the area would be greatly diminished.

PROSCIUTTO WITH MARINATED BABY ARTICHOKES IN BALSAMIC VINEGAR

Prosciutto e Carciofini al Balsamico

SERVES 6

Juice of 1 lemon

2 pounds baby artichokes

1 lemon, halved

Salt

Freshly ground black pepper to taste

⅓ to ½ cup extra virgin olive oil

3 to 4 tablespoons good-quality balsamic vinegar

¾ pound thinly sliced prosciutto

¼ pound Parmigiano-Reggiano, cut into slivers

Antica Trattoria Moretto, in the small town of Vignola in the province of Modena, tosses small marinated artichokes in balsamic vinegar and serves them over rosy slices of perfectly aged prosciutto di Parma, sprinkled with slivers of Parmigiano-Reggiano for a great country antipasto. The artichokes take a fair amount of work, but they can be prepared several hours ahead. A basket of Fried Flatbread Fritters (page 59), gnocco fritte, is the traditional accompaniment.

To prepare the artichokes, fill a large bowl with cold water and add the lemon juice. Remove the outer green leaves of the artichokes by snapping them off at the base, stopping when you reach the pale yellow inner leaves. Slice off the green tips. With a sharp knife, peel off the tough outer layer of the artichoke stems. As you work, rub the cut surfaces of the artichokes with the lemon halves. Add the trimmed artichokes to the lemon water.

BRING a medium saucepan of water to a boil and add a pinch or two of salt. Drain the artichokes, add to the boiling water, reduce the heat to medium, and cook, uncovered, until the artichoke bottoms can easily be pierced with a toothpick or a thin knife, 7 to 10 minutes. Drain the artichokes and place in a large bowl of ice water to stop the cooking. Drain again and slice lengthwise in half. Place cut side down on paper towels to drain.

TRANSFER the artichokes to a medium bowl, season with salt and pepper, and toss with the olive oil. Set aside to marinate at room temperature for an hour or two.

To serve, add the balsamic vinegar to the artichokes. Taste and adjust the seasoning. Arrange the prosciutto on individual serving plates. Pile a small mound of artichokes in the center of each plate, scatter the Parmigiano over the prosciutto, and serve.

FRIED ASPARAGUS

Asparagi Fritti

SERVES 4

1 pound asparagus

Salt

2 large eggs

⅛ teaspoon freshly
grated nutmeg

1 cup fine dried bread crumbs

⅓ cup freshly grated
Parmigiano-Reggiano

Olive oil for frying

Spring in Emilia-Romagna is the season of festivals. Every new crop of fruits or vegetables brings with it its own festival, whose origins often date back to medieval times. Altedo, a small town on the foggy Emilia plain, boasts an asparagus festival, as the rich farmland that surrounds it produces some of the most prized green asparagus in Italy. The night we dined at Antica Osteria di Buda, in the countryside near Medicina, a whole menu was dedicated to asparagus: Asparagus salad with oil, lemon, and slivers of Parmigiano. Risotto with asparagus. Baked asparagus. . . . I loved every single bite of food I had that night, but my favorite dish was the delectable crunchy fried asparagus. Serve it is as the promising beginning to a meal, or as a side dish next to grilled fish or meat.

TRIM off the bottom 1 or 2 inches of the tough, woody asparagus stalks. If the stalks are large, peel them with a potato peeler or a small sharp knife. Rinse well under cold water and drain.

BRING 2 inches of water to a boil in a large deep skillet. Add a large pinch of salt and the asparagus. Cook until the asparagus is barely tender to the touch, 1 to 2 minutes for thin asparagus, 3 minutes for thicker asparagus; do not overcook. Place a large bowl of ice water next to the pan and, with tongs, transfer the asparagus to the cold water to stop the cooking. Drain, place on paper towels, and pat dry with more paper towels. (The asparagus can be cooked up to a day ahead. Place on a large plate lined with paper towels, cover tightly, and refrigerate.)

BEAT the eggs in a shallow dish. Season with salt and the nutmeg. Combine the bread crumbs and Parmigiano and spread on a sheet of foil.

HEAT ½ inch of oil in a large skillet over medium-high heat. A few at a time, dip the asparagus into the eggs, letting the excess drip off, roll them in the bread crumb mixture, and add to the hot oil, without crowding the pan. Fry until they have a crisp golden brown crust. Drain on paper towels. Season generously with salt, place on a large shallow platter, and serve crisp and hot.

GRATINÉED ASPARAGUS
AND PROSCIUTTO

Asparagi e Prosciutto alla Parmigiana

SERVES 6

2 pounds asparagus

Salt

4 tablespoons (½ stick) unsalted butter

2 to 3 ounces thinly sliced prosciutto, cut into small strips

½ cup freshly grated Parmigiano-Reggiano

Cooked green or white asparagus is bathed in melted butter, covered with freshly grated Parmigiano, and baked until the cheese is melted and a golden crust forms on top. Nothing could be simpler or more delicious—except perhaps this version, which has the addition of strips of prosciutto.

CUT off the tough ends of the asparagus. If the asparagus stalks are thick, peel them with a vegetable peeler or small sharp knife. Rinse the asparagus and arrange it in 1 or 2 bunches, securing them with rubber bands or kitchen string.

BRING 2 to 3 inches of water to a boil in an asparagus cooker or in a narrow stockpot over medium heat. Add a nice pinch of salt and stand the asparagus in the pot. Cover the top of the asparagus loosely with foil or with the cooker lid and cook until tender but still a bit crunchy to the bite (it will finish cooking in the oven), 3 to 8 minutes, depending on the thickness. Place a large bowl of ice water next to the stove. Remove the asparagus from the pot, remove the rubber bands or string, and place in the ice water to stop the cooking. Drain again, place on a clean kitchen towel, and pat dry. (The asparagus can be cooked to this point up to a day ahead. Cover tightly and refrigerate.)

PREHEAT the oven to 400°F. Smear the bottom of a large baking dish with some of the butter.

MELT the remaining butter. Arrange a layer of the asparagus in the baking dish and season lightly with salt. Drizzle some of the melted butter over the asparagus, scatter the prosciutto over it, and sprinkle lightly with Parmigiano. Arrange another layer of asparagus on top and repeat as above, finishing with a generous sprinkling of cheese.

PLACE the baking dish on the middle rack of the oven and bake until the cheese has a nice golden color, 6 to 8 minutes. Remove from the oven and let stand for a few minutes before serving.

CHOOSING AND COOKING ASPARAGUS

Even though in some parts of the country asparagus is available most of the year, it is at its best in spring. When buying asparagus, look at the tips, which should be tightly closed, and their color, which should be a vivid green. Use asparagus as soon as you can; if you can't cook it right away, keep in the refrigerator, tightly wrapped, or stand the spears, just like flowers, in a vase with a few inches of water.

The method of cooking asparagus standing upright is typically Italian. While the thick asparagus stalks cook in the few inches of boiling water, the more delicate tips cook simultaneously in the steam above.

In this country, asparagus is usually cooked lying flat in a skillet of boiling water. If you use this method, make sure to keep the water to a gentle simmer so it won't break or damage the tips of the asparagus.

ROASTED MUSHROOMS

Funghi Ripieni

SERVES 6

1 pound large white
mushrooms, wiped clean

⅓ cup extra virgin olive oil,
plus extra for drizzling

1 garlic clove, finely minced

2 tablespoons chopped
flat-leaf parsley

3 to 4 ounces thinly sliced
mortadella or boiled ham,
very finely minced

¼ cup freshly grated
Parmigiano-Reggiano

3 tablespoons fine dried
bread crumbs

1 extra-large egg,
lightly beaten

Salt and freshly ground black
pepper to taste

My niece Daniela, who lives in Bologna with her husband, loves to cook and is always experimenting with what she calls piatti facili, *easy dishes. When my husband and I had dinner at Daniela's house, the food she prepared was typical of what a young, busy working woman would cook midweek. Simple but delicious. These stuffed mushrooms were accompanied by a lovely glass of chilled prosecco. The lamb that followed was served with roasted potatoes: both were perfect and simple.*

PREHEAT the oven to 400°F.

TRIM the mushrooms and separate the stems from the caps. Chop the stems very fine and set the caps aside.

PLACE the chopped stems in a small skillet with 2 tablespoons of the olive oil and cook, stirring, for a minute or two. Add the garlic and parsley, stir once or twice, and transfer to a small bowl. Add the mortadella, Parmigiano, bread crumbs, and egg. Season with salt and pepper and mix well. Stuff the mushroom caps with this mixture, mounding it slightly.

SMEAR the bottom of a baking dish large enough to hold the mushroom caps in a single layer with the remaining oil. Place the mushrooms in the dish and drizzle a bit of oil over each one.

PLACE the dish on the middle rack of the oven and bake for 15 to 20 minutes, or until the tops of the mushrooms are golden.

DEEP-FRIED PORCINI MUSHROOMS

Porcini Fritti

SERVES 4

1 pound fresh porcini,
shiitake, or portobello
mushrooms, wiped clean

3 large eggs

Salt

2 cups fine dried
bread crumbs

Olive oil or vegetable oil
for deep-frying

2 tablespoons finely chopped
flat-leaf parsley

Lemon wedges

talians are mushroom crazy. In the fall, when mushrooms of many different species are plentiful, restaurants and trattorie display large baskets of wild mushrooms to tempt their patrons. Fresh porcini, Boletus edulis, are without a doubt the Italian favorite mushroom. They can be sautéed, roasted, or stewed with meat or game. They are fabulous in soups, risottos, and pasta sauces. They are absolutely delicious thinly sliced raw in a salad, and immensely appetizing when dipped in egg, coated with bread crumbs, and deep-fried until they are golden and crisp. At Da Carlet, a well-known trattoria in the mountain town of Monghidoro, about forty-five minutes from Bologna, fried porcini were the irresistible opening of a memorable meal.

REMOVE the mushroom stems and save for another use. If using portobello mushrooms, scrape off the dark gills beneath the caps. You may use the stem close to the cap, but discard the base. Slice the mushrooms caps into ¼-inch-thick slices.

BEAT the eggs with a pinch of salt in a shallow bowl. Spread the bread crumbs on a sheet of aluminum foil. Dip the mushroom slices into the eggs, letting the excess drip back into the bowl, coat with the bread crumbs, and place on a cookie sheet lined with paper towels. (The mushrooms can be prepared up to this point a few hours ahead. Refrigerate, without covering them.)

PREHEAT the oven to 200°F.

HEAT 2 inches of oil in a deep large saucepan over high heat. When the oil is hot, slip several mushroom slices into the oil, without crowding, and fry until they are golden on both sides, about 1 minute. Remove from the oil with a slotted spoon and transfer to a platter lined with paper towels to drain. Keep warm in the oven while you fry the remaining mushrooms.

SEASON the mushrooms with salt, sprinkle with the parsley, and serve hot and crispy, with lemon wedges.

FRIED ZUCCHINI BLOSSOMS

Fiori di Zucchine Fritte

SERVES 4

For the batter

1 large egg

1¼ cups milk

1 cup all-purpose flour

Small pinch of salt

¼ pound (14 to 16) male
zucchini blossoms
(see box)

Olive oil

Salt to taste

In Italy, during the summer months, when large clusters of orange zucchini blossoms shine brightly in the open markets, they are eagerly snatched up by food lovers. And that is just what I did when browsing through the dazzling variety of fresh produce at Bologna's medieval open-air market. The blossoms I bought had probably been picked that morning, since they were still tightly closed. That night, at my brother's house, my sister-in-law, Emma, and I dipped the delicate blossoms into a light milk batter and quickly fried them to a golden crispness.

To prepare the batter, lightly beat the egg in a medium bowl, then whisk in the milk. Gradually sift in the flour, whisking well. Season the batter with the salt and set aside. When done, the batter should have a medium-thick consistency, not unlike sour cream.

REMOVE and discard the stems of the zucchini blossoms. Open the flowers gently and remove the pistils. Wash the blossoms quickly under cold running water and pat thoroughly dry with paper towels. (Don't worry if the flowers tear a bit.)

HEAT 1 inch of oil in a large skillet over high heat. Just before the oil begins to smoke, quickly dip a few blossoms at a time into the batter, letting the excess drip back into the bowl, and add to the hot oil. When the blossoms are lightly golden and have formed a crisp crust on one side, turn them over and fry the other side. With a slotted spoon, remove the blossoms from the oil and transfer to paper towels to drain. When all the blossoms have been fried, season lightly with salt and serve at once.

ZUCCHINI BLOSSOMS

The first thing you need to know about zucchini blossoms is that they are very delicate. They are generally available from the middle of July to the middle of September, and the best places to find them are specialty food markets and farmers' markets. Zucchini have both male and female blossoms. The male blossoms have long thin stalks; the female blossoms are sold attached to baby zucchini. The male blossoms seem to be better suited for deep-frying.

For perfectly crisp blossoms, make sure that your oil is hot enough. Fry only 2 or 3 blossoms at a time, and as they turn golden on the first side (it will happen in no time at all), turn them quickly to brown the other side. Keep the temperature of the oil constant, adjusting the heat as needed. If the oil is not hot enough, the blossoms will become soggy; if the oil is too hot, they will burn.

PARMIGIANO WITH BALSAMIC VINEGAR

In many trattorie of Bologna and its countryside, diners are often greeted with a plate of chunks of Parmigiano-Reggiano and cubes of rosy mortadella. In Parma, the locally produced prosciutto is served instead of mortadella, and in Modena, the Parmigiano chunks are drizzled with aged balsamic vinegar. These *antipasti* are generally served with a lively local wine such as Lambrusco or another sparkling wine.

Franca Pedroni, chef of the well-known Osteria di Rubiara in Modena's countryside, drizzles the Parmigiano with the prize-winning balsamico that her husband, Italo, produces. Keep in mind that if using artisanal balsamico, the older it is, the less you'll need to use. (See page 10.)

With a Parmigiano cutter or a short sturdy knife, break up about 6 ounces cheese into walnut-sized chunks. Place the cheese in a shallow dish, sprinkle with 1½ tablespoons balsamic vinegar and toss well. Let sit at room temperature for about 20 minutes, then toss with an additional 1½ tablespoons balsamic and serve.

TUNA AND RICOTTA MOUSSE

Spuma di Tonno e Ricotta

SERVES 6 TO 8

One 7-ounce can Italian tuna packed in olive oil, drained

7 ounces ricotta (about 1 cup), preferably whole-milk

½ teaspoon gelatin, softened in 3 tablespoons cold water

12 to 14 slices firm white bread

ietro Bondi was for many years the talented chef of Ristorante Diana, one of Bologna's most celebrated traditional restaurants. His passion for the classic food of the area was evident in every dish that came out of his kitchen. Eventually Pietro opened his own restaurant, where he continued cooking the great dishes of Bologna: heavenly tiny tortellini in a capon broth, green lasagne alla Bolognese, mixed boiled meats with the piquant salsa verde, mortadella mousse, and this tuna and ricotta mousse. Serve these small canapés before a sit-down dinner with a glass of chilled sparkling wine.

PLACE the tuna and ricotta in a food processor fitted with the metal blade and process to a smooth puree. Transfer to a medium bowl.

PUT the softened gelatin in a double boiler and stir over low heat until it has completely dissolved. Fold it into the tuna-ricotta mixture, then transfer to a small serving bowl. Cover with plastic wrap and refrigerate for a few hours. (The mousse can be prepared a day ahead. Let come to room temperature before serving.)

PREHEAT the oven to 400°F. Lightly oil a baking sheet.

TRIM the crusts from the bread. Cut rounds from each slice with a 2-inch cookie cutter, or cut them into triangles or rectangles. Place the bread on the baking sheet and bake on the middle rack of the oven until it has a light golden color, 3 to 5 minutes. Turn the pieces and brown the other side, 3 to 4 minutes.

PLACE the bowl of mousse on a large round serving dish. Arrange the toast around the bowl and let your guests help themselves.

JUMBO PRAWNS WITH
SWEET-AND-SOUR ORANGE SAUCE

Gamberoni con Salsa Agrodolce all'Arancio

SERVES 4

3 tablespoons unsalted butter

⅓ cup finely minced shallots

1 cup sesame seeds

12 jumbo prawns, or shrimp, peeled, deveined, rinsed, and patted dry

Salt to taste

¼ cup sugar

1 cup fresh orange juice

⅓ cup fresh lemon juice

My husband and I spent a week at Locanda del Lupo, a charming country hotel in the small town of Soragna in the Parma countryside, so we could visit the many excellent trattorie and restaurants of the area. Our first dinner was at the hotel's elegant restaurant, where this unusual antipasto was served. The sweet-and-sour flavors are a legacy of the cuisine of the Italian Renaissance.

PREHEAT the oven to 400°F. Lightly oil a baking sheet.

MELT 2 tablespoons of the butter in a medium skillet over medium-low heat. Add the shallots and cook, stirring, until pale yellow and very soft, 6 to 7 minutes. Turn off the heat.

SPREAD the sesame seeds on a sheet of aluminum foil. Season the prawns with salt and coat them lightly with the sesame seeds. Arrange the prawns on the prepared baking sheet, place on the middle rack of the oven, and bake for 5 to 6 minutes, until prawns are cooked all the way through and the sesame seeds are golden.

MEANWHILE, set the skillet over high heat, add the sugar, orange juice, and lemon juice, and cook, stirring, until the sauce has reduced by more than half and has a medium thick consistency and a rich glossy orange color, 8 to 10 minutes. Stir in the remaining 1 tablespoon butter. Arrange the prawns on individual warm plates, drizzle them generously with the sauce, and serve immediately.

WARM SALAD OF SHRIMP, RADICCHIO, ARUGULA, AND BALSAMIC VINEGAR

Scampi, Radicchio, e Rucola al Balsamico

SERVES 4

½ small head radicchio, washed, and dried

3 cups loosely packed arugula leaves, stems removed, washed, and dried

3 tablespoons balsamic vinegar

⅓ cup dry white wine

Salt

¼ to ⅓ cup extra virgin olive oil

16 medium shrimp, shelled, deveined, rinsed, and patted dry

Freshly ground black pepper to taste

Another antipasto from Giampaolo Ghilardotti, the talented young chef of the country hotel Locanda del Lupo in the Parma countryside, this pairs hot and cold ingredients in a delightful salad.

CUT the radicchio into thin julienne and place in a bowl. Add the arugula and toss to combine. Arrange the salad on four dinner plates.

IN a small bowl, combine the balsamic, wine, and a nice pinch of salt.

HEAT the oil in a large skillet over high heat. Add the shrimp and cook until they are lightly colored, 1 to 2 minutes. Add the balsamic mixture and cook, stirring, until the liquid has reduced by approximately half, about 2 minutes.

ARRANGE the shrimp over the salads and spoon the hot dressing over all. Serve at once, with a bit of freshly ground black pepper.

MUSSEL SALAD

Insalata di Cozze

SERVES 4 AS AN
APPETIZER, 2 OR 3 AS
AN ENTRÉE

4 pounds mussels, cleaned and debearded as instructed on page 213

1 garlic clove, halved

6 oil-cured black olives, pitted and quartered

1 tablespoon capers, drained

1 to 2 tablespoons chopped flat-leaf parsley

1 ripe plum tomato, seeded and diced

Salt and freshly ground black pepper to taste

⅓ cup extra virgin olive oil

3 to 4 tablespoons fresh lemon juice

The seafood salads one finds along the Adriatic coast may contain several varieties of fish and shellfish, or just one. The seafood may be tossed simply with flavorful extra virgin olive oil and lemon juice or be combined with other tempting ingredients. But no matter how the salad is made, its success depends simply on the freshness of the fish. At Al Pescatore Ristorante in Riccione, perhaps the most elegant of the small towns that dot Romagna's coast, I enjoyed a most delicious mussel salad. The plump mussels were tossed simply with a few capers, some black olives, chopped fresh parsley, and a handful of diced very ripe, bright red tomatoes, finished with the traditional dressing of light, fragrant olive oil and fresh lemon juice.

In Romagna, salads like this are served just barely chilled or at room temperature.

PUT the mussels in a large pot, cover, and cook over high heat, shaking the pot from time to time, until the mussels open; remove them with a slotted spoon as they open. (Some may take a bit longer than others to open; however, if after 3 to 4 minutes, any mussels are still firmly shut, discard them.)

RUB the inside of a salad bowl with the cut sides of the garlic clove; discard. Remove the mussels from the shells and place in the bowl. Let cool to room temperature. (The mussels can be prepared up to this point a few hours ahead and refrigerated, tightly covered. Bring to room temperature before serving.)

ADD the olives, capers, parsley, and tomatoes to the mussels and toss to mix. Season lightly with salt and pepper and toss with the oil and lemon juice. Taste and adjust the seasoning. Let the salad stand for 30 minutes before serving.

BROILED MUSSELS

Cozze Gratinate

SERVES 4

½ loaf Italian bread

¼ to ⅓ cup chopped flat-leaf parsley

1 tablespoon chopped oregano

1 garlic clove, finely minced

3 tablespoons freshly grated Parmigiano-Reggiano

Salt and freshly ground black pepper to taste

⅓ cup extra virgin olive oil

2 pounds mussels, cleaned and debearded as instructed on page 213

Lemon wedges

Mussels, a favorite along the Adriatic coast, are used in antipasti, salads, shellfish soups, and pasta sauces. They are also grilled, and when they are stuffed and broiled, they become a most perfect appetizer. Like most other seafood dishes of the Romagna seacoast, this is very simple. Take very fresh, plump mussels and cook them just long enough for them to open, then marinate them in an aromatic mixture of Parmigiano, bread, fresh herbs, and olive oil and broil them until they are golden brown. Serve these with a chilled crisp white wine.

REMOVE the crust from the bread and discard it. Chop the bread by hand or in a food processor fitted with the metal blade.

COMBINE 1½ cups of the bread (reserve any extra for another use), parsley, oregano, garlic, and Parmigiano in a medium bowl. Season with salt and pepper, stir in the oil, and mix just until the bread is evenly moistened; the mixture should be somewhat loose. Set aside.

PUT the mussels in a large heavy saucepan, add ½ cup water, cover, and place over high heat. Cook, shaking the pan from time to time, until all the mussels open; with a slotted spoon, transfer to a bowl as they open. (Some may take a bit longer to open; however, if after 3 to 4 minutes any mussels are still firmly shut, discard them.) Mussels can be cooked in several ways.

REMOVE the mussels from the shells and set aside one half of each shell. Add the mussels to the bread mixture and toss thoroughly to coat the mussels. Cover the bowl and let marinate at room temperature for 30 minutes.

PREHEAT the broiler.

PUT a mussel into each of the reserved shells and top them generously with the remaining bread mixture. Arrange the mussels on the broiler pan and broil until the topping is golden and crisp, about 2 minutes. Serve at once, with lemon wedges.

A Trio of Frittate

There are some dishes in Italy that transcend regional borders, and *frittata* is such a dish. A frittata is an open-faced omelet that looks like a large flat cake. While a frittata can be made with vegetables, cheeses, herbs, cured meats, or even leftover pasta and rice, it takes on a certain regionality when local ingredients are used. Two of the following frittatas do just that, and one was dictated by the availability of produce at the market.

Frittatas are perfect home food. My mother would make one a couple of nights a week and serve it as a light supper, following a bowl of clear broth with pastina. A few eggs, some Parmigiano, a handful of vegetables, and any leftover ingredient she had at hand would be turned into a golden frittata. My very favorite was made with leftover roasted potatoes.

I use the method I learned from my mother, who was a master at quickly turning the almost-cooked frittata out onto a dish, then slipping it back into the skillet to finish cooking, but there are other, simpler ways of making a frittata.

For an oven-baked frittata, pour the frittata mixture into a buttered ovenproof skillet or baking pan and bake in a preheated 350°F oven until the frittata has a nice golden color, 10 to 15 minutes, or until a thin knife inserted into the frittata comes out clean.

For a broiled frittata, cook the frittata mixture as instructed until the bottom is golden. Then instead of flipping it over, place the skillet briefly under a hot broiler until it is lightly golden.

A selection of frittatas makes a delicious appetizer. Prepare them a few hours ahead, then cut them into squares or wedges, arrange them on a platter, and serve with an *aperitivo* or a glass of sparkling wine.

FRITTATA WITH MUSHROOMS, ONIONS, AND BALSAMIC VINEGAR

Frittata di Funghi e Cipolle all'Aceto Balsamico

SERVES 4 AS AN
APPETIZER, 2 AS AN
ENTRÉE

⅓ cup extra virgin olive oil, plus more if needed

¼ pound porcini, chanterelle, or shiitake mushrooms, wiped clean and thinly sliced

1 tablespoon unsalted butter

2 medium yellow onions, thinly sliced

6 large eggs

⅓ cup freshly grated Parmigiano-Reggiano

Salt and freshly ground black pepper to taste

1 to 2 teaspoons good-quality balsamic vinegar (see page 10)

In and around the city of Modena, where balsamic vinegar is king, the precious condiment is used in many dishes. It enriches meat and fowl, it gives a sophisticated taste to sauces, it tops chunks of Parmigiano-Reggiano—and it makes the humble frittata dazzlingly appetizing. Italo Pedroni, whose country trattoria in Nonantola near Castelfranco is visited ritually by food lovers, makes his own balsamic. Using the year's first crop of porcini mushrooms, he made me a frittata that was generously sprinkled with a fifteen-year-old balsamic.

HEAT half of the oil in an 8-inch nonstick skillet over high heat. As soon as it is nice and hot, add the mushrooms, without crowding (cook them in batches if necessary), and cook, stirring, until lightly golden. With a slotted spoon, transfer the mushrooms to a bowl.

ADD the remaining oil, the butter, and onions to the skillet and reduce the heat to medium. Cook, stirring, until the onions are lightly golden and soft, 6 to 7 minutes.

WHILE the onions are cooking, break the eggs in the mushrooms. Add the Parmigiano, season with salt and pepper, and mix well with a fork.

WITH a slotted spoon, scoop up the onions and stir into the eggs. Put the skillet back over medium heat and add a bit more oil if needed, just enough to barely coat the bottom. When the oil is nice and hot, add the egg mixture. Cook, without stirring, until the frittata is lightly browned on the bottom and the top is beginning to set, 5 to 6 minutes.

REMOVE the skillet from the heat, invert a large flat plate over it, and carefully turn the frittata onto the plate. Slide the frittata back into the skillet and cook until the bottom is lightly browned, 2 to 3 minutes. Slide the frittata onto a serving plate and sprinkle generously with balsamic vinegar. Cut into wedges and serve warm.

FRITTATA WITH ASPARAGUS

Frittata di Asparagi

SERVES 4 AS AN
APPETIZER, 2 AS AN
ENTRÉE

2 pounds thin asparagus

Salt

¼ cup extra virgin olive oil

**½ cup finely minced
yellow onions**

6 large eggs

**⅓ cup freshly grated
Parmigiano-Reggiano**

On a warm late spring night in Bologna, when the humidity had reached a very uncomfortable level, my brother suggested we cancel our reservation at a local trattoria, which did not have air-conditioning, and just improvise something light to eat. He went into the kitchen and got to work. Our dinner that night consisted of this asparagus frittata, Swiss Chard with Butter and Parmigiano (page 332), and a selection of local cheeses and bread, from the panificio *down the street. The wine was the unpretentious effervescent Lambrusco of the region.*

We sat on the terrace, ate leisurely, and sipped wine, and the mood was nice, mellow, and relaxed, because no one had spent hours in the kitchen preparing this simple meal.

CUT off the asparagus tips; reserve the stalks for another preparation. You can also use 1 pound asparagus, using the stalks too. Bring a small saucepan of water to a boil. Add a nice pinch of salt and the asparagus tips and cook until tender but still firm to the bite, 2 to 3 minutes. Drain the asparagus and pat dry with paper towels.

HEAT 2 tablespoons of the oil in an 8-inch nonstick skillet over medium heat. Add the onions and cook, stirring, until pale yellow and soft, 5 to 6 minutes. Add the asparagus tips and stir for a minute or two.

MEANWHILE, lightly beat the eggs in a medium bowl. Add the Parmigiano, season with salt, and mix well. Pour the contents of the skillet into the eggs and mix thoroughly.

PUT the skillet back over medium heat and add the remaining oil. When the oil is nice and hot, add the egg mixture and cook until the frittata is lightly browned on the bottom and the top begins to set, 5 to 6 minutes.

REMOVE the skillet from the heat, invert a large flat plate over it, and turn the frittata out onto the plate. Slide the frittata back into the skillet and cook until the bottom is lightly browned, 2 to 3 minutes. Slide the frittata onto a serving plate. Let cool slightly, then cut it into wedges and serve warm or at room temperature.

FRITTATA WITH PAN-ROASTED
POTATOES AND PROSCIUTTO

Frittata di Patate e Prosciutto

SERVES 4 AS AN
APPETIZER, 2 AS
AN ENTRÉE

⅓ cup extra virgin olive oil

1 cup diced peeled boiling
potatoes, 2 to 3 small potatoes
or ½ large potato

2 to 3 ounces thinly
sliced prosciutto, cut into
small strips

1 sprig rosemary, stemmed,
finely chopped

1 garlic clove, finely minced

6 large eggs

⅓ cup freshly grated
Parmigiano-Reggiano

Salt and freshly ground black
pepper to taste

HEAT about half of the oil in an 8-inch nonstick skillet over medium heat. Add the potatoes and cook, stirring, until lightly golden and soft about 20 minutes. Add the prosciutto, rosemary, and garlic and stir for about a minute. The potatoes can be prepared a few hours ahead.

MEANWHILE, break the eggs into a medium bowl, stir in the Parmigiano, season lightly with salt and pepper, and mix well with a fork.

ADD the potatoes and prosciutto to the eggs and mix quickly to combine. Put the skillet back over medium heat and add the remaining oil if needed. When the oil is nice and hot, add the egg mixture and cook until the frittata is golden on the bottom and the top is beginning to set, 5 to 6 minutes.

REMOVE the skillet from the heat, invert a large flat plate over it and turn the frittata out onto the plate. Slide the frittata back into the skillet and cook the other side until the bottom is lightly browned, 2 to 3 minutes. Slide the frittata onto a serving plate, cut into wedges, and serve warm or at room temperature.

OSTERIA DE POETI

Years ago, starting well before the First and Second World Wars and for decades after that, the cities and small towns of Emilia-Romagna had a type of establishment that catered mostly, but not exclusively, to men. Called *osterie*, these were the Italian equivalent of English pubs, humble places patronized mostly by the hardworking blue-collar neighborhood people who would meet after work to socialize, drink a few glasses of local wine, play cards, and talk about sports, politics, and women. The food served consisted of the cured meats and cheeses of the region and of pickled vegetables and small onions marinated in oil or vinegar. There were always large loaves of rustic bread, which the men would break and pass around the table. Wine only was served in squat, stemless glasses.

Located in a medieval building on the narrow central street of Via De' Poeti, Osteria de Poeti was where my father could be found after work a couple of nights a week. Occasionally my mother sent my brother and me to the osteria to fetch him for dinner. The osteria was for me a dark, forbidding place, with high vaulted ceilings and very thick walls that had, I thought, menacing shadows on them. My brother and I would walk to the osteria and enter the cavernous space with apprehension; our father would come toward us and hug us and we would walk back home.

Today Osteria de Poeti, like many other osterie, has become hip. While the cavernous space has been preserved and retained some of its rusticity, it has been embellished and modernized. The large dark wooden tables have been replaced by smaller, more intimate tables covered by crisp white linens. The once-dark room now has soft lighting from wall sconces. A piano sits at one end of the room and music is played nightly. A large table, strategically located, showcases a tantalizing array of antipasti, while the modern-looking bar offers in addition to wine, various *apèritivi*.

While I was researching this book, my husband and I had dinner at the Osteria. As always when I am in Bologna, I began my meal with the traditional antipasto of prosciutto, culatello, and mortadella, which was presented elegantly on a beautiful plate. As I was eating, I thought about my father, who, fifty years earlier, had sat in the same space, eating the same food and sipping a glass of wine, just as I was doing now. And I understood what this place meant and offered to him: a few hours of respite from the struggles of everyday life. Suddenly I was grateful that the osteria had been preserved and embellished, allowing a younger generation to enjoy it.

SOFT POLENTA WITH MEAT RAGÙ

Polenta col Ragù alla Modenese

SERVES 6 TO 8 AS AN
APPETIZER, 4 AS AN
ENTRÉE

2 tablespoons unsalted butter

⅔ cup freshly grated
Parmigiano-Reggiano

½ recipe Polenta (page 206)
freshly cooked as instructed
on page 207 and still in the pot

½ to 1 cup milk, if needed

1 recipe meat ragù (page 188)

There are certain eateries where we feel more at ease with ourselves and more comfortable with everything around us. Perhaps it is the food and the aromas that come from the kitchen, or perhaps it is the friendliness of the owners and the informality of the place. Trattoria la Nicchia, in the small hamlet of Castelnuovo outside Modena, is such a place. The food is bold, well defined, and typical of the area. The last time my husband and I were there, fall was giving way to winter and it was downright cold and nasty outside. As the waiter was pouring us a nice glass of Lambrusco, he looked at us and said, "I think what you need tonight is comfort food." And what could have been better than steaming soft polenta topped by a fragrant meat ragù?

This is one of those dishes that belongs everywhere and nowhere in particular. It can be served in small portions as a heartwarming winter appetizer, or as a meal, followed perhaps only by a good green salad.

STIR the butter and about half of the Parmigiano into the hot polenta and mix well to combine. If the polenta is a little too thick, add some milk, and stir until it has a smooth, creamy consistency.

MEANWHILE, reheat the ragù in a medium saucepan.

SPOON the hot polenta onto serving plates and top with the ragù. Sprinkle with the remaining Parmigiano and serve.

FRIED POLENTA WITH PROSCIUTTO, PORCINI, AND MARSALA

Crostoni di Polenta Fritta con Prosciutto e Porcini

SERVES 4

1 ounce dried porcini mushrooms, soaked in 2 cups lukewarm water for 20 minutes

2 to 3 tablespoons extra virgin olive oil

¼ cup finely minced shallots or yellow onion

1 tablespoon chopped flat-leaf parsley

1 medium-thick slice prosciutto (about 2 ounces), diced

Salt and freshly ground black pepper to taste

1 tablespoon unsalted butter

½ cup dry Marsala

Olive oil for frying

½ recipe Polenta (page 206) cooked and chilled as instructed on page 207, then cut into 3- to 4-inch squares

ried, crisp polenta topped by a sauté of fresh porcini, diced prosciutto, and Marsala wine is hard to resist. This preparation, which is at home in the restaurants and trattorie of the region, is particularly appreciated in the fall when fresh porcini abound. Since fresh porcini are not always available in American markets, I have used the easily available, very flavorful dried porcini. Although the mushrooms can top grilled, roasted, or even soft polenta, I urge you to try it first on fried polenta, just as it is done in the countryside of the region.

DRAIN the porcini mushrooms (reserve the soaking water for another use if desired) and rinse well under cold running water.

HEAT the oil in a medium skillet over medium heat. Add the shallots and cook, stirring, until lightly golden and soft, 5 to 6 minutes. Add the parsley, prosciutto, and porcini and stir for about 1 minute. Season lightly with salt and pepper. Raise the heat to high, add the butter and Marsala, and cook, stirring, until most of the wine has evaporated and the mushrooms are glazed, about 2 minutes. Taste and adjust the seasoning; remove from the heat. (The mushrooms can be prepared several hours ahead and set aside at room temperature. Keep warm if you will be serving them right away.)

HEAT ½ inch of oil in a medium nonstick 8- to 10-inch skillet over medium-high heat until beginning to smoke. Add a few slices of polenta at a time and fry turning once, until golden brown and crusty on both sides, 3 to 4 minutes. Drain on paper towels.

MEANWHILE, reheat the mushrooms if necessary.

PLACE the polenta on individual plates spoon the mushrooms over the polenta, and serve.

FRIED POLENTA WITH PANCETTA, SAGE, AND VINEGAR

Crostoni di Polenta con Pancetta, Salvia, e Aceto

SERVES 4

2 tablespoons olive oil, plus oil for frying

½ recipe Polenta (page 206), cooked and chilled as instructed on page 207, then cut into 3- to 4-inch squares

5 ounces thickly sliced pancetta, cut into 3-inch-long strips

10 to 12 large sage leaves, roughly shredded

¼ cup red wine vinegar

*C**ountry food is not the most subtle food in the world. Its appeal relies on straightforward, unfussy preparations and basic everyday ingredients. Giancarlo, one of my brother's childhood friends, who lives in the foothills of Pianoro, twenty miles or so outside Bologna, prepared for us these two appetizers based on polenta. The golden, crusty, fried polenta with its succulent topping sent me straight to heaven. If fried food is a "no-no" for you, you can grill or roast the polenta, or even grill slices of crusty Italian bread. Nothing, however, equals the taste of hot fried, crusty polenta–except perhaps, soft, creamy polenta.*

PREHEAT the oven to 200°F.

HEAT ½ inch of oil in a medium nonstick skillet over medium-high heat until just beginning to smoke. Add a few slices of polenta at a time and fry, turning once, until golden brown and crusty on both sides, 3 to 4 minutes. Drain on paper towels. Keep the polenta warm in the oven while you cook the pancetta.

HEAT the 2 tablespoons oil in a medium nonstick skillet over medium heat. Add the pancetta and cook until it has a nice golden color. Discard most of the fat in the skillet. Add the sage and vinegar and stir over medium heat until most of the vinegar has evaporated.

PLACE the polenta on individual plates, top with the pancetta, and drizzle with the pan juices. Serve hot.

SAVORY BREADS
AND SAVORY FRITTERS
Crescente e Crescentine

lour, water, and yeast, three ingredients that when combined, produce the most ancient food known to man. Bread. Way before the oven was invented, bread was made without leavening, flattened and cooked on a hot stone or under the embers. These ancestral breads were the predecessors of the more modern leavened bread. Emilia-Romagna has an array of savory unleavened and leavened breads.

There is the *piadina* of Romagna, a thin circle of flatbread which, until a few decades ago, the women of Romagna baked on the *testo*, a thick terra-cotta slab that was placed on the hot coals. Today the *testo* has been replaced by a metal griddle that can efficiently cook the *piadine* on top of the stove. *Piadina* is, for the people of Romagna, soul food. It pairs perfectly with thick slices of prosciutto and salamis. It wraps around soft cheeses and sautéed savory greens.

There are the *tigelle* of Modena, small, muffin-like rounds of dough that have a crisp exterior and a soft interior. They are split open and rubbed with a traditional condiment of minced salt pork or lard, mixed with chopped garlic and fresh rosemary. *Tigelle* are often served at the opening of a rustic, informal meal, but they are equally wonderful anytime during the day.

There is the *crescente* of Bologna, a savory, soft leavened bread, seasoned with oil and salt and studded with bits of pancetta or prosciutto. Cut into squares or diamond shapes, it is generally served with cured meats and pickled vegetables. Large rounds or rectangles of freshly baked, crusty *crescente* embellish the windows of the bread stores of Bologna.

The *gnocco fritte* of Modena and the *crescentine fritte* of Bologna are made with a simple bread dough that has been rolled out very thinly, cut into traditional local shapes and fried until it puffs up into golden brown, light-as-air fritters. These fritters, which are absolutely impossible to resist, are quite often the opening of a traditional Emilian meal.

This food, which today is seldom made at home, can be found in country trattorie or in rustic establishments outside the larger cities. Nostalgic diners flock to these places longing for the type of food that mothers and grandmothers ritually made at home.

BOLOGNESE SAVORY BREAD

Crescente al Forno

SERVES 10 TO 12

2 teaspoons active dry yeast

Pinch of sugar

4 cups unbleached
all-purpose flour

⅓ cup melted lard or olive oil

2 ounces thickly sliced
pancetta, finely minced

2 ounces thickly sliced
prosciutto, finely minced

1½ teaspoons salt

Olive oil

1 large egg, lightly beaten

Generous pinch of
coarse salt

*C*rescente *is the savory bread of Bologna. Made with a yeast dough that is studded with bits of pancetta, kneaded with lard or oil, and seasoned generously with salt,* crescente *is shaped into a large, somewhat flat round or rectangle and baked until it puffs up and its crust is golden and crisp. Years ago, the custom was to knead* crescente *with bits of pig skin and cooking water reserved from cotechino. My mother loved* crescente *and made it from time to time, but she would also buy it at Atti, the most venerable bread shop of Bologna, as it came piping hot out of the oven, and bring it home for us to enjoy. I can't even begin to tell you how delicious that bread was.*

This savory bread is still found in most bread shops of Bologna and in restaurant and trattorie that cherish traditional cooking. If you are in Bologna, buy a large slice in the medieval central market of the city, then go next door to Tamburini, a heaven for all kinds of hams, sausages, and cheeses, and have them fill the crescente *with sweet prosciutto or any of the incomparable cured meats of Bologna. If you should dine at Ristorante Diana, Ristorante Rodrigo, or Trattoria Gigina, squares of this bread will probably greet you at the table, perhaps with cubes of mortadella and small chunks of Parmigiano. If you can't get to Bologna, just get in your kitchen and start baking.*

IN a small bowl, dissolve the yeast in ¾ cup lukewarm water with the sugar. Let sit for about 10 minutes.

To make the dough by hand, mound the flour on a large wooden board or other work surface. With your fingers, make a well in the center of the flour. Place the dissolved yeast, the melted lard or the oil, 1 cup lukewarm water, the pancetta, prosciutto, and salt in the well. Stir the ingredients briefly with a fork, then draw the flour, starting with the inside walls of the well, into the mixture. When all the flour has been incorporated, knead the dough for a few minutes, until smooth and pliable. Shape the dough into a ball.

To make the dough with a food processor, place the flour, the melted lard or oil, pancetta, prosciutto, and salt in a food processor fitted with the metal blade and pulse briefly to mix. Add 1 cup lukewarm water and pulse until the dough gathers loosely around the blade. Transfer the dough to a wooden board or other work surface and knead it for a few minutes, until smooth and pliable. Shape the dough into a ball.

LIGHTLY brush the inside of a large bowl with oil. Put the dough into the bowl, cover tightly with plastic wrap, and leave in a warm, draft-free place to rise until doubled in bulk, 1 to 1½ hours.

LIGHTLY oil a 12 × 14-inch baking sheet.

PLACE the dough on a lightly floured surface and flatten it with your hands. Place the dough on the prepared baking sheet and, with your fingers, starting from the center of the dough, stretch out the dough evenly to cover the baking sheet. Cover with plastic wrap and let rise in a warm, draft-free place until doubled in volume, 45 minutes to 1 hour.

PREHEAT the oven to 400°F.

WITH a razor blade or a thin sharp knife, slash a shallow diamond pattern crisscross all over the dough. Brush the dough lightly with the beaten egg and sprinkle with the coarse salt.

PLACE the pan on the middle rack of the oven and bake until the *crescente* is a rich golden brown, 30 to 35 minutes. Serve hot or at room temperature.

FRIED FLATBREAD FRITTERS

Gnocco Fritte Modenese

MAKES ABOUT
25 FRITTERS;
SERVES 6 TO 8

1½ teaspoons active dry yeast

¾ cup milk, heated until lukewarm

Pinch of sugar

2 cups unbleached all-purpose flour

3 tablespoons unsalted butter, at room temperature

Olive oil or vegetable oil for deep-frying

Salt

They are called gnocco fritte *in Modena,* torta fritta *in Parma,* crescentine *in Bologna, and* pinzin *in Ferrara. Different names, same preparation. A dough made with flour, yeast, milk or water, and lard or oil is rolled out into a large thin sheet, cut into triangles, and deep-fried. The result are crisp, golden fritters that puff up almost instantly as they cook, becoming as light as air and simply impossible to resist.*

Years ago, in the farmland around Modena, the typical breakfast for farmers, who began work at 4 in the morning, often consisted of grapes and gnocco fritte, *because it was inexpensive to prepare and filling. These fritters were also the treat that children came home to. They were the highlight of country festivals, where they were sprinkled generously with salt and served on sheets of brown paper. And they were the pride of country* trattorie, *which piled them up on large platters and served them with sliced cured meats.*

IN a small bowl, dissolve the yeast in the lukewarm milk with the sugar. Let sit for about 10 minutes.

To make the dough by hand, place the flour in a large bowl and, with your fingertips, rub the butter into the flour until the mixture has a crumbly consistency. Mound the mixture on a large wooden board or other work surface. With your fingers, make a round well in the center of the flour. Place the dissolved yeast in the well and, with a fork, draw the flour, starting with the inside walls of the well, into the liquid. When all the flour has been incorporated, knead the dough for a few minutes, until smooth and pliable. Shape the dough into a ball.

To make the dough with a food processor, place the flour, butter, and dissolved yeast in a food processor fitted with the metal blade and pulse until the dough gathers loosely around the blade. Transfer the dough to a board or other work surface and knead it for a few minutes, until smooth and pliable. Shape the dough into a ball.

LIGHTLY brush the inside of a large bowl with oil. Put the dough into the bowl, cover with plastic wrap, and let it rise in a warm draft-free place until doubled in bulk, about 1 hour.

LIGHTLY flour a wooden board or other work surface. Punch down the dough and roll it out into a large thin rectangle. With a scalloped pastry wheel, cut the sheet of dough into 5-inch-wide strips, then cut the strips crosswise into rectangles. Lay the rectangles on a tray lined with parchment paper.

HEAT 1 inch of oil in a wide, deep skillet over high heat. When the oil is very hot, slide 3 or 4 rectangles of dough at a time into the pan and fry until they are golden on the bottom, 20 to 30 seconds. Turn and fry the other side until golden. Transfer to paper towels to drain.

ARRANGE the fritters on a large warm serving plate, sprinkle lightly with salt, and serve hot.

FLATBREAD OF THE

"BREAD SISTERS" OF BOLOGNA

Crescentine al Forno

MAKES ABOUT 25
CRESCENTINE;
SERVES 6 TO 8

**1 recipe Fried Flatbread
Fritters dough (page 59),
allowed to rise**

*The incomparable "bread sisters" of Bologna, Margherita and Valeria
Simili, who began making bread at a very early age in their father's
bread shop, take the thin dough rectangles of* crescentine *(the same dough
used for Fried Flatbread Fritters, page 59), and bake them instead of frying them. Traditionally, to test the temperature of the ovens to determine if
they were hot enough to bake bread, the bakers of Bologna put flat scraps
of bread dough, brushed with olive oil, into the ovens. If these scraps baked
quickly and evenly, it was time to bake the bread. Margherita and Valeria
knew this trick well, and they also knew that those flat scraps of baked
dough were simply delicious, so they devised this lighter version of fritters.
I first tasted these as the crisp, golden* crescentine *came out of the oven of
their cooking school in Bologna. Margherita and Valeria serve them with
soft, creamy cheeses, but they can be paired equally well with a pâté or, of
course, the wonderful cured meats of the region.*

PREHEAT the oven to 400°F. Lightly brush a large baking sheet or two
sheets with oil.

ROLL out and cut the dough as directed on page 60. Place the dough rectangles ½ inch apart on the prepared pan and bake on the middle rack of
the oven for 8 to 10 minutes, or until golden brown and crisp. Serve piping hot.

Note: Margherita and Valeria think that the bread is at its best when just
baked. A compromise would be to bake the *crescentine* several hours
ahead, then reheat them briefly just before serving.

"LITTLE MUFFINS" WITH PESTO

Tigelle Modenesi con Il Pesto

MAKES ABOUT 15
TIGELLE

For the tigelle

2 teaspoons active dry yeast

½ cup milk, heated until lukewarm

Pinch of sugar

3 cups unbleached all-purpose flour

3 tablespoons unsalted butter, chilled

2 teaspoons salt

¾ cup sparkling water, at room temperature

For the pesto

2 ounces prosciutto fat, finely chopped, or prosciutto and pancetta, finely chopped, about ⅓ cup

1 garlic clove, finely chopped

2 tablespoons finely chopped rosemary

1 tablespoon freshly grated Parmigiano-Reggiano

1 tablespoon extra virgin olive oil

Salt and freshly ground black pepper to taste

Olive oil for the griddle

*T*igelle, *small, flat rounds of dough that, once fried, resemble miniature muffins, are typical of the Modena hills area and can be found occasionally also in the adjoining hills of Bologna. The name of this unusual bread comes from the special cooking pan originally used to cook* tigelle, *terra-cotta flat dishes joined together. Once cooked, the hot* tigelle *were split open and rubbed with a filling made of lard, finely chopped garlic, rosemary, and black pepper, called* pesto *in Emilia. Today, fat from prosciutto or a mixture of chopped prosciutto and pancetta is often used instead of lard. Maurizia, my nephew's wife, who was reared on this type of bread, cooks her* tigelle *in a* tigelliera, *a multicircle, cast-iron pan. In this country,* tigelle *can be cooked on a cast-iron griddle or in a cast-iron pan.*

Serve tigelle *as a casual, earthy appetizer or light luncheon, as a mid-afternoon pick-me-up, or at any meal instead of bread.*

IN a small bowl, dissolve the yeast in the lukewarm milk with the sugar. Let sit for about 10 minutes until foamy.

To make the dough by hand, place the flour in a large bowl and, with your fingertips, rub the butter into the flour until the mixture has a crumbly consistency. Mound the flour mixture on a large wooden board or other work surface. With your fingers, make a round well in the center of the flour. Place the dissolved yeast, the salt, and sparkling water in the well. Stir the ingredients briefly with a fork, then draw the flour, starting with the inside walls of the well, into the mixture. When all the flour has been incorporated, knead the dough for a few minutes, until pliable and smooth. Shape the dough into a ball.

To make the dough with a food processor, place the flour, salt, and butter in a food processor fitted with the metal blade and pulse briefly to mix. With the machine running, gradually pour in the dissolved yeast and the sparkling water and process just until the dough gathers loosely around the blade. Transfer the dough to a wooden board or other work surface and knead it for a few minutes, until smooth and pliable. Shape the dough into a ball.

LIGHTLY brush the inside of a large bowl with oil and put the dough into the bowl. Cover tightly with plastic wrap and let rise in a warm, draft-free place until doubled in bulk, 2 to 3 hours.

WHILE the dough is rising, prepare the pesto: Combine all the ingredients in a small bowl and mix well. Taste and adjust the seasoning. Cover and refrigerate; bring to room temperature before using.

DUST a working surface lightly with flour. Turn the dough out onto the work surface and flatten it with the palms of your hands. Roll it out into a large circle about ¼ inch thick. Cut the dough into disks with a 3-inch round cookie cutter and place on a parchment-lined tray.

HEAT a cast-iron griddle or large cast-iron skillet over medium-high heat until hot. To test the heat, sprinkle the pan with a few drops of water–if the drops skip and disappear almost instantly, the temperature is just right.

BRUSH the pan lightly with oil and place one or two circles of dough on it. Cook until their bottoms are speckled with small golden brown bubbles, about 10 to 15 seconds. Turn and cook on the other side for 10 to 15 seconds. Continue to cook, turning the rounds every 10 seconds or so, for a total of 2 to 3 minutes. (If the spots are black, not brown, the heat is too high.) Place the cooked *tigelle* in a single layer on a cookie sheet, cover with foil, and cook the remaining dough.

WITH a serrated knife, split each *tigelle* horizontally, as you would an English muffin, leaving just a small part attached. Brush lightly with the pesto and serve hot.

Note: While *tigelle*, like most of the savory breads in this chapter, are at their best as soon as they are cooked, they can be cooked a few hours ahead and reheated briefly in a hot oven. *Tigelle* can also be stuffed with sliced prosciutto, salame, or mortadella.

ROMAGNA'S FLAT GRIDDLE BREAD

Piadina Romagnola

MAKES 8 *PIADINE*

2 cups unbleached all-purpose flour

1 teaspoon salt

1 teaspoon baking soda

¼ pound lard, melted, or ⅓ cup olive oil

1 cup plus 2 tablespoons milk, heated until lukewarm

1 teaspoon honey

Olive oil for the griddle

un, sparkling blue water, fresh fish, and steaming-hot, fragrant piadina *were, when I was a teenager, the spectacular allures of a Romagna seacoast vacation. After a day of sun and a night of dancing, my friends and I would mellow out at an outdoor café with a* piada, *as it was called in those days, stuffed with a variety of appetizing concoctions. A hot, just-baked* piadina *wrapped around a few slices of prosciutto or salami, or sautéed leafy greens or wild herbs tossed in oil scented with garlic, is simply unforgettable.*

This flat unleavened bread was at one time the everyday bread of the peasants and laborers of Romagna. Made since the Middle Ages and originally baked by country women on large hot slabs of terra-cotta, piadina *is soul food to the people of Romagna.*

In Romagna, piadina *can be found in any traditional restaurant and trattoria worth its salt. There the* piadine *are generally still made by hand, and they come to the table piled high in a breadbasket, either whole or sliced into wedges, covered tightly with colorful cloth napkins to keep them warm. The little cafés that dot the long stretch of Romagna beaches sell* piadine *like hotcakes, and they are an omnipresent staple of food festivals. Unfortunately, today* piadina, *like other traditional regional dishes that require a bit of time and patience to prepare, is often factory made and lacks the taste of the authentic version.*

If you enjoy making bread, you will find making piadina *very relaxing. As you roll out the pieces of dough one by one into circles and see them puff up and brown in front of your eyes, you will experience the wonder of creating one of the most basic foods of Romagna just as it was done centuries ago. While* piadine *are at their best as soon as they are cooked, they can be prepared a few hours ahead and reheated briefly in a hot oven or under the broiler.*

To make the dough by hand, combine the flour, salt, and baking soda in a bowl, then mound the mixture on a large wooden board or other work surface. With your fingers, make a round well in the center of the flour. Place the melted lard, milk, and honey in the well. Stir the ingredients briefly with a fork, then draw in the flour, starting with the inside walls of the well, into the mixture. When all the flour has been incorporated, knead the dough until it is smooth and pliable, 6 to 7 minutes. Shape the dough into a ball.

To make the dough with a food processor, combine the dry ingredients in a food processor fitted with the metal blade. Add the lard, milk, and honey, and pulse until the dough gathers loosely around the blade. Transfer the dough to a wooden board or other work surface and knead it for a minute or two, until smooth and pliable. Shape the dough into a ball.

PLACE the dough in a lightly oiled large bowl, cover with plastic wrap, and let it rest for 10 to 15 minutes.

LINE a baking sheet with parchment paper. Punch down the dough and cut it into 8 pieces. Work with 1 piece at a time, keeping the remaining pieces covered with plastic wrap.

SPRINKLE a work surface lightly with flour. Flatten a piece of dough with the palm of your hand and then roll it out into a thin 7-inch circle. Place on the baking sheet and cover with plastic wrap. Repeat with the remaining dough.

HEAT a cast-iron griddle pan or large cast-iron skillet over medium-high heat until hot. To test the heat, sprinkle the griddle with a few drops of water–if the drops skip and disappear almost instantly, the temperature is just right.

LIGHTLY brush the pan with oil and place 1 circle of dough on it. Cook for 10 to 15 seconds, until the bottom has a sprinkling of golden brown bubbles. Turn and cook the other side for 10 to 15 seconds. Continue to cook, turning every 10 to 15 seconds, until the dough has a parched white surface and is speckled all over with golden brown spots, 2 to 3 minutes. (If the spots are black, not brown, the heat is too high.) As the *piadina* cooks, prick any bubbles that form with a fork. Place the *piadina* on a large ovenproof plate, cover with foil, and keep warm in a 200°F oven. Roll out and cook the remaining *piadine* in the same manner.

SERVE the hot *piadine* whole or cut into wedges, with any of the accompaniments suggested in the box on page 66.

ACCOMPANIMENTS FOR PIADINA

• Mild Italian sausage, split lengthwise and grilled or sautéed.

• Soft, creamy cheese. In Romagna, we use *squacquerone*, a local fresh cow's milk cheese, or *stracchino*, a soft, buttery cow's milk cheese from Lombardy. Stracchino is sometimes available in specialty food markets and cheese shops. Substitute any mildly sweet soft cheese.

• Prosciutto di Parma, salame, or coppa.

• Swiss chard, spinach, or broccoli rabe, sautéed with garlic in olive oil (or the filling for Griddle Bread Turnovers, page 67).

GRIDDLE BREAD TURNOVERS

Crescioni Romagnoli

MAKES 8 *CRESCIONI*

For the filling

½ pound Swiss chard

Salt

½ pound spinach

½ pound broccoli rabe

¼ cup extra virgin olive oil

1 to 2 garlic cloves,
finely minced

Freshly ground black pepper
to taste

½ cup freshly grated
Parmigiano-Reggiano

½ cup golden raisins, soaked
in lukewarm water for
20 minutes and drained

1 recipe Flat Griddle Bread
dough (page 64)

Olive oil for the griddle

In Romagna, the dough used for piadina *is also rolled out very thinly, stuffed with a savory vegetable filling, and cooked on a cast-iron griddle in just the same way. Looking somewhat like a Neapolitan calzone,* crescioni *are an ancient dish, with a sweet and salty juxtaposition of ingredients reminiscent of the food of the Renaissance. They can be served as an appetizer, a light lunch or supper, or, as in Romagna, a midday "pick-me-up."*

REMOVE the stems from the Swiss chard and reserve for another use. Wash the leaves thoroughly under cold running water. Bring a large pot of water to a boil. Add a generous pinch of salt and the Swiss chard and cook, uncovered, until the leaves are tender, 4 to 6 minutes. Drain, let cool slightly, then squeeze out any excess water and mince it roughly. Set aside.

REMOVE the stems from the spinach and wash it thoroughly under cold running water. Cook as instructed for the Swiss chard, until tender. Drain and squeeze out the excess water. Roughly mince and set aside.

TRIM any large woody stems and wilted leaves from the broccoli rabe. Wash well under cold running water. Cook as instructed for the chard until tender, 5 to 7 minutes. Drain and squeeze out any excess water. Roughly mince the broccoli rabe and set aside.

HEAT the oil in a large skillet over medium heat. Add the garlic and stir for 15 to 20 seconds, then add the Swiss chard, spinach, and broccoli rabe. Season with salt and pepper, stir for a minute or two, and transfer the mixture to a bowl. Add the Parmigiano and raisins and mix well to combine. Taste and adjust the seasoning, then let cool. (The greens can be prepared several hours ahead and kept at room temperature.)

LINE a baking sheet with parchment paper. Punch down the dough and cut it into 8 equal pieces. Work with 1 piece of dough at a time, keeping the remaining dough covered with plastic wrap.

LIGHTLY sprinkle a work surface with flour. Flatten a piece of dough with the palm of your hand and roll it out into a thin 8-inch circle. (The dough needs to be rolled quite thin, since it is going to be folded over.) Place on the baking sheet and cover with plastic wrap. Roll out the remaining dough.

PLACE a nice mound of sautéed greens on one-half of each circle of dough. Fold the other half of the dough over the filling, aligning the edges, fold the edges over slightly to form a border, and pinch the border with your fingertips or crimp with a fork to seal. Cover the *crescioni* with plastic wrap.

HEAT a cast-iron griddle or large cast-iron skillet over medium-high heat until hot. To test the heat, sprinkle the griddle with a few drops of water—if the drops skip and disappear almost instantly, the heat is just right.

PREHEAT the oven to 200°F.

LIGHTLY brush the pan with a bit of oil and place only as many *crescioni* as can fit comfortably on the griddle. Cook, turning every 10 to 15 seconds, until both sides have a parched white surface and are speckled with golden brown spots, 3 to 4 minutes. (If the spots are black, the heat is too high.) Place the *crescioni* on a baking sheet, cover loosely with aluminum foil and keep warm in the oven while you cook the remaining turnovers. Serve warm.

OTHER FILLINGS FOR CRESCIONI

- Cooked diced potatoes and diced squash tossed with onions sautéed in olive oil

- Swiss chard, spinach, or broccoli rabe sautéed with cubes of pancetta or prosciutto

- Any one of the above cooked greens with cubes of mozzarella or Fontina

- Radicchio sautéed in olive oil with crisp pancetta

SOUPS

Zuppe

The soups of Emilia-Romagna, while outstanding in their own right, are not many, perhaps because the Emiliani and Romagnoli have spent more of their energies in the creation of the many splendid pasta dishes of the region. However, if one sits down to a bowl of small home-made tortellini swimming in a golden, flavorful capon broth, chances are that, at least for a while, the memories of those great pastas will be all but forgotten.

In spite of their many names—*minestra, minestrina, minestrone, zuppa*, each denoting whether the style of the soup is thick, thin, hearty, etc.—the soups of Emilia-Romagna can be divided into two categories: the elegant, refined clear broth soups and the simpler, gutsier preparations rooted in the peasant tradition. The clear broth soups rely heavily on the quality of the homemade broth. When delicate, homemade pasta is cooked in homemade broth, nothing else is necessary, except perhaps a sprinkle of Parmigiano-Reggiano cheese.

The more substantial soups of *la cucina povera*, the cooking of the poor, depend heavily on *soffritto*, the traditional savory base of onion, parsley, garlic, pancetta, and herbs or other aromatic ingredients, chopped and sautéed together, which gives the soups their unique taste and identity. Pasta and Bean Soup, Rice and Cabbage Soup, and Pancotto are all perfect examples of *la cucina povera*. *Pancotto*, the humblest of all soups, which turns stale bread into a thick, porridge-like soup, filled the bellies of countless people during and immediately after the Second World War. Such soups were once made with water instead of broth, and used the most basic and modest ingredients, showing the creativity and resourcefulness of people who, in spite of lean times, would not settle for mediocre food.

There is today in Emilia-Romagna a renewed appreciation for this type of food. While the homogenization of Italy has reached many of the larger cities of the region, the smaller towns have retained more of their simple values and old ways with food. And it is in these little towns that I have come across soups whose flavors match the memory of flavors embedded deep within me. Perhaps it is still true that trends will come and go, but good food will never go out of style.

Broth
Il Brodo

At one time, every family in Emilia-Romagna routinely prepared homemade broth, usually on Sunday. In my house, it was a lazy day for most of the family, except for my mother, who rose earlier than usual to put up *la pentola del brodo*. The aroma of the slowly simmering broth would permeate the house in no time at all, making it almost impossible to continue sleeping. My brother, sister, and I would wander into the kitchen, slouch on the chairs around the kitchen table, and for a few minutes we would be quiet, inhaling that comfortable scent coming from the large bubbling pot. I loved Sunday mornings.

Broth is essential to many dishes of Emilia-Romagna and it is the vital ingredient in most soups. (Tortellini or tagliolini cooked in canned broth would be an abomination.) It is essential to risotto, to braised meats, and to stews. It is important to sauces and vegetables, and it is absolutely terrific on its own. My father loved broth, especially in winter. It comforted him, it warmed him, and it pleased him probably more than any other food.

Italian *brodo*, which has absolutely nothing to do with French stock, is made by putting a variety of meats, meat scraps, and bones in a large pot with a few vegetables, covering them with cold water, and bringing to a gentle simmer. The broth is skimmed of the impurities that come to the surface during the first minutes of cooking, then simmered very, very gently for no less than three hours. The long, slow cooking is needed to draw out all the flavor from the bones and vegetables. During this time, the broth needs only an occasional check or stir—nothing else. The best bones and meat scraps for *brodo* are beef, veal, capon, and chicken. Lamb and pork are generally not used because their flavors are too assertive. In Emilia-Romagna and throughout Italy, the traditional *brodo* is made in this way. We do not roast bones or use mixed herbs to flavor it, since those would overwhelm the broth's clean taste. Broth should be light and flavorful and have a great golden color. A good *brodo* is where much of the good cooking of the Emilia-Romagna region begins.

MEAT BROTH

Brodo di Carne

MAKES ABOUT
2 QUARTS

In making brodo, the impurities come to the surface as the water begins to simmer. The skimming is done at that point, and it might be necessary to do it a couple of times during the initial simmering.

2 pounds veal shanks, bones, and scraps

2 pounds beef scraps and bones, preferably knuckle bones

1 pound chicken bones and scraps

2 small carrots, peeled and cut into pieces

1 large celery stalk, cut into pieces

1 medium onion, quartered

A few sprigs parsley

2 small ripe tomatoes

Salt to taste

WASH the bones, meat scraps, and vegetables thoroughly under cold running water. Put all the ingredients except the salt in a large stockpot and add cold water to cover by 3 to 4 inches. Partially cover the pot and bring just to a boil over medium heat. As soon as the water begins to bubble, reduce the heat to low and skim off all the foam that has risen to the surface. Cook, at the gentlest of simmers, for about 3 hours.

SEASON with salt during the last few minutes of cooking.

IF you are planning to use the broth within a few hours, strain it through a fine-mesh strainer directly into another pot and remove the fat that comes to the surface of the broth as it cools with a spoon. If the broth is for later use, strain it, divide it among several small containers, and place the containers in a bowl of ice water to cool completely. It can be kept in the refrigerator, tightly covered, for 2 to 3 days or frozen for up to 2 months. Before using the broth, remove the fat that has solidified on the surface, and bring to a full boil.

CAPON BROTH

Brodo di Cappone

MAKES ABOUT
4½ QUARTS

One 7- to 8-pound capon

2 pounds veal bones or
veal shanks

2 to 3 pounds beef scraps
and bones, preferably
knuckle bones

2 carrots, peeled and
cut into pieces

2 celery stalks, cut into pieces

1 small onion, quartered

1 ripe tomato, quartered

Few sprigs parsley

Salt to taste

Chicken broth can't be made with just any chicken. A capon, a young neutered rooster, is the bird of choice in Emilia-Romagna. Usually weighing six to eight pounds, capon is known for its moist, delicate meat. Roasted capon is usually served at Christmas.

To extract all the flavor from the capon and the bones, the broth needs to simmer for a long time and, in doing so, it will cook the capon to the point where the bird will literally fall apart. That's fine, since the emphasis here is on the quality of the broth, not the perfect doneness of the capon. Just scoop up the capon, remove the meat from the bones, and use it as suggested in the note below. For the people of Bologna, nothing tastes better than homemade tortellini cooked in a fragrant capon broth.

WASH the capon, bones, and vegetables thoroughly under cold running water. Put all the ingredients except the salt in a large stockpot and add cold water to cover by 3 to 4 inches. Partially cover the pot and bring the liquid just to a boil over medium heat. As soon as the water begins to bubble, reduce the heat to low and skim off all the foam that has risen to the surface. Cook at the gentlest of simmers for 2 to 2½ hours. Season with salt during the last few minutes of cooking.

REMOVE the capon and set aside. If you are planning to use the broth within a few hours, strain it through a fine-mesh strainer directly into another pot and remove the fat that comes to the surface of the broth as it cools with a spoon, or by dragging a piece of paper towel over the broth surface.

IF the broth is for later use, strain it, divide it among several small containers, and place the containers in a bowl of ice water to cool completely. It can be kept in the refrigerator, tightly covered, for 2 to 3 days or frozen for up to 2 months. (See Freezing Broth for Later Use, page 73.) Before using, remove the fat that has solidified on the surface, and bring the broth to a full boil.

Note: Now, not only do you have a divine, flavorful broth to use for Tortellini in Capon Broth, Tagliolini in Broth, or Faccini's Anolini in Broth but you have the bonus of tender, moist meat that can be paired with a variety of vegetables.

REMOVE the meat from the bones and keep it warm in some of its hot strained broth until you are ready to use it. Serve it with one of the green sauces in this book and with Mashed Potatoes with Parmigiano (page 323). Or chill the meat, cut it into strips, and toss it with arugula, extra virgin olive oil, and balsamic vinegar.

CHICKEN BROTH Substitute a large plump, about 6 pounds, chicken for the capon and proceed as instructed.

FREEZING BROTH FOR LATER USE

Freezing gives you the advantage of having flavorful broth on hand to use on the spur of the moment. Freeze it in small containers, or freeze it in ice cube trays—when the broth is frozen, unmold the cubes, transfer to plastic bags, and freeze until ready to use.

TORTELLINI IN CAPON BROTH

Tortellini Bolognesi in Brodo di Cappone

SERVES 8

For the filling

1 tablespoon unsalted butter

¼ pound pork loin, trimmed of fat and cut into ½-inch cubes

2 ounces sliced prosciutto, cut into small pieces

2 ounces sliced mortadella, cut into small pieces

½ cup freshly grated Parmigiano-Reggiano

⅛ teaspoon freshly grated nutmeg, or more to taste

2 medium eggs, lightly beaten (plus 1 extra egg if necessary)

Salt to taste

For the tortellini

1¾ cups unbleached all-purpose flour

3 large eggs

2½ quarts Capon Broth (page 72) or Meat Broth (page 71)

¾ cup freshly grated Parmigiano-Reggiano

The authentic filling of tortellini is passionately debated in Bologna, pitting even members of the same family against each other. I remember one year while I was buying shoes in Bologna in one of Magli's many stores, I struck up a friendly conversation with the woman who managed the store. After hearing that I was a cooking professional, living in California and teaching the food of Bologna to eager Californians, she began drilling me on the subject. The true test came when she asked me what I put in the filling for tortellini. When I told her the ingredients I use and in what proportions, adding that the recipe and proportions were my mother's own, she looked at me with surprise and said, "Ah, brava, you know what you are doing." Curiously enough, my mother's tortellini filing is very similar to that of La Dotta Confraternità del Tortellino, a Bolognese fraternity that codified the ingredients and proportions that the true tortellini of Bologna should have and filed the recipe with the chamber of commerce.

To prepare the filling, melt the butter in a medium skillet over medium-high heat. When the butter begins to foam, add the pork loin and cook, stirring, until lightly golden, 3 to 4 minutes. Transfer the meat and cooking juices to a food processor fitted with the metal blade, add the prosciutto and mortadella, and pulse until the meat is finely ground but not pureed. Transfer the meat to a bowl, add the Parmigiano, nutmeg, and eggs and mix well with a wooden spoon or with your hands. Taste and adjust the seasoning, adding a bit more nutmeg and salt if needed. (Keep in mind that mortadella and prosciutto are salty.) The filling should be moist and just a bit sticky; if too dry, stir in another beaten egg. Cover the bowl and refrigerate for an hour or so to allow the mixture to firm up a bit. (The filling can be prepared up to 24 hours ahead.)

Using the flour and eggs, prepare the pasta dough as instructed on pages 95–97. Roll out the dough following the instructions on pages 97–98 and prepare the tortellini as instructed on page 99. Line a large tray or cookie sheet with a kitchen towel and place the tortellini in a single layer on it, making sure they do not touch each other, or they will stick together. They can be cooked immediately, or they can be refrigerated, uncovered, for several hours or overnight. In that case, turn them a few times so they dry evenly.

PUT the broth in a large pot and bring it to a boil over medium heat. Drop the tortellini gently into the pot and cook until tender but still a bit firm to the bite, 2 to 5 minutes, depending on their freshness. Ladle the tortellini and broth into individual serving bowls, sprinkle with the Parmigiano, and serve.

Preparing Ahead   To simplify this dish, you can prepare it in stages:

- Make the broth and the filling a few weeks ahead and freeze.

- Shape the tortellini a day ahead and refrigerate, uncovered.

- Bring the broth to a boil and cook the tortellini, just before serving.

TORTELLINI IN BOLOGNA

In spite of today's harried pace, several of the traditional Bolognese trattorie and restaurants still take pride in serving this time-honored preparation. At Trattoria Boni, Trattoria Gigina, Antica Trattoria del Pontelungo, Ristorante Diana, Sandro al Navile, and Franco Rossi, one can enjoy superb tortellini in broth or with Bolognese meat ragù. The tiny tortellini are made by the expert hands of the Bolognese *sfoglina*, the pasta maker, who, day after day, kneads and rolls out by hand large batches of dough and turns them into these delicate morsels. Unfortunately, the *sfoglina* is an institution that will soon vanish, since fewer and fewer women are interested in taking on this demanding task.

SOUP OF EGG AND PARMESAN STRANDS

Minestra di Passatelli

SERVES 6 TO 8

3 large eggs

Pinch of salt

Grated zest of 1 lemon

½ teaspoon freshly
grated nutmeg

1 tablespoon all-purpose flour

1 cup freshly grated
Parmigiano-Reggiano, plus
(optional) extra for serving

½ cup fine dried bread
crumbs, plus more if needed

2 quarts Meat Broth (page 71)

Passatelli, a soup made with an unusual soft dough of Parmigiano-Reggiano cheese, bread crumbs, nutmeg, and eggs that is riced directly into simmering homemade meat broth, was one of my father's favorite. He was a light eater and was at his happiest when he could linger over a large bowl of this flavorful soup, which, he would say, restored his spirit as well as his mind and body.

Passatelli is a specialty of the area that encompasses the cities of Modena, Bologna, and Ferrara, and it varies slightly from place to place. For example, my mother made the dough as described above, while Gigina in Bologna, one of my very favorite trattorie, adds a bit of flour and grated lemon zest. When the thin, golden strands of the passatelli cook in the hot broth, the aroma of the lemon infuses the broth with lightness and delicacy.

BEAT the eggs with the salt in a medium bowl. Add the lemon zest, nutmeg, flour, Parmigiano, and bread crumbs and mix well with a fork. When the mixture has the consistency of a soft dough, place it on a pastry board and knead it briefly, adding a bit more Parmigiano or bread crumbs if it should stick to the board. The dough should have a compact but tender, granular consistency. Place it on a plate, cover with plastic wrap, and set aside at room temperature for 30 minutes or so.

PUT the broth in a saucepan and bring to a gentle boil over medium heat.

DIVIDE the dough into two to three pieces. One piece at a time, put the dough in a potato ricer or a food mill fitted with the coarse disk and pass it directly into the simmering broth. Cook the strands for about 1 minute. Turn off the heat and let the soup rest for a few minutes. Serve with a sprinkling of additional Parmigiano if desired.

ANOLINI IN BROTH

Gli Anolini in Brodo

SERVES 4 TO 6

For the filling

¼ cup fine dried bread crumbs

2 to 3 tablespoons Chicken Broth (page 73) or canned low-sodium chicken broth

1 cup freshly grated Parmigiano-Reggiano

⅛ teaspoon freshly grated nutmeg

Salt to taste

1 extra-large egg, lightly beaten

2 to 3 tablespoons milk, optional

For the anolini

2¾ cups unbleached all-purpose flour

4 extra-large eggs

2 quarts Capon Broth (page 72) or Meat Broth (page 71)

⅓ to ½ cup freshly grated Parmigiano-Reggiano

*A*nolini a*re rounds of small, flat stuffed pasta that are generally served in broth and are a specialty of Parma, Piacenza, and the surrounding countryside. Served at Christmas, Easter, and other festive occasions, anolini are traditionally filled with meat and vegetables that have been braised slowly for many hours. But at Trattoria da Faccini in Castell' Arquato in the province of Piacenza, we found anolini stuffed with Parmigiano-Reggiano. This lighter version, which came to our table in a fragrant capon broth, was so flavorful that I stopped talking (not an easy task for me), so that I could concentrate and enjoy the soup to its fullest.*

TO prepare the filling, place the bread crumbs in a bowl, add the broth, and mix well. Add the Parmigiano and nutmeg and season lightly with salt. Stir in the beaten egg and mix well with a wooden spoon. The filling should be moist and a bit sticky; if it is too dry, add a few tablespoons of milk. Taste and add salt if needed. Cover and refrigerate. (The filling can be prepared up to 1 day ahead. Bring it to room temperature before using.)

USING the flour and eggs, prepare the pasta dough as instructed on pages 95–97. Roll out the pasta dough following the methods on pages 97–98. Prepare the anolini. Line a large tray or cookie sheet with a kitchen towel and place the anolini on it in a single layer, making sure they do not touch each other. The anolini can be cooked immediately, or they can be refrigerated, uncovered, for several hours or overnight. In that case, turn them once or twice so they dry evenly.

PUT the broth in a large pot and bring to a boil over medium heat. Drop the anolini gently into the pot and cook until tender but still a bit firm to the bite, 2 to 5 minutes, depending on their freshness. Ladle the anolini and broth into individual serving bowls, sprinkle with the Parmigiano, and serve.

Preparing Ahead

- Prepare the broth a few weeks ahead and freeze.

- Prepare the anolini a day ahead and refrigerate, uncovered.

- Bring the broth to a boil and cook the anolini at the last moment.

ANOLINI WITH BUTTER AND SAGE Anolini are also delicious served *asciutti* (literally, as a pasta), tossed simply with butter, chopped fresh sage, and freshly grated Parmigiano.

ANOLINI WITH TRUFFLES Anolini are spectacular tossed with butter and Parmigiano and topped with shavings of fresh white truffle.

FREEZING STUFFED PASTA

Because of their relatively dry filling, tortellini and anolini freeze better than most other stuffed pastas. Spread the tortellini or anolini on a cookie sheet in a single layer, without touching, and place in the freezer. When they are completely frozen, put them in one or several plastic bags, secure tightly, and return them to the freezer, where they can be kept for a couple of months. Do not defrost tortellini or anolini before cooking or the pasta will become sticky—just add them to the simmering broth still frozen.

MINESTRONE OF MODENA

Minestrone Modenese

SERVES 8 TO 10

2 quarts cold water, Chicken Broth (page 73), or canned low-sodium chicken broth

⅓ to ½ cup extra virgin olive oil

3 ounces sliced pancetta, chopped

3 ounces sliced prosciutto, chopped, optional

1 cup minced yellow onions

½ cup minced celery

½ cup minced carrots

Generous 1 tablespoon chopped flat-leaf parsley

2 cups diced ripe tomatoes or minced drained canned tomatoes

½ cup dried cannellini beans or borlotti beans, picked over, soaked overnight in plenty of water, drained, and rinsed

2 medium boiling potatoes, peeled and diced

¼ pound green beans, ends trimmed and cut into ½-inch pieces

2 medium zucchini, ends trimmed and diced

¼ pound white mushrooms, wiped clean, trimmed, and diced

2 cups shredded Savoy cabbage

¼ pound asparagus, tough bottoms removed and diced

*M*inestrone *(meaning "big soup") is the generic Italian name for vegetable soup. Minestrone is generally a thick soup, and it may contain, besides an array of fresh seasonal vegetables, beans, chickpeas, tomatoes, garlic, and herbs. It may also have the addition of small pasta or rice, and can be served hot, at room temperature, or chilled, topped with olive oil or Parmigiano.*

Most of the minestroni *of Emilia-Romagna begin with a* soffritto, *onions, celery, carrots, and parsley, garlic, or other fresh herbs sautéed together in oil or lard. While the choice of vegetables and legumes that go into a minestrone is dictated by the season and by personal preference, the cook's intuition is responsible for balancing the soup's flavor. A good minestrone should have a hardy but mellow flavor, with no sharp edges. Modena, a city that is at once refined and earthy, prepares a minestrone enriched with an aromatic* soffritto *of pancetta, prosciutto, onion, carrot, celery, parsley, and tomatoes. The minestrone, which is simmered slowly for no less than two and a half hours, becomes densely thick and absolutely irresistible. Serve it as the Modenesi do, hot in winter, warm in the spring and fall, and at room temperature in summer.*

HEAT the water in a medium saucepan and keep warm over low heat.

HEAT the oil in a large pot over medium heat. Add the pancetta, the prosciutto, if using, the onions, celery, carrots, and parsley and cook, stirring, until the vegetables are lightly golden and soft, 8 to 10 minutes. Add the tomatoes and stir until they begin to soften, about 5 minutes.

ADD the cannellini beans, potatoes, green beans, zucchini, mushrooms, cabbage, asparagus, peas, and basil to the pot, season with salt and pepper, and stir for 2 to 3 minutes to coat the vegetables well with the savory base. Add the water and the Parmigiano rind, if using, and bring just to a boil. Reduce the heat to low, partially cover the pot, and simmer, stirring from time to time, for 2 to 2½ hours, until the minestrone has a dense, thick consistency. If the soup should thicken too much, add a bit more

1 cup fresh or frozen small green peas

8 to 10 basil leaves, shredded

Salt and freshly ground black pepper to taste

Rind from a small piece of Parmigiano-Reggiano, scraped clean, optional

⅓ to ½ cup freshly grated Parmigiano-Reggiano

water. Remove the cheese rind if you used it, and adjust the seasoning.

TURN off the heat and let the soup stand for about 30 minutes. Serve with a sprinkling of Parmigiano.

RICE OR SMALL PASTA such as ditalini can be added to the soup during the last minutes of cooking. (Add rice 10 minutes before you turn off the heat, pasta 3 to 5 minutes before.) The rice or pasta will keep cooking as the soup rests.

"LA NEBBIA"

If you should happen to travel through the Emilia side of the region during the autumn, you will probably encounter a habitual guest, *la nebbia*, the fog. The fog, which can be devastatingly thick, envelops the flat, fertile farmland, its trees, houses, and people like a dark mantle, penetrating through even layers of clothing all the way to the bone. As evening falls, the locals, who know the fog very well, scurry home, trying to beat the darkness. Others who are caught in it drive slowly and defensively (very unusual for Italians) in order to reach their destination safely. The next morning, the fog slowly and lazily disappears, but she will be back in a few hours. After all, this is her season to shine.

The Many Faces of "Pasta e Fagioli"

Pasta e fagioli (pasta and bean soup), one of Italy's most popular food combinations, is convivial food. It is unassuming, basic, filling, and comforting.

Beans have always been synonymous with the food of the poor, since poor people got their protein requirements from inexpensive beans rather than from costly meat, which at one time would appear on their tables only on Sunday or on special occasions.

In Emilia-Romagna, *pasta e fagioli* is a dish that is always yet never the same, since, in preparing it, the cook relies on her own instincts, not on written recipes. But although the variations of *pasta e fagioli* are as numerous as the people who inhabit the region, the cooking procedure follows a traditional pattern. The beans are cooked in water or broth. A *soffritto*, the traditional savory base of cured meats, vegetables, and/or herbs that gives soup its own identity, is added to the beans (or the cooked beans are added to the *soffritto*). Sometimes the cooked beans are pureed, other times they are only partially pureed or left whole. Sometimes the rind of a piece of Parmigiano-Reggiano or a prosciutto rind is added for additional flavor. Often homemade or small dried pasta is added to the soup and cooked. While the cooking techniques required for these soups are minimal and the modest ingredients will not break anyone's bank, the cooking sequence, with its layering of savory ingredients, builds up the soup's flavor and richness.

QUICK-SOAK METHOD FOR DRIED BEANS

If you forget to soak dried beans overnight, this is what you can do: Pick over the beans, place them in a large saucepan, and add cold water to cover by 2 to 3 inches. Bring to a gentle boil over medium heat and simmer the beans, uncovered, for 2 to 3 minutes. Turn off the heat and leave the beans in the water for 1 to 2 hours, then drain. Cook as instructed.

COOKING DRIED BEANS

Italians love beans and use them in myriad dishes. Because fresh beans have a very short life span, most cooks rely heavily on dried beans. While regional preferences dictate the choice of dried beans, the method for cooking them is basically the same throughout Italy.

- Pick over the beans, put them in a large bowl, add cold water to cover generously, and let soak for several hours, or overnight. (The long soaking softens the beans and they will cook more evenly.)

- Drain the beans and rinse them under cold running water. Put the beans in a large pot and add cold water to cover them by 3 to 4 inches. Partially cover the pot and bring to a gentle simmer. Simmer the beans gently over low heat, stirring occasionally, until tender, 40 minutes to 1 hour. (Do not let the water boil, or the skins will burst.)

- Add salt only at the end of cooking, or the beans skins will crack as they cook.

- Toward the end of cooking, taste the beans often to determine their doneness.

- If you are not using the beans right away, transfer them to a bowl with their liquid. Cool them to room temperature, then cover and refrigerate them for up to a day or two. (The beans' cooking liquid is sometimes added to sauces and ragùs to flavor and thicken them.)

- 2 cups dried beans weigh approximately ¾ pound.

- 2 cups dried beans make approximately 4 cups cooked beans.

The beans used most frequently in Emilia-Romagna are called "borlotti." These plump, meaty beans with beige, pink, and brown marbling are generally available in Italian markets or health food stores. The bland flavor of canned beans will give you an equally bland dish.

PASTA AND BEAN SOUP

Maltagliati con Fagioli

SERVES 6

2 cups dried borlotti beans or cranberry beans, picked over, soaked overnight in cold water to cover generously, drained, and rinsed

1 medium boiling potato, peeled and cut into large pieces

¼ cup extra virgin olive oil

1 cup finely minced yellow onions

2 garlic cloves, minced

2 tablespoons chopped parsley flat-leaf

3 to 4 ounces pancetta, chopped or very finely diced

2 cups Homemade Tomato Sauce (page 22) or 2 tablespoons double-concentrated Italian tomato paste, diluted in 2 cups Meat Broth (page 71), or canned low-sodium chicken broth, or cold water

Salt and freshly ground black pepper to taste

1 recipe Maltagliati (page 84) or 6 ounces dried small tubular pasta, such as ditalini

½ cup freshly grated Parmigiano-Reggiano

*M*altagliati, *literally meaning "badly cut," are small pieces of pasta scraps from the rolled-out dough used to make tortellini, tortelloni, and tagliatelle. Since, in the frugal kitchens of Emilia-Romagna, nothing ever went to waste, these irregular pieces of dough were added to bean or lentil soups. The soft egg pasta, with its light consistency, paired so well with these soups that later the women of the region would roll out pasta specifically to make* maltagliati. *Today,* maltagliati *are often store-bought.*

PUT the beans in a medium pot, add 2½ quarts water and the potato, and bring just to a boil over medium heat. As soon as the water begins to bubble, reduce the heat to low and simmer, uncovered, stirring from time to time, until the beans are tender, 45 minutes to 1 hour.

WHILE the beans are cooking, prepare the savory base. Heat the oil in a small saucepan over medium heat. Add the onions, garlic, parsley, and pancetta, and cook, stirring, until the onions and pancetta are lightly golden, 5 to 6 minutes. Stir in the tomato sauce and season with salt and pepper. Simmer, uncovered, until the sauce is reduced by approximately half, 12 to 15 minutes. Turn off the heat.

PUREE the beans and potato, with their liquid, in a food processor or using a food mill and return to the pot. Add the savory base, place the pot over low heat, and simmer for 5 to 6 minutes. Taste and adjust the seasoning.

ADD the pasta and cook, stirring from time to time, until it is tender but still firm to the bite. Turn off the heat and let the soup stand for 5 to 10 minutes.

SERVE with the Parmigiano.

Preparing Ahead The soup can be prepared 1 day ahead, but in that case, do not add the pasta. Let cool, cover, and refrigerate. When you are ready to serve, bring the soup to a gentle boil, then add and cook the pasta.

MALTAGLIATI

2 large eggs

1½ cups all-purpose flour

PREPARE the pasta dough with the eggs and flour called for here as instructed on pages 95–97. Roll out the pasta by hand or by machine (pages 97–98).

LET the pasta sheets dry for a few minutes on the counter, then fold the sheets loosely into 3-inch-wide flat rolls, or fold lengthwise in half if you used a machine. Cut off one corner of the rolled-up pasta diagonally to form a triangle, then cut off the other corner the same way. Now cut the pasta straight across, turning the pointed part of the pasta roll into another triangle. (If this seems a bit confusing, just remember that the pasta shape is called "badly cut," so don't worry how badly you cut the rolled-out dough.) Repeat the process with the remaining dough. Unfold and spread out the *maltagliati* so they don't stick to each other. They can be cooked immediately or dried and used at a later time.

KEEP IN MIND

Bean soups, just like lentil and chickpea soups, have a propensity for becoming very thick after they sit because the starch in the beans quickly absorbs the liquid in the soup.

After adding the pasta to the soup, let the soup stand for no more than 10 minutes, or the pasta will overcook, absorb the broth, and swell considerably in size.

If you omit the pasta, however, allow the soup to stand for 20 minutes or more so it will thicken and its flavors will become more pronounced.

ITALO'S PASTA AND BEAN SOUP

Pasta e Fagioli di Italo

SERVES 6

3 cups dried borlotti beans or cranberry beans, picked over, soaked overnight in cold water to cover generously, drained, and rinsed

⅓ cup extra virgin olive oil

1 cup finely minced yellow onions

¼ pound sliced pancetta, chopped or very finely minced

4 to 5 medium sage leaves, chopped

1 garlic clove, finely minced

Salt and freshly ground black pepper to taste

6 ounces dried small tubular pasta, such as ditalini

⅓ cup freshly grated Parmigiano-Reggiano

ere we have another version of the humble bean and pasta soup from Italo Pedroni, owner of the well-known Osteria di Rubbiara, in the countryside of Modena, which, in the old peasant tradition, uses water, not broth.

PUT the beans in a large pot, add 2½ quarts water, and bring just to a boil over medium heat. As soon as the water begins to bubble, reduce the heat to low and simmer, uncovered, stirring from time to time, until the beans are tender, 45 minutes to 1 hour.

MEANWHILE, prepare the savory base: Heat the olive oil in a medium saucepan over medium heat. Add the onions and pancetta and cook, stirring, until lightly golden, 5 to 6 minutes. Add the sage and garlic and cook for a minute or two longer. Season with salt and pepper and turn off the heat.

ADD the savory base to the beans and simmer for 4 to 5 minutes, then add the pasta. Cook over medium heat, stirring from time to time, until the pasta is tender but still a bit firm to the bite. Turn off the heat, taste, and adjust the seasoning. Let the soup stand for a few minutes.

SERVE sprinkled with the Parmigiano-Reggiano.

YESTERDAY LARD, TODAY OLIVE OIL

Years ago, the most popular cooking fat of Emilia-Romagna was chemical-free, sweet lard. I still remember my mother's potatoes cooked in a large black skillet with lard. They were awesome. While some traditional cooks, such as Ivan and Barbara of Hostaria da Ivan in Parma's countryside, still make their own lard and use it in many of their dishes, the majority of people have replaced lard with olive oil.

LENTIL AND BREAD SOUP

Zuppa di Lenticchie e Pane

SERVES 8 TO 10

2½ cups dried brown lentils (about 1 pound), picked over and rinsed well

2½ quarts Meat Broth (page 71), or canned low-sodium chicken broth, or cold water

Rind from a small piece Parmigiano-Reggiano, scraped clean, optional

⅓ cup extra virgin olive oil

1 cup very finely minced yellow onions

2 tablespoons chopped flat-leaf parsley

Pinch of dried thyme

Mamma Albertina, my nephew's mother-in-law, is an old-fashioned country cook. As she was preparing this soup in the beautifully appointed large kitchen of her newly remodeled country home, she reminisced about the time in her life, during and after the Second World War, when ingredients and money were scarce and imagination and resourcefulness were needed to prepare food. "We thickened the soup by pureeing lentils, beans, or potatoes, or we added old stale bread. Stale bread also took the place of the pasta. Water was used instead of broth, which was seldom affordable. A few ounces of sausage or pancetta would flavor the soup." Then, smiling, she continued, "Today when I make soup, I use rich, flavorful broth, and I splurge on the quality of the oil, which must be extra virgin. I still add to the soup the rind of Parmigiano, which I first scrape thoroughly with a knife, because, in our peasant tradition, nothing ever went to waste. It gives the soup a delicious, delicate taste of Parmigiano."

PUT the lentils in a large pot, add the broth and the Parmigiano rind, if using, and bring just to a boil over medium heat. As soon as the liquid

THE VIRTUES OF A THICK SOUP

The virtues of a thick soup are many. They nourish, they comfort, they fill and satisfy. Why anyone would opt for a thin, watery soup instead of a densely gratifying soup is beside me.

ANONYMOUS

Lentil soup, like bean and potato soups, becomes thicker as it sits. If you are preparing this soup a day ahead, you will probably need to add a bit more broth or water when you reheat it. Keep in mind that the bread the soup is served with will also soak up broth, making it even thicker.

begins to bubble, reduce the heat to low, partially cover the pot, and simmer, stirring from time to time, until the lentils are tender, 40 to 50 minutes. Remove from the heat.

PUREE about two-thirds of the lentils with some of their liquid in a food processor or using a food mill and return to the pot. Set aside.

WHILE the lentils are cooking, prepare the savory base. Heat the oil in a small saucepan over medium heat. Add the onions, parsley, and thyme and cook, stirring, until the onions begin to color, 3 to 4 minutes. Raise the heat a bit, add the sausage and pancetta, and stir until the meat has a nice golden color, 3 to 4 minutes. Stir in the diluted tomato paste and season with salt and pepper. As soon as the base begins to bubble, reduce the heat to low and simmer, uncovered, until it has a medium-thick consistency, 15 to 20 minutes.

STIR the base into the cooked lentils, set over medium-low heat, and simmer for 8 to 10 minutes. Taste and adjust the seasoning. Remove the soup from the heat and let stand for 10 to 15 minutes.

PLACE a slice of bread in each soup bowl and ladle the soup over. Sprinkle generously with the Parmigiano.

1 link (about ¼ pound) Homemade Bolognese Sausage (page 267) or mild Italian pork sausage (containing no fennel seeds chile peppers, or strong spices), casing removed and finely chopped

1 thick slice pancetta (2 to 3 ounces), very finely minced

3 tablespoons double-concentrated Italian tomato paste, diluted in 2 cups Meat Broth (page 71), canned low-sodium chicken broth, or cold water

Salt and freshly ground black pepper to taste

8 slices Italian bread, grilled or toasted

⅓ to ½ cup freshly grated Parmigiano-Reggiano

MUSHROOM SOUP

Zuppa di Porcini

SERVES 6 TO 8

The luscious hills of Emilia-Romagna are richly gifted with the most prized wild mushroom, Boletus edulis, *porcini. In the fall and spring, most restaurants use them with abandon. One of the many porcini preparations I came across was a wholesome, flavorful soup, which was done slightly different by two very different cooking establishments, the award-winning La Frasca Restaurant in Castrocaro Terme, a small resort town in the province of Forlì, and the more humble Da Carlet, a trattoria in the hill town of Monghidoro. Since fresh porcini mushrooms are hard to come by in this country, prepare the soup as I have done here, with a combination of dried porcini and fresh shiitakes.*

2 ounces dried porcini mushrooms, soaked in 2 cups lukewarm water for 20 minutes

1 pound shiitake mushrooms

½ cup extra virgin olive oil

½ cup finely minced shallots

⅓ cup chopped flat-leaf parsley

Salt to taste

7 cups Meat Broth (page 71) or canned low-sodium beef broth

½ cup heavy cream

2 cups ½-inch cubes 2- to 3-day-old Italian bread, crusts removed

1 tablespoon unsalted butter

⅓ to ½ cup freshly grated Parmigiano-Reggiano

DRAIN the porcini mushrooms and reserve the soaking water. Rinse the mushrooms well under cold running water and mince them. Strain the soaking water through a sieve lined with paper towels into a small bowl; Reserve the water.

RINSE the shiitakes quickly under cold running water and pat dry with paper towels. Remove and discard the tough stems. Cut the caps into thin slices.

HEAT ⅓ cup of the oil in a large saucepan over medium heat. Add the shallots and parsley and cook, stirring, until the shallots are lightly golden and soft, about 5 minutes. Add the porcini and shiitake mushrooms, season with salt, and stir well for a minute or two. Add about 1 cup of the reserved porcini liquid and cook, stirring occasionally, until most of the liquid has evaporated. Add the remaining porcini water and cook, stirring, until only a few tablespoons of liquid are left in the pan. Remove from the heat.

PUREE the mushrooms with the cooking juices using a food mill or in a food processor and return to the pan. Put the pan back over medium heat, add the broth, and bring just to a boil. As soon as the broth begins to bubble, reduce the heat to low and add the cream. Cook, stirring occasionally, until the soup has a medium-thick consistency, about 20 minutes. Remove from the heat and let stand for 10 to 15 minutes before serving.

MEANWHILE, heat the butter with the remaining oil together in a medium skillet over medium heat. Add the bread cubes and cook, stirring, until golden on all sides. Transfer to paper towels to drain.

LADLE the soup into individual soup bowls, scatter the croutons over the top, sprinkle with grated Parmigiano, and serve.

A RUSTIC VARIATION For the porcini soup of Trattoria Da Carlet add a few ounces of chopped pancetta to the base of shallots and parsley and omit the cream. Serve the soup with grilled bread instead of sautéed bread cubes.

BREAD SOUP

Pancotto

SERVES 8

4 tablespoons (½ stick) unsalted butter

1½ cups finely minced yellow onions

1 pound 3- to 4-day-old Italian bread, cut into medium cubes

⅓ cup shredded sage leaves or chopped flat-leaf parsley

2 quarts Meat Broth (page 71) or canned low-sodium beef broth

½ cup freshly grated Parmigiano-Reggiano, plus more for serving

Salt to taste

*P*ancotto, *or* paneda, *literally, "cooked bread," is a thick peasant bread soup that was created to use up stale bread.*

When I told my daughters that this was a dish of my childhood, they looked at me suspiciously and said, "Right, and you also walked to school in the snow without shoes." While luckily enough I always had shoes to wear, food, particularly during the war, was often scarce, and it was almost impossible to find and afford basic everyday ingredients, so my mother put pancotto *on the table several times a week. She made a vegetable broth with a few pieces of onion, carrots, celery, and a potato or two (meat broth at that time was not even a consideration) and added leftover stale bread. As the bread cooked in the light broth, absorbing it, it became soft and creamy and swelled into a thick, dense soup.*

The amazing thing was that this humblest of soups was so tasty. So good, in fact, that long after the war had ended, many families kept making the soup, and country trattorie prepared it regularly, enriching it with flavorful homemade broth, superlative Parmigiano, and fresh herbs.

MELT 3 tablespoons of the butter in a large saucepan over medium-low heat. Add the onions and cook, stirring a few times, until pale yellow and very soft, 5 to 6 minutes. Add the bread, half of the sage, and 2 cups of the broth and stir well for a minute or two. Add the remaining 6 cups broth, raise the heat to medium, and bring just to a boil. As soon as the broth begins to bubble, reduce the heat to low and cook, uncovered, stirring from time to time, until the bread is very soft and has broken down completely and the soup is very thick, about 20 minutes.

STIR ¼ cup of the Parmigiano, the remaining 1 tablespoon butter and the remaining sage into the soup. Taste and add a bit of salt if needed. Cook, stirring constantly, for a minute or two, then serve with the remaining Parmigiano.

RICE AND CABBAGE SOUP

Riso e Verze in Brodo

SERVES 6 TO 8

2 tablespoons unsalted butter

2 tablespoons extra virgin olive oil

½ cup finely minced yellow onions

⅓ cup finely minced carrots

1 garlic clove, finely minced

2 tablespoons chopped flat-leaf parsley

1 thick slice (2 to 3 ounces) pancetta, chopped or very finely minced

2 tablespoons double-concentrated Italian tomato paste, diluted in 2 cups Meat Broth (page 71), canned low-sodium beef broth, or water

Salt to taste

½ large (2½- to 3-pound) head Savoy cabbage, cored and roughly chopped

6 cups Meat Broth (page 71), canned low-sodium beef broth, or cold water

1 cup Arborio rice

½ cup freshly grated Parmigiano-Reggiano

Barbara Aimi, who, with her husband, Ivan, runs the delightful Hostaria da Ivan in Roccabianca in Parma's countryside, defines this preparation as a cross between a rice and cabbage dish and a very thick soup. And, in the old peasant tradition, she uses lard instead of butter and oil, and water instead of broth.

HEAT the butter and the oil together in a large pot over medium heat. Add the onions, carrots, garlic, parsley, and pancetta and cook, stirring from time to time, until a light golden color, 5 to 6 minutes. Add the diluted tomato paste, season with salt, and bring to a gentle boil. Reduce the heat to medium-low and simmer, uncovered, until the base has a medium-thick consistency, 10 to 12 minutes.

ADD the cabbage to the base and cook, stirring from time to time, until it begins to soften, 5 to 6 minutes. Add the broth. As soon as the broth begins to bubble, partially cover the pot and simmer, stirring occasionally, until the cabbage is completely soft, 20 to 25 minutes.

ADD the rice and cook, uncovered, stirring from time to time, until it is tender but still firm to the bite. Remove from the heat and let the soup stand for a few minutes.

ADJUST the seasoning and serve, generously sprinkled with the Parmigiano.

CHICKPEA SOUP WITH ROSEMARY

Zuppetta di Ceci al Rosmarino

SERVES 8

2 cups (1 pound) dried chickpeas, picked over soaked overnight in cold water to cover generously, drained, and rinsed

1 boiling potato

1 carrot plus ½ cup finely minced carrots

¼ to ⅓ cup extra virgin olive oil

1 cup finely minced yellow onions

2 tablespoons finely minced fresh rosemary or 1 tablespoon crumbled dried rosemary

1 tablespoon minced fresh sage or 1 teaspoon finely crumbled dried sage

Salt and freshly ground black pepper to taste

Extra virgin olive oil

*D*olce e Salato, in the small town of San Pietro in Casale, about fifteen miles outside Bologna, is an unusual restaurant, as it specializes in first courses, pasta, risotto, and soups. Paola Martelli, the chef-owner of the restaurant, is a creative cook. She mixes and matches ingredients with an uncanny ability and the innate aptitude of one who has been around food for many years. This is one of Paola's soups, which is almost pristine in its execution and yet delivers satisfying, aromatic flavors.

PUT the chickpeas, potato, and whole carrot in a large pot, add enough cold water to cover by 3 to 4 inches, and bring to a boil. Reduce the heat to low, partially cover the pot, and cook, stirring from time to time, until the chickpeas are tender, 40 to 50 minutes. With a large slotted spoon, remove the potato and carrot, and reserve. Drain the chickpeas, reserving the cooking water, and set aside.

HEAT the oil in a large saucepan over medium heat. Add the onions, minced carrots, rosemary, and sage and cook, stirring, until the vegetables are lightly golden and soft, 5 to 6 minutes.

MEANWHILE, puree half of the chickpeas with the potato and carrot using a food mill or in a food processor.

ADD the puree to the savory vegetable base together with the remaining chickpeas and stir for a minute or two, then add 6 to 7 cups of the reserved cooking water (just enough to cover by 2 inches). Season with salt and pepper and bring to a gentle simmer over medium heat. Cook, stirring from time to time, until the soup has thickened slightly, 10 to 12 minutes. Serve hot with a few drops of extra virgin olive oil drizzled over each serving.

ENRICHING SOUP WITH BREAD

If you like really thick soups, place 1 or 2 small slices of grilled or toasted Italian or French bread in each bowl and sprinkle some grated Parmigiano over the bread. Ladle the soup over the bread, and let it sit for a minute or two. The bread will absorb some of the liquid, thus thickening the soup.

If you would like to add the bread but want a less rustic presentation, remove the crusts from good-quality sliced white bread and cut the slices into 1-inch squares. Fry the bread in extra virgin olive oil until golden and drain on paper towels. Add to the soup when serving.

COOKING EXTRA CHICKPEAS FOR LATER USE

When preparing chickpea, bean, or lentil soup, cook double the amount of the legume you are using and reserve half, to be used in a salad or to enrich a meat stew.

PASTA

milia-Romagna takes its pasta seriously. That is probably why the cooks of the region prepare as many homemade pasta dishes as they do. Emilia-Romagna's tortellini, tortelloni, lasagne, ravioli, tortelli, cappelletti, tagliatelle, pappardelle, and tagliolini are admired throughout Italy and set the standard of excellence for pasta making.

Years ago, many restaurants in Bologna had their *sfogline* (pasta makers) make fresh pasta in the front window, or in a strategically located working area inside the restaurant, so that customers and passersby could see that the pasta was indeed made on the premises. It was fascinating to see the *sfogline,* dressed all in white, their hair covered by a white net, knead masses of dough with secure, steady strokes, roll it out with a long rolling pin into very large sheets of pasta, and, in no time at all, cut it into long, golden tagliatelle or stuff and shape it into tiny tortellini.

The fresh pasta of Emilia-Romagna is made only with unbleached all-purpose flour and eggs. No semolina flour, no salt, and no oil is ever used. The superlative soft wheat of the region, the eggs, and the expert hands of the pasta maker produce delicate, golden, silky pasta that is wrapped voluptuously around mouthwatering fillings, or layered into lasagne, or cut into tagliatelle.

Traditionally, the only tools needed to make fresh pasta were a large wooden board, your hands, and a long rolling pin. This was a craft passed down from mother to daughter for generations. My mother, a superlative cook who excelled at pasta making, made tagliatelle several times a week and, with a minimal investment of time and money, fed the family well. I must have been eleven or twelve years old when my mother, with a white apron tied around her waist, piled flour onto our large wooden board, made a well in the center, cracked the eggs into it, and said to me, "Today you are going to learn how to make pasta."

Making pasta entirely by hand is not difficult, but, it requires time and commitment. Try to knead pasta dough by hand if possible, because the texture and consistency produced by hand kneading is far superior to that of dough made by machine. You will also find the experience of kneading the dough therapeutic and relaxing. It is wonderful to see how a mound of flour and a few eggs are transformed into a velvety dough in a matter of minutes. Keep in mind that the purpose of homemade fresh pasta is to enjoy it at its very best–fresh! That is why the cooks of Emilia-Romagna generally make the pasta in the morning and eat it the same day.

In this chapter, you will find three ways of making pasta dough: by hand, with a food processor, and with an electric mixer. You will also find instructions for how to roll out the dough with a rolling pin and with a hand-cranked pasta machine. If you are thinking about buying a pasta machine that makes the dough and extrudes it as spaghetti, penne, and other shapes, forget it. The pasta produced with those machines has a gummy, sticky texture that has absolutely nothing to do with the real thing.

Homemade Pasta

The Ingredients

- Unbleached all-purpose flour and eggs (see the individual recipes for proportions)

Equipment for Making Pasta by Hand

- A large wooden board; a polyethelene board can be used if necessary, and marble can be used in a pinch, but it is really too cold for pasta making

- A fork for mixing

- A long Italian rolling pin for pasta (check with your gourmet kitchen store for this) or a regular rolling pin

- A plastic or metal dough scraper to clean the board

- A scalloped pastry wheel to cut the pasta into the desired shapes

Equipment for Making Pasta by Machine

- A food processor or electric mixer

- A hand-cranked pasta machine

- A scalloped pastry wheel to cut the pasta into the desired shapes

Making Pasta Dough by Hand

Mound the flour on a large wooden board or other work surface. With your fingers, make a round well in the center of the flour. Break the eggs into the well. Stir the eggs thoroughly with a fork, then gradually draw the flour, starting with the inside walls of the well, into the eggs, mixing it with the fork, until a soft paste begins to form.

With a dough scraper, push all the remaining flour to one side of the board (if you have a flour sifter, sift the flour clean just as they do in Italy). Scrape off and discard the bits and pieces of dough attached to the board. Add some of the flour you have pushed aside to the dough and begin kneading gently. As you keep incorporating more flour, the dough will become firmer and your kneading will need to become more energetic. Do not add too much flour, though; you may not need it all.

The moment you have a soft, manageable dough, clean the board again and wash your hands. Flour the work surface lightly and begin to knead the dough, pushing it away from you with the palms of your hands and then folding half of the dough back over itself. As you knead, keep turning the dough: push, fold over, and turn. Knead the dough for 8 to 10 minutes, adding a bit more flour if it sticks to the board and your hands.

Press one finger into the center of the dough. If it comes out barely moist, the dough is ready to be rolled out. If the dough is quite sticky, knead it a bit longer, adding more flour. When it is ready, the dough will be compact, pliable, smooth, and moist.

If you are going to roll out the dough with a pasta machine, it can be used immediately. If you are going to roll it out with a rolling pin, wrap it first in plastic wrap, and set it aside to rest for about 30 minutes. After that time, the gluten in the dough will have relaxed and it will be easier to roll it out. If the dough is too soft and limp when you remove the plastic wrap, knead it for a minute or so to a firmer consistency.

Tip: The amount of flour needed to make a perfect dough depends on many things: the altitude, the humidity, the temperature of the room, the size of the eggs. Always start with a little less flour than the recipe calls for. Knead the dough thoroughly, adding only a small amount of flour at a time. Keep in mind that you can always add flour but you can't take any away.

Making Pasta Dough in a Food Processor

Break the eggs into a food processor fitted with the metal blade and process briefly to mix them. Add the flour in a few batches and pulse until dough firms and gathers loosely around the blade. (Don't let the dough form a ball, or it will be tough.) At this point, the dough should be moist and slightly sticky.

Put the dough on a lightly floured wooden board or other work surface. Dust your hands with flour and knead the dough for a few minutes, adding a bit more flour if the dough is sticky. Dough made in a food processor will not be as elastic as dough kneaded by hand; however, it should still be smooth and pliable. If it seems too firm, wrap it in plastic wrap and let rest at room temperature for 20 to 30 minutes, then knead the dough again for about a minute.

Making Pasta Dough with an Electric Mixer

Break the eggs into the bowl of an electric mixer fitted with the dough hook and beat briefly at low speed. Add the flour in a few batches, beating well after each addition. Increase the speed and knead the dough for 5 to 6 minutes, until smooth, soft, and pliable.

Transfer the dough to a lightly floured wooden board or other work surface. Flour your hands lightly and knead the dough for a minute or two. If the dough seems too firm, wrap it in plastic wrap and let it rest at room temperature for 20 to 30 minutes, then knead the dough again for about a minute.

Tip: Making the dough with a machine requires a little less flour than making it by hand. Reserve ½ cup or so of the flour called for in the recipe. After the dough has been kneaded, touch it. If it is silky and slightly moist, it is ready; if it is too sticky, work in the reserved flour.

Rolling Out Pasta Dough by Hand

Dust a large wooden board or other work surface very lightly with flour. Flatten the dough with your hands and, using a long pasta rolling pin, start rolling from the center of the dough out, away from you, toward the edges. Rotate the dough slightly and roll out again from the center toward the edges; don't push down on the dough as you roll it out. Keep rolling and turning the dough to produce a circular sheet of dough. If the dough sticks to the work surface, roll it loosely around the rolling pin, lift up the rolling pin, and dust the work surface lightly with flour.

Once you have a nice circle of dough, about the size of an individual pizza, roll the far edge of the pasta sheet up around the rolling pin. Hold the dough near you with one hand while, with the palm of the other hand, you push the rolling pin with the rolled dough gently away from you. Turn the dough a quarter turn and repeat a few more times, keeping the circular shape by rotating the dough a quarter turn each time. If the dough sticks to the board or to the rolling pin, dust the board and the pasta sheet very lightly with flour; do not use too much flour, or the dough will be too dry.

When the circle of dough has doubled in size, starting from the far edge, roll up half of the pasta sheet snugly around the rolling pin. Put the palms of your hands at the center of the rolling pin and gently roll the pin back and forth while stretching the dough outward under your palms; your hand should never remain in the same position, but should move from the center out to the sides in a continuous motion. This action will stretch the dough sideways as well as forward. Keep stretching the dough this way, working as fast as you can, or the pasta will dry out and will be impossible to stretch. While part of the dough is wrapped around the rolling pin, rotate the sheet a quarter turn. Unroll the dough, then starting from the far edge roll up half of the pasta sheet snugly around the rolling pin, and roll and stretch the dough as described above, rotating it as needed. When the sheet of pasta is very thin, almost transparent, it is ready.

The rolled-out sheet should be used immediately if you are making stuffed pasta. Allow it to dry for 8 to 12 minutes before cutting it into noodles.

Tip: If rolling out a large batch of dough by hand seems too daunting, roll out half or a quarter of the dough at a time keeping the rest covered with plastic wrap. In this case, you can use a regular rolling pan rather than a long pasta pin. If the dough tears, simply patch it with a scrap of dough and go over it with the rolling pin.

Rolling Out Pasta Dough with a Hand-Cranked Pasta Machine

Set the rollers of the pasta machine at their widest opening. Cut off a piece of dough about the size of a large egg and flatten it under the palm of your hand. Keep the rest of the dough wrapped in plastic wrap. Dust the flattened piece of dough lightly with flour and run it once through the machine. Fold the dough in half, pressing down on it with your fingertips, and run it through the machine again. Repeat this step four to five times, dusting the dough lightly with flour if needed, until the dough is smooth and no longer sticky; the dough will become firmer since the machine is actually kneading the dough. Do not skimp on this step, or, as you thin the pasta, it may stick to the rollers.

Adjust the rollers to the next setting and run the dough through once; do not fold the dough again. Adjust the rollers to the next setting and run the pasta sheet through the rollers once; continue to adjust the rollers and roll the pasta through the machine until it reaches the desired thinness.

If you are making stuffed pasta, cut and stuff the dough immediately, before rolling out another piece. For string pasta or ribbon noodles, roll out the remaining dough and allow the sheets to dry before cutting them into noodles.

Tip: If the sheet of dough sticks to the pasta machine, dust it lightly with flour. Be sure to run the sheet of dough once through each setting; don't skip a setting or the dough may tear.

Making Stuffed Pasta

If the dough was rolled out by hand, cut a strip from the large sheet and keep the remaining sheet covered with plastic wrap. Cut, stuff, and shape the dough, then repeat the process with the remaining dough.

If the dough was rolled out with a pasta machine, cut, stuff, and shape each sheet of dough as soon as it has been rolled out.

Ravioli: Trim a thin sheet of dough as necessary so that it has straight edges and is 5 inches wide. Starting 1¼ inches from one end, place 1 tablespoon of filling every 2½ inches down the center of the sheet of dough. Stop when you get halfway down the length of the dough. Fold the empty dough over the filling, aligning the edges, and seal the dough around each mound of filling, pressing out any air pockets with your fingertips. Cut the dough between the filling into individual ravioli and press the edges to seal.

Tortelli: Follow the instructions for ravioli.

Tortelloni: Cut a thin sheet of dough into 3-inch squares. Place 1 tablespoon of filling in the center of each square and fold in half to form a triangle. Seal the dough around each mound of filling and press the edges firmly together to seal. One at a time, bend each *tortellone* around your finger, placing one point slightly over the other, and press to seal.

Tortellini: Cut a thin sheet of dough into 1½-inch squares. Place a scant teaspoon, or less, of filling in the center of each square and fold in half to form a triangle. Seal the dough around each small mound of filling and press the edges firmly together to seal. One at a time, bend each *tortellino* around your finger, placing one point slightly over the other, and press to seal.

Cannelloni: Cut a thin sheet of dough into 4 × 5-inch rectangles. Parboil the pasta and stuff and shape it as instructed in the individual recipe.

Lasagne: Cut thin wide sheets of dough to fit your lasagne pan. Parboil the sheets as instructed in the individual recipe.

Pappardelle: Using a fluted pastry wheel, cut a thin sheet of pasta into 8- by 1-inch ribbons. (No pasta machine that I know of has cutters for pappardelle.) Pappardelle, like the other noodles below, can be cooked immediately or allowed to dry on a tray at room temperature.

Garganelli: These small grooved handmade *maccheroni* are typical of the Romagna side of the region. There, garganelli are made with a special ridged tool called a *pettine*, comb, but a clean new regular comb with long teeth works very well. Cut the sheet of dough into 1½-inch squares. Place the comb in front of you, with the teeth pointing away from you. Lay a pasta square over the comb, with one corner pointing toward you. Place a long pencil over the pasta square and, starting with the corner closest to you, wrap the pasta square up around the pencil. Press gently as you roll, pushing the pencil away from you over the comb. Gently slide the garganelli off the pencil and place on a dry cloth. Repeat with the remaining squares. Garganelli are best when cooked a few hours after they are made; drying them overnight will make them brittle.

Stricchetti: These bow ties are a pretty, easy pasta to make by hand. Cut the sheet of dough into 1 × 1½-inch rectangles. Firmly pinch the center of each rectangle together to make a bow tie shape. *Stricchetti* can be cooked immediately or allowed to dry for several hours, or overnight.

Tagliatelle or Tagliolini: Before the sheet of pasta is cut into noodles, it needs to dry.

If the dough was rolled out by hand, place a tablecloth on your work surface and lay the sheet of dough on it. Let dry until the surface is no longer sticky, 8 to 15 minutes, depending on the temperature and the thickness of the pasta. Turn the sheet gently to dry on the other side until no longer sticky. Don't let the pasta dry too much, or it will become brittle and impossible to cut.

When the pasta sheet is no longer sticky, fold it loosely into a flat roll about 3 inches across. With a large sharp knife, cut the roll across into ½-inch-wide ribbons for tagliatelle or ¼-inch-wide ribbons for tagliolini. Unravel the noodles and place them in loose bundles on a wooden board or on the tablecloth. The noodles can be cooked immediately or allowed to dry, uncovered, and cooked later; they can be kept at room temperature, uncovered, for several days.

If the pasta was rolled out with a pasta machine, spread a clean tablecloth on a large work surface and lay the rolled-out sheets of pasta on it. Let dry for 8 to 10 minutes, depending on the temperature of the room, until the sheets of pasta are no longer sticky and are beginning to curl up slightly at the edges.

Run the sheets of pasta through the widest setting of the pasta machine for tagliatelle or the narrow setting for tagliolini. Arrange the noodles in bundles on a wooden board or tablecloth. They can be cooked immediately or allowed to dry, uncovered, and cooked later; they can be kept at room temperature, uncovered, for several days.

Tip: Today many shapes of egg pasta that used to be religiously made at home, such as tagliatelle, tagliolini, pappardelle, stricchetti, and garganelli, are made commercially and are widely available. Factory-made egg pasta is a modern luxury—a luxury that can be particularly appreciated in busy households.

Dried Pasta

If homemade pasta relies on soft all-purpose flour, eggs, and the experienced hands of the pasta maker to be outstanding, good factory-made dried pasta—spaghetti, penne, linguine, etc.—owes its superior taste to golden yellow semolina (a hard durum-wheat flour), water, and the manufacturer's know-how.

Durum-wheat flour has a high gluten content, which makes it ideal for factory-made pasta, since it is gluten that gives pasta a firm, springy texture. Factory-made pasta is produced by huge machines that knead the dough. The dough is extruded through *trafile*, perforated dies, into various shapes and the shaped pasta is dried in temperature-controlled chambers.

Today there are so many wonderful brands of imported Italian pasta on the market that choosing can be a bit confusing. In selecting dried pasta, look for "100 percent semolina flour" on the box. This pasta has the golden color of wheat and, when properly cooked, swells in size yet maintains its firmness. Some excellent large producers of pasta are Barilla, Agnesi, and De Cecco. Today truly superior pasta made by artisan makers is also available in the market. Made in small quantities, artisanal pasta is more expensive than most of the well-known brands. Look for Martelli, Artigiano Pastaio, and Latini.

Whether made by large companies or small artisans, dried pasta, with its firmer texture, is the perfect vehicle for straightforward, uncomplicated olive oil–based and tomato, vegetable, and seafood sauces. This pasta has always been more popular in southern Italy. However, now that the majority of women work outside the home, and experienced pasta makers are slowly disappearing, the consumption of dried pasta has increased all over the country, especially in the north. My brother and his wife, Emma, who were raised on a steady diet of homemade pasta, today eat as much spaghettini as they do tagliatelle.

Unfortunately, in this country, there are still misconceptions about pasta, with many believing that homemade pasta is better than factory-made. The truth is that they are two entirely different products that lend themselves to different preparations, and neither one is better than the other. Just as it would be very hard to make light, delicate stuffed pasta using semolina flour, it would also be difficult to make rigatoni with soft all-purpose flour. Most of the time, good dried pasta is vastly preferable to the often sad, limp, so-called "fresh pasta" available in many markets.

Cooking, Saucing, and Serving Pasta

Italians might spend less time in the kitchens these days, but when they cook pasta, the ritual they engage in is the same as the one their mothers and grandmothers followed. My mother used to say, "Quick, come to the table. The pasta is ready, and pasta does not wait for anyone!" And she was right. There is a precise set of actions during the last moments of pasta cooking that takes place in all Italian kitchens, transcending regional lines. Once the large pot of boiling water is going at full speed, the salt and pasta are added. The pasta is stirred and checked. It is tasted when cooked, it is drained in a large colander and vigorously shaken. It is stirred quickly with the hot sauce. Then, at last, it is served and brought to the table where the family waits.

The basic rules of pasta cooking apply to both fresh and dried pasta. Nothing could be simpler or more logical. This is how to do it:

- Use a big pot. One pound of pasta needs 4 to 5 quarts of water to cook, so that it can move around and be stirred comfortably. (In Italy, one pound of pasta generally feeds 6, since it is usually served as a first course. In America, it may serve 4 to 6 because it is often served as an entrée.)

- When the water boils, add the salt and pasta. The salt will season the pasta lightly, and bring out its flavor. (Italians prefer coarse salt because it has a purer, cleaner taste than regular table salt, which can taste very metallic.) Cover the pot and bring the water back to the boil, then remove the lid.

- Stir the pasta a few times as it cooks. If you have plenty of water in the pot and stir it occasionally, the pasta will not stick together. Do not add oil to the water–it would make the pasta slippery, making it impossible for the sauce to properly adhere to it.

- The cooking time will depend on the type, size, and shape of the pasta. Fresh homemade pasta will cook in a matter of minutes. Large, sturdy dried pasta such as rigatoni can take as long as 14 minutes. Stay with the pasta, check it, and taste it to determine its doneness. Remove the pasta from the pot when it is tender but still firm to the bite, *al dente*, because it will finish cooking in the sauce.

- It is a good idea to scoop out and reserve a bit of the cooking water before draining the pasta. It will come in handy if a sauce needs to be stretched or loosened a bit. The starch in the water will also give body to a sauce.

- When the pasta is cooked, drain it and immediately toss it with the sauce. *Never* rinse pasta. It will wash off the layer of starch that helps bind the sauce with the pasta.

- *Never* precook pasta unless you are making lasagne or cannelloni.

- Toss the pasta and sauce together thoroughly. Don't serve pasta naked, with the sauce on top, because the pasta will stick together in an unattractive mass.

- And, finally, sit back and enjoy one of the most gratifying dishes in the world. *Buon appetito!*

SWISS CHARD-RICOTTA RAVIOLI
WITH BALSAMIC VINEGAR

Ravioli di Ricotta al Balsamico

SERVES 4 TO 6

For the filling

½ pound Swiss chard

Salt

About 1¼ cups ricotta cheese

½ to ⅔ cup freshly grated
Parmigiano-Reggiano
(to taste)

1 large egg, lightly beaten

¼ teaspoon freshly
grated nutmeg

For the pasta dough

2 cups unbleached
all-purpose flour

3 extra-large eggs

For the sauce

4 tablespoons (½ stick)
unsalted butter

⅓ cup very finely minced
shallots or yellow onions

½ cup Chicken Broth
(page 73) or canned low-
sodium chicken broth

4 to 5 tablespoons good-
quality balsamic vinegar
(see page 10)

½ cup freshly grated
Parmigiano-Reggiano

1 tablespoon coarse salt

Salt to taste

Da Amerigo is a well-known trattoria in the small hill town of Savigno, about twenty-five miles outside Bologna. The kitchen, which, not by design, is open for everyone to see, is staffed by local women and family members. The front of the house is the responsibility of Alberto, a thirty-five-year-old dynamo who was literally raised in the trattoria and embraces his work with enthusiasm, dedication, and knowledge. Noticing that we were very interested in the food, Alberto kept sending us small tastes of special dishes, from crescentine, *deep-fried thin squares of dough topped with culatello, the prized ham of the region, to chunks of Parmigiano-Reggiano drizzled with aged balsamic vinegar. But when the Swiss chard ravioli I had ordered came to the table, coated with an intoxicating, aromatic sauce of locally produced sweet butter, balsamic vinegar, and Parmigiano, I knew I had struck gold. For this dish, use the oldest balsamic vinegar you can afford, and real Parmigiano-Reggiano, imported from Italy.*

To prepare the filling, remove the chard stalks from the leaves, reserving them for another use. Wash the leaves well in several changes of cold water, drain, and put them in a large saucepan with only the water that clings to the leaves. Add a pinch of salt, turn the heat to medium, and cover the pot. Cook until the leaves are tender, 8 to 10 minutes. Drain the chard, squeeze out the excess water, and finely chop it.

PUT the Swiss chard, ricotta, Parmigiano, egg, and nutmeg in a medium bowl or in the bowl of an electric mixer fitted with the paddle attachment, season with salt, and mix until thoroughly combined. Taste and adjust the seasoning. Cover the bowl and refrigerate for about 1 hour. (The filling can be prepared up to a day ahead so flavors can meld.)

USING the flour and eggs prepare the pasta dough as instructed on pages 95–97. Roll out the dough and prepare the ravioli as instructed on pages 97–100. Cover a large tray with a clean kitchen towel and place the ravioli on it in a single layer, leaving space between them. The ravioli can be cooked immediately or refrigerated, uncovered, for several hours.

To prepare the sauce, melt 3 tablespoons of the butter in a large skillet over medium heat. Add the shallots and cook, stirring with a wooden spoon, until pale yellow and very soft, 6 to 7 minutes. Add the chicken broth and stir until reduced by approximately half. Add the balsamic vinegar, stir once or twice, and turn off the heat.

Bring a large pot of water to a boil over high heat. Add the coarse salt and the ravioli and cook, stirring a few times, until the ravioli are tender but still a bit firm to the bite. Scoop out and reserve a bit of the pasta cooking water. Turn off the heat and, with a large skimmer or slotted spoon, remove the ravioli, draining the excess water back into the pot, and place in the skillet with the sauce. Add the remaining 1 tablespoon butter and about half of the Parmigiano. Stir quickly but gently over medium heat until the pasta and sauce are well combined. Stir in a bit of the reserved pasta water if the pasta seems a bit dry. Taste, season with salt, and serve with the remaining Parmigiano.

THE INTERNET AND FOOD, AN INSTANT CONNECTION

During my second visit to Da Amerigo, Alberto and I were chatting about food in general and about the efforts that people like Alberto make in trying to preserve the traditional dishes and customs of the area when they are constantly challenged by fast food and an even faster pace of life. Suddenly he stopped talking and looked at me as if he had just seen me for the first time, then he turned around and disappeared briefly. When he came back, he had in his hands a cookbook and said, "*Signora*, I did not realize that it was you, look, I have one of your cookbooks, which I purchased on the Internet!" I asked him why in the world he would want a book written in the United States when obviously *he* was the expert, and he answered, "Well, I probably will not use it often, but I love to buy cookbooks on the Internet, because now, whether we like it or not, we are all connected and I want to see how people cook in other countries and whether our food is represented honestly." Then, with a mischievous smile, he continued, "And you pass the test."

BUTTERNUT SQUASH TORTELLI

Tortelli di Zucca

SERVES 4 TO 6

For the filling

**1 medium butternut squash
(2 to 2½ pounds)**

**¾ cup freshly grated
Parmigiano-Reggiano**

**⅛ teaspoon freshly
grated nutmeg**

Salt to taste

For the pasta dough

**2 cups unbleached
all-purpose flour**

3 extra-large eggs

1 tablespoon coarse salt

For the sauce

**3 to 4 tablespoons
unsalted butter**

8 to 10 sage leaves, shredded

**½ cup freshly grated
Parmigiano-Reggiano**

Salt to taste

Leaving Bologna and Modena behind, land of scrumptious tortellini, tortelloni, and stuffed lasagne, my husband and I were very much looking forward to a dish that is the undisputed star of several northeastern towns of Emilia-Romagna—squash tortelli. Tortelli di zucca, or cappellacci, *as tortelli are called in and around Parma, Piacenza, and Ferrara, is a glorious pasta stuffed with the very sweet local squash, Parmigiano-Reggiano, nutmeg, and, sometimes, crushed amaretti cookies and occasionally,* mostarda di Cremona, *large pieces of plump fruit preserved in a sweet, mustardy thick syrup. According to many traditional cooks, the best, and* only, *sauce for these divine tortelli is sweet, creamy butter, fresh sage, and Parmigiano—nothing else. Others disagree, insisting that the perfect sauce is a lovely aromatic meat ragù. My preference is the butter and sage version; it allows the squash filling to stand out. But I have included the ragù in a variation below.*

To prepare the filling, preheat the oven to 350° F.

Cut the squash lengthwise in half and remove and discard the seeds. Wrap the squash in a sheet of foil, place on a baking sheet, and bake on the middle rack of the oven until it is tender and can be easily pierced with a knife, about 1 hour. Let cool slightly.

Scoop out the flesh from the squash and place on a large clean cloth napkin (not a kitchen towel, because the soft squash would stick to the porous cloth). Wrap the napkin around the squash and squeeze out about ½ cup of the watery juices (see box, page 106). Place the squash in a bowl and mash it with a spoon. Add the Parmigiano and nutmeg, season with salt, and mix well. Taste and adjust the seasoning. Cover and refrigerate for an hour or two.

Using the flour and eggs, prepare the pasta dough as instructed on pages 95–97. Roll out the dough and prepare the tortelli as instructed on pages 97–100. Cover a large tray with a clean kitchen towel and place the tortelli on it in a single layer, making sure they do not touch each other. The tortelli can be cooked immediately or refrigerated, uncovered, for a few hours, or overnight.

BRING a large pot of water to a boil over high heat. Add the coarse salt and tortelli, stir once or twice, and cook, until the tortelli are tender but still firm to the bite, 2 to 3 minutes.

WHILE the pasta is cooking, prepare the sauce. Melt the butter in a small skillet over medium heat. Add the sage and stir for about 1 minute. Keep warm over low heat.

TURN off the heat under the pasta pot and, with a large skimmer or slotted spoon, scoop up the tortelli, draining the excess water back into the pot, and place in a large heated bowl. Add the sauce, season lightly with salt, and add about half of the Parmigiano. Mix gently and serve at once, with the remaining Parmigiano.

TORTELLI WITH BOLOGNESE RAGÙ Substitute ½ recipe Bolognese Ragù (page 122) for the butter sauce. While the tortelli are cooking, reheat the sauce if necessary. Place the tortelli in a large heated bowl. Gently toss with the meat sauce and serve with freshly grated Parmigiano-Reggiano.

LIQUID GOLD

At my restaurant, we take the wrung-out juices of the squash and cook them over high heat until they are reduced to a dark, golden thick essence that resembles caramel, then cool it slightly and fold it into the squash mixture. It adds sweetness and body to the filling. The only tricky thing is to make sure that the juices are thickened enough so they won't make the filling watery, but not so thick that they will clump up in the filling. On a day when you are not pressed for time, try it.

SQUASH RAVIOLI WITH SQUAB RAGÙ
AND BALSAMIC VINEGAR

Ravioli di Zucca con Ragù di Piccione e Balsamico

SERVES 4 TO 6

For the filling

**1 medium butternut squash
(2 to 2½ pounds)**

**¾ cup freshly grated
Parmigiano-Reggiano**

**⅛ teaspoon freshly
grated nutmeg**

Salt to taste

For the pasta dough

**2 cups unbleached
all-purpose flour**

3 extra-large eggs

For the marinade

**Salt and freshly ground black
pepper to taste**

**Enough extra virgin olive oil
to coat the squab generously,
about ¼ cup**

7 to 8 sage leaves, shredded

1 small sprig rosemary

**2 fresh or frozen (and
defrosted) squabs
(about 1 pound each)**

For the sauce

**⅓ cup very finely minced
shallots**

**Salt and freshly ground black
pepper to taste**

*T*his is a very elegant dish that combines the delicate taste of butternut squash ravioli filling with the slightly gamy flavor of marinated squab. Fresh sage and a final touch of balsamic vinegar round out the flavors of the quick, delicious sauce. The dish, which combines tradition with creativity, comes from Alessandra, the immensely talented chef of Ristorante Buriani. The restaurant, one of the best in Emilia-Romagna, is located in Pieve di Cento, a very small town between the cities of Ferrara and Modena. (The dish can be prepared in stages.)

TO prepare the filling, preheat the oven to 350° F. Cut the squash lengthwise in half and remove and discard the seeds. Wrap the squash in a sheet of foil, place on a cookie sheet, and bake on the middle rack of the oven until it is tender and can easily be pierced with a knife, about 1 hour.

SCOOP out the flesh from the squash and place on a large clean cloth napkin (not a kitchen towel, because the squash will stick). Wrap the napkin around the squash and squeeze out about ½ cup of the watery juices (see page 106). Place the squash in a bowl and mash it with a spoon. Add the Parmigiano and nutmeg, season with salt, and mix well. Taste and adjust the seasoning. Cover the bowl and refrigerate for an hour or two.

USING the flour and eggs, prepare the pasta dough as instructed on pages 95–97. Roll out the dough and prepare the ravioli as instructed on pages 97–100. Cover a large tray with a clean kitchen towel and place the ravioli on it in a single layer, making sure they do not touch each other. The ravioli can be cooked immediately or refrigerated, uncovered, for several hours.

REMOVE and discard all the innards of the squabs. Using a sharp knife, split the skin of each squab down the backbone and pull to remove the backbone. Remove the breasts and place in a medium bowl. (Removing

6 to 7 sage leaves, finely shredded

½ cup dry white wine

2 tablespoons unsalted butter

¼ cup good-quality commercial balsamic vinegar or 2 to 3 tablespoons artisan-made balsamic (see page 10)

1 tablespoon coarse salt

⅓ cup freshly grated Parmigiano-Reggiano

the breasts is not difficult, because the birds are very small and tender. However, if this task is not appealing to you, have the butcher do it.) Reserve the squab legs/thighs for another use. Season the breasts with salt and pepper, place in a shallow dish, and cover with olive oil. Add the sage and rosemary and marinate the breasts for 1 to 1½ hours in the refrigerator.

To prepare the sauce, remove the breasts from the marinade, pat dry with paper towels, and cut into pieces about the size of peas. Set aside. Heat 3 tablespoons of the oil from the marinade in a large skillet over medium heat. Add the shallots and cook, stirring with a wooden spoon, until pale yellow and very soft, 6 to 7 minutes. Add the meat, season with salt and pepper, and cook until it has a nice golden color, 3 to 4 minutes. Stir in the sage, raise the heat to high, and add the wine. Cook, stirring constantly, until only a few tablespoons of wine are left in the skillet. Add the butter. As soon as it has melted, add the balsamic vinegar and stir briefly just until it is incorporated into the sauce. Turn off the heat.

MEANWHILE, bring a large pot of water to a boil over high heat. Add the coarse salt and ravioli and cook, until the ravioli are tender but still firm to the bite. Scoop out about ½ cup of the pasta water, add it to the sauce, and turn the heat to medium.

TURN the heat off under the pasta pot. With a large skimmer or slotted spoon, scoop up the ravioli, draining the excess water back into the pot, and place in the skillet. Stir quickly but gently until the pasta and sauce are well combined. Taste, adjust the seasoning, and serve sprinkled with the Parmigiano-Reggiano.

Preparing Ahead

- Make the butternut filling a day ahead; cover and refrigerate.

- Make the ravioli up to a day ahead.

- Marinate the breasts several hours ahead, then dice the meat and keep tightly covered in the refrigerator. (Do not marinate the meat *after* it has been diced, or it will soak up too much oil.)

- Make the sauce a half hour or so ahead. Set aside at room temperature.

RICOTTA AND GOAT CHEESE TORTELLONI

Tortelloni di Ricotta e Capra

SERVES 4 TO 6

For the filling

1 large egg

4 cups ricotta cheese

¼ pound fresh goat cheese

⅓ cup freshly grated
Parmigiano-Reggiano

¼ cup chopped flat-leaf
parsley

Salt to taste

For the pasta dough

2 cups unbleached
all-purpose flour

3 extra-large eggs

For the sauce

3 tablespoons unsalted butter

2 to 3 ounces thickly sliced
pancetta, diced

8 to 10 sage leaves, shredded

Salt to taste

1 tablespoon coarse salt

½ cup freshly grated
Parmigiano-Reggiano

*I*t was at Antica Trattoria Moretto on the outskirts of Vignola, a small town in the province of Modena, that we enjoyed some of the best food of Emilia. The trattoria, which looked more like a country restaurant than a mom-and-pop establishment, was quite large and had a beautiful light interior with inviting table settings. But what caught my eyes the moment we walked in was the large table that displayed an array of mouthwatering dishes. We sat and began ordering food in the leisurely Italian manner, determined to try as many dishes as we could. Of all the dishes we sampled, perhaps the most outstanding was this tortelloni. The tortelloni, made with the eggs of free-range chickens, had a bright golden color and were plump with a delicate, creamy cheese stuffing, and the simple sauce of sweet butter, crisp pancetta, and fresh sage made them all the more appetizing.

To prepare the filling, put the egg in a medium bowl or the bowl of an electric mixer fitted with the paddle attachment and beat lightly. Add the ricotta, goat cheese, Parmigiano, and parsley, season with salt, and mix until thoroughly combined. Taste and adjust the seasoning. Cover the bowl with plastic wrap and refrigerate for an hour or so to allow the mixture to firm up. (The filling can be prepared up to a day ahead.)

USING the flour and eggs, prepare the pasta dough as instructed on pages 95–97. Roll out the dough and prepare the tortelloni as instructed on pages 97–100. Cover a large tray with a clean kitchen towel and place the tortelloni on it in a single layer, without letting them touch one another. The tortelloni can be cooked immediately or refrigerated, uncovered, for a few hours, or overnight.

To prepare the sauce, melt the butter in a medium skillet over medium heat. As soon as it begins to foam, add the pancetta and cook, stirring, until lightly golden, 1 to 2 minutes. Add the sage and a small pinch of salt, stir for about 1 minute, and turn off the heat.

MEANWHILE, bring a large pot of water to a boil over high heat. Add the coarse salt and tortelloni and cook, stirring a few times, until the tortelloni are tender but still firm to the bite. Turn off the heat.

WITH a large skimmer or a slotted spoon, scoop out the tortelloni, draining the excess water back into the pot, and place them in the skillet. Add a small handful of the Parmigiano and mix gently over medium heat until the pasta and sauce are well combined. Taste, adjust the seasoning, and serve with the remaining Parmigiano.

TORTELLI WITH POTATOES

Tortelli di Patate

SERVES 4 TO 6

For the filling

2 medium boiling potatoes (about ¾ pound)

About ½ cup ricotta cheese

⅓ cup freshly grated Parmigiano-Reggiano

⅛ teaspoon freshly grated nutmeg

Salt to taste

For the pasta dough

2 cups unbleached all-purpose flour

3 extra-large eggs

For the sauce

½ pound shiitake mushrooms

¼ to ⅓ cup extra virgin olive oil

1 garlic clove, finely minced

In the Apennine mountains in Emilia, pasta stuffed with potatoes was once typical fare, perhaps because potatoes were cultivated more extensively in the high terrain than leafy vegetables were.

At Ristorante Cocchi in Parma, the tortelli were topped with a mixture of fresh porcini mushrooms quickly and simply sautéed in oil, garlic, and fresh herbs. Here, fresh shiitakes take the place of porcini, which are seldom available in America.

TO prepare the filling, put the potatoes in a medium saucepan and cover with cold water. Bring to a gentle boil over medium heat and cook until tender. Drain the potatoes and cool slightly, then peel and put through a food mill or potato ricer into a bowl. Add the ricotta, Parmigiano, and nutmeg, season with salt, and mix well with a wooden spoon. Taste and adjust the seasoning. Cover the bowl with plastic wrap and refrigerate for an hour or two. (The filling can be prepared several hours ahead.)

USING the flour and eggs, prepare the pasta dough as instructed on pages 95–97. Roll out the dough and prepare the tortelli as instructed on pages 97–100. Cover a large tray with a clean kitchen towel and place the tortelli on it in a single layer, without letting them touch one another. The tortelli can be cooked immediately or refrigerated, uncovered, for several hours, or overnight.

1 to 2 chopped tablespoons flat-leaf parsley

Salt and freshly ground black pepper to taste

1 cup Chicken Broth (page 73) or canned low-sodium chicken broth

1 tablespoon unsalted butter

1 tablespoon coarse salt

½ cup freshly grated Parmigiano-Reggiano

To prepare the sauce, discard mushroom stems. Wipe the caps clean with a damp towel or wash them quickly under cold running water and dry thoroughly with paper towels.

HEAT the oil in a large skillet over high heat. As soon as the oil is almost smoking, add the mushrooms, without crowding (if necessary, sauté them in two batches), and cook, stirring, until they have a nice golden color, about 2 minutes. Add the garlic and parsley and stir once or twice. (Remember that the skillet is *very* hot and the garlic, which should be lightly colored, will turn too brown in no time at all.) Season with salt and pepper, then add the broth and butter. Cook, stirring, until the broth is reduced by approximately half and the sauce has a creamy consistency. Turn off the heat.

MEANWHILE, bring a large pot of water to a boil over high heat. Add the coarse salt and tortelli and cook, stirring a few times, until the tortelli are tender but still firm to the bite. Turn off the heat under the pasta pot and, with a slotted spoon, scoop out the tortelli, draining the excess water back into the pot, and place in a large heated bowl. Add the mushrooms, season lightly with salt, and sprinkle with about half of the Parmigiano. Stir gently to combine. Serve hot with remaining cheese.

MUSHROOMS

It is amazing what a handful of mushrooms can do to a dish. Perhaps that is why Italians are obsessed with the aroma of fresh porcini mushrooms and, when in season, use them with abandon. Fresh porcini are occasionally available in this country, though their flavor is not as appealing as that of their Italian counterparts.

Shiitakes, the brown Japanese mushrooms, are a great substitute and, when cooked in the Italian manner, with olive oil, garlic, and parsley, become fragrant and succulent. White button mushrooms, which are always available in American markets, are a third option for this dish, but their flavor is not as intense as that of porcini and shiitake. Choose small white mushrooms and clean them well.

TORTELLINI WITH PROSCIUTTO

Tortellini al Prosciutto

SERVES 4 TO 6

For the filling

1 tablespoon unsalted butter

¼ pound pork loin, trimmed of fat and cut into ½-inch cubes

2 ounces sliced prosciutto, cut into pieces

2 ounces sliced mortadella, cut into pieces

½ cup freshly grated Parmigiano-Reggiano

⅛ teaspoon freshly grated nutmeg

2 medium eggs, lightly beaten (plus 1 extra egg if necessary)

Salt to taste

For the pasta dough

1¾ cups unbleached all-purpose flour

3 large eggs

1 tablespoon coarse salt

For the sauce

3 to 4 tablespoons unsalted butter

¼ pound thickly sliced prosciutto, diced

Salt to taste

*W*hile the splendid traditional Tortellini in Capon Broth (page 74) is a treat not to be missed, tortellini are also exceptionally good when tossed in a rich Bolognese meat ragù, with this simple sauce of butter, prosciutto, and Parmigiano. The sauce, which often has the addition of cream, is a favorite of Bolognese teenagers, who seem to be able to ingest huge portions of tortellini while remaining extremely slender.

To prepare the filling, melt the butter in a medium skillet over medium-high heat. When the butter begins to foam, add the cubed pork and cook, stirring, until lightly golden, 3 to 4 minutes. Transfer the meat and cooking juices to a food processor fitted with the metal blade. Add the prosciutto and mortadella and pulse until the meat is finely ground; do not puree.

TRANSFER the ground meat to a bowl, add the Parmigiano, nutmeg, and eggs and mix well with a wooden spoon. Season with salt. (The filling should be moist and just a bit sticky. If it is too dry, stir in another beaten egg.) Cover the bowl with plastic wrap and refrigerate for a few hours to allow the mixture to firm up a bit. (The filling can be prepared up to 24 hours ahead.)

USING the flour and eggs, prepare the pasta dough as instructed on pages 95–97. Roll out the dough and prepare the tortellini as instructed on pages 97–100. Cover a large tray with a clean kitchen towel and place the tortellini on it in a single layer, without letting them touch one another. They can be cooked immediately or refrigerated, uncovered, for 5 to 6 hours, or overnight.

BRING a large pot of water to a boil over high heat. Add the coarse salt and tortellini and cook, stirring a few times, until the tortellini are tender but still a bit firm to the bite. Scoop out and reserve about 1 cup of the pasta cooking water.

**½ cup freshly grated
Parmigiano-Reggiano**

WHILE the tortellini are cooking, make the sauce: melt the butter in a large skillet over medium heat. As soon as the butter foams, add the prosciutto and stir for a minute or two.

DRAIN the tortellini and add to the skillet with the sauce. Season lightly with salt and add about half of the Parmigiano. Toss gently and quickly over medium heat until the pasta and sauce are well combined. Add a bit of the reserved pasta water if the tortellini seem a bit dry. Serve at once, with the remaining Parmigiano.

TORTELLINI WITH BOLOGNESE MEAT RAGÙ Substitute 2 to 2½ cups of any of the Bolognese meat ragùs in this chapter for the prosciutto sauce. Place the sauce in a large skillet and heat until hot. Add the drained tortellini to the sauce and stir over medium heat until the tortellini and sauce are well combined. Serve with a sprinkling of Parmigiano-Reggiano.

SPINACH LASAGNE WITH
BOLOGNESE RAGÙ

Lasagne Verdi alla Bolognese

SERVES 6 TO 8

For the lasagne

**2 cups unbleached
all-purpose flour**

3 extra-large eggs

**2 tablespoons finely chopped
fresh cooked or frozen
spinach, squeezed dry**

1 tablespoon coarse salt

For the ragù

**1 cup Béchamel Sauce
(page 28)**

**1 recipe Bolognese Ragù
(page 122)**

**¾ cup freshly grated
Parmigiano-Reggiano**

**1 to 2 tablespoons cold
unsalted butter, cut into
small cubes**

L asagne alla Bolognese, with its slowly simmered, flavorful ragù, creamy béchamel sauce, and delicate homemade pasta, is one of the most beautiful and sumptuous dishes of the region. It used to be made regularly on Sundays, on holidays, and for special celebrations that brought large families together around the dinner table. The arzdoura *(the woman of the house) would get up particularly early to prepare the lasagne. While her family slept, she completed the ragù, whipped up the béchamel sauce, layered the pasta, and turned the dish into a small masterpiece. Today this immensely pleasing dish is not made at home as often as it used to be, and people of the region seek out restaurants and trattorie that make lasagne as good as the ones their mothers used to make.*

In Emilia-Romagna, lasagne is always made with homemade pasta. In Bologna, the pasta has the addition of spinach. The spinach dough is rolled out paper-thin and layered sparingly with meat ragù, béchamel, and Parmigiano-Reggiano. Although several steps are necessary to produce this dish, it is perfect for a dinner party or family gathering, since it can be assembled a day or two ahead and baked at the last moment.

USING the flour, eggs, and spinach, prepare the pasta dough as instructed on pages 95–97, adding the spinach along with the eggs. Roll out the dough as instructed on pages 97–98 and cut it to fit your lasagne pan.

PLACE a bowl of cold water on a counter near the stove and spread out some kitchen towels near the bowl. Bring a large pot of water, preferably one with a pasta insert, to a boil. Add the coarse salt and 3 to 4 sheets of pasta (no more). After the water comes back to a boil, cook the pasta for no longer than 20 to 25 seconds. Lift out the sheets with the pasta insert or a large skimmer, trying not to tear them, and plunge them into the bowl of cold water to cool. Immediately remove the pasta sheets, lay them out on the towels, and pat dry with another towel. Repeat with the remaining pasta.

PREHEAT the oven to 400°F. Generously butter the bottom and sides of a lasagne pan.

ADD the béchamel sauce to the ragù and mix well to combine. Cover the bottom of the lasagne pan with a layer of pasta sheets, trimming the pasta to fit the pan if necessary. Spread a thin layer of ragù over the pasta and sprinkle with Parmigiano-Reggiano. Repeat the process—one layer of pasta, one layer of ragù, and a sprinkle of Parmigiano. Dot the top with the butter. (The lasagne can be assembled 1 to 2 days ahead and refrigerated, tightly covered with plastic wrap. Remove from the refrigerator an hour or two before baking.)

PLACE the lasagne pan on the middle rack of the oven and bake until the top of the lasagne is lightly golden, 15 to 20 minutes. Remove from the oven and let settle for a few minutes before serving.

HOW "LASAGNE ALLA BOLOGNESE" LAUNCHED MY COOKING CAREER

I can truly say that this is the dish that started my cooking career. In 1970, a year or so after my husband and I and our two-year-old daughter, Carla, moved from New York to Sacramento, I began hosting dinner parties. The dishes I served were the ones I grew up eating. And lasagne alla Bolognese was the undisputed winner. I will always remember the first time I made it for several doctors who were in practice with my husband, and their wives. As I put the large lasagne pan on the table, with its golden brown top still bubbling from the heat and its sumptuous, rich aroma engulfing the room, everyone stopped talking. As my guests began eating, they marveled at the lightness and succulence of the dish and wanted to know how to do it. And the next day my telephone began ringing with requests for the recipe for those splendid lasagne alla Bolognese.

SPINACH LASAGNE WITH MEAT-SAUSAGE RAGÙ

Lasagnette Verdi con Ragù alla Romagnola

SERVES 6 TO 8

For the lasagne

2 cups unbleached
all-purpose flour

3 extra-large eggs

2 tablespoons finely chopped
cooked fresh spinach or
defrosted frozen spinach,
squeezed dry and finely
chopped

1 tablespoon coarse salt

For the béchamel sauce

1 cup milk

2 tablespoons unsalted butter

2 tablespoons
all-purpose flour

Pinch of salt

1 recipe Meat-Sausage Ragù
(page 188)

1 to 2 tablespoons cold
unsalted butter, cut into
small cubes

¾ cup freshly grated
Parmigiano-Reggiano

*B*risighella is a charming little town on the Romagna side of the region that boasts a small central square, two cafés, a few restaurants, some fairly stylish boutiques, two legendary medieval castles perched at the top of two of the hills that surround the town, and Gigiolé. I had a wonderful meal here! Gigiolé is the best restaurant of the area, and it is a destination for food lovers. The food of Gigiolé is steeped in tradition. The spinach lasagne, layered with the traditional meat-sausage ragù, is light and delicate with only five layers. The trick, I was told by Tarcisio, the chef-owner of the restaurant, was to spread each sheet of homemade pasta "very lightly" with the long-simmered, full-bodied meat ragù.

USING the flour, eggs, and spinach, prepare the pasta dough as instructed on pages 95–97, adding the spinach with the eggs. Roll out the dough as instructed on pages 97–98 and cut it to fit your lasagne pan.

PLACE a bowl of cold water on a counter near the stove and spread out some kitchen towels near the bowl.

BRING a large pot of water, preferably one with a pasta insert, to a boil. Add the coarse salt and 3 to 4 sheets of pasta (no more). After the water comes back to the boil, cook the sheets for no longer than 20 to 25 seconds. Scoop out the sheets with the pasta insert or a large skimmer, trying not to tear them, and plunge them into the cold water to cool. Immediately remove the pasta sheets, lay out on the towels, and pat dry with another towel. Repeat with the remaining pasta.

PREPARE the béchamel sauce as instructed on page 28 using the proportions called for in this recipe. Let cool slightly.

PREHEAT the oven to 400 °F. Generously butter the bottom and sides of a lasagne pan.

ADD the béchamel sauce to the ragù and mix well. (Reserve the leftover béchamel for another use; see box, page 119.) Line the bottom of the pan with a layer of pasta sheets. Spread a thin layer of sauce over the pasta and sprinkle lightly with Parmigiano. Repeat with one layer of pasta, one of meat sauce, and one of Parmigiano. Dot the top layer of pasta with the butter. (The lasagne can be assembled 1 day ahead and refrigerated, tightly covered with plastic wrap. Remove the lasagne from the refrigerator a couple of hours before baking.)

THE number of layers in the lasagne depends on the size of the baking pan. However, lasagne should have no fewer than 5 layers and no more than 8.

BAKE the lasagne on the middle rack of the oven for about 15 minutes, until the top has a nice golden color. Remove from the oven and let it set for a few minutes before serving.

ONLY FRESH PASTA WILL DO

I wish I could tell you to go ahead and buy dried lasagne, but I can't. To appreciate this dish in all its delicacy, you have to make it with fresh, thinly stretched, homemade pasta. To simplify this dish, make the ragù a day ahead. Prepare the pasta and the béchamel and assemble the lasagne several hours or a day ahead. Then bake it, and sit back to enjoy a dish that has a few centuries of tradition.

CANNELLONI WITH MEAT STUFFING

Cannelloni di Carne al Forno

SERVES 8 TO 10

For the filling

2 tablespoons unsalted butter

½ pound pork loin, trimmed of fat and cut into 3 or 4 thick slices

1 thick slice mortadella (about ¼ pound), cut into cubes

1 thick slice prosciutto (about ¼ pound), cut into cubes

½ cup freshly grated Parmigiano-Reggiano

Pinch of freshly grated nutmeg

Salt to taste

2 large eggs, lightly beaten

For the cannelloni

1¾ cups unbleached all-purpose flour

3 large eggs

1 tablespoon coarse salt

*M*any of the traditional stuffed pasta dishes of Emilia-Romagna, such as lasagne and cannelloni, are sumptuous, rich, and positively irresistible. These are the dishes that used to be on the tables of the people of the region, if not daily, then certainly weekly and always on holidays and special occasions. What a joy to see them on the menus of some restaurants and trattorie. Ristorante Rodrigo in Bologna makes cannelloni with a filling similar to the one used for tortellini, and tops them with a light béchamel sauce. Trattoria Il Testamento del Porco in Ferrara makes a similar version, but tops the cannelloni lightly with a Bolognese meat sauce and drizzles them with a bit of delicious béchamel. Rich? Of course. But, oh, boy, are they good.

Cannelloni is perhaps one of the easiest stuffed pastas to make. It is also one of the loveliest and most elegant. Do not worry about the several steps in this recipe. You can make the filling a few days ahead. Make the pasta, stuff the cannelloni, and coat them with béchamel a day ahead, then bake them at the last moment.

TO prepare the filling, melt the butter in a medium skillet over medium heat. As soon as the butter begins to foam, add the pork loin and cook turning once, until golden on both sides, 2 to 3 minutes.

TRANSFER the meat to a cutting board and cut it into 1-inch pieces. Place in the food processor together with the mortadella and prosciutto and pulse until the meat is finely minced but not pureed. Transfer to a bowl, add the Parmigiano and nutmeg, and season lightly with salt (keep in mind that the prosciutto is salty). Add the eggs and mix to incorporate.

USING the flour and eggs, prepare the pasta dough as instructed on pages 95–97. Roll out the dough and cut into rectangles for cannelloni as instructed on pages 97–99.

For the béchamel sauce

2 cups milk

3 tablespoons unsalted butter

**3 tablespoons
all-purpose flour**

Salt to taste

**½ to ¾ cup freshly grated
Parmigiano-Reggiano**

**2 tablespoons unsalted butter,
cut into small cubes**

PLACE a bowl of cold water on a counter near the stove and spread out some kitchen towels near the bowl. Bring a large pot of water to a boil, preferably a pot with a pasta insert, and add the coarse salt and 5 to 6 pasta rectangles. After the water comes back to the boil, cook the pasta for no longer than 20 to 25 seconds. Scoop out the pasta with the pasta insert or a skimmer and plunge it into the cold water to cool. Immediately remove the pasta and lay it out on the kitchen towels. Pat dry with another towel. Repeat with the remaining pasta.

ONE at a time, lay the rectangles of pasta on a work surface and place 1 heaping tablespoon of the meat filling along the long edge of the pasta nearest you. Roll up the pasta loosely around the filling to make a tube. Generously butter a large baking dish (or two smaller ones) that can accommodate the cannelloni in a single layer and lay the cannelloni next to each other, leaving a little space between them.

PREPARE the béchamel sauce as instructed on page 28, using the proportions called for in this recipe. Let cool slightly, taste, and correct for salt. (Makes approximately 2 cups.)

VERSATILE BÉCHAMEL

Smooth, creamy béchamel is the "secret" binding sauce of many Italian dishes, and it is one of the essential components of lasagne.

Leftover béchamel can be used in a variety of ways. Add it to a simple garlic-free tomato sauce, and it will become luxurious. Or add it to blanched vegetables and turn them into a succulent gratin. Stir it into the meat mixture for meat loaf and meatballs, and they will emerge lusciously tender. Or toss it with cooked sturdy pasta such as rigatoni, spread in a baking dish, and broil or bake in a hot oven until a brown crust forms.

Reheat leftover béchamel in a saucepan over low heat or in a double boiler, stirring constantly; add a few tablespoons of milk if the sauce is too thick.

SPOON the béchamel sauce over the cannelloni, coating them generously. (The cannelloni can be prepared up to this point a day ahead. Cover the dish tightly with plastic wrap and refrigerate until ready to use.) Bring back to room temperature before baking.

PREHEAT the oven to 400°F.

SPRINKLE the Parmigiano over the cannelloni and dot with the butter. Bake on the middle rack of the oven until the cannelloni are lightly golden, 10 to 12 minutes. Remove from the oven and allow the cannelloni to settle for a few minutes before serving.

CANNELLONI TOPPED WITH BOLOGNESE RAGÙ Prepare ragù with the proportions and as instructed on Tagliatelle with Bolognese Ragù (page 122). Set aside until ready to use.

Assemble the cannelloni as directed and place in the baking dish. Spread 1 to 2 tablespoons of meat sauce over each *cannellone*, and drizzle some of the béchamel over the meat sauce. Sprinkle with a bit of Parmigiano and bake as directed.

PASTA DOUGH

Pasta all'Uovo

MAKES ABOUT 1 POUND
PASTA DOUGH

3 cups unbleached
all-purpose flour

5 large eggs

Tagliatelle, tagliolini, pappardelle, garganelli, and strichetti are at their best when made with fresh pasta. The pasta dough can be made with one of the methods given on pages 95–97.

PREPARE the pasta dough as instructed on pages 95–97 using the flour and eggs in this recipe. Roll out the pasta dough, as on pages 97–98, and cut it into the shape called for in the recipe, pages 98–100.

TAGLIATELLE COL RAGÙ

If one had to select a dish that best typifies the succulent food of Emilia-Romagna, tagliatelle with ragù would probably win hands down. Tagliatelle with ragù is to the people of Emilia-Romagna what apple pie is to Americans—quintessential comfort food. This love for one of the most celebrated dishes of Italy originated in the kitchens of the region, where simple, everyday magic took place and where the ritual of pasta making and of the Sunday ragù was an established fact. It is a love that stems from the reassuring image of mothers kneading large batches of dough, rolling it out into perfect golden circles, and cutting it by hand into wide enticing noodles. It is from the comfort of the rhythmical sound of the *mezzaluna* (half-moon–shaped chopping knife) used to chop the vegetables that became the savory base of the ragù, from the inviting aroma of the ragù slowly simmering on the stove for hours, reducing and concentrating in flavor. From the tossing of the tagliatelle with the ragù, with the sauce clinging to the wide noodles, to the grating of the Parmigiano over the steaming pasta, serving the dish is a ritual that warms the hearts just as much as the food does.

While the preparation of the tagliatelle is pretty much the same all over the region, the making of the ragù is not. Ragù is a long-cooked sauce of ground meat and vegetables simmered in liquid. The type of meat and liquid changes from area to area and often from family to family. What generally does not change is the base of chopped onion, carrot, and celery that browns slowly in butter and oil, releasing their sweet flavors; the browning of the meat, which is added to the vegetable base, and the long, slow cooking which produces the intensely flavored ragù.

So, if you are traveling through Emilia-Romagna, don't be surprised to find this much-celebrated, much-loved dish on the menu of many restaurants and trattorie. Order it wherever you are, because, there on your plate, invisibly tangled with golden strands of tagliatelle and the perfume of the meat ragù, rest several hundred years of superlative cooking traditions.

TAGLIATELLE WITH BOLOGNESE RAGÙ

Tagliatelle col Ragù alla Bolognese

SERVES 4 TO 6

For the ragù

3 tablespoons extra virgin olive oil

2 tablespoons unsalted butter

¼ cup finely minced yellow onions

¼ cup finely minced carrots

¼ cup finely minced celery

2 to 3 ounces thickly sliced pancetta, finely minced

¾ pound ground beef chuck

¼ pound ground pork loin

½ cup medium-bodied red wine, such as a Chianti Classico

3 tablespoons double-concentrated Italian tomato paste, diluted in 3 cups Meat Broth (page 71) or canned low-sodium chicken broth

Salt and freshly ground black pepper to taste

½ cup milk, preferably whole milk

1 tablespoon coarse salt

1 recipe Pasta Dough (page 120), rolled out and cut into tagliatelle (see page 100), or 1 pound imported dried tagliatelle

½ cup freshly grated Parmigiano-Reggiano

An unassuming entrance in a pleasantly unassuming building led us to a beautiful, well-appointed dining room. We were late for our 1 P.M. lunch reservation and we were hungry, especially my son-in-law Brian, who seems to be able to eat as much as he wants while remaining fit and trim. Less than a minute after we were seated, a waiter appeared with four crystal glasses of Champagne. I drew a deep breath, sipped a bit of Champagne, and sat back knowing instinctively and immediately that all the raves I had heard about this restaurant were true. Ristorante Buriani, located in the small historical town of Pieve di Cento in the province of Bologna, has a national reputation. Alessandra Buriani, a shy young thirty-something, is the talented chef, who oversees an equally talented kitchen crew made up mostly of other family members. Alessandra's husband, Fabio, whose warmth and wine expertise charms you instantly, is the wine master.

Our lunch lasted three hours. We savored one terrific dish after the other, but the one that is vividly etched in my memory is the homemade tagliatelle with Buriani's meat ragù.

To make the ragù, heat the oil and 1 tablespoon of the butter together in a medium saucepan over medium heat. As soon as the butter begins to foam, add the minced vegetables and pancetta. Cook, stirring occasionally, until the vegetables and pancetta have a nice golden color, about 5 minutes. Add the ground beef and pork, raise the heat to high, and cook, stirring and breaking up the meat with a wooden spoon, until the meat and vegetables have a rich brown color and the bottom of the pan is glazed, 7 to 8 minutes.

ADD the wine and cook, stirring, until most all of it has evaporated. Stir in the diluted tomato paste and season with salt and pepper. As soon as the liquid comes to a boil, reduce the heat to low, partially cover the pan, and simmer for about 2 hours, stirring and checking the sauce every 20 minutes or so. The sauce should be thick, with an appealing nutty brown color, and just slightly liquid. Add a bit more broth or water if the sauce looks too dry.

ADD the milk, partially cover, and simmer for 10 to 15 minutes longer. Taste and adjust the seasoning. Turn off the heat. (Makes approximately 3 cups.)

MEANWHILE, bring a large pot of water to a boil over high heat. Add the coarse salt and tagliatelle and cook until the pasta is tender but still firm to the bite. Drain the pasta and place in a large heated bowl.

ADD the remaining 1 tablespoon butter, about two-thirds of the sauce, and a small handful of the Parmigiano. Toss quickly until the pasta and sauce are well combined. Add more sauce if needed. Serve at once, with the remaining Parmigiano.

PREPARING A RAGÙ AHEAD OF TIME

My mother routinely made a double batch of ragù. One night she would toss it with tagliatelle, and a day or two later she would use it over gnocchi or over layered slices of polenta. Let any extra ragù cool to room temperature, then refrigerate it in a tightly sealed container for a few days, or freeze it. If it has been frozen, defrost the ragù slowly in the refrigerator, then reheat it gently, allowing it to simmer for 5 to 6 minutes, before tossing it with the pasta.

TAGLIATELLE WITH RAGÙ

Tagliatelle col Ragù della Gigina

SERVES 4 TO 6

For the ragù

4 tablespoons (½ stick) unsalted butter plus 1 tablespoon

½ cup finely minced yellow onions

½ cup finely minced carrots

½ cup finely minced celery

1 pound ground beef chuck

Salt and freshly ground black pepper to taste

½ cup medium-bodied red wine

1 cup whole milk

1 tablespoon double-concentrated Italian tomato paste, diluted in 1 cup Meat Broth (page 71) or water

1 tablespoon coarse salt

1 recipe Pasta Dough (page 120), rolled out and cut into tagliatelle (see page 100), or 1 pound imported dried tagliatelle

½ cup freshly grated Parmigiano-Reggiano

*W*hile some cooks add pork, veal, prosciutto, or pancetta to their Bolognese ragù, the ragù of Trattoria Gigina uses only beef. The ragù has a direct, straightforward flavor and a meatier and denser consistency than the other ragùs in this chapter. Nadia, Gigina's daughter, claims that their ragù is very traditional, and that her mother and grandmother have been making it in the same manner for generations.

To make the ragù, melt 3 tablespoons of the butter in a medium saucepan over medium heat. As soon as the butter begins to foam, add the minced vegetables and cook, stirring occasionally, until lightly golden and soft, 5 to 6 minutes. Raise the heat to high and add the beef. Cook, stirring and breaking up the meat with a wooden spoon, until it has a nice rich brown color, 8 to 10 minutes. Season with salt and pepper.

Add the wine and stir until most of it has evaporated. Add the milk. As soon as the milk begins to bubble, reduce the heat to the barest simmer, partially cover the pan, and simmer, stirring from time to time, until the milk has been completely absorbed and no liquid is left in the pan, 40 to 45 minutes.

Add the diluted tomato paste. As soon as the sauce begins to simmer again, partially cover the pan and cook, stirring and checking the sauce every 20 minutes or so, for 1 to 1½ hours, until most of the liquid has been absorbed. The sauce should have a dense texture and a moist but not liquid consistency. If the sauce reduces too much as it cooks, stir in a bit of water or broth.

Stir 1 tablespoon butter into the sauce, taste, and adjust the seasoning. Turn off the heat. (Makes approximately 3 cups.)

Meanwhile, bring a large pot of water to a boil over high heat. Add the coarse salt and tagliatelle and cook until the pasta is tender but still firm to the bite.

DRAIN the pasta and place in a large heated bowl. Add the remaining tablespoon butter, about two-thirds of the sauce, and a small handful of the Parmigiano. Toss quickly until the pasta and sauce are well combined. Add more sauce if needed. Serve at once, with the remaining Parmigiano.

A LITTLE RAGÙ GOES A LONG WAY

A meat ragù that has simmered slowly for a few hours acquires an intensity of flavor that is round and rich, without being heavy. Use the ragù with restraint, because a little of this flavorful sauce goes a long way. Keep in mind that ragù (just as any other sauce) should barely coat the pasta, not drown it. Use approximately ⅓ cup of ragù per serving.

TAGLIATELLE WITH WALNUT, RICOTTA, AND GARLIC PESTO

Tagliatelle all'Agliata

SERVES 6 TO 8

For the sauce

¾ cup walnuts

1 garlic clove, peeled

Salt to taste

½ cup ricotta cheese

⅓ cup freshly grated
Parmigiano-Reggiano

¼ cup chopped
flat-leaf parsley

⅓ cup extra virgin olive oil

Freshly ground black pepper
to taste

1 tablespoon coarse salt

1 recipe Pasta Dough
(page 120), rolled out and cut
into tagliatelle (see page 100),
or 1 pound imported dried
tagliatelle

2 tablespoons unsalted butter,
at room temperature

Freshly grated Parmigiano-
Reggiano for serving, optional

*T*rattoria da Gianni, in the Apennine mountain town of Rocca dei Corvi near the Ligurian border, prepares a splendid walnut-ricotta pesto, of obvious Ligurian origin, and pairs it with tagliatelle, the typical noodles of Emilia-Romagna. The thick, creamy sauce mixed with delicate homemade tagliatelle makes for an incredibly satisfying dish. Because it is quite filling, it can be stretched to serve 8.

To make the pesto, put the walnuts, garlic, and a pinch of salt in a food processor fitted with the metal blade. Pulse the machine until the walnuts are chopped very fine but not pulverized. Transfer the mixture to a bowl. Add the ricotta, Parmigiano, parsley, and olive oil. Season with salt and pepper. (The pesto will have a firm, thick consistency; don't worry—it will be thinned down later on.) (Makes 1 cup.) Cover the bowl and set aside. (The pesto can be prepared several hours ahead and refrigerated. Bring it to room temperature before using.)

BRING a large pot of water to a boil over high heat. Add the coarse salt and tagliatelle and cook until the pasta is tender but still a bit firm to the bite. Scoop out 2 cups of the pasta cooking water and stir about 1 cup of it into the walnut pesto.

DRAIN the pasta and place in a large heated bowl. Add the butter and pesto and toss together quickly until the pasta and sauce are well combined. Add some more of the pasta water if the tagliatelle seem a bit dry. Taste, adjust the seasoning, and serve with some Parmigiano if desired.

Note: This is a dish that cannot be allowed to wait because the homemade pasta will absorb the creamy sauce quickly. When you are ready to drain the pasta, make sure that everyone is at the table. Drain the pasta, toss it with the sauce, and sit down to enjoy it.

TAGLIATELLE WITH BEANS AND PROSCIUTTO

Tagliatelle con Fagioli e Prosciutto

SERVES 4 TO 6

The unusual and winning combination of beans and pasta is not new at all. In fact, dishes such as pisarei e fasò, *a typical pasta of Faenza's countryside, and* pasta e fagioli, *a very thick soup of beans with the home-made dough called* maltagliati, *are much-loved traditional dishes of the region. Today the combination of pasta and beans has been rediscovered by young chefs and touted for its exceptional nutritive value.*

This somewhat more refined variation of the ubiquitous pasta-and-bean combination tosses homemade tagliatelle with a deliciously rich sauce of butter, prosciutto, beans, tomatoes, and cream.

For the sauce

½ cup dried borlotti beans or cranberry beans, picked over, soaked overnight in cold water to cover generously, or 1½ cups canned beans, rinsed and drained

¼ pound prosciutto, in 2 or 3 thick slices

3 tablespoons unsalted butter

⅓ cup finely minced yellow onions

3 tablespoons double-concentrated Italian tomato paste, diluted in 3 cups Chicken Broth (page 73) or canned low-sodium chicken broth

¼ cup heavy cream

Salt to taste

1 tablespoon coarse salt

1 recipe Pasta Dough (page 120), rolled out and cut into tagliatelle (see page 100), or 1 pound imported dried tagliatelle

½ cup freshly grated Parmigiano-Reggiano

IF using dried beans, drain and rinse under cold running water, put them in a medium pot, and cook as instructed on page 82. Scoop out about 1 cup of the bean cooking water and set aside. Drain the beans and set aside until ready to use.

TO make the sauce, separate the fat from the prosciutto, reserving it, and dice the prosciutto. Dice the prosciutto fat, put it in a large skillet with the butter, and place over medium heat. When the butter begins to foam, add the onion and cook, stirring, until the onion and prosciutto fat are lightly golden, 5 to 6 minutes. Add the diced prosciutto and the beans and stir for a minute or two.

ADD the diluted tomato paste and the cream, season with salt, and bring to a gentle boil. Reduce the heat to medium-low and simmer, uncovered, stirring from time to time, until the sauce has a medium-thick consistency, 12 to 15 minutes. Taste and adjust the seasoning. (Makes approximately 3 cups.)

WHILE the sauce is cooking, bring a large pot of water to a boil over high heat. Add the coarse salt and tagliatelle and cook, uncovered, until the pasta is tender but still a bit firm to the bite.

DRAIN the pasta, making sure to leave a bit of water clinging to the noodles, and add it to the skillet with the sauce. Add about half of the Parmigiano and mix quickly over medium heat until the pasta and sauce are well combined. Stir in some of the reserved bean cooking water if the pasta seems a bit dry, or pasta water (if you used canned beans). Taste, adjust the seasoning, and serve with the remaining Parmigiano.

TOSSING PASTA IN THE SKILLET

Think of your large skillet as your serving bowl. When the pasta is added to the skillet and tossed quickly with the hot sauce, the sauce will thicken and cling to the pasta in no time at all, and the pasta will get to the table perfectly cooked and piping hot. The drawback of this technique is that an inexperienced cook may linger too long over the tossing and overcook the pasta and reduce the sauce too much. So, if you are a beginner, here is what to do:

- Make sure to have enough sauce in the skillet and keep it over low heat.

- Undercook your pasta slightly, so you have a little time to practice mixing the pasta with the sauce.

- Toss the pasta quickly, as you would a salad. The moment the sauce clings to the pasta "loosely," turn off the heat.

- Always keep some of the pasta water (or bean cooking water) at hand. Remember, this is the "fixer" of many dry sauces.

- And, finally, bring the pasta to the table *"pronto."*

TAGLIATELLE WITH
TOMATO SAUCE AND CREAM

Tagliatelle al Burro e Oro

SERVES 4 TO 6

For the sauce

3 to 4 tablespoons unsalted butter

½ cup very finely minced yellow onions

3 cups Homemade Tomato Sauce (page 22) or canned Italian plum tomatoes, with their juice, put through a food mill to remove the seeds

¼ cup heavy cream

Salt to taste

1 tablespoon coarse salt

1 recipe Pasta Dough (page 120), rolled out and cut into tagliatelle (see page 100), or 1 pound imported dried tagliatelle

½ cup freshly grated Parmigiano-Reggiano

*B*urro e oro *(butter and gold) is a traditional sauce of Emilia that is often paired with plump, homemade stuffed pasta pillows such as tortelloni and tagliatelle. The sauce, which was one of my father's favorites, is fresh, light, and flavorful. It is also the epitome of simplicity—unsalted butter, onions, tomatoes, and cream are simmered briefly together, creating a sauce with a rich golden color. This is a sauce that can be made in the time it takes the water to come to a boil.*

TO make the sauce, melt the butter in a large skillet over medium heat. Add the onions and cook, stirring, until very, very soft, about 8 minutes. Add the tomato sauce and cream and season with salt. As soon as the sauce comes to a boil, reduce the heat to medium-low and let bubble gently, uncovered, for about 5 minutes. Taste, adjust the seasoning, and turn off the heat. (Makes about 2½ cups.) (The sauce can be prepared a few hours ahead.)

BRING a large pot of water to a boil over high heat. Add the coarse salt and tagliatelle and cook until the pasta is tender but still firm to the bite.

DRAIN the pasta and add it to the skillet. Add a small handful of the Parmigiano and toss quickly over medium heat until the pasta and sauce are well combined. Taste, adjust the seasoning, and serve with the remaining Parmigiano.

TAGLIATELLE WITH PROSCIUTTO AND PEAS Sauté the onions in the butter as directed. Add 3 ounces prosciutto, diced, and 1 cup fresh peas blanched in boiling salted water for 1 to 2 minutes and stir for a minute or two. Add the tomato sauce and cream, season with salt, and proceed as instructed above.

CHESTNUT FLOUR TAGLIATELLE
WITH PANCETTA AND SAGE

Tagliatelle di Farina di Castagne con Pancetta e Salvia

SERVES 4

For the tagliatelle

1⅓ cups unbleached
all-purpose flour

1 cup fine chestnut flour
(available at Italian and
specialty food markets and
health food stores)

3 large eggs

3 to 4 tablespoons milk

For the sauce

3 to 4 tablespoons
unsalted butter

3 ounces thickly sliced
pancetta or prosciutto, diced

½ to 1 cup Chicken Broth
(page 73) or canned low-
sodium chicken broth

Salt to taste

10 to 12 sage leaves, finely
shredded

1 tablespoon coarse salt

Salt to taste

½ cup freshly grated
Parmigiano-Reggiano

There was a time when the people who lived in the mountain towns of Emilia-Romagna supplemented their meager diet with the nut of the chestnut tree. The trees were abundant and abundantly rich, and the nuts harvested in the fall were turned into myriad delicious dishes. Even in the flat countryside of Emilia, chestnuts were immensely popular. I have memories of a large dark brown cake called castagnaccio, *which my mother made for us children. I also remember my very favorite aunt, Zia Rina, who had a farm outside Bologna, rolling out chestnut flour dough with an old broom handle. The dough, which was later cut into tagliatelle, was thick and yielding and had a rich grayish color. The tagliatelle, cooked and tossed with just a bit of butter and some fresh herbs, was filling and quite delicious.*

I had almost forgotten about that tagliatelle until I found a recipe in an old cookbook belonging to my sister-in-law's mother, then the memories came rushing back. Here is the recipe, chestnut tagliatelle dressed simply with butter, crisp pancetta, and fresh sage. Make it in winter and enjoy with a glass of really good red wine.

USING the flours, eggs, and milk, prepare the pasta dough as instructed on pages 95–97. Roll out the dough as instructed on pages 97–98, and cut it into tagliatelle. (See box.)

TO prepare the sauce, melt the butter in a large skillet over medium heat. As soon as the butter begins to foam, add the pancetta and stir until lightly golden, 1 to 2 minutes. Add ½ cup of the broth, season with salt, and bring to a simmer. Simmer until the broth has reduced by about half, 2 to 3 minutes. Stir in the sage and turn off the heat.

MEANWHILE, bring a large pot of water to a boil over high heat. Add the coarse salt and tagliatelle and cook until the pasta is tender but still firm to the bite. (Remember, pasta that is freshly made will cook in less than a minute.)

DRAIN the pasta and add it to the skillet. Season the pasta lightly with salt and stir in a small handful of the Parmigiano. Mix gently but quickly over medium heat until the pasta and sauce are well combined. Add some of the remaining ½ cup broth if pasta is a bit dry and stir to incorporate. Taste, adjust the seasoning, and serve with the remaining Parmigiano.

TAGLIATELLE WITH AN ATTITUDE

The dough for chestnut tagliatelle is a bit more temperamental than the dough made with all-purpose flour because chestnut flour is high in starch (that is why one feels comfortably full after eating a bowl of this pasta). Follow these simple steps, and you will have an unusual, absolutely delicious plate of noodles.

- When making the dough, follow the proportions given in the recipe to the letter. Cover the dough in plastic wrap and let it rest at room temperature for about half an hour or so.

- Roll out the dough a bit thicker than for regular tagliatelle. If you are using a pasta machine, stop at number 3.

- Let the pasta sheets dry for 15 to 20 minutes before cutting them into noodles. They can be cooked immediately or rolled up into loose bundles, placed on a tray, and refrigerated, uncovered, for several hours or overnight.

- Treat the noodles gently as you drain and toss them with the sauce, so they won't break.

TAGLIOLINI WITH MIXED MUSHROOMS

Tagliolini con Funghi Misti

SERVES 4 TO 6

1 ounce dried porcini mushrooms, soaked in 2 cups lukewarm water for 20 minutes

½ pound mixed fresh mushrooms, such as chanterelle, shiitake, and oyster mushrooms (or white button mushrooms), wiped clean

⅓ cup extra virgin olive oil

2 garlic cloves, finely minced

2 to 3 tablespoons chopped flat-leaf parsley

Salt and freshly ground black pepper to taste

1 tablespoon coarse salt

1 recipe Pasta Dough (page 120), rolled out and cut into tagliolini (see page 100), or 1 pound imported dried tagliolini

1 to 2 tablespoons unsalted butter

If you are a porcini mushroom lover, fall is the perfect time to travel to Italy, because that is when this prized Italian mushroom is at its best, and exuberantly abundant.

At Antica Trattoria Moretto, outside the town of Vignola in the Emilia region, we had a most glorious plate of thin homemade tagliolini tossed with fresh, meaty porcini. The porcini had been diced and sautéed in the classic flavor base of oil, garlic, and parsley. They were golden brown and their aroma made your head swirl. Since porcini are not an everyday occurrence in our markets, I have used dried porcini mushrooms and shiitakes. The dried porcini impart their earthy fragrance to the dish, and the other mushrooms, when cooked in the Italian manner, bestow succulence.

DRAIN the porcini mushrooms and reserve the soaking liquid. Rinse the mushrooms well under cold running water and roughly chop them. Line a strainer with paper towels and strain the liquid into a bowl. Set aside.

CUT the fresh mushrooms into thin slices, then cut the slices into medium dice.

HEAT the oil in a large skillet over high heat until very hot. Add the fresh mushrooms, without crowding, in batches if necessary, and cook, stirring, until lightly golden, 2 to 3 minutes. Add the porcini, garlic, and parsley and season with salt and several grinds of pepper. Add about 1 cup of the reserved mushroom liquid and bring to a fast boil. Cook, stirring, until the liquid has reduced by approximately half. Taste, adjust the seasoning, and turn off the heat. (The mushrooms can be sautéed 1 hour or so ahead of time.)

BRING a large pot of water to a boil over high heat. Add the coarse salt and tagliolini and cook, stirring a few times, until the pasta is tender but still a bit firm to the bite.

DRAIN the pasta and place in the skillet with the mushrooms. Add the butter, season lightly with salt, and mix quickly over medium heat until the pasta and sauce are well combined. Stir in more of the reserved mushroom liquid if the pasta seems a bit dry. Taste, adjust the seasoning, and serve.

WATCH YOUR TAGLIOLINI . . .

Because the thin homemade pasta cooks in no time at all. Keep it *al dente*, since it will continue to cook as it is tossed with the sauce.

Tagliolini should not be allowed to wait, since, when cooked, it will absorb the sauce quickly and dry out somewhat. Do what Italians do; summon everyone to the table, then sauce and serve the pasta.

TAGLIOLINI WITH ONION SAUCE

Tagliolini con le Cipolle

SERVES 4 TO 6

For the sauce

3 tablespoons unsalted butter

2 tablespoons extra virgin olive oil

4 yellow onions (about 2 pounds medium), thinly sliced

3 tablespoons double-concentrated Italian tomato paste, diluted in 3 cups Chicken Broth (page 73) or canned low-sodium chicken broth

Salt and freshly ground black pepper to taste

1 tablespoon coarse salt

1 recipe Pasta Dough (page 120), rolled out and cut into tagliolini (see page 100), or 1 pound imported dried tagliolini

½ cup freshly grated Parmigiano-Reggiano

*S*andoni is a modest country trattoria on the outskirts of Bologna where one can eat large portions of homemade pasta, grilled ribs, and sausages with grilled polenta for very little money. One of Sandoni's most popular dishes is tagliolini with onion sauce. The sauce is of the utmost simplicity, yet it is immensely appetizing and heartwarming. The only trick is to cook the onions very gently over low heat until they are meltingly soft and the liquid in the pan has reduced to a thick glaze, or essence, that coats the onions.

To make the sauce, heat 2 tablespoons of the butter and the oil together in a large skillet over medium heat. Add the onions and cook, stirring from time to time, until golden and very soft, 12 to 15 minutes.

Raise the heat to high, add the diluted tomato paste, and season lightly with salt and pepper. As soon as the liquid comes to a boil, reduce the heat to low and partially cover the skillet. Cook, stirring occasionally, until the onions are meltingly soft and the liquid in the pan has reduced to a thick glaze, 30 to 35 minutes. If the sauce is too thin, remove the lid, raise the heat to high, and cook, stirring, until the sauce has a dense consistency, 3 to 5 minutes. (Makes about 3 cups.) (The sauce can be prepared a few hours ahead. Reheat gently before using.)

Bring a large pot of water to a boil over high heat. Add the coarse salt and tagliolini and cook, stirring a few times, until the pasta is tender but still firm to the bite.

Drain the tagliolini and place in a large heated bowl. Add the remaining 1 tablespoon of butter, about two-thirds of the onion sauce, and half of the Parmigiano. Mix quickly until the pasta and sauce are well combined. Stir in additional sauce if needed. Taste, adjust the seasoning, and serve with the remaining Parmigiano.

TAGLIOLINI WITH PROSCIUTTO AND BALSAMIC VINEGAR

Tagliolini al Prosciutto e Aceto Balsamico

SERVES 4 TO 6

For the sauce

¼ pound prosciutto, in 2 or 3 thick slices

4 tablespoons (½ stick) unsalted butter

½ cup very finely minced red onions

½ cup dry white wine

½ cup Chicken Broth (page 73) or canned low-sodium chicken broth

Salt to taste

3 to 4 tablespoons balsamic vinegar (see page 10)

1 tablespoon coarse salt

1 recipe Pasta Dough (page 120), rolled out and cut into tagliolini (see page 100), or 1 pound imported dried tagliolini or tagliatelle

½ cup freshly grated Parmigiano-Reggiano

One of my favorite restaurants in Bologna is Antica Trattoria del Cacciatore. Originally a trattoria, today it is an elegant, bustling restaurant on the outskirts of Bologna. It has been able to evolve and refine itself while maintaining high standards and serving impeccable food, and all the pasta is still made by a sfoglina, a local woman who makes it by hand. The pasta is golden yellow, with a porous, nonslippery texture that absorbs sauces beautifully. I love to dine there, especially when I am served dishes like this that are a bit unusual though simple to execute, and absolutely delicious.

To make the sauce, separate the fat from the prosciutto and set the prosciutto aside. Chop the fat very fine and place in a large skillet with 3 tablespoons of the butter. Put the skillet over medium heat. As soon as the butter begins to foam, add the onions and cook, stirring, until lightly golden and soft, 5 to 6 minutes.

While the onions are cooking, dice the prosciutto.

Add the prosciutto to the skillet and stir for a minute or two, then add the wine and cook briskly until almost all the wine has evaporated. Add the broth, season with salt, and bring to a gentle boil. Cook, stirring occasionally, until the sauce has a medium-thick consistency, about 3 minutes. Add the remaining 1 tablespoon butter and the balsamic vinegar, stir once or twice, and turn off the heat.

Meanwhile, bring a large pot of water to a boil over high heat. Add the coarse salt and taglioline and cook until the pasta is tender but still firm to the bite. (Fresh tagliolini will be done in about 30 seconds.)

Drain the pasta, making sure to leave a bit of water clinging to the noodles, and add it to the skillet. Toss quickly over medium heat until the pasta and sauce are well combined. Taste, adjust the seasoning, and serve with a sprinkling of the Parmigiano.

TAGLIOLINI WITH WHITE TRUFFLES

Taglioline al Tartufo Bianco

SERVES 4 TO 6

2 ounces white truffles

1 tablespoon coarse salt

1 recipe Pasta Dough (page 120), rolled out and cut into tagliolini (see page 100), or 1 pound imported dried tagliolini

4 tablespoons (½ stick) unsalted butter, at room temperature

Salt to taste

½ cup freshly grated Parmigiano-Reggiano

*W*hite truffles, shaved over delicate homemade pasta, are an exceptionally luxurious treat. Late fall and part of winter are the season for truffles and, in Italy, any restaurant and trattoria that can afford this delectable fungi showcases it prominently in large baskets, next to that other fall delicacy, wild porcini mushrooms.

Truffles can be used in many preparations. My father would shave just a little bit over eggs, and for him that was the ultimate treat. For me, however, the ultimate indulgence is a plate of homemade tagliolini, or a creamy, buttery risotto lavishly blanketed with shaved fresh, aphrodisiacal, aromatic white truffles.

CLEAN the truffle, if necessary, by gently scraping away any dirt with a stiff brush. Wipe the truffle clean with a barely moist paper towel; do not rinse under water.

BRING a large pot of water to a boil over high heat. Add the coarse salt and tagliolini and cook until the pasta is tender but still firm to the bite.

WHILE the pasta is cooking, melt the butter in a large skillet over medium heat.

SCOOP out and reserve about 1 cup of the pasta cooking water. Drain the pasta and add it to the skillet. Season lightly with salt and stir in about half of the Parmigiano. Toss quickly until the butter and cheese thoroughly coat the pasta. Add some of the pasta cooking water if the tagliolini seems a bit dry.

PLACE the pasta on heated plates. Using a truffle slicer or a potato peeler, shave 10 to 12 thin slivers of truffle onto each portion. Serve at once.

VARIATION: When fresh truffles are not available, cook the pasta and toss it with the butter and cheese. You will then have one of the simplest and purest dishes of Italy.

ABOUT FRESH TRUFFLES

Truffles are fungi that grow underground near the roots of oak, hazelnut, and poplar trees. White and black truffles are found in many parts of Italy, including Emilia-Romagna, Piedmont, Tuscany, and the Marches. The white truffle of Alba in Piedmont is particularly prized for its quality and fragrant aroma.

Late fall and part of winter are truffle season. The quantity of truffles harvested in any given year is determined in part by the amount of rain that falls during late summer and early fall, among other factors. The more rain, the more truffles are harvested. The truffles are sniffed out and unearthed by trained dogs, whose owners search for this underground treasure very cautiously, keeping the location of their hunt a well-guarded secret. Truffles are very expensive, especially if the harvest is low.

Good white or black truffles should be firm and compact, with no softness whatsoever, and they should have a strong fragrance. To store truffles properly, wrap them in newspaper, then wrap tightly in aluminum foil and keep in the refrigerator. Use truffles as soon as you can, since they are perishable and lose their aroma rather quickly.

Imported fresh truffles can be found from time to time in specialty food markets.

Cleaning Truffles: The best way to clean truffles is with a stiff brush. If the dirt is entrenched in the peaks and valleys of the truffle, it may need to be removed with a small paring knife. After the dirt has been removed, rub the surface with a barely moist (not wet) paper towel. Never wash truffles.

Cooking with Truffles: If you don't have a special truffle slicer, slivers of very thinly sliced truffle can be made with a sharp potato peeler. Slice the truffle raw directly over the dish you are serving. In Emilia-Romagna, we shave white truffles over tagliolini, risotto, and fried eggs and over cutlets *alla Bolognese.*

PAPPARDELLE WITH SAUSAGE, MUSHROOMS, AND CREAM

Pappardelle con Salsiccia, Funghi, e Panna

SERVES 4 TO 6

For the sauce

⅓ cup extra virgin olive oil

¾ pound fresh porcini, shiitake, or chanterelle mushrooms, wiped clean and thinly sliced

1 garlic clove, minced

1 tablespoon chopped flat-leaf parsley, plus 1 tablespoon finely chopped parsley

3 tablespoons unsalted butter

½ cup finely minced yellow onions

1 link (about ¼ pound) Homemade Bolognese Sausage (page 267) or mild Italian pork sausage (containing no fennel seeds, chile pepper, or strong spices), casing removed and finely chopped

½ cup dry white wine

½ cup Chicken Broth (page 73) or canned low-sodium chicken broth

½ cup heavy cream

Salt to taste

1 tablespoon coarse salt

Bologna, like Florence, sits in a large valley surrounded by luscious, high green hills. The hills, which are dotted with small quaint towns and hamlets, are the summer retreat of many Bolognese families, who eagerly escape the oppressive humid heat of the valley for the crisp, fresh air and peaceful surroundings of the mountains. Monghidoro, one of the largest towns with a population of two thousand, is a popular destination point. Besides a few boutiques, artisan shops, and outdoor cafés, the town also has several very good trattorie. At Da Carlet, a popular rustic trattoria, we were served superlative pasta. I loved the homemade wide pappardelle, topped by the first crop of intensely fragrant porcini mushrooms, from the nearby woods. The mushrooms, prepared in the typical Italian way, were tossed in a large skillet with hot, fragrant oil and sprinkled with a bit of garlic and parsley. Then they were added to a simple sauce of onion, sausage, and cream and tossed with the pappardelle.

To make the sauce, heat the oil in a large skillet over high heat until very hot. Add the mushrooms, without crowding (cook in batches if necessary), and cook, stirring, until lightly golden, 2 to 3 minutes. Add the garlic and 1 tablespoon chopped parsley and stir for 30 to 40 seconds, then transfer the mushrooms to a bowl with a slotted spoon.

WIPE the skillet clean with paper towels. Add 2 tablespoons of the butter and put over medium heat. As soon as the butter begins to foam, add the onions and cook, stirring, until lightly golden and soft, 5 to 6 minutes. Raise the heat to high and add the sausage. Cook, stirring and breaking up the sausage with a wooden spoon, until it has lost its raw color, 2 to 3 minutes. Return the mushrooms to the skillet and add the wine. Stir until the wine has reduced by approximately half. Add the broth and cream, season with salt, and reduce the heat to medium. Simmer until the sauce has a medium-thick consistency, 4 to 5 minutes. Stir in the remaining

1 recipe Homemade Pasta (page 120), rolled out and cut for pappardelle (page 99), or 1 pound imported dried pappardelle

½ cup freshly grated Parmigiano-Reggiano

1 tablespoon butter and the finely chopped parsley and turn off the heat. (The sauce can be prepared a few hours ahead. Reheat gently before using.)

BRING a large pot of water to a boil over high heat. Add the coarse salt and pappardelle and cook, stirring a few times, until the pasta is tender but still a bit firm to the bite.

SCOOP out and reserve about 1 cup of the pasta cooking water. Drain the pasta and place in the skillet with the sauce. Add about half of the Parmigiano and mix over medium heat until the pasta and sauce are well combined. Stir in some of the reserved pasta water if the pasta seems a bit dry. Serve at once, with the remaining Parmigiano.

INSTEAD OF FRESH PORCINI

Although fresh porcini mushrooms are beginning to appear more often in specialty food markets, the truth is that in many parts of the country, they are hard to come by. Thankfully, shiitake and chanterelle mushrooms are readily available in many markets. When these mushrooms are sautéed in the manner of porcini—with oil, garlic, and parsley—they become an acceptable substitute. The sausage, which in this dish is used in a small amount as a flavoring agent, just as prosciutto or pancetta would be, should be fresh and mild, with no fennel, dried herbs, or hot chile pepper added to it. This versatile sauce can be used over tagliatelle, rigatoni, penne, and potato gnocchi.

GARGANELLI WITH SAUSAGE SAUCE

Garganelli con il Sugo di Salsiccia

SERVES 4 TO 6

For the sauce

4 tablespoons (½ stick) unsalted butter

½ cup finely minced yellow onions

1 garlic clove, finely minced

½ pound Homemade Bolognese Sausage (page 267) or mild Italian pork sausage (containing no fennel seeds, chile pepper, or strong spices) casings removed and finely chopped

½ cup dry white wine

3 tablespoons double-concentrated Italian tomato paste, diluted in 2½ cups Chicken Broth (page 73) or canned low-sodium chicken broth

⅓ cup milk

Salt and freshly ground black pepper to taste

1 tablespoon coarse salt

1 recipe Pasta Dough (page 120), rolled out and cut into garganelli (see page 99), or 1 pound imported dried garganelli, penne, tagliatelle, or rigatoni

⅔ cup freshly grated Parmigiano-Reggiano

*O*ne of the most loved dishes that appears consistently on the menus of the trattorie of Bologna is gramigna *with sausage.* Gramigna *("little weeds") is a short, somewhat curly fresh egg pasta, made by pressing the dough through a small hand-operated extruder. While years ago, many Bolognese families prided themselves on making their own* gramigna, *today most people buy it from the local* panificio *(bread and pasta store) or buy a factory-made product. The traditional sauce for this pasta, with fresh homemade sausage, wine, milk, tomatoes, and just a bit of cream, is deliciously decadent. Here, the sauce is paired with* garganelli, *small, grooved homemade* maccheroni *that are typical of the Emilia-Romagna region and are today available in Italian specialty stores. Penne, tagliatelle, or rigatoni can also be used.*

To make the sauce, melt 3 tablespoons of the butter in a large skillet over medium heat. As soon as the butter begins to foam, add the onions and cook, stirring, until lightly golden and soft, 5 to 6 minutes. Add the garlic and stir once or twice. Raise the heat to high and add the sausage. Cook, stirring and breaking up the sausage with a wooden spoon, until it is a rich golden color, 5 to 7 minutes.

ADD the wine and cook, stirring briskly, until almost all of it has evaporated. Stir in the diluted tomato paste and milk and season lightly with salt and several grinds of pepper. As soon as the liquid comes to a boil, reduce the heat to medium-low and simmer, uncovered, stirring occasionally, until the sauce has a medium-thick consistency and pale golden color, about 15 minutes. Turn off the heat. (The sauce can be prepared a few hours ahead. Reheat gently before using.)

MEANWHILE, bring a large pot of water to a boil over high heat. Add the coarse salt and pasta and cook until the pasta is tender but still firm to the bite.

Scoop out and reserve about 1 cup of the pasta cooking water. Drain the pasta and place in the skillet with the sauce. Add the remaining 1 tablespoon butter and a small handful of the Parmigiano. Stir quickly over medium heat until the pasta and sauce are well combined. If the pasta seems a bit dry, add some of the reserved pasta water and stir once or twice. Taste, adjust the seasoning, and serve with the remaining Parmigiano.

GARGANELLI WITH MEAT RAGÙ

Garganelli col Ragù

SERVES 4 TO 6

For the sauce

2 tablespoons extra virgin olive oil

3 tablespoons unsalted butter

¼ cup finely minced yellow onion

¼ cup finely minced carrots

¼ cup finely minced celery

1 link (about ¼ pound) Homemade Bolognese Sausage (page 267) or mild Italian pork sausage (containing no fennel seeds, chile pepper, or strong spices), casing removed and finely chopped

½ pound ground pork loin

¼ pound thinly sliced prosciutto, finely minced

1½ cups Homemade Tomato Sauce (page 22) or canned Italian plum tomatoes, with their juice, put through a food mill to remove the seeds

La Nicchia is a pleasant, family-owned trattoria in the countryside of Modena that serves mostly traditional food. What drove us there was the allure of stinco al forno, *braised whole veal shank, for which the trattoria is famous. However, that evening, fate was not with us, and this tantalizing dish was sold out. So, upon the recommendation of the owner, we ordered garganelli, with the trattoria's long-simmered meat ragù. The dish that came to our table, preceded by a most appetizing aroma, was homey and sophisticated at the same time, with a delicious, delicate flavor that lingered on the palate.*

To make the sauce, heat the oil and 2 tablespoons of the butter together in a medium saucepan over medium heat. As soon as the butter begins to foam, add the onion, carrots, and celery and cook, stirring, until lightly golden and soft, 5 to 6 minutes. Raise the heat to high and add the sausage and pork. Cook, stirring to break up the meat with a large wooden spoon, until it is lightly golden, about 6 minutes. Add the prosciutto and stir for a minute or two.

Add the tomato sauce and broth and season with salt. As soon as the sauce begins to bubble, reduce the heat to low, partially cover the pan, and cook at the barest simmer, stirring from time to time, for about 2 hours, until most of the liquid has been absorbed and the sauce is just slightly liquid. If the sauce reduces too much during cooking, stir in a bit of additional broth.

½ cup Meat Broth (page 71) or canned low-sodium chicken broth, plus more if needed

Salt to taste

⅓ cup milk

1 tablespoon coarse salt

1 pound imported dried garganelli or penne rigate

½ cup freshly grated Parmigiano-Reggiano

ADD the milk and simmer for 10 to 15 minutes longer. Taste and adjust the seasoning; turn off the heat. (Makes approximately 2½ cups.)

BRING a large pot of water to a boil over high heat. Add the coarse salt and garganelli and cook until the pasta is tender but still firm to the bite.

DRAIN the pasta and place in a large heated bowl. Add the remaining 1 tablespoon butter, about half of the sauce, and a small handful of the Parmigiano and toss quickly until the pasta and sauce are well combined. Add more sauce if needed. Serve at once, with the remaining Parmigiano.

SLOW COOKING DOES IT

This rich, flavorful ragù has a surprisingly light, delicate taste. In making it, keep in mind the following: Cook the vegetables until they are soft and golden. Brown the meat over high heat so that its juices will bestow taste on the vegetables. Add the liquid and, as it begins to bubble, reduce the heat and simmer the ragù *very slowly* for a minimum of 2 hours, until it has a shining, glazed appearance and a just slightly liquid consistency.

GARGANELLI WITH LOBSTER AND FRIED ZUCCHINI

Garganelli con Astice e Zucchine

SERVES 4 TO 6

For the sauce

2 fresh or thawed frozen lobster tails (8 to 9 ounces each)

½ cup extra virgin olive oil, plus more if needed

1 garlic clove, lightly crushed

½ cup dry white wine

1 pound ripe tomatoes, seeded and diced

Salt to taste

Small pinch of dried red chile pepper, optional

3 medium zucchini (about ¾ pound), ends trimmed and cut into small cubes

1 tablespoon coarse salt

1 recipe Pasta Dough (page 120), rolled out and cut into garganelli (see page 99), or 1 pound imported dried garganelli or tagliolini

*T*o be at a seaside resort town at the end of summer, when most tourists have left and life has slowed to a leisurely, mellow pace, can be good for one's soul. I was in Cesenatico at the end of September with nothing to do but stare at the beautiful blue ocean, take long walks, read a few good novels, and try as many local dishes as humanly possible, a job that my husband, my daughter, Paola, and her husband, Brian, shared enthusiastically with me. It was in Cesenatico that we found Trattoria da Pippo, which served, appropriately enough, nothing but seafood dishes. This is one of their delicious dishes, which follows the basic cooking philosophy of Romagna. Keep it fresh, keep it simple, keep it clean and uncluttered. It is food that sings.

To make the sauce, with a large knife or poultry shears, cut the shells of the lobster tails in half down the underside of the tail. Grasping the cut shells with a kitchen towel, pry them open and remove the meat. Cut it into ¼-inch dice.

HEAT about half of the oil in a large skillet over medium heat. Add the garlic and cook until it is golden brown on all sides, then discard it. Add fresh or frozen lobster and stir until lightly golden, 1 to 2 minutes. Scoop out the lobster with a slotted spoon and transfer to a bowl.

ADD the wine and stir to release the browned bits attached to the bottom of the skillet. When almost all the wine has evaporated, add the tomatoes, season with salt and the chile pepper, if using, and stir until the tomato juices begin to thicken, 3 to 4 minutes. Return the lobster to the skillet, stir once or twice, and turn off the heat.

HEAT the remaining oil in a medium skillet over high heat. When the oil is hot, add the zucchini and cook until golden brown and a bit crisp, 2 to 3 minutes. With a slotted spoon, transfer the zucchini to paper towels to drain.

MEANWHILE, bring a large pot of water to a boil over high heat. Add the coarse salt and pasta and cook until the pasta is tender but still firm to the bite.

SET the skillet of sauce over medium heat. Scoop out and reserve about ½ cup of the pasta cooking water. Drain the pasta and add it to the sauce. Season lightly with salt. Add the fried zucchini and mix quickly until the pasta and sauce are well combined. If the sauce seems a bit dry, stir in a bit of the pasta cooking water or some olive oil. Taste, adjust the seasoning, and serve at once.

LOBSTER TAILS

Frozen lobster tails are now available at most markets. They vary greatly in weight. The larger the tail, the meatier it is going to be.

If you are starting with live lobsters, drop them into a large pot of boiling water and cook until done (the cooking time will be determined by the weight of the lobster; ask your fishmonger). When the lobsters are cooked, remove from the pot and split them in half. Remove the claws and the joints (knuckles) and crack them open and split the tails in half. Remove the meat with a narrow knife or spoon and cut it into small dice. Since the lobster is already cooked, omit the sautéing. Simply sauté the tomatoes as instructed above, then add the lobster and proceed as directed.

BOW TIES WITH PROSCIUTTO SAUCE

Strichetti con il Sugo di Prosciutto

SERVES 4 TO 6

For the sauce

1 cup fresh peas or thawed frozen peas

Salt

3 tablespoons unsalted butter

1 tablespoon extra virgin olive oil

¼ cup finely minced yellow onion

¼ cup finely minced carrots

¼ cup finely minced celery

¼ pound prosciutto, in 1 thick slice, minced

½ cup dry white wine

2 cups Homemade Tomato Sauce (page 22) or canned Italian plum tomatoes, with their juice, put through a food mill to remove the seeds

⅓ cup milk, preferably whole milk

1 tablespoon coarse salt

1 recipe Pasta Dough (page 120), rolled out, cut and shaped into *strichetti*, or bow ties (see page 100), or 1 pound imported dried bow ties, garganelli, or tagliatelle

½ cup freshly grated Parmigiano-Reggiano

*G*raziella, the oldest sister of my sister-in-law, cooks with the assurance of someone who has spent a great deal of time around a stove. One of her favorite sauces is this traditional prosciutto ragù, which is standard in many kitchens of the region. She serves it over homemade tagliatelle, bow ties, or garganelli.

IF you are using fresh peas, bring a small saucepan of water to a boil. Add a pinch of salt and the peas. Cook, uncovered, until tender, 5 to 10 minutes, depending on their size. Drain and set aside.

To make the sauce, heat the oil and 2 tablespoons butter together in a large skillet over medium heat. As soon as the butter begins to foam, add the onion, carrots, and celery and cook, stirring occasionally, until golden and soft, 8 to 10 minutes.

ADD the prosciutto and stir for a minute or two, then raise the heat to high and add the wine. Stir until almost all the wine has evaporated. Add the tomato sauce and season lightly with salt. As soon as the sauce comes to a boil, reduce the heat to low and simmer, uncovered, until the sauce has a medium-thick consistency, about 15 minutes. Stir the milk and peas into the sauce and simmer for 2 to 3 minutes longer. Turn off the heat. (Makes approximately 2½ cups.)

BRING a large pot of water to a boil over high heat. Add the coarse salt and pasta and cook until the pasta is tender but still a bit firm to the bite.

SCOOP out and reserve about ½ cup of the pasta cooking water. Drain the pasta and place in the skillet with the sauce. Add the remaining 1 tablespoon butter and a handful of the Parmigiano. Stir quickly over medium heat until the pasta and sauce are well combined. Add a bit of the reserved cooking water if the pasta seems dry. Taste, adjust the seasoning, and serve with the remaining Parmigiano.

BOW TIES WITH RABBIT RAGÙ

Strichetti con Ragù di Coniglio

For the sauce

1 rabbit (2½ to 3 pounds), cut into serving pieces

¼ to ⅓ cup extra virgin olive oil

Salt to taste

½ cup finely minced yellow onions

1 thick slice pancetta (about 2 ounces), finely minced

½ cup dry white wine

3 tablespoons double-concentrated Italian tomato paste, diluted in 3 cups Chicken Broth (page 72) or canned low-sodium chicken broth

1 tablespoon unsalted butter

1 tablespoon coarse salt

1 recipe Pasta Dough (page 120), rolled out and shaped into *stricchetti*, or bow ties (see page 100), or 1 pound imported dried bow ties, garganelli, or tagliatelle

⅓ to ½ cup freshly grated Parmigiano-Reggiano

*T*he city of Modena is famous for many things: Luciano Pavarotti, for one. Ferrari sport cars, balsamic vinegar, zampone (the locally made sausage stuffed into a pig's foot), Lambrusco wine, and great, succulent food. Modena is also the home of Trattoria la Bianca, one of the oldest trattorie of the city, which has been in the same family for almost fifty years. This trattoria, serving the traditional food of the area, makes its superlative pasta the old-fashioned way—with a long rolling pin and a lot of elbow grease. My choice the night my husband and I were there was strichetti with rabbit ragù. The bright golden homemade bow ties were large and a bit thick. Topped with a sauce of slowly braised rabbit ragù, the dish was sweet, light, and simply delicious.

This delightful ragù really has two lives. First, the rabbit is braised slowly with onion, pancetta, and broth until it is tender and succulent. It is then served as an entrée with polenta (grilled, fried, or soft).

In its second life, any leftover braised rabbit is removed from the bones, minced very fine, and put back into the sauce. The sauce is simmered for a few minutes and tossed with pasta. Just think how logical this is. Serve the braised dish one night, and the day after, make a sauce with what is left. Of course, braised chicken, braised veal shanks, or any alla cacciatora preparation can be used in the same way.

To make the sauce, wash the rabbit in several changes of cold water and pat dry with paper towels.

HEAT the oil in a large skillet over medium heat. Add the rabbit, season with salt, and cook, turning once, until lightly golden on both sides, 6 to 7 minutes. Transfer the rabbit to a plate.

DISCARD about half of the fat in the skillet if necessary, reduce the heat a bit, and add the onions and pancetta. Cook, stirring, until the onions and pancetta are lightly golden, 5 to 6 minutes. Return the rabbit to the skillet, raise the heat to high, and add the wine. Cook, stirring and moving the rabbit pieces around, until the wine is reduced approximately by half. Add the diluted tomato paste. As soon as the liquid comes to a boil, reduce the heat to low, partially cover the skillet, and simmer very gently for 15 to 20 minutes. Turn off the heat.

TRANSFER the rabbit to a cutting board and, as soon as it is cool enough to handle, remove the meat from the bones. Mince the meat very fine, making sure to remove all the small pieces of bone and cartilage. Return the meat to the skillet, place over low heat, and simmer for a few minutes longer. Stir the butter into the sauce and taste and adjust the seasoning. (Makes approximately 3 cups.) (The sauce can be prepared several hours or a day ahead. Reheat it gently just before using.)

MEANWHILE, bring a large pot of water to a boil over high heat. Add the coarse salt and pasta and cook until the pasta is tender but still a bit firm to the bite.

DRAIN the pasta and place it in the skillet. Add a small handful of the Parmigiano and mix quickly over medium heat until the pasta and sauce are well combined. Taste, adjust the seasoning, and serve with the remaining Parmigiano.

THE SECRET INGREDIENT

The cooking water of pasta and beans is the "secret ingredient" of the good Italian cook. If a sauce is too thin, the addition of some pasta or bean cooking water, which is loaded with starch, will thicken it. It will also impart body and a rounder flavor to the sauce.

PASTA WITH BEAN SAUCE

Pasta con Intingolo di Fagioli

SERVES 4 TO 6

For the sauce

½ cup dried borlotti beans or cranberry beans, picked over and soaked overnight in cold water to cover generously, drained, and rinsed, or 1½ cups canned beans, rinsed and drained

3 tablespoons double-concentrated Italian tomato paste

¼ cup extra virgin olive oil

⅓ cup finely minced yellow onion

1 garlic clove, minced

1 tablespoon finely minced rosemary or chopped flat-leaf parsley

2 to 3 ounces sliced pancetta, finely chopped

Salt and freshly ground black pepper to taste

1 tablespoon coarse salt

1 pound imported dried rigatoni or penne rigate

½ cup freshly grated Parmigiano-Reggiano

*F*ew dishes in Emilia-Romagna are as basic, hearty, and uncompromisingly plebeian as this one. It has become a classic of *la cucina povera, the humble food of laborers and peasants, because beans were once "the meat of the poor" and it validates the notion that good food can be created with a handful of basic but delicious ingredients. At Trattoria Vernizzi, located in the small hamlet of Frascarolo di Busseto in the farmland between Parma and Piacenza, this sauce was served over* pisarei, *small flour-and-bread dumplings that looked like little shells.*

IF using dried beans, put them in a medium pot and cover generously with cold water. Cook as instructed on page 82. Drain the beans and reserve their cooking water. Stir the tomato paste into 3 cups of the reserved bean water. Set aside.

TO make the sauce, heat the oil in a large skillet over medium heat. Add the onion, garlic, rosemary, and pancetta and cook, stirring, until the mixture is lightly golden and soft, 5 to 6 minutes. Add the beans and stir once or twice, then add the diluted tomato paste and season with salt and pepper. Bring the sauce to a boil, reduce the heat to medium-low, and cook, stirring from time to time, until the sauce has a medium-thick consistency, 13 to 15 minutes. Taste and adjust the seasoning. (Makes 2½ to 3 cups.) (The sauce can be prepared several hours ahead, but when you reheat it, you will need to add a bit of the reserved bean cooking water or pasta water, because the beans will have soaked up a lot of the liquid.)

WHILE the sauce is cooking, bring a large pot of water to a boil over high heat. Add the coarse salt and pasta and cook until the pasta is tender but still firm to the bite.

DRAIN the pasta and add it to the skillet with the sauce. Add about half of the Parmigiano and mix quickly over medium heat until the pasta and sauce are well combined. Stir in ¼ cup or so of the reserved bean cooking water or tap water if the pasta seems a bit dry. Taste and adjust the seasoning. Serve with the remaining Parmigiano.

Mixed Cured Meats with Fried Flatbread
Fritters and Romagna's Flat Griddle Bread

Gratinéed Asparagus and Prosciutto

Tortellini in Capon Broth

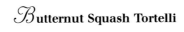
Butternut Squash Tortelli

$\mathscr{S}$pinach Lasagne with
Bolognese Ragù

$\mathscr{R}$igatoni with Sausage,
Peas, Tomatoes, and Cream

Saffron-Ricotta Gnocchi with Walnut Sauce

Squash Risotto

Cooked Vegetable Salad
with Prosciutto

*S*eafood Salad with Arugula

*G*rilled Skewers of
Calamari and Shrimp

Roasted Capon with Roasted Potatoes and Swiss Chard with Butter and Parmigiano

Roasted Stuffed Fillet of Beef

My Mother's Pastry Fritters

Sweet Spinach–Almond–Ricotta Pie

*C*ornmeal Cookies, Pears Baked in Lambrusco

THE PASTA OF THE
OVER-THE-HILL-FISHERMEN GANG

La Pasta dei Pescatori Pensionati

SERVES 4 TO 6

**3 to 4 tablespoons
unsalted butter**

**⅓ cup very finely minced
yellow onion**

**2 ounces pancetta, in
1 or 2 thick slices, finely diced**

**2 ounces prosciutto, in
1 thick slice, finely diced**

**2 ounces mortadella, in
1 thick slice, finely diced**

**1½ cups fresh peas or thawed
frozen peas**

Salt to taste

1 tablespoon coarse salt

**1 pound imported dried
garganelli or bow ties**

3 large eggs

⅓ to ½ cup heavy cream

**½ cup freshly grated
Parmigiano-Reggiano**

**Freshly ground black pepper
to taste**

I magine a group of retired fishermen, who, when they actually catch a fish, throw it back in the water, and who spend more time eating than fishing. My brother, Gianni, is such a fisherman, and so are his old friends. In their younger years, they were very serious about their beloved sport and would drive great distances to reach the perfect spot on the Po River, where they would fish for hours. Today their fishing expedition takes them to a small man-made lake just outside Bologna. There they fish a little (always throwing back the fish they catch in the lake), bond in camaraderie, and eat–a lot. Giancarlo, one of my brother's childhood friends, is the assigned cook. Nicknamed "the King of Pasta," Giancarlo cooks a different pasta every week. The cooking facilities at the laghetto are rudimentary. An old grill and a two-burner butane stove are all they have, so the food Giancarlo prepares has to be simple. This is one of his pastas, which can be prepared on the spur of the moment.

HEAT the butter in a medium saucepan over medium heat. As soon as the butter begins to foam, add the onion and cook, stirring, until lightly golden and soft, 5 to 6 minutes. Add the pancetta, proscuitto, and mortadella and cook, stirring, until lightly golden, 2 to 3 minutes. Add the peas, season lightly with salt, and stir for a minute or two. Turn off the heat. (The sauce can be prepared to this point a few hours ahead.)

BRING a large pot of water to a boil over high heat. Add the coarse salt and pasta and cook until the pasta is tender but still firm to the bite.

WHILE the pasta is cooking, beat the eggs, cream, and about half of the Parmigiano together in a large pasta bowl. Season with salt and a generous amount of pepper.

DRAIN the pasta, add it to the bowl, and stir quickly. Pour the sauce into the bowl and mix well until the pasta and sauce are well incorporated. Taste and adjust the seasoning. Serve at once, with the remaining Parmigiano.

PASTA WITH MUSHROOM RAGU

Pasta con Intingolo di Funghi

SERVES 4 TO 6

1 ounce dried porcini mushrooms, soaked in 2 cups lukewarm water for 20 minutes

4 to 5 ounces mixed mushrooms (such as chanterelle, shiitake, and/or oyster mushrooms, wiped clean. (Discard shiitake and oyster stems, but use the chanterelle stems.)

⅓ to ½ cup extra virgin olive oil

1 garlic clove, finely minced

1 to 2 tablespoons chopped flat-leaf parsley

Salt and freshly ground black pepper to taste

1 cup dry white wine

⅓ cup finely minced shallots or yellow onion

2 to 3 ounces sliced pancetta, finely minced

2 cups Homemade Tomato Sauce (page 22) or canned Italian plum tomatoes, with their juice, put through a food mill to remove the seeds

1 tablespoon coarse salt

1 pound dried penne or rigatoni or fresh tagliatelle, page 100

For Italian food lovers, the seasons are probably identified more by what can be found in the markets than by the weather patterns. Fall is my favorite time of the year, the season for game dishes and chestnuts, for thick soups and long-simmered stews and ragùs, for pasta loaded with fresh porcini mushrooms or white truffles. It is the time for serious food. My husband and I love to go to Italy in the fall when the air is crisp, the crowds are gone, and Italians are more relaxed and hospitable. And I eat mushrooms every chance I have.

Mushrooms cooked in a sauce are a pretty standard preparation, though the cooks of the region add to it what they have at hand and what they feel is right for the sauce. The most important ingredient in a mushroom sauce is, of course, the mushrooms. Here a variety of mushrooms is sautéed in the traditional combination of oil, garlic, and parsley, then added to a flavorful tomato sauce, on which they bestow their woodsy fragrance.

To make the sauce, drain the porcini mushrooms and reserve the soaking liquid. Rinse the mushrooms well under cold running water and roughly chop them. Line a strainer with paper towels and strain the liquid into a bowl. Set aside.

CUT the fresh mushrooms into thin slices, then cut the slices into medium dice.

HEAT about half of the oil in a large skillet over high heat until very hot. Add the mixed mushrooms, without crowding (cook in batches if necessary), and cook, stirring, until lightly golden, 2 to 3 minutes. Add the porcini, garlic, and parsley, season with salt and pepper, and stir a few times. With a large slotted spoon, transfer the mushrooms to a bowl.

PUT the skillet back over high heat and, when nice and hot, add ½ cup of the wine. Stir with a wooden spoon, scraping the bottom of the skillet to release the browned particles attached to it. When almost all of the wine has evaporated, add the contents of the skillet to the mushrooms. Set aside.

**½ cup freshly grated
Parmigiano-Reggiano**

HEAT the remaining oil in a medium saucepan over medium heat. Add the shallots and pancetta and cook, stirring from time to time, until the mixture is lightly golden and soft, 5 to 6 minutes. Add the remaining ½ cup wine and cook until almost all of it has evaporated. Add the tomato sauce and 1 cup of the reserved porcini liquid and cook, uncovered, at a gentle simmer until the sauce has a medium-thick consistency, about 15 minutes. Season the sauce lightly with salt and add the mushrooms. Simmer, stirring from time to time, until the sauce has a medium-thick consistency again, about 10 minutes longer. Taste, adjust the seasoning, and turn off the heat. (Makes approximately 3⅓ cups.) (The sauce can be prepared up to a day ahead. Reheat gently before using.)

BRING a large pot of water to a boil over high heat. Add the coarse salt and the pasta and cook until the pasta is tender but still a bit firm to the bite.

DRAIN the pasta and place in a large heated bowl. Add about half of the sauce and stir until the pasta and sauce are well combined. Stir in more sauce if needed. Taste, adjust the seasoning, and serve sprinkled with the Parmigiano.

PASTA WITH MONKFISH AND FRESH TOMATO

Pasta con Sugo di Rana Pescatrice e Pomodoro

SERVES 4 TO 6

For the sauce

1 cup fresh peas or thawed frozen peas

Salt

⅓ cup extra virgin olive oil

1 large garlic clove lightly smashed

¾ pound monkfish fillet, cleaned of any membrane and cut into pieces about the size of a small green olive

⅓ cup very finely minced shallots or yellow onion

½ cup dry white wine

1 pound ripe tomatoes, peeled, seeded, and diced (see page 217)

Freshly ground black pepper to taste

1 to 2 tablespoons chopped flat-leaf parsley

1 tablespoon coarse salt

1 pound imported dried penne or garganelli

On the Romagna side of the region, particularly in the many small, quaint coastal towns lined with wide, sandy beaches, pasta and seafood are combined daily in blissful union. Here is a simple but delicious way of preparing a seafood pasta sauce: take the freshest fish available, dice it, and toss it quickly in extra virgin olive oil, then combine it with meaty, ripe tomatoes, wine, and fresh peas. This is the type of food that makes my taste buds percolate and satisfies me most.

IF using fresh peas, drop them into a small saucepan of boiling salted water and cook until tender but still a bit firm. Drain and set aside.

To make the sauce, heat the oil in a large skillet over medium heat. Add the garlic and brown on all sides; discard the garlic. Add the fish and cook, stirring, until lightly golden, about 2 minutes. With a slotted spoon, transfer the fish to a dish.

ADD the shallots and cook, stirring, until lightly golden and soft, 4 to 5 minutes. Raise the heat to high and stir in the wine. Cook, scraping the bottom of the pan with a wooden spoon to release the browned bits, until almost all the wine has evaporated. Add the tomatoes and cook until the juices have thickened, 3 to 5 minutes. Return the fish to the skillet, season with salt and pepper, add the parsley, and stir for about 1 minute. Taste and adjust the seasoning, then turn off the heat.

BRING a large pot of water to a boil over high heat. Add the coarse salt and pasta and cook until the pasta is tender but still firm to the bite.

SCOOP out and reserve about 1 cup of the pasta cooking water. Drain the pasta and place in the skillet with the sauce. Mix over medium heat until the pasta and sauce are well combined, adding some pasta water if necessary. Taste, adjust the seasoning, and serve.

PASTA WITH POTATO-TOMATO SAUCE

Minestra Contadina

SERVES 4 TO 6

For the sauce

⅓ cup extra virgin olive oil

2 to 3 garlic cloves, finely minced

⅓ cup chopped flat-leaf parsley

2 small boiling potatoes, peeled and cut into pieces about the size of a small olive

3 cups Homemade Tomato Sauce (page 22) or canned Italian plum tomatoes, with their juices, put through a food mill to remove the seeds

1 cup Chicken Broth (page 73) or canned low-sodium chicken broth, plus more if needed

Salt and freshly ground black pepper to taste

1 tablespoon coarse salt

½ pound imported dried small tubular pasta such as ditali or ditalini

½ cup freshly grated Parmigiano-Reggiano

*Y*ears ago, before and after the Second World War, when Italy was struggling economically, many farmers, peasants, and laborers fed their families with very little money and lots of imagination. Amazingly, some of these dishes were so good that, in spite of the few basic ingredients used in making them, they have stood the test of time. My niece, Daniela, who lives in Bologna, shared with me one of her mother-in-law, Mafalda's, favorite pasta dishes, which, she says, "is a link to her humble peasant tradition."

To make the sauce, heat the oil in a medium saucepan over medium heat. Add the garlic and parsley and stir for about 1 minute. Add the potatoes and cook, stirring, until they are well combined with the savory base, about 2 minutes. Add the tomato sauce and broth and season generously with salt and pepper.

As soon as the sauce comes to a boil, reduce the heat to medium-low and simmer, uncovered, stirring occasionally, until the potatoes are very tender, about 20 minutes (the potatoes should be cooked until falling apart so they will thicken the sauce and coat the pasta thoroughly). If, during cooking, the sauce reduces too much, make small additions of broth or water.

MEANWHILE, bring a large pot of water to a boil over high heat. Add the coarse salt and pasta and cook until the pasta is tender but still firm to the bite.

SCOOP out and reserve about 1 cup of the pasta cooking water. Drain the pasta and place in a large heated bowl. Add the sauce and stir in a nice handful of the Parmigiano. Add a few tablespoons of the reserved pasta water if the pasta seems a bit dry. Mix well and serve at once with the remaining Parmigiano.

MAFALDA'S SECRETS

The "poorer," original version of this dish was made with lard, garlic, parsley, potatoes, tomatoes, and water. Today, Mafalda, who lives comfortably in Bologna, omits the lard and enriches the dish with extra virgin olive oil, homemade tomato sauce, and Parmigiano-Reggiano cheese.

In preparing this dish, Mafalda suggests the following:

• Cook the potatoes in the sauce, not separately, until they are very soft and will break when pressed with a fork. The starch of the potatoes will enrich and thicken the sauce.

• Keep adding small amounts of water or broth to the sauce if needed as it cooks and thickens.

• Season generously with salt and pepper, and don't be stingy with the Parmigiano either.

PENNE WITH SPICY ANCHOVY SAUCE

Penne con Sugo Piccante di Acciughe

SERVES 4 TO 6

1 tablespoon coarse salt

1 pound imported dried penne rigate or rigatoni

For the sauce

2 tablespoons unsalted butter

2 to 3 tablespoons extra virgin olive oil

6 to 8 anchovy fillets packed in oil, finely chopped

2 large garlic cloves, finely minced

Chopped fresh chile pepper or red pepper flakes to taste

1 heaping tablespoon chopped flat-leaf parsley

Salt to taste

⅓ to ½ cup freshly grated Parmigiano-Reggiano, plus extra for serving if desired

A gas station, a small church, four houses, and Trattoria del Cacciatore comprise the tiny hamlet of Frassinara, in the farmland around Parma. Here in the land of butter, prosciutto, Parmigiano, and succulent stuffed pastas, we found a dish that was more in tune with the unpretentious cooking of southern Italy than with that of Emilia-Romagna. Gramigna, *a short homemade pasta from Bologna, was paired with a spicy anchovy sauce. The unusual combination, which strayed blatantly from tradition, was too tempting to dismiss. The very spicy sauce that coated the delicate homemade pasta proved to be a winner. When we asked the owner of Trattoria del Cacciatore how he came about the dish, he said that, after spending a week in Naples, he came back with the desire to try something different, so he paired this basic southern Italian sauce with* gramigna, *and he loved it.*

Perhaps this is fusion cooking Italian-style!

BRING a large pot of water to a boil over high heat. Add the coarse salt and pasta and cook until the pasta is tender but still firm to the bite.

WHILE the pasta is cooking, make the sauce: Heat the butter and oil together in a large skillet over medium-low heat. Add the anchovies, garlic, chile pepper, and parsley and cook, stirring and making sure the garlic does not color, until the anchovies and garlic are cooked into a soft paste, about 5 minutes. Season lightly with salt.

SCOOP out and reserve about 1 cup of the pasta cooking water. Drain the pasta and place in the skillet with the sauce. Add the Parmigiano and a few tablespoons of the pasta water if the pasta seems a bit dry. Toss together over medium heat until the pasta and sauce are well combined. Taste, adjust the seasoning, and serve with additional Parmigiano if desired.

LEFTOVER PASTA–FRIED, BAKED, AND AS A FRITTATA

Years ago, when Italy was less prosperous than it is today, nothing went to waste in an Italian kitchen, not even leftover pasta. Served reheated, pasta has never held any special appeal for me, but leftover pasta tossed in hot oil until crisp and crusty is, for me, the ultimate treat. The perfect pasta for this improvisation needs to be thick and sturdy, such as rigatoni or penne, even though my mother had absolutely no qualms about using anything she had at hand. Here are three simple ways of using leftover penne and rigatoni:

Fried   Pour a thin layer of olive oil into a heavy skillet, preferably a nonstick one. When the oil is hot add the pasta and whatever sauce clings to it and cook over medium-high heat without stirring until the bottom is crisp. Now stir and cook the pasta until each piece is golden and crisp on all sides. Sprinkle with salt.

Baked   Reheat leftover pasta and toss it with some béchamel or with some butter and Parmigiano and bake it until the top is golden brown.

As a frittata   Bring the leftover pasta to room temperature, then combine it with some beaten eggs and a handful of Parmigiano and cook it just like a frittata.

RIGATONI WITH SAUSAGE, PEAS, TOMATOES, AND CREAM

Rigatoni con la Salsiccia, Piselli, Pomodori, e Panna

SERVES 4 TO 6

For the sauce

1 cup fresh peas or thawed frozen peas

Salt

2 tablespoons unsalted butter

1 tablespoon extra virgin olive oil

⅓ cup finely minced yellow onion

1 link (about ¼ pound) Homemade Bolognese Sausage (page 267) or mild Italian pork sausage (containing no fennel seeds, chile pepper, or strong spices) casing removed and finely chopped

2 to 3 ounces sliced pancetta, finely minced

½ cup dry white wine

3 cups Homemade Tomato Sauce (page 22) or canned Italian plum tomatoes, with their juices, put through a food mill to remove the seeds

¼ cup heavy cream

1 tablespoon coarse salt

1 pound imported dried rigatoni, penne rigate, garganelli, or shells

½ cup freshly grated Parmigiano-Reggiano

The women of Emilia-Romagna cook on the spur of the moment. They look into the refrigerator, take out what they have, and, with the secure instinct that comes from years of cooking, whip up some pretty delicious dishes.

My sister, Carla, prepared this dish in about fifteen minutes one night when we had returned home late after an afternoon of shopping.

IF using fresh peas, drop them into a small saucepan of boiling salted water and cook until tender but still a bit firm. Drain and set aside.

To make the sauce, heat the butter and oil together in a large skillet over medium heat. Add the onion and stir until lightly golden and soft, about 6 minutes. Raise the heat to high, add the sausage and pancetta, and cook, stirring and breaking up the sausage with a wooden spoon, until the sausage has a golden brown color, 3 to 4 minutes.

ADD the wine and stir until almost all of it has evaporated. Add the tomato sauce and cream and season with salt. As soon as the sauce comes to a boil, reduce the heat to low and cook at the slowest of simmers, uncovered, until it has a medium-thick consistency, 13 to 15 minutes.

STIR in the peas, simmer for another minute or two, and turn off the heat. Taste and adjust the seasoning. (The sauce can be prepared several hours ahead. Reheat gently before using.)

MEANWHILE, bring a large pot of water to a boil over high heat. Add the coarse salt and pasta and cook until the pasta is tender but still firm to the bite.

DRAIN the pasta and place in the skillet with the sauce. Add a small handful of the Parmigiano and mix over medium heat until the pasta and sauce are well combined. Taste, adjust the seasoning, and serve hot, with the remaining Parmigiano.

SPAGHETTINI WITH SHRIMP, TOMATOES, AND PESTO

Spaghettini con Gamberetti, Pomodori, e Pesto

SERVES 4 TO 6

For the sauce

¼ to ⅓ cup extra virgin olive oil

1 pound medium shrimp, shelled, deveined, and cut into pieces about the size of a small olive

1 pound ripe tomatoes, peeled, seeded, and diced (see page 217)

Salt to taste

1 tablespoon coarse salt

1 pound imported dried spaghettini or spaghetti

2 to 3 tablespoons Pesto (page 178)

When I was a teenager growing up in Bologna, seafood was not something that made an appearance on our table on a regular basis. But during our annual vacation to the splendid beaches of Romagna, that was practically all we ate. What I loved then—and love even more today—is the simplicity of the food, which relies entirely on the freshness of the fish, and the unpretentiousness of the trattorie and restaurants that serve it. At Da Pippo, a charming small trattoria located on the pier of Cesenatico, this dish, combining flavorful shrimp with fresh tomatoes and light, fragrant pesto, was served over strozzapreti, a local pasta that looks like twisted ribbons of short thick tagliatelle.

Here, I have substituted spaghettini for strozzapreti, which are too labor intensive to prepare. To keep the dish clean and fresh tasting, a bit of restraint is needed. Make the pesto with only a very small garlic clove. Select the ripest tomatoes, the freshest shrimp, and a light extra virgin olive oil.

To make the sauce, heat the oil in a large skillet over medium-high heat. Add the shrimp and stir quickly until lightly golden, about 1 minute. With a slotted spoon, transfer the shrimp to a bowl.

PUT the skillet back over high heat, add the tomatoes, and stir until their juices have thickened, 3 to 5 minutes. Return the shrimp to the skillet, season lightly with salt, and stir for about a minute. Taste, adjust the seasoning, and turn off the heat.

BRING a large pot of water to a boil over high heat. Add the coarse salt and spaghettini and cook until the pasta is tender but still firm to the bite.

DRAIN the pasta and place in the skillet with the sauce. Mix quickly over medium heat until the pasta and sauce are well combined. Remove from the heat, add the pesto, and toss quickly to distribute it evenly. Taste, adjust the seasoning, and serve at once.

SPAGHETTINI WITH WHITE CLAM SAUCE

Spaghettini con le Vongole

SERVES 4 TO 6

For the sauce

5 pounds clams (the smallest you can find), cleaned (see page 160)

1 cup dry white wine

⅓ cup extra virgin olive oil, plus extra if needed

1 small garlic clove, finely minced

1 tablespoon chopped flat-leaf parsley

Salt and freshly ground black pepper to taste

1 tablespoon coarse salt

1 pound imported dried spaghettini or spaghetti

8 to 10 basil leaves, very finely shredded, or 1 tablespoon chopped flat-leaf parsley, optional

Pinch of red pepper flakes, optional

This recipe proves that when the ingredients are good, the less one puts in a dish, the better it tastes—at least, that is the Italian philosophy with food. At Ristorante da Pippo, in the small coastal town of Cesenatico, I had a plate of perfectly cooked thin spaghetti loaded with the delicious small clams of the Adriatic. The sauce of extra virgin olive oil had just a bit of garlic, some parsley, wine, and the flavorful cooking liquid from the clams. Nothing else. And because of that restraint, the dish was light, fresh, and unforgettable.

To make the sauce, put the clams and ½ cup of the wine in a large skillet over medium heat, cover, and cook until the clams open. Transfer them to a bowl as they open. (If some clams do not open, cook them a little longer; however, if they still fail to open in 3 or 4 minutes, discard them.)

REMOVE the clams from the shells and place in a bowl. Line a small strainer with paper towels and strain the clam juices; set aside.

WIPE the skillet clean with paper towels, put it over medium heat, and add the oil. Add the garlic and parsley and stir just long enough for the garlic to lightly color, 30 to 35 seconds. Add the remaining ½ cup wine and the reserved clam juices, season with salt and pepper, and let the liquid cook briskly until it is reduced by about half. Add the clams, stir once or twice, and turn off the heat.

MEANWHILE, bring a large pot of water to a boil over high heat. Add the coarse salt and spaghettini and cook until the spaghettini is tender but still firm to the bite.

DRAIN the pasta and add to the skillet. Add the basil and the red pepper flakes, if using, and toss over medium heat until the pasta and sauce are well combined. Taste and adjust the seasoning. If the pasta seems a bit dry, add a nice splash of good extra virgin olive oil, and serve.

SPAGHETTINI WITH CLAMS AND TOMATOES

Spaghettini con Vongole e Pomodoro

SERVES 4 TO 6

For the sauce

5 pounds clams (the smallest you can get), cleaned as instructed, or cockles

½ cup dry white wine

¼ cup extra virgin olive oil, plus extra if desired

⅓ cup very finely minced yellow onion

1 garlic clove, finely minced

2½ cups canned Italian plum tomatoes, with their juice, put through a food mill to remove the seeds

Salt and freshly ground black pepper to taste

2 tablespoons chopped flat-leaf parsley

1 tablespoon coarse salt

1 pound imported spaghettini or spaghetti

One of the joys of going to the Adriatic coast of Romagna is to eat the very small, round clams of the area. I love these tiny clams, especially when they are simply cooked and tossed with spaghettini. To clean clams, soak them in a large bowl of cold salted water for 30 minutes. Scrub the clams well under cold running water to remove all dirt. Discard any open clams. Place the clams in a bowl, cover with a wet towel, and refrigerate. (Even though very fresh clams can be kept in the refrigerator for a few days, I make a point to use mine the day I buy them.)

To make the sauce, put the clams, ½ cup water, and the wine in a large skillet over medium heat, cover, and cook until the clams open. Transfer them to a bowl as they open. (If some clams do not open, cook them a little longer; if they still fail to open in 3 or 4 minutes, discard them.)

REMOVE the clams from the shells and place in a bowl. Line a small strainer with paper towels and strain the clam juices into another bowl; set aside.

HEAT the oil in a large skillet over medium heat. Add the onion and cook, stirring, until lightly golden and soft, 5 to 6 minutes. Add the garlic and stir a few times. Add the tomatoes and the reserved clam juices and season with salt and pepper. As soon as the sauce comes to a boil, reduce the heat a bit and simmer, stirring occasionally, until the sauce has a medium-thick consistency, 10 to 12 minutes. Stir in the clams and parsley. Taste, adjust the seasoning, and turn off the heat.

MEANWHILE, bring a large pot of water to a boil over high heat. Add the coarse salt and the spaghettini and cook until the pasta is tender but still firm to the bite.

DRAIN the pasta and add to the skillet. Toss well over medium heat until the pasta and sauce are well combined. Taste, adjust the seasoning, and serve with a few drops of olive oil if desired.

SPAGHETTI WITH TUNA
FOR CHRISTMAS EVE

Spaghetti con il Tonno della Vigilia di Natale

SERVES 4 TO 6

For the sauce

¼ to ⅓ cup extra virgin oil

1 large garlic clove, lightly smashed

½ cup finely minced yellow onions

2 tablespoons chopped flat-leaf parsley

One 7-ounce can white tuna packed in olive oil, drained and minced

3½ to 4 cups Homemade Tomato Sauce (page 22) or canned Italian plum tomatoes, with their juice, put through a food mill to remove the seeds

Salt and freshly ground black pepper to taste

1 tablespoon coarse salt

1 pound imported dried spaghetti

When I was growing up in Bologna, eating fish was not a daily event. On some Fridays, following the church guidelines, my mother would buy fish that had arrived that day from the nearby Adriatic. She prepared it simply, pan-fried with just some lemon and capers, or with the addition of a sauce. We children soaked up the sauce with bread and left the whole fish on the plate. Needless to say, we disliked fish intensely—except in spaghetti with tuna, which my mother prepared ritually on Christmas Eve. Perhaps the tuna, which was canned in olive oil, did not register in our young minds as "fish," or perhaps we considered the spaghetti a treat, since my mother prepared it only a few times a year.

During my last visit to Bologna, my brother cooked spaghetti with tuna for me, and it was just as good as the dish my mother used to prepare for us.

To make the sauce, heat the oil in a large skillet over medium heat. Add the garlic and cook, stirring, until golden brown on all sides; discard the garlic. Add the onions and cook, stirring, from time to time, until lightly golden and soft, 5 to 6 minutes. Add the parsley and tuna and stir for a minute or two.

ADD the tomato sauce, season with salt and a generous amount of pepper, and bring to a gentle simmer. As soon as the sauce comes to a boil, reduce the heat, stirring occasionally, until the sauce has a medium-thick consistency, 12 to 15 minutes. Taste, adjust the seasoning, and turn off the heat. (Makes about 3 cups.) (The sauce can be prepared up to a day ahead. Reheat gently before using.)

MEANWHILE, bring a large pot of water to a boil over high heat. Add the coarse salt and spaghetti and cook until the pasta is tender but still a bit firm to the bite.

DRAIN the pasta and place in the skillet with the sauce. Mix over medium heat until the pasta and sauce are well combined. Taste, adjust the seasoning, and serve.

Note: When a dish is as simple to prepare as this and tastes so good, there is probably a catch, right? But of course. And the catch is simply this: Choose the best possible ingredients—extra virgin olive oil from Liguria, Tuscany, or Umbria; tunafish canned in olive oil, imported from Italy; canned Italian plum tomatoes from San Marzano or, better yet, wonderful homemade tomato sauce. These are the ingredients that turn a simple sauce into a most appetizing dish.

Canned tuna packed in olive oil is an indispensable item in the Italian pantry and cooks all over rely on it for impromptu preparations. Buy white tuna; its color should be uniform, without any dark parts.

RISOTTO, GNOCCHI, AND POLENTA

Risotti, Gnocchi, e Polenta

While superlative homemade pasta is, and has always been, the trademark of Emilia-Romagna, other dishes, such as risotto, gnocchi, and polenta, though they have always been staples in the kitchen of the region, have been less widely heralded. I grew up with these dishes and they made for a very pleasant change from the almost daily pasta. Risotto was my favorite dish after pasta. My mother's risottos were traditional–with Bolognese meat ragù, with cabbage, or with butter and

Parmigiano (*alla parmigiana*), and only when we vacationed on the Adriatic coast could I indulge in magnificent seafood risottos.

Risotto

When I started teaching Italian cooking in Sacramento more than twenty-five years ago, a stereotypical image of Italian food was still quite prevalent, and most people had never heard of, let alone tasted, a risotto. This beautiful, versatile, elegant dish, one of the glories of Italian gastronomy, was nowhere to be seen. Even though this is no longer the case, there are still a lot of people in this country who seem to think that a risotto can be cooked in a double boiler, in the oven, in the microwave, or in a covered pan. The fact, of course, is, that a true risotto is cooked only with the immutable, traditional cooking technique explained below.

Risotto is made with Italian short-grain rice. The rice, which is extensively cultivated in Piemonte, the Veneto, and Emilia-Romagna, is cooked using a method that slowly draws out the natural starches in the rice, turning them into a creamy substance that coats the rice.

Risotto begins by stirring the large, plump grains of starchy Italian rice briefly with minced onions that have been sautéed in butter or, occasionally, olive oil. This step, which coats the rice with the fat in the pan, is called *tostatura*, "toasting the rice." The rice is then cooked with small additions of hot, flavorful broth and constant stirring until all the broth has been absorbed. The constant stirring of the rice is what coaxes the starches out of the grains and binds them with the other ingredients. Herbs, vegetables, meats, shellfish, game, etc., are added to the pan at different stages, giving the risotto its own particular identity.

For most risottos, with the exception of seafood and some vegetable risottos, butter and Parmigiano are added during the last few minutes of cooking and stirred vigorously into the rice. This important step, which we call *mantecare*, "to stir and blend together," gives the risotto a velvety, creamy consistency. This simple touch turns an already delicious risotto into a perfect one.

The Vital Ingredients: Broth and Rice

The good clean taste of broth is an important element of risotto. The broth for risotto should be light and flavorful. If it is too strong and assertive, it will overpower the overall taste of the dish. If necessary, dilute the broth with some water.

To make the perfect risotto, you need the appropriate rice. Some years back, a woman complained to me that even though she had followed the recipe for risotto in one of my books "to the letter," her risotto was not as good as mine. Why? I later found out that the rice she used was long-grain rice and the broth was canned. While canned broth, diluted in some water, can, on the spur of the moment, be used, long-grain rice will result in nothing but a sticky, gooey mess.

The following short-grain rice varieties are perfect for risotto and are easily available in this country:

Arborio: A nice, plump rice, rich in soft starches, which dissolves easily in cooking

Carnaroli: High in soft starches, like Arborio; often the choice of chefs in Italy

Vialone Nano: A medium-grain rice very popular in the Veneto, a region that takes its risotto very seriously

If you have never made a risotto in your life but love the dish, I suggest you start with Risotto with Prosciutto, Butter, and Parmigiano (page 167). It is the most basic of all risottos. The ingredients are few, which will allow you to concentrate on the cooking. Before you begin, read Tips for a Perfect Risotto. After you have cooked risotto a few times, you will begin to understand its timing and sequences, and you will start to relax. At that point, the fun begins. Risotto is a highly visual dish to prepare because you have to be on top of it and stir all the time. Look into the pan and see the changes that occur during the cooking. The rice turns from chalky white to translucent as it "toasts" with the soft, golden onions, absorbing the flavors of the butter and onions. Watch how quickly the wine is absorbed by the rice, and how the rice grains turn large and plump as they cook. It is almost magical to see the raw material transformed within minutes into a hearty dish.

Tips for a Perfect Risotto

- Chop, dice, and measure all your ingredients, and place them on a tray in the order in which you are going to use them, even the butter and cheese that you are going to swirl in at the end.

- Bring the broth to a boil, and keep it warm over low heat. Make sure the broth stays hot, but not boiling. Cold broth will slow down the cooking.

- Select a wide heavy pot so that your rice has space to expand. At home I use a 14-inch Calphalon skillet. At my restaurant, I use a heavy aluminum restaurant skillet or sauté pan.

- Begin cooking the risotto 18 to 20 minutes before you want to sit down for dinner. The exact cooking time of a risotto depends on many things: the size of your burner, the type of heat you are using, whether your broth is really hot or just warm, whether the pan you are using conducts heat evenly, etc.

- Risotto is always cooked uncovered.

- Stir risotto constantly, preferably with a wooden spoon.

- The ratio of broth to rice is generally 3 to 1 (3 cups of broth to 1 cup of rice). However, always have a little more broth at hand. If you run out of broth, you can heat up some water and use it in place of broth.

- Go easy with the salt, because most of the time the broth is already seasoned and so are many ingredients that are added to the rice.

- Undercook the risotto slightly, since it will keep cooking as it sits and waits to be served.

- Watch risotto carefully during the last few minutes of cooking. Stir constantly and add the broth a very, very little at a time. Taste the rice to determine its doneness.

- Risotto, like pasta, should not be prepared ahead of time, or the rice will become overcooked and sticky when reheated. What you can do, however, is sauté the onion, add the rice, and sauté for a minute or two, until it is translucent and completely coated with the fat in the skillet, then turn off the heat and cover the skillet with a lid. You can prepare the rice up to this point a few hours ahead. Fifteen minutes before you want to serve the risotto, reheat the rice and continue cooking, adding ladlefuls of hot broth.

RISOTTO WITH PROSCIUTTO, BUTTER, AND PARMIGIANO

Risotto al Prosciutto e Parmigiano

SERVES 4 TO 6

6 cups Chicken Broth (page 73) or canned low-sodium chicken broth

4 tablespoons (½ stick) unsalted butter

½ cup finely minced yellow onion

2 cups Arborio, Carnaroli, or Vialone Nano rice

1 thick slice prosciutto (about ¼ pound), diced

1 cup dry white wine

½ cup freshly grated Parmigiano-Reggiano

Salt and pepper to taste

Risotto with butter and Parmigiano is a favorite dish in Parma. At Ristorante Cocchi, the risotto, which was creamy and perfectly cooked, also contained small cubes of prosciutto. In spring and summer, I like to add all that is fresh and seasonal—sweet small peas, asparagus tips, ripe tomatoes, or small, tender zucchini. In fall and winter, I add one or several varieties of mushrooms.

HEAT the broth in a medium saucepan, keep warm over low heat.

MELT 3 tablespoons of the butter in a large skillet over medium heat. When the butter begins to foam, add the onions and cook, stirring, until pale yellow and soft, about 5 minutes. Add the rice and stir quickly for a minute or two, until the rice is translucent and well coated with the butter. Add the prosciutto and stir for about 1 minute, then add the wine. Cook, stirring, until almost all the wine has evaporated. Add about ½ cup of the hot broth and cook until it has been almost completely absorbed. Continue cooking and stirring the rice in this manner, adding broth ½ cup or so at a time, until the rice is tender but still firm to the bite, about 18 minutes.

WHEN almost all of the last addition of broth is incorporated, add the remaining 1 tablespoon butter and about half of the Parmigiano. Stir quickly until the butter and cheese are melted and the rice has a moist, creamy consistency. Taste, adjust the seasoning, and serve immediately, with the remaining Parmigiano.

RISOTTO WITH FRESH HERBS

Risotto alle Erbe Aromatiche

SERVES 4 TO 6

6 cups Vegetable Broth (page 169) or 3 cups low-sodium chicken broth mixed with 3 cups water

3 tablespoons extra virgin olive oil

½ cup finely minced shallots or yellow onions

2 cups Arborio, Carnaroli, or Vialone Nano rice

1 cup dry white wine

2 to 3 tablespoons finely chopped mixed herbs (flat-leaf parsley, marjoram, basil and/or mint)

1 tablespoon unsalted butter

¼ cup freshly grated Parmigiano-Reggiano, optional

My sister's son, Marcello, who lives on a beautiful farm about twenty miles outside Bologna, is almost a vegetarian. And not only does he eat meat very, very rarely, he almost never drinks wine—something unheard of in my family! Fortunately, though, on occasion Marcello likes to cook. During my last visit to their farmhouse, Marcello and his fianceé, Maurizia, prepared for me a delicious, almost fat-free herb risotto, which used vegetable broth in place of chicken, extra virgin olive oil instead of butter, and shallots instead of onion. The herbs, which came from their large garden, were added to the risotto during its last few minutes of cooking so they retained their color and freshness. It was a lovely, easy-to-prepare dish, which I enjoyed thoroughly.

HEAT the vegetable broth in a medium saucepan; keep warm over low heat.

HEAT the oil in a large skillet over medium heat. Add the shallots and cook, stirring, until pale yellow and soft, 5 to 6 minutes. Add the rice and stir quickly for a minute or two, until the rice is translucent and well coated with the oil. Add ½ cup of the wine and stir until almost all of it has evaporated. Stir in the remaining ½ cup wine and cook in the same manner. Add about ½ cup of the hot broth or just enough to barely cover the rice. Cook, stirring, until the broth has been almost completely absorbed. Continue cooking and stirring the rice in this manner, adding broth ½ cup or so at a time, until the rice is tender but still a bit firm to the bite, about 18 minutes.

WHEN almost all of the last addition of broth is incorporated, add the herbs, butter, and Parmigiano, if using. Stir quickly until the butter and cheese are melted and the rice has a moist, creamy consistency. If the risotto seems a bit dry, stir in a little more broth. Taste, adjust the seasoning, and serve immediately.

VEGETABLE BROTH

Brodo Vegetale

MAKES ABOUT 2
QUARTS

3 carrots

3 celery stalks

2 medium zucchini,
ends trimmed

2 tomatoes, cored

1 large onion, peeled

Salt to taste

A flavorful vegetable broth can be used as an alternative to the traditional meat and chicken broths. Its light quality is perfect for vegetable risotti and for spring and summer vegetable soups. This broth takes no effort to prepare, since it can be made with most basic vegetables. Make a large batch and freeze it in ice-cube trays. Then divide the ice cubes among small plastic bags to use as needed.

CUT the vegetables into small pieces. Put them in a pot and add cold water to cover by 3 inches. Partially cover the pot and bring to a boil over medium heat. Reduce the heat to low and simmer for 1 to 1½ hours, skimming off the foam that comes to the surface of the water. Season with salt.

LINE a mesh strainer with paper towels and strain the broth, a few ladles at a time, into a large bowl. If you are not planning to use the broth right away, let it cool to room temperature. It can be refrigerated for a few days or be frozen for 2 months.

RISOTTO WITH SANGIOVESE

Risotto al Sangiovese di Romagna

SERVES 4 TO 6

4 cups homemade Meat Broth
(page 71) or canned low-
sodium beef or chicken broth

4 tablespoons (½ stick)
unsalted butter

⅓ cup finely minced
yellow onion

1 thick slice pancetta (about
2 ounces), very finely minced

When the people of Emilia-Romagna are not eating pasta, they might opt for a soup, a gnocchi, or a risotto dish. While in the homes of the region today the dish might be the meal, in restaurants and trattorie, it is still traditionally served as a first course. In Bologna, when I need a fix of risotto, I go to Trattoria Battibecco. Battibecco, which is not in fact a trattoria but a very elegant, expensive restaurant, serves simply divine risotto. It was cooked with a Sangiovese wine from Romagna, and everything about the dish was perfect. The rice, which had an appealing medium red color, was moist and creamy and firm to the bite, and its taste had the floral quality of the good Sangiovese wine.

1 garlic clove, minced

Generous 1 tablespoon finely chopped fresh rosemary or 1 teaspoon dried rosemary

2 cups Arborio, Carnaroli, or Vialone Nano rice

2 cups Sangiovese di Romagna or California Sangiovese

½ cup freshly grated Parmigiano-Reggiano

1 to 2 tablespoons chopped flat-leaf parsley, optional

Salt to taste

HEAT the broth in a medium saucepan, keep warm over low heat.

MELT 3 tablespoons of the butter in a large skillet over medium heat. When the butter begins to foam, add the onion and pancetta. Cook, stirring, until lightly golden, about 5 minutes. Add the garlic and rosemary and stir for about 1 minute. Add the rice and stir quickly until the rice is translucent and well coated with the butter, about 2 minutes. Add ½ cup of the wine and stir until almost all of it has evaporated. Add ½ cup more wine and cook in the same manner. Add ½ cup of the broth, or just enough to barely cover the rice and cook, stirring constantly, until the broth has been almost completely absorbed. Continue cooking and stirring the rice in this manner, adding the broth ½ cup or so at a time, for 14 to 15 minutes.

WHEN the last addition of broth has been completely incorporated, add the remaining 1 cup wine, ½ cup at a time, and cook and stir until it has been almost completely absorbed, and the rice is tender but still a bit firm to the bite. Stir in the remaining 1 tablespoon butter, a small handful of the Parmigiano, and the parsley, if using, and stir quickly until the butter and cheese are melted and the rice has a moist, creamy, and slightly loose consistency. Taste, adjust the seasoning, and serve sprinkled with the remaining Parmigiano.

RISOTTO WITH SANGIOVESE AND SAUSAGE Add ¼ pound mild Italian pork sausage, casing removed and finely chopped, along with the onions and pancetta and sauté everything together until golden. Proceed as instructed above.

RISOTTO WITH SANGIOVESE AND DRIED PORCINI Soak 1 ounce dried porcini mushrooms in lukewarm water to cover for 20 minutes. Drain the mushrooms (reserve the water for another use if desired). Rinse the mushrooms under cold running water and chop them fine. Sauté the onions and pancetta as instructed above, then add the mushrooms and stir for about 1 minute. Proceed as instructed above.

SUMMER RISOTTO

Risottino Estivo

SERVES 4 TO 6

6 cups Vegetable Broth
(page 169)

¼ cup extra virgin olive oil

⅓ cup finely minced shallots

2 cups Arborio, Carnaroli,
or Vialone Nano rice

1 pound ripe tomatoes,
peeled, seeded, and minced
(see page 217)

Salt to taste

¼ cup finely minced herbs
(basil, oregano, flat-leaf
parsley, mint and/or
marjoram)

1 tablespoon unsalted butter

¼ cup freshly grated
Parmigiano-Reggiano

Rodrigo is one of the oldest and best known restaurants of Bologna. The two owners, Renzo and Gilberto, began working there as teenagers about forty years ago and when, after several years, the original owner, Rodrigo, retired, they bought the restaurant. It was then that I met them, and throughout the years I have witnessed their hard work and well-deserved success. Rodrigo is a restaurant that dances to its own tune. The place is casual yet elegant. The food is traditional yet innovative and, in a city that serves some of the best homemade pasta of Italy and richly prepared second courses, Rodrigo dares to be different, because it emphasizes risotto more than homemade pasta and light, straightforward seafood preparations. This is one of Rodrigo's risottos, which is cooked in a flavorful vegetable broth and uses milder, sweeter shallots instead of onion. The tomatoes must be fresh, ripe, and flavorful, and the herbs freshly picked. Butter is swirled sparingly into the risotto just before serving. If you have access to fresh herbs and off-the-vine tomatoes, I urge you to make this dish.

HEAT the broth in a medium saucepan; keep warm over low heat.

HEAT the oil in a large heavy skillet over medium heat. Add the shallots and cook, stirring, until translucent and soft, 6 to 7 minutes. Add the rice and stir for a minute or two. Add the tomatoes and all their juices, season lightly with salt, and cook, stirring, until the juices have thickened, 3 to 4 minutes. Add a small ladleful of the hot broth (about ½ cup), or just enough to barely cover the rice, and cook, stirring, until the broth has been almost completely absorbed. Continue cooking and stirring the rice in this manner, adding a small ladleful of broth at a time, until the rice is tender but still a bit firm to the bite, about 18 minutes.

WHEN almost all of the last addition of broth is incorporated, add the herbs, butter, and Parmigiano and stir quickly until the butter and cheese are melted and the rice has a moist, creamy consistency. Stir in just a bit more broth if the rice seems a bit dry. Taste, adjust the seasoning, and serve immediately.

SQUASH RISOTTO

Risotto con la Zucca

SERVES 4 TO 6

7 cups Vegetable Broth (page 169) or canned low-sodium chicken broth

4 tablespoons (½ stick) unsalted butter

⅓ cup finely minced shallots

1 pound butternut squash, peeled, seeded and cut into pea-sized dice

2 cups Arborio, Carnaroli, or Vialone Nano rice

1 cup dry white wine

1 tablespoon chopped flat-leaf parsley

½ cup freshly grated Parmigiano-Reggiano

The cooks of Parma, Piacenza, and Ferrara, three major cities on the Emilia side of the region, love squash and use it in terrific pasta fillings, in risotto, and roasted with butter and Parmigiano. At Il Testamento del Porco, a trattoria in Ferrara, I had a sublime squash risotto that looked as if it had been laced with gold nuggets. The sweet taste of the squash, enriched with butter and Parmigiano, makes this risotto quite memorable.

HEAT the broth in a medium saucepan; keep warm over low heat.

MELT 3 tablespoons of the butter in a large skillet over medium heat. When the butter begins to foam, add the shallots and cook, stirring, until lightly golden and soft, about 5 minutes. Add the squash and mix well. Add about ½ cup of the broth and stir until almost all of the broth has evaporated, 3 to 4 minutes. Add the rice and stir for a minute or two, then add the wine all at once. When the wine has completely evaporated, add another ½ cup of the broth and cook, stirring constantly, until the broth has been almost completely absorbed. Continue cooking and stirring the rice in this manner, adding ½ cup or so broth at a time, until the rice is tender but still a bit firm to the bite, about 18 minutes.

WHEN almost all of the last addition of broth is incorporated, add the parsley, the remaining 1 tablespoon butter, and about half of the Parmigiano and stir quickly until the butter and cheese are melted and the rice has a moist, creamy consistency. Taste, adjust the seasoning, and serve with the remaining Parmigiano.

RISOTTO WITH CABBAGE

Risotto col Cavolo

SERVES 4 TO 6

½ pound Savoy cabbage

2 to 3 ounces prosciutto, cut into ⅛-inch-thick slices

3 tablespoons unsalted butter

2 tablespoons extra virgin olive oil

⅓ cup finely minced yellow onion

¼ cup finely minced carrots

¼ cup finely minced celery

1 tablespoon double-concentrated Italian tomato paste, diluted in 1 cup Vegetable Broth (page 169), Chicken Broth (page 73), or canned low-sodium chicken broth

5 cups Vegetable Broth (page 169), Chicken Broth (page 73), or canned low-sodium chicken broth

2 cups Arborio, Carnaroli, or Vialone Nano rice

1 cup dry white wine

⅓ cup freshly grated Parmigiano-Reggiano

Strategically located between Emilia and Romagna, Imola, a lovely, small Emilian city, reaches the borders of Tuscany through the Apennine mountains. Because of its location, Imola is equally comfortable serving the food of Emilia and of Romagna, while tapping into the straightforward food of Tuscany. While the richness of the risottos of Emilia-Romagna does not match its pastas, there are some dishes that in their delicious simplicity are instantly associated with a place. Risotto with cabbage is synonymous with Imola. There is nothing fancy about the ingredients that go into this dish of obvious peasant tradition, but when onions, carrots, cabbage, and pancetta or sausage cook slowly together, they become the source of considerable flavor. And when the rice is added and cooked with the slow addition of the flavorful hot broth, the flavors grow in intensity, resulting in an almost voluptuous dish. This is a satisfying risotto that befits the foggy winter nights of the region.

REMOVE and discard any bruised outer cabbage leaves. Slice the cabbage in half and remove the core. Cut the cabbage into thin strips, then finely chop it.

REMOVE the fat from the prosciutto and finely chop the fat. Dice the prosciutto and set aside.

HEAT 2 tablespoons of the butter and the oil together in a large skillet over medium heat. Add the prosciutto fat, onion, carrots, and celery and cook, stirring, until the vegetables are lightly golden and soft, 7 to 8 minutes. Add the prosciutto and stir for about a minute, then add the cabbage and cook for 2 to 3 minutes. Add the diluted tomato paste, cover the skillet, reduce the heat to medium-low, and simmer, stirring occasionally, until the cabbage is soft, about 15 minutes. (The dish can be prepared up to this point several hours ahead.)

MEANWHILE, heat the broth in a medium saucepan; keep warm over low heat.

REMOVE the lid of the skillet and raise the heat to medium. Add the rice and stir for a minute or two. Add the wine and stir until almost all of it has evaporated. Add about ½ cup of the hot broth and cook, stirring, until it has been almost completely absorbed. Continue cooking and stirring the rice in this manner, adding the broth ½ cup or so at a time, until the rice is tender but still firm to the bite, about 18 minutes.

WHEN almost all of the last addition of broth is incorporated, add the remaining tablespoon butter and the Parmigiano and stir quickly until the butter and cheese are melted and the rice has a moist, creamy consistency. Taste, adjust the seasoning, and serve immediately.

RISOTTO WITH CABBAGE AND SAUSAGE After the onion, carrot, and celery are golden and soft, add ¼ pound mild Italian pork sausage (omit the prosciutto), casing removed and finely chopped, and cook, breaking it up with a wooden spoon, until it begins to lose its raw color. Add the rice and proceed as instructed above.

THE "WAVE" MAKES THE DIFFERENCE

For me the consistency of a risotto should be *all'onda*, "to the wave," which means that it should be moist but not soupy. It should be creamy and voluptuous, with each grain of rice barely firm to the bite.

BARLEY AND SAUSAGE RISOTTO

Orzotto di Salsiccia

SERVES 4

3 to 4 cups Chicken Broth (page 73), or canned low-sodium chicken broth

3 tablespoons unsalted butter

1 cup pearl barley, washed in several changes of cold water

2 tablespoons extra virgin olive oil

½ cup finely minced yellow onions

1 link (about ¼ pound) mild Italian pork sausage (with no fennel seeds, chile pepper, or strong spices), casing removed and finely chopped

2 ounces sliced pancetta, finely minced

½ cup medium-bodied red wine, such as a Sangiovese from Emilia-Romagna or California

1 tablespoon double-concentrated Italian tomato paste, diluted in 1 cup of the broth

Salt and freshly ground black pepper to taste

⅓ cup freshly grated Parmigiano-Reggiano

Fontanelle di Roccabianca, a tiny community on the flat, fertile plains of Emilia between Parma and Piacenza, is the home of Hostaria da Ivan. Barbara and Ivan, the owners, cook food that is strongly rooted in tradition but presented with flair and creativity. There, just as in most country trattorie we visited, there are no written menus, no computers or calculators, just the warm, personable couple whose passion for food is evident in the food they serve. My husband and I liked this little place so much that we dined there three nights in a row, and each time we discovered a new little gem. The night we had this delicious barley risotto, Barbara came to our table and said, almost apologetically, "I know that barley is not a native ingredient of the area, but because I like its nutty flavor so much, I cooked it just like a risotto. But, of course, the sausage is homemade." Who was I to argue?

HEAT the broth in a medium saucepan; keep warm over low heat.

MELT 2 tablespoons of the butter in a large skillet over medium heat. When the butter begins to foam, add the barley and stir for a minute or two, until the barley is well coated with the butter. Add 2½ cups of the hot broth and bring to a boil. Reduce the heat to medium-low, partially cover, and simmer, stirring occasionally, until the barley has absorbed almost all of the broth and is tender but still firm to the bite, about 20 minutes. (If the broth is absorbed too fast, add a bit more, as necessary.)

WHILE the barley is cooking, prepare the sauce: Heat the oil in a small skillet over medium heat. Add the onions and cook, stirring, until pale yellow and translucent, 6 to 7 minutes. Add the sausage and pancetta and stir with a large wooden spoon, breaking up the sausage, until the sausage is lightly golden, 2 to 3 minutes. Raise the heat to high and add the wine. Stir until almost all of the wine has evaporated. Add the diluted tomato paste, bring to a gentle simmer, and cook over medium-low heat, stirring occasionally, until the sauce has a medium-thick consistency, 7 to 8 minutes. Season lightly with salt and pepper.

ADD the sauce to the cooked barley and cook and stir over medium heat until the sauce has been almost completely absorbed, 2 to 3 minutes. Taste the barley, which should be tender but still a bit firm to the bite. If it seems too firm, add a little more broth and cook it for a few minutes longer, until most of the liquid has been absorbed. Add the remaining 1 tablespoon butter and the Parmigiano and stir until the butter is melted and the barley has a moist, creamy consistency. Taste, adjust the seasoning, and serve immediately.

SELECTING BARLEY

Pearl barley, available in most markets, has been husked and polished and cooks in 20 to 25 minutes. Barley bought at health food stores might still retain its husk. In that case, the cooking time ranges between 40 and 50 minutes. Barley is also available in supermarkets in 10-minute-cooking brands.

The Italian word *orzotto* is a contraction of the words *orzo* (barley) and *risotto*. *Orzotto* thus means that the barley is cooked in the style of a risotto.

SHRIMP, POTATO, AND PESTO RISOTTO

Risotto con Patate, Gamberi, e Pesto

SERVES 6

6 cups Fish Broth (page 178)

1½ cups peeled and finely diced boiling potatoes

¼ cup extra virgin olive oil

⅓ cup finely minced shallots or yellow onions

2 cups Arborio, Carnaroli, or Vialone Nano rice

1 cup dry white wine

20 medium shrimp, shelled, deveined, and cut into small pieces

1 tablespoon unsalted butter, optional

2 to 3 tablespoons Pesto (page 178)

Buriani is simply the best restaurant on the Emilia side of the region. Pieve di Cento, a small town in the farmland about twenty miles from Bologna, is the home of Buriani. There, a group of young people who took over the restaurant from their parents prepares food that is rooted in tradition yet brilliantly innovative, light, and absolutely delicious. The menu, which emphasizes the superlative ingredients of the area, was so tempting that my husband and I, and my daughter and her husband, kept ordering course after course. This risotto, a specialty of neighboring Liguria, was delicate and absolutely delicious.

HEAT the broth in a medium saucepan; keep warm over low heat until ready to use.

BRING a small saucepan of water to a boil. Add the diced potatoes and cook for 3 to 4 minutes. Drain and set aside.

HEAT the oil in a large skillet over medium heat. Add the shallots and cook, stirring, until pale yellow and soft, 4 to 5 minutes. Add the potatoes and stir once or twice, then add the rice and stir until the rice is well coated with the oil, about 2 minutes. Stir in the wine. When the wine has completely evaporated, add about ½ cup of the hot broth and cook, stirring constantly, until the broth has been almost completely absorbed. Continue cooking and stirring the rice in this manner, adding ½ cup or so of broth at a time, for about 16 minutes.

WHEN almost all of the last addition of broth is incorporated, add the shrimp and a little more broth and cook, stirring, for 2 to 3 minutes longer, until the rice is tender but still a bit firm to the bite and has a moist, creamy consistency. If it is too dry, stir in a bit more broth.

TURN off the heat. Add the butter, if using, and 2 tablespoons of the pesto, and stir quickly to incorporate. Taste, adding more pesto if you like, and serve immediately.

PESTO

2 cups loosely packed
basil leaves

⅓ to ½ cup extra virgin
olive oil

2 tablespoons pine nuts

1 garlic clove, peeled

Salt and freshly ground black
pepper to taste

¼ cup freshly grated
Parmigiano-Reggiano

PUT all the ingredients except the cheese in a food processor fitted with the metal blade or a blender and process until smooth. Pour the sauce into a bowl and stir in the Parmigiano. Taste and adjust the seasoning. Tightly cover the bowl with plastic wrap and refrigerate until ready to use. (Makes 1 cup.)

FISH BROTH

Brodo di Pesce

MAKES ABOUT
2 QUARTS

1 large yellow onion, peeled

2 small carrots

1 celery stalk

2 fresh bay leaves or 1 dried
bay leaf

2 to 3 sprigs parsley

3 pounds fish heads and
bones, thoroughly rinsed

1 cup dry white wine

3 quarts cold water

1 tablespoon salt

This light, delicate broth will impart additional flavor to any seafood risotto, sauce, or stew.

COARSELY dice the vegetables. Combine all the ingredients in a large pot and bring to a boil over medium heat. Skim off any foam that rises and reduce the heat to low. Simmer, uncovered, skimming the foam, for about 1 hour.

LINE a strainer with a few layers of paper towels and strain the broth into another pot or a large bowl. If you are not planning to use the broth right away, let cool to room temperature, then refrigerate for a few days or freeze for up to a couple of months. (Bring the broth to a full boil before using.)

SHELLFISH RISOTTO

Risotto di Pesce

SERVES 4 TO 6

4 cups Fish Broth (page 178)

¾ pound whole squid, cleaned (see box, page 232), or ½ pound cleaned squid

⅓ cup extra virgin olive oil

⅓ cup finely minced yellow onions

2 cups Arborio, Carnaroli, or Vialone Nano rice

½ cup dry white wine

½ pound shrimp, peeled, deveined, rinsed, and cut into pea-sized dice

2 tablespoons chopped flat-leaf parsley

1 tablespoon unsalted butter, optional

liseo is the reserved but attentive, courteous owner of Ristorante Quattro Colonne of Rimini. The restaurant is quaintly located on the pier, a shot away from fishermen's vessels and recreational boats. The food at Quattro Colonne is that of the Romagna seacoast, simple, straightforward, and absolutely irresistible. This risotto, which was studded with very small pieces of shrimp and squid, had a savory base of onion and finely chopped squid, which, Eliseo said, gave the risotto added flavor and personality.

COMBINE the fish broth and 2 cups water in a medium saucepan and bring just to a simmer. Keep warm over low heat.

SLICE the squid into ¼-inch rings. Finely chop 8 to 10 of the rings and set aside. Cut the remaining squid into small pieces and set aside. Reserve the tentacles for another use.

HEAT the oil in a large skillet over medium heat. Add the onion and the finely chopped squid and cook, stirring, until a light golden color, 5 to 6 minutes. Add the rice and stir until it is well coated with the oil, about 2 minutes. Add the wine and stir until almost all of it has evaporated. Add ½ cup of the hot broth, or just enough to barely cover the rice, and cook, stirring, until the broth has been almost completely absorbed. Continue cooking and stirring the rice in this manner, adding broth ½ cup or so at a time, for 15 to 16 minutes.

WHEN almost all of the last addition of broth is incorporated, add the diced squid and the shrimp and cook and stir until the shrimp are lightly golden and the squid are chalky white, 2 to 3 minutes. Stir in the parsley and the butter, if using, and stir until the butter melts. The rice should be tender but still a bit firm to the bite and have a moist, creamy consistency; if it is too dry, stir in a little more broth. Taste, adjust the seasoning, and serve immediately.

RISOTTO WITH CLAMS AND TOMATOES

Risotto con Vongole e Pomodoro

SERVES 4 TO 6

3 pounds littleneck clams or cockles (the smallest you can get), cleaned as instructed on page 162

For the sauce

3 tablespoons extra virgin olive oil

1 garlic clove, finely minced

2 tablespoons chopped flat-leaf parsley

1 cup canned Italian plum tomatoes, with their juice, put through a food mill to remove the seeds

Salt to taste

Chopped fresh red chile pepper or red pepper flakes to taste

For the risotto

3 cups Fish Broth (page 178)

2 to 3 tablespoons extra virgin olive oil

⅓ cup finely minced shallots or yellow onion

2 cups Arborio, Carnaroli, or Vialone Nano rice

½ cup dry white wine

1 tablespoon chopped flat-leaf parsley

*M*y mother's love of risotto was, at best, lukewarm. She would prepare it a few times a month at most, and, when she did, it was at my father's insistence or because she had some leftover meat sauce that needed to be used up. She was most comfortable kneading the dough for pasta or gnocchi, which she would turn into mouthwatering dishes. I loved risotto, but since as a teenager I had no interest whatsoever in cooking, I had to enjoy it at someone else's house, or at a restaurant or trattoria. The seafood risottos of the Adriatic seacoast were the absolute best.

This preparation adds a savory tomato-clam sauce to risotto during its last few minutes of cooking. The amount of tomatoes is just enough to tinge the risotto lightly with red, without overpowering it. (A larger amount of this sauce would be great tossed with spaghettini.) This type of sauce offers many options, since it can be made not only with clams, but with mussels, squid, shrimp, scallops, or even cuttlefish, which in turn will give your risotto a new identity.

PUT the clams and ½ cup water in a large skillet, cover the skillet, and place over medium heat. Cook just until the clams open. (Some may take a bit longer than others to open.) Transfer the clams to a bowl as they open. Discard any that will not open. Line a strainer with paper towels and strain the cooking liquid into a bowl.

REMOVE the clams from the shells and, if large, cut each into 2 to 3 pieces. Set aside.

TO prepare the sauce, heat the oil in a small saucepan over medium heat. Add the garlic and parsley. As soon as the garlic begins to color, less than a minute, add the tomatoes and the reserved clam liquid. Season with salt, add the chile pepper, reduce the heat to medium-low, and cook, uncovered, stirring occasionally, until the sauce is reduced by approximately half, 4 to 6 minutes. Stir in the clams and turn off the heat. (The sauce can be prepared an hour ahead.)

To prepare the risotto, combine the fish broth and 3 cups water in a medium saucepan and bring to a simmer; keep warm over low heat.

Heat the oil in a large skillet over medium heat. Add the shallots and cook, stirring, until pale yellow and soft, 4 to 5 minutes. Add the rice and stir quickly for a minute or two, until the rice is translucent and well coated with the oil. Add the wine and stir until almost all of it has evaporated. Add ½ cup of the hot broth, or just enough to barely cover the rice, and cook, stirring, until the broth has been almost completely absorbed. Continue cooking and stirring the rice in this manner, adding the broth as needed ½ cup or so at a time, for 16 minutes.

When the last addition of broth has been completely incorporated and the rice looks somewhat dry, add the sauce. Cook, stirring constantly, until most of the liquid has been absorbed, and the rice is tender but still a bit firm to the bite and has a moist, creamy consistency, 2 to 3 minutes. Stir in the last parsley. Taste, adjust the seasoning, and serve immediately.

RISOTTO WITH CLAMS
AND CHILE PEPPER

Risotto con Vongole e Peperoncino

SERVES 4 TO 6

3 pounds littleneck clams or cockles (the smallest you can get), cleaned as instructed on page 162

1 cup dry white wine

3 cups Fish Broth (page 178)

3 to 4 tablespoons extra virgin olive oil

⅓ cup finely minced shallots or yellow onion

1 garlic clove, finely minced

2 cups Arborio, Carnaroli, or Vialone Nano rice

Salt to taste

Finely minced fresh red chile pepper or red pepper flakes to taste

2 tablespoons chopped flat-leaf parsley

1 tablespoon unsalted butter, optional

*R*isotto with clams is a favorite dish of the Romagna seacoast. While the variations are many, my preference is for this traditional, straightforward preparation, which produces a most delicate risotto. At Ristorante al Pescatore, in the elegant seaside town of Riccione, the risotto, which was loaded with very small, tasty clams, had been spiced up a bit by the addition of some peperoncino, red chile pepper. Walter, the owner of the restaurant, offered a few words of advice: "Make sure the clams are fresh and very small; if not, cut them into a few pieces. Make sure you cook the risotto in a very light fish broth. If the broth is too strong, it will overpower the dish. And make sure to add only a little bit of garlic and chile pepper, so you will have a dish with perfectly balanced flavors." Grazie, *Walter.*

PUT the clams and ½ cup of wine in a large skillet, cover the skillet, and place over medium heat. Cook just until the clams open (some may take longer than others to open). Transfer the clams to a bowl as they open. Discard any that won't open. Line a strainer with paper towels and strain the cooking liquid into a bowl.

REMOVE the clams from the shells and cut each into 2 or 3 pieces. Add the clams to the strained juices, cover, and set aside until ready to use. (The clams can be prepared a few hours ahead. Refrigerate until ready to proceed.)

COMBINE the broth and 3 cups water in a medium saucepan and bring to a simmer; keep warm over low heat.

HEAT the oil in a large skillet over medium heat. Add the shallots and cook, stirring, until pale yellow and soft, 5 to 6 minutes. Stir in the garlic and cook for about 1 minute. Add the rice and stir until it is thoroughly coated with the oil, about 1 minute. Add the remaining ½ cup wine and cook, stirring, until almost all the wine has evaporated. Season lightly with salt and the chile pepper. Add ½ cup of the hot broth, or just enough to barely cover the rice, and cook, stirring, until the broth has been almost completely absorbed. Continue cooking and stirring the rice in this manner, adding broth ½ cup or so at a time, for 15 to 16 minutes.

WHEN almost all of the last addition of broth is incorporated and the rice looks somewhat dry, add the parsley, the butter, if using, and the clams with their liquid. Cook, stirring constantly, until the liquid has been almost completely absorbed and is tender but still a bit firm to the bite and has a moist, creamy consistency. Taste, adjust the seasoning, and serve immediately.

Note: Most of the time Italians do not pair cheese with seafood, because the taste of the cheese would overpower the delicate taste of the fish or shellfish. That is why Parmigiano is not used in these seafood risottos. In Emilia-Romagna, the amount of butter used in seafood risottos is also kept to a bare minimum, with many cooks preferring the lighter taste of olive oil. A very small pat of butter stirred into the risotto at the last moment, however, is quite acceptable.

Gnocchi

Gnocchi are no-nonsense food—hearty, straightforward, and heartwarming. Just like a good stew or a steaming plate of pasta, gnocchi are comfort food. I know I am my mother's daughter if for no other reason than that I love gnocchi and love to make them, just as my mother did. My mother was at her very best when she kneaded something. Pasta and gnocchi would begin in her hands as individual unrelated ingredients, and by the time she was done, they had been transformed into splendid preparations.

I, just as many people in northern Italy and in Emilia-Romagna, grew up with gnocchi, especially potato gnocchi. During affluent times, the gnocchi were tossed with a rich Bolognese meat ragù, or with a sauce of porcini mushrooms. In leaner times, a few tablespoons of butter or oil and a very light sprinkling of Parmigiano was all that coated them. This was a dish that was easy to make, inexpensive to prepare, and could feed and satisfy the hunger of a large family quite easily.

In Emilia-Romagna, gnocchi are traditionally made with either potatoes or ricotta. A skillful, seasoned gnocchi maker never adds eggs to the dough because it makes gnocchi rubbery, though the addition of an egg does make the dough easier to handle.

While potato gnocchi are the perfect vehicle for satisfying meat sauces, the more delicate ricotta gnocchi are best suited to lighter sauces, or simply toss them with sweet butter, fresh sage, and Parmigiano.

Making gnocchi is not really hard. There are a few things, however, that should be understood. I have compiled a short list of tips that will help you with your first batch of homemade gnocchi.

TIPS

- *The potatoes.* Potato gnocchi require floury potatoes, which contain very little water. Russet potatoes, also known as baking potatoes, work perfectly for me. Do not use new potatoes; they are too moist.

  The best and easiest way to mash potatoes is with a potato ricer. Do not use a food processor or a hand mixer; they will make the potatoes gummy and sticky.

- *The flour.* Because it is hard to know just how much moisture there is in the potato or the ricotta you are using, when you add the flour to the other ingredients, always start with a bit less than the recipe suggests, then add more if the dough sticks too much to the work surface.

- *The dough.* Do not knead the dough for more than a few minutes. The longer the dough is kneaded, the more flour it will absorb, resulting in heavier gnocchi. After a few minutes of kneading, the dough should have a compact but moist consistency, and it should be easy to roll out on the board.

- *Testing the gnocchi.* Before rolling out the gnocchi, take a small piece of the dough and drop it into boiling water. If, after a minute or two, it comes to the surface intact, your dough is ready; if it disintegrates in the water, you must knead in just a bit more flour. If, on the other hand, it is chewy and heavy, you have probably added too much flour, and the gnocchi will be on the heavy side.

- *Storing gnocchi.* Uncooked potato gnocchi can be kept in the refrigerator, uncovered, for several hours. Ricotta gnocchi can be refrigerated, uncovered, overnight. Do not freeze gnocchi; when cooked, they will be unappetizingly mushy.

- *Cooking gnocchi.* Use a large, wide pan that can accommodate 5 to 6 quarts of water. The wider the pan, the less chance there is that the gnocchi will stick together. After a minute or two, the gnocchi will come floating to the surface of the water. Give them 20 to 30 seconds, then scoop them out with a slotted spoon, or they will become soggy.

POTATO GNOCCHI

Gnocchi di Patate

SERVES 4 TO 6

4 large russet potatoes (about 2 pounds), scrubbed and dried

2 teaspoons salt

1½ to 2 cups unbleached all-purpose flour

2 teaspoons salt

PREHEAT the oven to 375°F.

TO make the dough, make a deep slit in each potato with a large knife. Put the potatoes on a baking sheet, place on the center rack of the oven, and bake until tender, about 1 hour.

LET the potatoes cool briefly, then peel them while they are still quite warm, cut them into rough pieces, put them through a potato ricer into a large bowl and season with the salt. Let the potatoes cool a bit, then add 1½ cups of the flour, a little at a time, mixing well with your hands until the flour and potatoes come together into a rough dough.

TRANSFER the mixture to a work surface and knead lightly, gradually adding the remaining ½ cup flour if the dough sticks too much to the board and to your hands. Then knead the dough for 2 to 3 minutes, dusting it lightly with flour if needed, until it is smooth, pliable, and just a bit sticky.

TO shape the gnocchi, cut off a piece of dough about the size of an orange. Flour your hands lightly. Using both hands, roll out the piece of dough with a light back-and-forth motion into a rope about the thickness of your index finger. Cut the rope into 1-inch pieces.

HOLD a fork with its tines against the work surface, the *curved* part of the fork facing away. Starting from the bottom of the tines of the fork, press each piece of dough with your index finger firmly upward along the length of the tines, then let the gnocchi fall back onto the work surface. Repeat with the remaining dough until all the gnocchi have been formed.

LINE a large tray with a clean kitchen towel and lightly flour the towel. Place the gnocchi on the towel, without crowding them. They can be cooked immediately or be refrigerated, uncovered, for several hours.

TO cook the gnocchi, bring a large pot of water to a boil over high heat. Add the salt and gnocchi and cook, until all the gnocchi rise to the surface, 1 to 2 minutes. After 20 to 30 seconds, remove the gnocchi with a slotted spoon or a skimmer, draining the excess water back into the pot, and place in the sauce or a heated bowl (see individual recipes).

RICOTTA GNOCCHI

Gnocchi di Ricotta

SERVES 4 TO 6

1 pound whole-milk ricotta

⅓ cup freshly grated
Parmigiano-Reggiano

2 teaspoons salt

1 large egg, lightly beaten

1 to 1½ cups unbleached
all-purpose flour

2 teaspoons salt

To make the dough, combine the ricotta, Parmigiano, salt, and 1 cup of the flour in a large bowl. Mix together well with your hands until the ingredients are evenly blended and the mixture comes together into a rough dough.

TRANSFER the dough to a wooden board or other work surface and knead lightly, gradually adding the remaining ½ cup flour if the dough sticks too much to the board and to your hands. Then knead the dough for 2 to 3 minutes, dusting it lightly with flour if needed, until it is smooth, pliable, and just a bit sticky.

To shape the gnocchi, cut off a piece of dough about the size of an orange. Flour your hands lightly (do not flour the work surface, or the dough will not slide smoothly). Using both hands, roll out the piece of dough with a light back-and-forth motion into a rope about the thickness of your index finger. Cut the roll into 1-inch pieces.

HOLD a fork with its tines against the work surface, the curved part of the fork facing away from you. Starting from the bottom of the tines of the fork, press each piece of dough with your index finger firmly upward along the length of the tines, then let the gnocchi fall back onto the work surface. Repeat with the remaining dough until all the gnocchi have been formed.

LINE a large tray with a clean kitchen towel and flour the towel lightly. Place the gnocchi on the towel, without crowding them. They can be cooked immediately or be refrigerated, uncovered, for several hours.

To cook the gnocchi, bring a large pot of water to a boil over high heat. Add the salt and gnocchi and cook until all the gnocchi rise to the surface, 1 to 2 minutes. After 20 to 30 seconds, remove the gnocchi with a slotted spoon or a skimmer, draining the excess water back into the pot, and place in the sauce or a heated bowl (see individual recipes).

POTATO GNOCCHI WITH

MEAT-SAUSAGE RAGÙ

Gnocchi di Patate con Ragù alla Romagnola

SERVES 4 TO 6

For the ragù

¼ cup extra virgin olive oil

⅓ cup finely minced
yellow onions

⅓ cup finely minced carrots

⅓ cup finely minced celery

6 ounces ground beef

6 ounces ground pork

1 link (about ¼ pound)
Homemade Bolognese
Sausage (page 267) or
mild Italian pork sausage
(containing no fennel seeds,
chile peppers or strong
spices), casing removed and
finely chopped

2 ounces thinly sliced
pancetta, finely minced

2 ounces thinly sliced
prosciutto, finely minced

1 cup dry white wine

2 cups Homemade Tomato
Sauce (page 22) or canned
Italian plum tomatoes, with
their juice, put through a food
mill to remove the seeds

Salt and freshly ground black
pepper to taste

1 tablespoon unsalted butter

1 tablespoon coarse salt

1 recipe Potato Gnocchi
(page 186)

In the fall of 1999, our daughter, Paola, and her husband, Brian, joined us in Emilia-Romagna for a week. After spending a few days on the Adriatic coast, we headed for the small hill town of Brisighella, where we stayed at Gigiolé, a charming hotel whose restaurant has a regional reputation. During our brief stay, we experienced some truly horrific rain that made it impossible for us to go anywhere. The first night, seated in the dramatic grotto-like dining room of Gigiolé, with the heat of the fireplace and the glow of the candles warming the room, I ordered the potato gnocchi with meat-sausage ragù, not unlike the ragù my mother used to make. The dish of plump gnocchi, lightly coated with the rich brown, flavorful ragù, was simply outstanding.

TO prepare the ragù, heat the oil in a medium saucepan over medium heat. Add the vegetables and cook, stirring, until lightly golden and soft, 5 to 6 minutes. Raise the heat to high, add the beef, pork, sausage, pancetta, and prosciutto, and cook, stirring and breaking up the meat with a wooden spoon, until the meat is a nice golden color, 7 to 8 minutes. Stir in the wine and cook until almost all of it has evaporated. Add the tomato sauce and season with salt and pepper. As soon as the sauce begins to bubble, reduce the heat to low, partially cover the pan, and cook the ragù at the slowest of simmers for 1½ to 2 hours, checking it and stirring it every 20 minutes or so, until the sauce is thick, with a rich reddish color, and just slightly liquid. If the sauce reduces too much as it cooks and begins to stick to the bottom of the pan, stir in a bit of water or chicken or beef broth.

STIR the butter into the sauce, taste, and adjust the seasoning. Turn off the heat. (Makes about 3½ cups.)

MEANWHILE, bring a large pot of water to a boil over high heat. Add the coarse salt and gnocchi and cook until the gnocchi rise to the surface of the water, 1 to 2 minutes. After 20 to 30 seconds, remove the gnocchi with

**½ cup freshly grated
Parmigiano-Reggiano**

a large slotted spoon or skimmer, draining the excess water back into the pot, and place in a large heated bowl.

ADD about half of the sauce and a small handful of the Parmigiano and stir until the gnocchi and sauce are well combined. Add more sauce if needed. Serve at once, with the remaining Parmigiano.

Note: Every time I make a ragù, I double the recipe, so a few days later I can toss the ragù with some pasta or stir it into a risotto. It can be refrigerated for a few days and frozen for up to 2 months.

SPINACH-POTATO GNOCCHI

Chicche della Nonna

SERVES 4 TO 6

For the gnocchi

¼ cup very finely chopped cooked fresh or thawed frozen spinach, squeezed dry

1 large egg

4 large russet potatoes (about 2 pounds), baked until tender and put through a potato ricer

2 teaspoons salt

1½ to 2 cups unbleached all-purpose flour

For the sauce

4 tablespoons (½ stick) unsalted butter

⅓ cup very finely minced yellow onion

3 ounces thickly sliced prosciutto, diced

3 cups Homemade Tomato Sauce (page 22) or canned Italian plum tomatoes, with their juice, put through a food mill to remove the seeds

Salt to taste

1 tablespoon coarse salt

2 teaspoons salt

½ cup freshly grated Parmigiano-Reggiano

*L*e Roncole is an unassuming, homey trattoria located in Roncole Verdi, near Busseto. The legendary composer Giuseppe Verdi was born there in 1813. Roncole, and most of Parma's plain, is a shrine to Verdi. Every café, wine tavern, and trattoria in the area displays Verdi memorabilia, and Verdi operas are played loudly everywhere. At Trattoria le Roncole, Verdi's portrait was prominently positioned at the entrance. The spinach gnocchi, made without the typical ridges, were called chicche della nonna, *or grandma's candies. They were smaller than regular gnocchi and lighter.*

To prepare the gnocchi, lightly beat the egg in a large bowl, then stir in the spinach. Add the potatoes, salt, and 1½ cups of the flour and make the dough as instructed on page 186.

SHAPE the gnocchi as instructed on page 186, and cut each rope of dough into 1-inch pieces. (The gnocchi can be cooked immediately or refrigerated, uncovered, for several hours.)

To prepare the sauce, melt 3 tablespoons of the butter in a large skillet over medium heat. When it begins to foam, add the onion and cook, stirring occasionally, until lightly golden and soft, 5 to 6 minutes. Add the prosciutto and stir for a minute or two. Add the tomato sauce and season with salt. As soon as the sauce begins to bubble, reduce the heat to medium-low and simmer, uncovered, until the sauce has a medium-thick consistency, 6 to 7 minutes. (The sauce can be prepared several hours ahead.)

MEANWHILE, bring a large pot of water to a boil over high heat. Add the coarse salt and gnocchi and cook until the gnocchi rise to the surface, 1 to 2 minutes. After 20 to 30 seconds, remove the gnocchi with a large slotted spoon or skimmer, draining the excess water back into the pot, and place in the skillet.

ADD the remaining 1 tablespoon butter and a small handful of the Parmigiano and mix briefly over low heat until the gnocchi and sauce are well combined. Taste, adjust the seasoning, and serve with the remaining Parmigiano.

POTATO GNOCCHI WITH

CREAM-TOMATO SAUCE

Gnocchi di Patate al Burro e Oro

SERVES 4 TO 6

For the sauce

4 tablespoons (½ stick) unsalted butter

1 garlic clove, peeled

3 cups Homemade Tomato Sauce (page 22) or canned Italian plum tomatoes, with their juice, put through a food mill to remove the seeds

3 to 4 sage leaves, shredded, or basil leaves, shredded

Salt to taste

¼ cup heavy cream

1 tablespoon coarse salt

1 recipe Potato Gnocchi (page 186)

½ cup freshly grated Parmigiano-Reggiano

The Italian burro e oro *implies a sauce made with butter, cream, and tomatoes. The classic tomato sauces of Emilia-Romagna are never bright red. Whether made from fresh ripe tomatoes, homemade preserved tomato sauce, or canned tomatoes, they generally have the addition of a few tablespoons of milk, cream, or butter, which lightens the sauce in color and flavor and reduces the assertiveness of the tomatoes. At the venerable Ristorante Diana, a bastion of traditional Bolognese cooking, this light sauce was served over melt-in-your-mouth potato gnocchi, and lightly blanketed with freshly grated Parmigiano-Reggiano.*

To prepare the sauce, melt 3 tablespoons of the butter in a large skillet over medium heat. When it begins to foam, add the garlic and cook until it is lightly golden on all sides. Discard the garlic, add the tomato sauce and sage, and season with salt. As soon as the sauce begins to bubble, reduce the heat to low and simmer, uncovered, stirring occasionally, until the sauce has a medium-thick consistency, 6 to 8 minutes. Add the cream and the remaining 1 tablespoon butter and stir for a minute or two. Taste, adjust the seasoning, and set aside until ready to use. (The sauce can be prepared a few hours ahead.)

MEANWHILE, bring a large pot of water to a boil over high heat. Add the coarse salt and gnocchi and cook until the gnocchi rise to the surface, 1 to 2 minutes. After 20 to 30 seconds, remove the gnocchi with a large slotted spoon or skimmer, draining the excess water back into the pot, and place in the skillet.

STIR over medium heat until the gnocchi and sauce are well combined. Taste, adjust the seasoning, and serve with a generous sprinkling of the Parmigiano.

RICOTTA GNOCCHI WITH PROSCIUTTO AND PORCINI MUSHROOM SAUCE

Gnocchi con Sugo di Prosciutto e Funghi Porcini

SERVES 4 TO 6

For the sauce

1 ounce dried porcini mushrooms, soaked in 2 cups lukewarm water for 20 minutes

1 heaping teaspoon double-concentrated Italian tomato paste

2 tablespoons unsalted butter

2 tablespoons extra virgin olive oil

⅔ cup finely minced yellow onions

1 garlic clove, finely minced

¼ pound prosciutto, in 1 thick slice, finely diced

½ cup dry white wine

Salt and freshly ground black pepper to taste

1 tablespoon coarse salt

1 recipe Ricotta Gnocchi (page 187)

½ cup freshly grated Parmigiano-Reggiano

Fanano is a charming small mountain town located in the magnificent Apennine mountains of Emilia. In the fall and spring, the richly wooded forests around Fanano supply a seemingly inexhaustible bounty of fresh porcini mushrooms. And porcini mushrooms are what you get when you eat at Il Fungo d'Oro Trattoria (The Golden Mushroom Trattoria), which celebrates the porcini season by dedicating its whole menu to them. The simple, straightforward dishes of the area become utterly delicious and grand when enriched with fresh porcini. But what happens when the porcini season ends? Do Italian go into shock? Of course not. They simply change gears. They open their pantry and reach for a bag of aromatic, woodsy dried porcini.

This dish is an adaptation of the one I had at Il Fungo d'Oro, which was made with fresh porcini. The sauce has a tempting aroma and wholesome taste that pairs particularly well with potato gnocchi, penne, or rigatoni. Because of its concentrated aroma, a little of this sauce goes a long way.

To prepare the sauce, drain the porcini mushrooms and reserve the soaking water. Rinse the mushrooms well under cold running water and roughly chop them; set aside. Line a strainer with paper towels and strain the liquid into a bowl. Pour 1½ cups of the strained liquid into a small bowl, stir in the tomato paste, and set aside.

HEAT 1 tablespoon of the butter and the oil together in a large skillet over medium heat. When the butter begins to foam, add the onions and cook, stirring, until lightly golden and soft, 5 to 6 minutes. Add the garlic, porcini, and prosciutto and stir for a minute or two. Raise the heat to high and add the wine. Cook, stirring briskly, until the wine is reduced by approximately half. Add the diluted tomato paste, season with salt and pepper, and reduce the heat to medium-low. Simmer, uncovered, stirring occasionally, until the sauce has a medium-thick consistency,

12 to 15 minutes. Taste and adjust the seasoning. (Makes about 1½ cups.) (The sauce can be prepared several hours ahead. Reheat gently before proceeding.)

WHILE the sauce is cooking, bring a large pot of water to a boil over high heat. Add the coarse salt and the gnocchi and cook until the gnocchi rise to the surface, 1 to 2 minutes. After 20 to 30 seconds, remove the gnocchi with a slotted spoon or a skimmer, draining the excess water back into the pot, and place the gnocchi in the skillet with the sauce.

ADD the remaining 1 tablespoon butter and about half of the Parmigiano. Mix well over medium heat until the gnocchi and sauce are well combined. Taste, adjust the seasoning, and serve with the remaining Parmigiano.

ASPARAGUS-POTATO GNOCCHI
WITH FRESH TOMATOES

Gnocchi di Patate e Asparagi con Dadolata di Pomodoro

SERVES 4 TO 6

For the gnocchi

4 large russet potatoes (about 2 pounds), scrubbed and dried

2 pounds asparagus

2 teaspoons salt

2 to 2½ cups unbleached all-purpose flour

For the sauce

3 to 4 tablespoons extra virgin olive oil

⅓ cup finely minced shallots or yellow onion

1 pound ripe tomatoes, seeded and finely diced

Salt to taste

1 tablespoon unsalted butter

⅓ to ½ teaspoon dried tarragon or 1 to 2 tablespoons chopped flat-leaf parsley

1 tablespoon coarse salt

⅓ cup freshly grated Parmigiano-Reggiano

A member of my family in Italy, knowing I was researching yet another book, told me that in the small town of Castel San Pietro, about fifteen miles outside Bologna, there was a restaurant called Dolce e Salato that served over forty types of homemade pasta, in addition to risotto and gnocchi. He raved so much about the place that the next day, my husband and half of my Italian family drove to Castel San Pietro.

The owner came to our table, told us what his restaurant was all about, and, without missing a beat, said he "would order for us and would keep going until we told him to stop, but not to worry, because the portions were going to be very small." The dishes we tried were truly outstanding, and so, we realized, was our capacity to eat as much as we did. This is one of the gnocchi of Dolce e Salato, which was as light as a feather and as pretty to look at as it was delicious.

TO prepare the gnocchi, preheat the oven to 375°F. Make a deep lengthwise slit in each potato with a large knife. Put the potatoes on a baking sheet and bake until tender, about 1 hour.

MEANWHILE, cut off the tough asparagus bottoms. With a potato peeler or a small sharp knife, peel the stalks. Rinse the asparagus gently under cold running water.

BRING a medium saucepan of salted water to a boil. Add the asparagus and cook until very tender, 5 to 10 minutes, depending on the size. (Make sure to cook the asparagus until very tender, because it is going to be pureed.) Drain the asparagus, cut into 1- or 2-inch pieces, and place in a food processor fitted with the metal blade. Pulse until the asparagus is pureed but not soupy. Put the puree in a large kitchen towel (not terrycloth) and squeeze out approximately ⅓ to ½ cup of the watery juices. Place the puree in a large bowl until you are ready to use it. (The puree can be prepared several hours ahead.)

REMOVE the potatoes from the oven and let cool slightly, then peel them while they are still warm. Put them through a potato ricer and in the bowl with the asparagus. Add the salt and 2 cups of the flour. Make the dough and shape the gnocchi as instructed on page 186. (The gnocchi can be cooked immediately or refrigerated, uncovered, for several hours.)

To prepare the sauce, heat the oil in a large skillet over medium heat. Add the shallots and cook, stirring, until lightly golden and soft, 4 to 5 minutes. Raise the heat to high, add the tomatoes, and season with salt. Cook, stirring constantly, until the tomatoes are soft and their juices have thickened, 3 to 6 minutes, depending on the ripeness of the tomatoes. Add the butter and tarragon and stir briefly.

MEANWHILE, bring a large pot of water to a boil over high heat. Add the coarse salt and gnocchi and cook until the gnocchi rise to the surface, 1 to 2 minutes. After 20 to 30 seconds, remove the gnocchi with a large slotted spoon or skimmer, draining the excess water back into the pot, and place in the skillet.

ADD about half of the Parmigiano and stir over medium heat until the gnocchi and sauce are well combined. Taste, adjust the seasoning, and serve with the remaining Parmigiano.

GNOCCHI WITH ASPARAGUS TIPS, HAM, AND BUTTER
Melt 3 to 4 tablespoons unsalted butter in a large skillet and toss in 2 cups asparagus tips, blanched, and 2 ounces thinly sliced prosciutto or ham, cut into thin strips. Season with salt and pepper and toss with the cooked gnocchi and a bit of freshly grated Parmigiano.

PLAYING WITH DOUGH

The dough for this gnocchi requires a little more flour than usual because of the moisture in the asparagus. When making the dough, start by working in only 2 cups of the flour. If your dough is very sticky, add a little of the remaining flour. Resist the temptation to add the flour all at once, or your gnocchi will be as dense as bricks.

POTATO GNOCCHI WITH SAUSAGE RAGÙ

Gnocchi di Patate con Sugo di Salsiccia

SERVES 4 TO 6

1 ounce dried porcini
mushrooms, soaked in
2 cups lukewarm water for
20 minutes

2 tablespoons unsalted butter

1 to 2 tablespoon extra virgin
olive oil

⅓ cup finely minced
yellow onion

½ pound Homemade
Bolognese Sausage
(page 267) or mild Italian
pork sausage (containing no
fennel seeds, chile pepper, or
strong spices), removed
casing and very finely
chopped

1 thick slice pancetta (about
2 ounces), very finely minced

1½ to 2 cups canned Italian
plum tomatoes, with their
juice, put through a food mill
to remove the seeds

Salt and freshly ground black
pepper to taste

1 tablespoon coarse salt

1 recipe Potato Gnocchi
(page 186)

½ cup freshly grated
Parmigiano-Reggiano

*I*n the farmhouses of Emilia-Romagna, women used to make not only pasta, gnocchi, and breads but also sausages, pickled vegetables, jams, and tomato sauces that were put away for winter use. The fields provided a generous supply of vegetables, and the hills a harvest of wild mushrooms. Albertina, the mother of my nephew's future wife, was born and raised on a farm, where she still lives today with her husband, younger daughter, and her ninety-year-old mother. Albertina doesn't need to go far to shop for ingredients—she has what she needs in her pantry or in her fields. This is one of her ragùs, which uses fresh porcini, homemade sausage, and homemade tomato sauce.

To prepare the sauce, drain the porcini mushrooms, reserving the soaking water. Rinse the mushrooms well under cold running water and roughly chop them. Line a strainer with paper towels and strain the liquid into a bowl. Set aside until ready to use.

HEAT the butter and oil together in a medium saucepan over medium heat. As soon as the butter begins to foam, add the onion and cook, stirring, until lightly golden and soft, 5 to 6 minutes. Add the chopped sausage and pancetta and cook, stirring a few times, until the meat has a rich golden brown color, 6 to 7 minutes. Add the porcini mushrooms and stir once or twice, then add 1 cup of the reserved porcini water. Cook and stir for a minute or two, then add the tomatoes and simmer, uncovered, stirring occasionally, until the sauce has a medium-thick consistency, about 15 minutes. Season with salt and pepper. (Makes 2 to 2½ cups.) (The sauce can be prepared several hours ahead. Reheat gently before using.)

MEANWHILE, bring a large pot of water to a boil over high heat. Add the coarse salt and gnocchi and cook until the gnocchi rise to the surface, 1 to 2 minutes. After 20 to 30 seconds, remove the gnocchi with a slotted spoon, draining excess water into the pot, and place in a large heated bowl.

ADD about half of the sauce and a small handful of the Parmigiano. Stir until the gnocchi and sauce are well combined. Add more sauce if needed. Serve at once, with the remaining Parmigiano.

RICOTTA-SQUASH GNOCCHI

Gnocchi di Lucca

SERVES 4

The sweet orange squash of the region bequeaths its wonderful flavor to stuffed pasta and gnocchi. The best way to enjoy these savory morsels is to toss them simply with sweet butter, sage, and Parmigiano, but occasionally a bolder sauce such as a ragù is preferred. (See the variation, page 198.)

For the gnocchi

2 pounds butternut squash

1 large egg, lightly beaten

1 cup whole-milk ricotta

¾ cup freshly grated Parmigiano-Reggiano

2 teaspoons salt

1⅓ to 1⅔ cups unbleached all-purpose flour

1 tablespoon coarse salt

To prepare the gnocchi, preheat the oven to 375°F. Cut the squash lengthwise in half, place on a baking sheet, cut side up, cover with a sheet of aluminum foil, and bake until tender, 1 to 1½ hours. Let cool slightly, then remove and discard the seeds and scrape the pulp from the skin. Put the pulp in a large kitchen towel (not terrycloth), wrap it around the squash, and squeeze out approximately ¾ cup of the watery juices.

In a large bowl, combine the squash pulp, egg, ricotta, Parmigiano, salt, and 1⅓ cups of the flour. Mix with a wooden spoon or your hands until thoroughly blended together.

For the sauce

3 to 4 tablespoons unsalted butter

6 to 7 sage leaves, finely shredded

Salt to taste

⅓ to ½ cup freshly grated Parmigiano-Reggiano

TRANSFER the mixture to a lightly floured wooden board and, with your hands, work gently into a dough, gradually adding a little more flour if the dough sticks too much to your hands and to the board. Dust the dough lightly with flour and place in a bowl. Cover the bowl with a kitchen towel and refrigerate for 2 to 3 hours.

FORM the gnocchi as instructed on page 186, but cut each rope of dough into ½-inch pieces; shaping them against the tines of a fork is optional (see box). (The gnocchi can be cooked immediately or be refrigerated, uncovered, overnight.)

BRING a large pot of boiling water to a boil over high heat. Add the coarse salt and gnocchi and cook until the gnocchi rise to the surface, 1 to 2 minutes. Let cook for just 20 to 30 seconds longer.

AS the gnocchi are cooking, make the sauce: Melt the butter in a large skillet over medium heat. When it begins to foam, add the sage and stir a few times.

REMOVE the gnocchi from the pot with a slotted spoon or a skimmer, draining the excess water back into the pot, and place in the skillet. Season lightly with salt and add a small handful of the Parmigiano. Stir over medium heat until the gnocchi are well coated with butter. Taste, adjust the seasoning, and serve with the remaining Parmigiano.

RICOTTA-SQUASH GNOCCHI WITH SAUSAGE RAGÙ Romano Rossi, the chef-owner of Il Testamento del Porco Trattoria in Ferrara, likes to pair squash ravioli or gnocchi with a sausage ragù. The sausage ragù from Potato Gnocchi with Sausage Ragù (page 196) is absolutely wonderful tossed with these gnocchi.

GNOCCHI UNLIKE ANY OTHER

Ricotta-squash gnocchi are not hard to make, but they do require a bit of tender loving care. This is what I do:

- Because squash has a great deal of moisture, some of its juices must be removed after it is cooked, or the dough will be very sticky and impossible to work with.

- Even after you have incorporated the amount of flour given in the recipe, the dough will be sticky and soft. Resist the urge to add more flour, or your gnocchi will be tough and chewy.

- Work the dough quickly and gently. Do not handle it for more than a few minutes. The more you handle it, the more flour you will need to add.

- Refrigerate the dough for a few hours before making the gnocchi. This will facilitate the shaping of the gnocchi.

- Before shaping the gnocchi, take a small piece of the dough and drop it in boiling water. If the piece stays together and comes to the surface of the water, your dough is OK. If it disintegrates in the water, a little more flour needs to be worked into the dough.

- Because ricotta-squash gnocchi are delicate, they may be made without the traditional ridges given by the tines of a fork. However, if you feel comfortable with the dough, go ahead and shape them as instructed on page 186.

- Ricotta-squash gnocchi will be firmer after they are cooked.

SAFFRON-RICOTTA GNOCCHI
WITH WALNUT SAUCE

Gnocchetti allo Zafferano con Noci

SERVES 4 TO 6

For the gnocchi

1 large egg

⅛ teaspoon powdered saffron

1 pound whole-milk ricotta

½ cup freshly grated
Parmigiano-Reggiano

2 teaspoons salt

1 to 1½ cups unbleached
all-purpose flour

For the sauce

½ cup walnuts

3 tablespoons unsalted butter

⅓ cup finely minced shallots

1 cup heavy cream

Salt to taste

1 tablespoon coarse salt

½ cup freshly grated
Parmigiano-Reggiano

*I*n and around Bologna ricotta is used not only as a table cheese but also in cooking. Ricotta gnocchi are lighter and more delicate than potato gnocchi, and so are the sauces that are paired with them. In this dish, saffron-ricotta gnocchi are tossed with a shallot-walnut cream sauce and dusted with Parmigiano-Reggiano cheese. I first had this terrific dish at Trattoria Battibecco in Bologna. Later, at Ristorante la Romantica in Ferrara, I enjoyed a version that used hazelnuts instead of walnuts.

TO prepare the gnocchi, lightly beat the egg in a large bowl and stir in the saffron. Add the ricotta, Parmigiano, salt, and 1 cup of the flour. Make the dough and roll out the gnocchi as instructed on page 187.

TO prepare the sauce, preheat the oven to 375°F.

PUT the walnuts on a lightly oiled baking sheet and toast in the oven until a light golden color, 3 to 4 minutes. Remove from the oven and place in a food processor fitted with the metal blade. Pulse until the walnuts are finely chopped. Transfer to a small bowl.

MELT the butter in a large skillet over medium-low heat. When the butter begins to foam, add the shallots and cook, stirring occasionally, until lightly golden and very soft, 5 to 7 minutes. Add the walnuts and stir a few times, then add the cream. Season with salt and simmer, stirring occasionally, until the sauce has a medium-thick consistency, 3 to 4 minutes.

MEANWHILE, bring a large pot of water to a boil over high heat. Add the coarse salt and gnocchi and cook until the gnocchi rise to the surface, 1 to 2 minutes. After 20 to 30 seconds, scoop out and reserve about ½ cup of the cooking water. With a large slotted spoon, remove the gnocchi, draining the excess water back into the pot, and place the gnocchi in the skillet with the sauce. Mix briefly over low heat until the gnocchi and sauce are combined. Stir in some of the gnocchi cooking water if the sauce seems dry. Taste, adjust the seasoning, and serve with the Parmigiano.

BREAD GNOCCHI WITH BEAN AND MUSHROOM SAUCE

Pisarei con Sugo di Porcini e Fagioli

SERVES 6

For the bread gnocchi

1¼ cups unbleached all-purpose flour

1 cup semolina flour

1 cup fine dried bread crumbs (see box, page 203)

1 teaspoon salt

For the sauce

½ cup dried red kidney beans, picked over, soaked overnight in cold water to cover, drained, and rinsed, or 1 cup canned beans, rinsed and drained

1 ounce dried porcini mushrooms, soaked in 2 cups of lukewarm water for 20 minutes

2 tablespoons double-concentrated Italian tomato paste

2 tablespoons unsalted butter

2 tablespoons extra virgin olive oil

⅓ cup finely minced yellow onion

1 small garlic clove, finely minced

5 to 6 sage leaves, finely minced

Pisarei, small flour-and-bread gnocchi, are the unique specialty of the northern part of the Emilia-Romagna region and, in particular, of the city of Piacenza and its countryside. Pisarei are sturdy, chewy little dumplings with none of the more delicate qualities that properly made potato gnocchi or ricotta gnocchi have.

Patrizia, the chef-owner of Ristorante la Fiaschetteria in the small town of Besenzone in the province of Piacenza, shared with me her tips for this gutsy dish:

"First, accept the fact that pisarei *are chewier and firmer than most gnocchi. That is what the dish is all about. Make the dough with the exact proportions listed in the recipe. After the dough has been kneaded for a few minutes, it should feel pliable, yielding, and just a bit sticky, and, when pressed with a finger, it should leave a small 'dimple.' If too firm, it probably means that too much flour or bread crumbs have been used. Wrap the dough in plastic wrap and let it rest for thirty minutes or so. The dough will then relax a bit and it will be easier to roll it out."*

I did exactly as she instructed. The dumplings were easy to roll out and, when tossed with a traditional bean, tomato, and mushroom sauce, the dish was rich and utterly satisfying. A most perfect dish for long, cold winter nights.

To prepare the gnocchi, combine 1 cup of the all-purpose flour, the semolina, bread crumbs, and salt in a large bowl and mix thoroughly. Make a well in the center, add ¾ cup very warm water, and, with your hands or a fork, start to mix in the flour mixture. Add ¾ cup more warm water and mix with your hands until the flour is incorporated and the mixture sticks together easily and forms a dough.

LIGHTLY flour a work surface and place the dough on it. Lightly flour your hands and knead the dough until it is soft, pliable, and just a bit

1 to 2 tablespoons chopped
flat-leaf parsley

Salt and freshly ground black
pepper to taste

1 tablespoon coarse salt

½ cup freshly grated
Parmigiano-Reggiano cheese

sticky, 5 to 6 minutes. If the dough sticks too much to the work surface, knead in just a bit of the remaining flour. Wrap the dough in plastic wrap and let it rest for 20 to 30 minutes at room temperature.

CUT off a piece of dough about the size of an orange and keep the larger piece wrapped in plastic wrap. Flour your hands lightly (do not flour the work surface, or the dough will not slide smoothly). Using both hands, roll out the piece of dough with a light back-and-forth motion into a long rope about the thickness of your little finger. Cut the roll into ½-inch pieces. Press your index finger into each small piece of dough while pulling it toward you on the board. The indentation made by your finger in the dough will shape it into a little shell. (This indentation will also help the gnocchi absorb the sauce.) Repeat with the remaining dough.

LINE a tray with a clean kitchen towel and flour the towel lightly. Place the gnocchi on the towel, leaving enough space between them so they won't stick together. Let stand at room temperature, uncovered, for an hour or two. (The gnocchi can also be refrigerated, uncovered, for a few hours; however, their texture will become a bit firmer.)

TO prepare the sauce, if you are using dried beans, place them in a saucepan, cover them abundantly with cold water, and cook over low heat until tender, 40 to 50 minutes. Reserve 1 cup of the cooking water, and drain the beans. Set aside until needed.

DRAIN the porcini mushrooms, reserving the soaking water. Rinse the mushrooms well under cold running water and roughly chop them. Line a strainer with paper towels and strain the soaking water into a bowl. Stir the tomato paste into the porcini water and set aside.

HEAT the butter and oil together in a medium saucepan over medium heat. When the butter begins to foam, add the onion and cook, stirring, until lightly golden, 5 to 6 minutes. Add the garlic, sage, parsley, and porcini and stir for a minute or two. Add the diluted tomato paste and the reserved bean cooking water (or 1 cup tap water if using canned beans) and season with salt and pepper. Reduce the heat to medium-low and simmer, uncovered, stirring from time to time, for 15 to 20 minutes.

ADD the beans and simmer for a few minutes longer, until the sauce has a nice thick consistency. Taste and adjust the seasoning. (Makes about

2 to 2½ cups.) (The sauce can be prepared several hours ahead. Reheat gently before using.)

BRING a large pot of water to a boil over high heat. Add the coarse salt and gnocchi and cook until the gnocchi rise to the surface, 10 to 12 minutes. (These gnocchi take considerably longer to cook than regular gnocchi.) Remove the gnocchi with a slotted spoon or a skimmer, draining the excess water back into the pot, and place in a large heated bowl.

ADD about half of the sauce and a small handful of the Parmigiano. Stir until the gnocchi and sauce are well combined. Add more sauce if needed, and serve with the remaining Parmigiano.

DRIED BREAD CRUMBS

In Emilia-Romagna, bread crumbs are a vital ingredient in many dishes. They are essential both to *pisarei* and to *passatelli,* the bread crumb–Parmigiano soup of Romagna. They are used to give consistency and crispness to meat loaves and meatballs, and they coat cutlets and vegetable fritters.

Two- to three-day-old good, crusty Italian bread makes excellent bread crumbs. (Do not buy the little packages sold in supermarkets, which often have the consistency of sawdust and extraneous flavorings.) Make sure your bread is very dry. Cut it into pieces and grind it into fine crumbs in a food processor. Use as needed. (I freeze mine in several plastic bags.)

Polenta

Polenta is comfort food. Cornmeal, water, salt, and elbow grease are all that is needed to make it, at least if you want to make it with the traditional stirring technique. Many non-Italian cooks seem to associate polenta with cornmeal mush. But for most Italians, especially from regions such as Veneto, Friuli–Venezia Giulia, and Lombardy, who grew up on it, polenta is a wonderful, versatile, body-warming food that sustains life.

Polenta was quite important in the diet of the people of Emilia-Romagna, especially before, during, and immediately following the Second World War, when the country suffered terrible hardships. In most northern Italian kitchens, polenta was traditionally made in a large copper kettle called *paiolo*. My mother would put the big *paiolo* on our large wood-burning stove and, as the water began to simmer, take handfuls of coarse, golden cornmeal and let it stream from her fingers into the simmering water. As the cornmeal cooked, it absorbed the water, gradually becoming firmer and harder to stir. Somehow, though, my mother never seemed to notice that, for she kept stirring the mixture tirelessly, reaching all the way to the bottom of the *paiolo* with a long wooden paddle, until the cornmeal was transformed into a rich, thick golden mass. In affluent times, she cooked the polenta using a mixture of water and milk, then, when it was done, stirred in butter and a handful or two of Parmigiano, making the polenta soft and creamy and impossible to resist. She spooned the polenta directly onto our plates, or poured it onto our large wooden board and shaped into a steaming golden mound. Then she let it settle and cool a bit before cutting it into slices with a long piece of string and piling it on our plates.

It is hard to believe, considering the popularity of polenta, that corn is not an Italian ingredient. In fact, corn was a gift of the New World to the old—and, in Italy, it was transformed into polenta. This down-to-earth food has become indispensable to the cuisine of northern Italy.

Polenta can be used in myriad ways. It can be served as an appetizer, a first course, an entrée, a side dish, and even a dessert. In most cases, it is filling enough to take the place of bread or pasta. Creamy, soft polenta served straight out of the pot is mesmerizing next to fish stews and braised meats. But it is also impossible to resist when it is fried to a golden crisp, or baked, or grilled.

After a few decades of neglect, polenta is back in fashion. Countryside trattorie serve it in the traditional manner, perhaps with Rabbit Hunter-Style (page 255) or with Salt Cod with Shallots and Tomatoes (page 229). Elegant restaurants serve it in small portions, generally as an appetizer or side dish. I love Fried Polenta with Pancetta, Sage, and Vinegar (page 54).

It is wonderful to know that the trattorie and restaurants of Emilia-Romagna worth their salt still make polenta by hand, because, as one cook said to me, "The fragrance and consistency of polenta stirred by hand is unsurpassed." It is also nice to know that it is possible to make very acceptable polenta by using the modern, nonstirring method given here, which produces a smooth, delicious polenta.

Cooking Tips for Hand-Stirred Polenta

The cornmeal: Polenta can be made with coarse or fine cornmeal or, as is the case in these recipes, with a mixture of the two, which produces a lovely medium-textured polenta.

The pot: Since the *paiolo*, the large unlined copper kettle typically used for polenta making, is not easily available in this country, use a large, heavy pot or a heavy copper-bottomed stainless-steel pot. Since, during cooking, some of the polenta will stick to the bottom of the pot, fill the empty pot right away with cold water and leave it overnight. This will make cleaning it much easier.

The heat: Polenta should be cooked over gentle, medium-low heat. If polenta is cooked over high heat, it will bubble up and spit back at you with a vengeance. It will also stick heavily to the bottom of the pot. Medium-low heat will allow you to stir the polenta more easily.

The stirring: Stirring polenta is very important; otherwise, you will find yourself with burned cornmeal. However, this does not mean you have to stay glued to the pot stirring without stop for the entire cooking time. Yes, it is okay to detach yourself briefly from the pot. But keep it short.

The consistency: The consistency of the polenta is determined by the ratio of dry to liquid ingredients and by the cooking time. If you love softer polenta, increase the liquid in these recipes by about 1 cup. If you prefer thicker, sturdier polenta, add ½ cup more cornmeal. Do not skimp on the cooking time; using the traditional stirring method, it will take 40 minutes to make perfectly cooked polenta.

POLENTA: THE TRADITIONAL METHOD

SERVES 8 TO 10

2 cups coarse cornmeal

1 cup fine cornmeal

1 tablespoon coarse salt

2 tablespoons unsalted butter, optional

½ cup freshly grated Parmigiano-Reggiano, optional

BRING 9 cups water to a boil in a large heavy pot over medium heat. Combine both cornmeals in a bowl and place it near the pot. As soon as the water begins to simmer, add the salt, then start pouring in the cornmeal by the handful in a slow, thin stream, stirring constantly with a long wooden spoon or a wire whisk to prevent lumps. When all the cornmeal has been incorporated, reduce the heat a bit and cook the polenta at a steady simmer, stirring constantly with the wooden spoon, reaching all the way to the bottom and the sides of the pot. As it cooks, the polenta will thicken considerably and will bubble and spit back at you. Reduce the heat slightly as necessary to avoid being splattered. Continue to cook and stir the polenta for about 40 minutes; it is done when it comes away effortlessly from the side of the pot.

IF using the butter and Parmigiano, add them to the polenta and stir until well incorporated and the polenta is smooth and creamy. Use as directed in the individual recipes.

POLENTA: THE ALMOST NO STIR METHOD Add the cornmeal to the water as instructed above. As soon as all the cornmeal has been incorporated, pour the mixture into a large stainless steel bowl and put the bowl over a double boiler or a large pot containing 3 to 4 inches of simmering water. Make sure that the bowl does not touch the water. Cover the bowl completely with a sheet of aluminum foil, making sure that no steam can escape, and cook at a steady simmer for about 1½ hours. Stir the polenta every 30 minutes or so, reaching all the way to the bottom of the bowl and covering the bowl again with foil. Make sure there is always enough simmering water in the pot. If the polenta becomes too thick and you have a tough time stirring it, add a bit of hot water, broth, or milk. The polenta is done when it is thick and smooth and comes away effortlessly from the side of the bowl.

IF using the butter and Parmigiano, add them to the polenta and stir until well incorporated. Use as instructed in the individual recipes.

HOW TO SERVE POLENTA

For soft polenta: As soon as the polenta is done, spoon it into serving dishes. (If the polenta is too firm, stir in some hot water, milk, or broth to achieve the consistency you prefer.)

For soft polenta prepared ahead: Transfer the cooked polenta to a large stainless-steel bowl, place the bowl over a double boiler or a large pot containing 3 to 4 inches of slowly simmering water—make sure that the bowl does not touch the water—and cover the bowl tightly with a sheet of aluminum foil. The polenta will stay soft for 2 to 3 hours. Stir occasionally and check the water occasionally.

For firm warm polenta: Pour the cooked soft polenta onto a large board and shape it with a large wet spatula into a mound, or spread it evenly with a wet spatula to a ½-inch thickness. Let the polenta cool until it is firm enough to cut into slices, about 15 minutes. Slice the polenta while it is warm and serve.

For grilled, baked, or fried polenta: Turn the cooked polenta onto a large baking sheet and spread it evenly with a wet spatula to a ½-inch thickness. Let cool to room temperature. Refrigerate, uncovered, for several hours, or overnight.

Turn the polenta over onto a cutting board and cut it into rectangles or squares. Bake, fry, or grill the polenta as instructed in the individual recipes.

IMPROVISING A MEAL
FOR MY ITALIAN FAMILY

My brother, my sister, and all the other members of my Italian family know I have written six cookbooks. And when they came to visit me a few years ago, they all dined at my restaurant in Sacramento and loved the food. Yet, somehow, they were not fully convinced of my "culinary abilities." So, one day, during my last visit to Bologna, I told them I was going to cook a meal for them. When I saw their perplexed looks, I decided I would dazzle them. I sent my brother to the store to buy a large boneless pork roast. I seasoned the roast with the traditional local mixture of garlic, rosemary, and sage and put it in the oven (see Pork Roast with Sweet-and-Sour Onions, page 288). Then I kicked everyone out of the kitchen, rolled up my sleeves, and whipped up a large batch of Saffron-Ricotta Gnocchi. I made the sauce for the gnocchi, cooked onions for the roast, and browned the pancetta, then I strolled into the dining room as cocky and confident as one who has just won an important culinary award.

Luckily for me, everything turned out great. My family gave me a standing ovation, and now they expect me to cook a meal or two each time I am in Bologna. Maybe I should have left them to wonder whether I could really cook or not.

SEAFOOD

Pesce e Frutti di Mare

By the time I was a young teenager, I knew how to make perfect tagliatelle, even though cooking was not high on my list of priorities. So I was not completely lost in the kitchen– except when it came to fish. Perhaps the reason was that I was born and raised in Bologna, the landlocked capital of Emilia-Romagna. The Emilia side–home of Bologna, Modena, Parma, and Piacenza–is inland, while the Romagna side has miles of breathtakingly beautiful seacoast. At that time, geography often defined what we ate, so, before refrigeration and superhighways, the consumption of fresh fish in Emilia was somewhat limited. In my family, fish was generally eaten on Friday, the "lean" day of the week, and it didn't necessarily come from the Adriatic. My brother, Gianni, an avid fisherman, who made weekly fishing expeditions to the nearby Po River, would return home with more freshwater fish than we could possibly use. However, in the summertime, when my family spent a few weeks in a little *pensione* on the Adriatic coast, eating fish once or even twice a day was routine, since it was fresh, plentiful, and inexpensive.

Whether we ate in the *pensione,* or in any of the humble *trattorie* facing the sea, the fish was always simply prepared. I can still recall the taste of the local sole, with its firm, compact texture and sweet taste, which had been grilled and drizzled only with olive oil and lemon juice. And the small, peppery Adriatic clams, served in their aromatic juices, with just a hint of garlic, parsley, oil, and chile pepper. And the golden, crunchy, yet tender fried calamari that came piled up on a plate. This was, and still is, Romagna's coastal home cooking. It is also the food of the many *trattorie* and restaurants of the seacoast. This food is so firmly etched in my memory that I still can taste it, and can reproduce it without the aid of recipes. For you, I have written down recipes for Sautéed Breaded Monkfish, Clams with Garlic and Chile Pepper, and Pan-Roasted Fish with Pancetta and Potatoes.

Now that Italy has superhighways, supertrains, and cargo planes, and fish can be safely and quickly transported from one part of the country to another, the popularity of fresh fish has increased tremendously, particularly inland. (When in Bologna, visit the many fish stores in the city's medieval open market, then go to Rodrigo Restaurant for the best *grigliata di pesce misto*, mixed grill of fresh fish, this side of the Adriatic.)

In spite of this increased popularity, many seafood preparations are still strongly anchored to traditional themes. Dried cod, *baccalà*, a favorite with the older generation, can be found in the *trattorie* of the countryside, fried in the manner of Bologna and sprinkled with lemon and parsley, or stewed in an aromatic tomato sauce, as it is prepared in Modena, or simmered with onions, raisins, butter, and tomato paste, as it is done in Parma. This dish is almost always served with polenta.

Catfish used to be plentiful in the streams and rivers of the region, but today most of this rich-tasting fish is farm-raised. Then there is eel, the elongated freshwater or saltwater fish that is the pride of the Valle di Comacchio, an area of lagoons and gloomy landscape near the city of Ferrara. In Comacchio and Ferrara, eel, or its larger cousin, *capitone*, is typically served as a part of Christmas dinner. In Ferrara and the surrounding areas, eel is roasted, fried, or stewed, and it is often added to a risotto with great results. Don't let the look of eel prevent you from trying it; its firm texture and mild taste are sure to win you over.

Most of the dishes in this chapter are straightforward and simple to prepare, and rely on the freshness of the fish and on the Italian way of treating and flavoring them, as well as the desire of the cook to do it right.

SUMMERTIME ON THE ROMAGNA SEACOAST

The large, white sandy beaches of the Romagna seacoast are, in the summer months, filled to capacity with throngs of vacationers. Each person stakes out his or her territory, lays down a towel, and takes his or her rightful spot in the sun or under a colorful umbrella. Tanned bodies are everywhere. Children make sand castles or splash in the water, while parents keep a vigilant eye on them. Older people stroll along the water's edge. Teenagers strut around in skimpy bathing suits like glorious peacocks, basking in the admiration and envy that their perfect shapes elicit. The many little cafés that line the edges of the beaches dish out *gelati*, sodas, juices, espresso, cappuccino, and loud music, as well as tempting *panini* and *piadina*, the local thin, flat griddled bread, stuffed with cheeses, prosciutto, *salame*, or marinated vegetables. These snacks keep the vacationers satisfied until lunch. Then, as lunchtime approaches, a slow exodus begins. People gather their sandy beach towels and retrace their steps back to their hotel or to a trattoria that faces the sea for their well-deserved and much-anticipated meal.

This is the time for seafood. Seafood on pasta, in risotto, on crostini, in salads, simply grilled, poached, steamed, fried, or in seafood stews. The delicious aroma of grilled fish is everywhere. After lunch, most vacationers, with the exception perhaps of teenagers, who are forever restless, retreat to the privacy of their rooms for the *pisolino*, the Italian nap, which restores one's strength and aids digestion.

The sunny afternoons, spent in a variety of leisurely activities, lead inevitably to dinner. Afterward, the ritual of the *passeggiata* begins. Smartly, although casually, clad people, sporting their tans as a badge of honor, stroll along the fashionable streets eating colorful *gelati*. This is the time to meet friends and relax at outdoor cafés with an espresso or a digestivo and catch up on the local gossip. For the very young, this is the time to go to a *discoteca*.

The great movie director Federico Fellini, who was born and raised on the Romagna seacoast, depicted this joyous, carefree summer lifestyle in one of his best movies, *I Vitelloni*, more than forty years ago. Have things changed at all during these forty years? Not much. Today the beaches of Romagna appear more crowded than ever with vacationers who seem to be determined to soak up every ray of sun, eat every strand of spaghetti left on the plate, dance until the wee hours of the morning, and enjoy their vacations on the seacoast before returning to the routine of their lives in the city.

FISH SOUP

Brodetto Romagnolo

SERVES 4 TO 6

1/3 cup extra virgin olive oil

1/3 cup chopped yellow onion

1 garlic clove, finely minced

2 tablespoons chopped
flat-leaf parsley

2 anchovy fillets, minced,
optional

1/2 cup dry white wine

1/4 cup red wine vinegar

2 cups canned Italian plum
tomatoes, with their juice,
put through a food mill to
remove the seeds

Salt to taste

Freshly ground black pepper
to taste or a small pinch of red
pepper flakes

1 pound whole squid, cleaned
as instructed on page 232, or
1/2 pound cleaned squid, bodies
cut into 1/2-inch-thick rings

1 pound assorted firm-fleshed
fish fillets, such as halibut,
turbot, sturgeon, and/or cod,
cut into 2- to 3-inch pieces

1/2 pound medium shrimp

1/2 pound sea scallops

1 pound clams, cleaned as
instructed on page 162

1 pound mussels, cleaned and
debearded (see box)

Slices of Italian bread, grilled
or toasted

*P*erhaps the most famous dish of Romagna's Adriatic coast is brodetto, *a thick seafood soup that, like so many other regional dishes, has innumerable permutations. Some feel that* brodetto *should be made with a large variety of locally caught fresh fish and shellfish. For them, the more varied the fish, the better and more interesting the dish. Others cherish the virtue of a simple shellfish-only* brodetto, *even though originally this humble fisherman's dish did not include shellfish at all.*

In each one of the small coastal cities, each village and each household claims to make the best, most authentic brodetto. *As you move around the region, the soup changes its identity and becomes* brodetto di Cesenatico, di Rimini, di Riccione, *and so on. Then the permutations of each one of these soups is multiplied further as they are prepared by the individual restaurants and trattorie, whose chefs compete for the honor of preparing the very best* brodetto *of the seacoast.*

A brodetto *generally begins with a* soffritto, *the savory base of oil, onion, garlic, parsley, wine, and vinegar. Often fresh tomatoes, tomato paste, or canned tomatoes are added to this base, which is generally seasoned with a bit of hot chile pepper. Then comes the seafood, which is added beginning with those that need the longest cooking time, such as octopus and calamari. Fish and shellfish follow in their respective order and, as everything simmers and the sauce thickens, the intense aroma of the* brodetto *signals that the soup has achieved its balance of flavors.*

A more elaborate brodetto *can be made with the addition of a fish broth made with fish bones and heads and a few basic vegetables. The broth is simmered for about an hour, the bones and vegetables are removed, and the head meat is pureed with the remaining liquid.*

When I make a brodetto, *I use a large deep heavy pot so that the fish has ample space to cook, a pot I can take straight to the table. Few things taste as good as a slice of crusty Italian bread dipped into this rich seafood soup.*

HEAT the olive oil in a heavy pot over medium heat. Add the onion and cook, stirring, until lightly golden and soft, 5 to 6 minutes. Add the garlic, parsley, and the anchovies, if using. As soon as the garlic begins to color, less than 1 minute, add the wine and vinegar and cook briskly, stirring from time to time, until the liquid is reduced by approximately half. Add the tomatoes and season with salt and pepper. As soon as the sauce begins to bubble, add the squid, cover the pan, and reduce the heat to low. Cook at the gentlest of simmers, stirring occasionally, until the squid is very tender, about 40 minutes. Add a bit more of the sauce made by the tomatoes or water if the sauce has reduced too much. (The dish can be made up to this point a few hours ahead. Bring back to a gentle simmer before proceeding.)

ADD the thicker pieces of fish to the pan, cover, and simmer for 2 to 3 minutes. Add the remaining fish, the shrimp, and the scallops and simmer for 2 to 3 minutes. Lastly, stir the clams and mussels gently into the sauce, cover the pan, and simmer until they have opened. Discard any clams or mussels that will not open. Let the soup sit for a few minutes before serving.

TASTE the soup, adjust the seasoning, and ladle into warm deep bowls. Serve with slices of grilled, crusty Italian bread.

HOW TO CLEAN MUSSELS

Soak the mussels in a large bowl of cold salted water for 30 minutes. (The salt will help draw out the sand from the mussels.) Scrub the mussels well, with a hard brush if possible, under cold running water to remove all dirt. Remove each mussel's beard by pulling it off. Discard any mussels that are open. Place the mussels in a large bowl, cover with a wet towel, and refrigerate until ready to use. If your shellfish is quite fresh (ask your fishmonger when you buy them), they can be kept in the refrigerator for a couple of days.

SAUTÉED HALIBUT WITH OLIVES, CAPERS, AND TOMATOES

Rombo alle Olive, Capperi, e Pomodoro

SERVES 4

5 tomatoes (1½ pounds), peeled and seeded

⅓ cup extra virgin olive oil

1 cup all-purpose flour

4 halibut steaks or sea bass fillets (7 to 8 ounces each), about ¾ inch thick

Salt to taste

1 cup dry white wine

4 small green olives, pitted and minced

1½ teaspoons capers, drained and minced

1 small garlic clove, minced

1 teaspoon thyme leaves or 1 tablespoon chopped flat-leaf parsley

At Saporetti Trattoria, on the outskirts of Ravenna, I was served a delicious preparation of whole branzino, *striped bass, in a flavorful sauce of wine, fresh tomatoes, capers, and olives. The small amount of capers and olives, which were finely minced, gave the sauce only a bare hint of their presence, allowing the fresh flavor of the fish to shine through.*

What would I serve after this appetizing dish? Nothing more than refreshing, palate-cleansing arugula salad.

MINCE the tomatoes and place in a bowl, with all their juices, until ready to use.

PREHEAT the oven to 200°F.

HEAT the oil in a large skillet over medium heat. Spread the flour on a sheet of aluminum foil. Season the fish with salt, dredge it lightly in the flour on both sides, and add to the skillet. Cook until golden on both sides but still a bit translucent on the inside, 6 to 7 minutes. Using a large metal spatula, carefully transfer the fish to heatproof serving plates. Place the plates in the oven while you prepare the sauce.

PUT the skillet back over high heat, add the wine, and stir until it is reduced by approximately half. Add the olives, capers, garlic, tomatoes, and thyme and season lightly with salt. (Remember, the capers and olives are already salty.) Cook, stirring, until the tomatoes juices have thickened, 4 to 5 minutes. Taste and adjust the seasoning. Spoon the sauce over the fish and serve immediately.

BAKED HALIBUT WITH POTATOES

Rombo e Patate al Forno

SERVES 4

3 medium boiling potatoes (about 1½ pounds)

Salt and freshly ground black pepper to taste

⅓ cup extra virgin olive oil, plus extra for brushing

2 garlic cloves, sliced

1 medium onion, thinly sliced

½ pound cherry tomatoes, any stems removed

4 halibut steaks (7 to 8 ounces each), about ¾ inch thick

What a beautiful dish this is, beautiful because it roasts potatoes with fresh cherry tomatoes and onion and, when the potatoes are golden and tender and the tomatoes are beginning to split and release their sweet juices, they are topped with fish steaks and cooked until the fish is meltingly tender. The result is a dish that draws all the flavors together in a simple, quick, yet most appetizing preparation. This dish is an adaptation of one I had a few years ago at Ristorante lo Squero in Rimini.

PEEL the potatoes and slice them ¼ inch thick. Soak the potatoes in cold water for about 30 minutes, then drain and dry them thoroughly with a kitchen towel.

PREHEAT the oven to 400°F.

PLACE the potatoes in a large baking pan that can later accommodate the fish comfortably. Season the potatoes with salt and pepper and toss with the oil. Put the pan on the middle rack of the oven and bake until the potatoes are lightly golden and about half-cooked, 12 to 15 minutes.

SPRINKLE the garlic, onion, and cherry tomatoes over the potatoes and season lightly with salt. Cook until the skins of the tomatoes begin to split, 8 to 10 minutes.

BRUSH the fish steaks with a bit of oil and season with salt. Place the fish steaks, without overlapping them, over the vegetables and bake until the fish is chalky white on the outside but still a bit translucent on the inside, about 10 minutes. (The cooking time for fish is generally 10 to 12 minutes per inch of thickness.)

REMOVE the pan from the oven and let stand for a minute or two before serving. Place the steaks on individual warm plates and serve with the vegetables.

POACHED SEA BASS WITH GREEN SAUCE

Branzino Lesso con la Salsa Verde

SERVES 4

1 recipe Light Vegetable Broth (recipe follows)

4 sea bass steaks (7 to 8 ounces each), about ¾ inch thick

Salt to taste

1 to 2 tablespoons extra virgin olive oil

1 recipe Piquant Green Sauce with Shallots (page 25)

The comment I hear most from people who have visited Italy for the first time is "I can't believe how thin Italians are, especially the women. How can they do it, when they are surrounded by all that good food?" The answers, of course, are many, but knowing my countrymen and countrywomen, I can tell you that most of the time (barring special occasions), they are selective about what they eat. Seafood, grilled, roasted, boiled, poached, or steamed, is a favorite, because it can be prepared with a minimal amount of fat or no fat whatsoever. I love poached fish, cooked briefly in water that has simmered with a mixture of onion, carrot, celery, parsley, and lemon juice, or vinegar, for it allows the fish to retain its own clear identity.

PUT the broth in a large skillet that can accommodate the fish in a single layer, or in a fish poacher and bring to a gentle boil over medium heat. Add the fish and, as soon as the broth comes back to a boil, reduce the heat a bit and simmer the fish for about 5 minutes. Turn off the heat and let the fish sit in the hot broth for 4 to 6 minutes longer, until its flesh is chalky white and the inside is no longer translucent.

WITH a large metal spatula, transfer the fish to individual serving plates. Pat the fish dry with paper towels. Season with salt and drizzle with olive oil. Serve warm or at room temperature, accompanied by the green sauce.

LIGHT VEGETABLE BROTH

Brodo Vegetale

MAKES 7 TO 8 CUPS

1 small onion, quartered

2 medium carrots,
cut into pieces

2 celery stalks, cut into pieces

Sprig or two of flat-leaf parsley

Juice of 1 lemon

Pinch of salt

PUT 2 quarts water, the vegetables, parsley, lemon juice, and salt in a medium pot, place over medium heat, and bring to a boil. Reduce the heat to low and simmer, uncovered, for 30 to 40 minutes. Strain the broth into a large bowl.

IF you are not planning to use the broth right away, let it cool to room temperature, then refrigerate for up to a few days or freeze for several months.

HOW TO PEEL AND SEED TOMATOES

Cut an X in the bottom of each tomato and drop them into a pot of boiling salted water. Boil until the skins begin to split, about 1 minute. Transfer to a bowl of ice water. As soon as you can handle them, peel off the skin. Place the tomatoes on a cutting board and cut them crosswise in half. Squeeze out the seeds or pull them out with your fingers.

SEAFOOD "MEATBALLS"

Polpette di Pesce

SERVES 4 AS AN
ENTRÉE, 6 AS AN
APPETIZER

3 large eggs

2 cups plus 2 to 3 tablespoons
fine dried bread crumbs

2 to 3 tablespoons freshly
grated Parmigiano-Reggiano

⅓ cup chopped
flat-leaf parsley

1 small garlic clove,
finely minced

3 tablespoons extra virgin
olive oil

1 pound firm-fleshed fish
fillets, such as sturgeon,
monkfish, or halibut

Salt and freshly ground black
pepper to taste

Olive oil for frying

Lemon wedges

*P*olpette *(meatballs), made with meat, seafood, or vegetables, have been a staple of* la buona cucina casalinga, *good home cooking, from the time when necessity turned leftover ingredients into savory morsels. Today now that Italy has become quite affluent, these savory dishes are almost forgotten. However, in Rimini, at Quattro Colonne, an unpretentious restaurant on the pier that serves very good food, I had a plate of golden, crisp seafood* polpette *that brought back happy memories of my childhood.*

BEAT 1 of the eggs in a medium bowl. Add 2 tablespoons of the bread crumbs, the Parmigiano, parsley, garlic, and oil and mix well.

CHOP the fish very fine, preferably by hand, or in a food processor. If using a food processor, pulse the machine until the fish is chopped to a granular consistency; do not puree. Add the fish to the bowl, season with salt and pepper, and mix with a rubber spatula until thoroughly blended. The mixture should be soft and a bit moist, but not wet. Mix in an additional 1 tablespoon bread crumbs, if needed. (The mixture can be prepared several hours ahead. Refrigerate tightly covered with plastic wrap.)

LINE a baking sheet with parchment or wax paper. Spread the remaining 2 cups bread crumbs on a sheet of aluminum foil. Lightly beat the remaining 2 eggs in a shallow bowl. Divide the fish mixture into 12 equal parts and shape each one into a ball. Dip the balls in the eggs and roll each one in the bread crumbs, flatten it lightly with the palms of your hands, and place on the baking sheet. Refrigerate the *polpette*, uncovered, for about 1 hour.

HEAT 1 inch of oil in a medium heavy skillet over medium-high heat. When the oil is quite hot, lower a few *polpette* at a time into the oil with a slotted spoon and cook until one side has a light golden crust, 1 to 2 minutes. Turn them gently and cook the other side until golden brown.

Remove with a slotted spoon and place on towels to drain. Serve hot, with lemon wedges.

SEAFOOD POLPETTINE By shaping the seafood mixture into very small balls, you will have delicious, crunchy *polpettine* to serve before a meal. Shape heaping teaspoons of the mixture into small balls and dip them into the eggs and roll in the bread crumbs. Fry until golden on all sides. Insert a wooden tooth pick into each ball, place on a large platter, and let your guests help themselves.

MIXED GRILL OF FISH

Grigliata di Pesce Misto

SERVES 4

For the marinade

2 to 3 tablespoons chopped flat-leaf parsley

2 garlic cloves, thinly sliced

⅓ cup extra virgin olive oil

¼ cup fresh lemon juice

Salt and freshly ground black pepper to taste

2 pounds mixed sea bass, swordfish, and/or halibut fillets or steaks, cut into 3-ounce pieces

Salt and freshly ground black pepper to taste

About ¾ cup plain dried bread crumbs

Lemon wedges

*O*n the Romagna seacoast, whole fish or fish steaks are marinated in a mixture of chopped parsley, garlic, olive oil, and lemon juice, then sprinkled with dried bread crumbs and grilled until the coating is golden brown and slightly charred, but the inside is still moist and juicy. If you should find yourself in one of the lovely resort towns—Rimini, Riccione, Cattolica, Cesenatico, or Milano Marittima—during the summer, make sure to eat at a trattoria or restaurant that faces the sea and serves a grigliata di pesce misto. *If you can't get there, make this at home.*

To prepare the marinade, combine the parsley, garlic, oil, and lemon juice in a medium bowl and season with salt and pepper.

PLACE the fish in a large shallow dish. Pour the marinade over the fish, turning to coat each piece well. Cover with plastic wrap and marinate at room temperature for 1 hour, turning and basting the fish with the marinade a few times.

PREHEAT a gas grill or prepare a charcoal fire.

REMOVE the fish from the marinade, season both sides with salt and pepper, and sprinkle on both sides with the bread crumbs to cover evenly. Place on the hot grill and cook until the fish has a nice golden brown color, about 3 to 4 minutes. Turn and cook on the other side, until golden brown and no longer translucent on the inside, 2 to 3 minutes longer. Serve at once, with lemon wedges.

BROILING INSTEAD OF GRILLING Preheat the broiler. Remove the fish from the marinade, sprinkle on one side with bread crumbs, and place under the hot broiler, breaded side up. Broil until the fish is golden brown, about 3 minutes. Turn the fish, sprinkle with more bread crumbs, and broil until the coating is golden brown and the inside is no longer translucent, about 2 minutes.

SAUTÉED BREADED MONKFISH

Rana Pescatrice Impanata

SERVES 4

1 garlic clove, finely minced

¼ to ⅓ cup chopped
flat-leaf parsley

½ cup plain dried bread
crumbs

½ to ⅔ cup extra virgin
olive oil

2 pounds monkfish or other
firm-fleshed fish, fillets,
cut into 2-inch pieces

Salt and freshly ground black
pepper to taste

Lemon wedges

On the Romagna seacoast, shellfish is often coated and marinated in an aromatic mix of parsley, garlic, bread crumbs, and olive oil, then skewered and grilled. I use the same mixture to coat and marinate morsels of monkfish, then brown them quickly in oil and finish cooking them in the oven. The fish has a crisp, golden exterior and is moist and tender on the inside. Complement the dish with a light, refreshing arugula salad.

COMBINE the garlic, parsley, bread crumbs, and ¼ cup of the oil in a bowl. Stir until well blended. The mixture should be somewhat loose; if it is too dry, add a bit more oil. Add the monkfish, season with salt and pepper, and toss to coat the pieces thoroughly. Cover the bowl with plastic wrap and let marinate for 20 to 30 minutes at room temperature.

PREHEAT the oven to 400°F.

IN a large ovenproof skillet that can accommodate the fish in a single layer, heat ⅓ cup oil over high heat. When the oil is hot, add the fish and cook until a light golden crust forms on the bottom, about 2 minutes. Turn the pieces over and brown on the other side, 1 to 2 minutes longer. (As you put the fish in the hot skillet, some of the coating may fall off and burn; don't worry, it will be discarded.) Cook in batches if necessary, then return all the fish to the pan.

TRANSFER the skillet to the middle rack of the oven and cook until the fish is cooked all the way through, 3 to 5 minutes.

REMOVE from the oven and sprinkle the fish lightly with salt. Arrange on warm serving plates and serve with lemon wedges.

GRILLED SKEWERED MONKFISH Marinate the fish as instructed above and preheat the grill or broiler. Thread the fish pieces onto metal or wooden skewers, pressing on the bread crumb mixture so it adheres to the fish. Grill or broil the fish until a golden crust forms on the first side, 3 to 4 minutes. Turn and cook on the other side, 2 to 3 minutes longer. Serve hot, with lemon wedges.

PAN-ROASTED FISH WITH
PANCETTA AND POTATOES

Pesce in Padella con Pancetta e Patate

SERVES 4

3 medium boiling potatoes (about 1½ pounds)

½ cup extra virgin olive oil

2 to 3 ounces thickly sliced pancetta, diced

1 garlic clove, finely minced

6 to 7 sage leaves, shredded, or 1 teaspoon finely crumbled dried sage

Salt to taste

Four 6-ounce pieces sole or turbot fillet

*W*hen my husband and I approached Lido-Lido, considered the best and most elegant restaurant in Cesenatico, we could not find the door. And when we did find it, we couldn't open it. So we knocked and knocked, and finally a waiter, with his nose stuck up in the air, appeared and let us in. Our reservation was for eight o'clock, and since we had arrived two to three minutes early, they did not answer right away. A not-too-propitious sign, we thought. We were seated in the still-empty dining room and promptly ordered a nice, expensive bottle of wine, which pleased our waiter immensely. Within half an hour the tables began to fill, and by nine-thirty the place was hopping. The food was terrific, the decor was gorgeous, and the waiter became our best buddy. This is one of the dishes we had.

PEEL the potatoes and slice them ¼ inch thick. Place in a saucepan of boiling salted water and cook over medium heat until tender but still a bit firm to the bite, 5 to 6 minutes. Drain gently and pat dry with paper towels.

HEAT 3 to 4 tablespoons of the oil in a large skillet over medium heat. Add the pancetta and cook, stirring, until a nice golden color, 1 to 2 minutes. Add the garlic and sage, stir once or twice, and add the potatoes. Season with salt and stir for about 1 minute, then turn off the heat. (The dish can be prepared up to this point a few hours ahead.)

HEAT the remaining 4 to 5 tablespoons oil in a large nonstick skillet over medium heat. When the oil is just beginning to smoke, season the fish lightly on both sides with salt, add to the skillet, and cook until the bottom is golden brown, 2 to 3 minutes. Turn the fish and cook until golden brown on the other side, about 2 minutes.

WHILE the fish is cooking, put the skillet with the potatoes back over medium heat and stir gently until heated through.

ARRANGE the potatoes on warm plates, top with the fish, and serve hot.

SALT-CRUSTED ROASTED STRIPED BASS

Branzino al Sale

SERVES 4

2 striped bass (about 2 pounds each), cleaned and scaled

3 to 3½ cups coarse salt

Freshly ground black pepper to taste

Extra virgin olive oil

Fresh lemon juice

1 tablespoon chopped flat-leaf parsley

alt-crusted roasted fish is now very popular in Emilia-Romagna, where it comes to the table in all its majestic glory. The thick layer of salt that encases the fish not only allows it to be cooked without any fat, it also produces tender, succulent, delicate meat.

Don't be intimidated by the fact that this whole fish needs to be skinned and boned after cooking, because the process is much easier than it appears.

PREHEAT the oven to 400°F.

RINSE the sea bass thoroughly inside and out under cold running water. Pat dry with paper towels.

PLACE the salt in a small bowl and drizzle with 1 to 2 tablespoons water. Spread a thin layer of the salt over a large baking sheet. Place the fish on the salt, leaving some space between them. Cover the tops and sides of the fish with the remaining salt, pressing it lightly so it adheres.

SET the baking sheet on the middle rack of the oven and bake for 30 minutes. The salt should have a light golden color and be as firm as a slab of concrete. Remove from the oven and let the fish cool for 5 to 6 minutes.

WITH a large metal spatula, scrape off the crusted salt from around and underneath the fish, to detach it from the pan. Using two metal spatulas, transfer the fish to a work surface. Cut off the heads and tails.

WITH a sharp boning or other thin knife, make a long incision along the backbone of each fish, cutting through the skin. Pull off the skin and the salt attached to it. (Because the fish is still warm, the skin will come off quite easily.) Brush off any salt that may have fallen onto the meat. Remove the top fillet and place on a large serving plate. Remove and discard the large central bone, being careful not to pull away any flesh with it. Turn the fish over, pull off the skin, and place the remaining fillets on the serving dish.

SEASON the fillets with pepper, drizzle with olive oil and lemon juice, and sprinkle with the parsley. Serve warm or at room temperature.

FILLET OF SOLE WITH WHITE WINE

Filetti di Sogliole al Vino Bianco

SERVES 4

⅓ cup olive oil

4 sole fillets
(7 to 8 ounces each)

Salt to taste

1 cup all-purpose flour

1 cup dry white wine

¼ cup fresh lemon juice

1 tablespoon unsalted butter

1 tablespoon chopped
flat-leaf parsley

A delicious way of cooking sole on the Adriatic coast is to sauté it quickly in olive oil until it is golden and crisp and to serve it simply with a few drops of lemon juice. At La Lampara Ristorante in Cattolica, a small resort town about ten miles from Rimini, the sole was topped with a few tablespoons of wine-enriched pan juices. The beautiful thing about this elegant dish is that it can be put together in a matter of minutes.

Since American sole doesn't have the firm, compact consistency of Adriatic sole, and the thinner part of the sole at the tail end breaks easily during cooking, at my restaurant in Sacramento, we fold the tail under the sole, then flour it and cook it briskly in hot oil.

PREHEAT the oven to 200°F.

HEAT the oil in a large skillet over medium-high heat. Season the sole on both sides with salt, fold the thin tail section under itself, and dust lightly with flour, shaking off the excess. When the oil is nice and hot, add the sole, folded part up, without crowding, and cook, turning once, until the fish is golden brown on both sides and opaque all the way through, 6 to 8 minutes. Transfer the fish to individual heatproof plates using a large metal spatula and keep warm in the oven while you finish the sauce.

RAISE the heat under the skillet to high. Add the wine, lemon juice, and butter and cook, stirring, until the sauce has a medium-thick consistency. Stir in the parsley, taste, and adjust the seasoning. Spoon the sauce over the fish and serve at once.

TUNA BAKED IN PARCHMENT

Tonno al Cartoccio

SERVES 4

3 leeks, white part only, thinly sliced

¼ cup extra virgin olive oil, plus extra for brushing

½ pound cherry tomatoes

Salt to taste

4 tuna steaks (about 8 ounces each), about ¾ inch thick

Freshly ground black pepper to taste

everal years ago, my brother, Gianni, and his wife, Emma, decided it was time to lose some weight. And so, wisely, they began eating smaller portions and they turned to seafood instead of meat for their major protein source and to fresh vegetables. When they reached the goal they had set for themselves, they had adapted so well to their new style of eating that they decided to stay with it. My brother, who, for years, could not even boil water, began to fiddle in the kitchen and became hooked on the rewards that preparing a meal gave him. This is one of his dishes; it is a great dish for a lazy Sunday. Prepare the bundles a few hours ahead and refrigerate, then go to a movie or play a few sets of tennis. Bring the bundles back to room temperature before putting them in the very hot oven.

PREHEAT the oven to 500°F.

WASH the leeks well under cold running water. Place on a clean kitchen towel and dry thoroughly.

HEAT about half of the oil in a small skillet over medium heat. Add the leeks and cook, stirring, until lightly golden and soft, 6 to 7 minutes. Transfer the leeks to a small plate until ready to use.

CUT the cherry tomatoes in half and place in a bowl. Season lightly with salt, and drizzle with the remaining oil.

PLACE four 12 × 16-inch sheets of parchment paper or aluminum foil on a work surface and brush lightly with oil. Put a tuna steak in the center of one half of each sheet. Season the fish with salt and pepper and top with the leeks and cherry tomatoes. Fold the other half of each sheet over the fish and tightly fold the edges together to seal making a 1-inch border. Place the bundles on two large baking sheets. Bake for about 8 minutes, or until the bundles have puffed up.

PUT the bundles on individual serving plates and let your guests unwrap or cut the bundles open with a knife or scissors (be careful of the hot steam that will pour out).

Baccalà

Baccalà and *stoccafisso*. These names identify a single fish, cod (*merluzzo*). They also identify the fact that this fish, which reached Italy from the icy waters of Norway, has for centuries been preserved throughout Europe, either by salting it or by drying it in the sun. Salt-preserved cod is called *baccalà*, sun-dried cod is called *stoccafisso*. In Italy, *baccalà* and *stoccafisso* are often used interchangeably. Apparently preserved cod became known to Italians in 1431 when Piero Querini, a Venetian sea captain who was shipwrecked on the island of Rost, in the Norwegian archipelago, encountered preserved fish for the first time. A few centuries later, dried cod was a staple in many Italian homes.

There was a time when *baccalà* and *stoccafisso* were considered poor man's food because they were abundant and inexpensive. (That is no longer the case.) My mother, following the church dogma of not eating meat on Friday, would routinely prepare *baccalà* on that day, as she favored it over the fresh but expensive fish from the nearby Adriatic.

Baccalà shows up in many cooking preparations and it is still very popular in some regions, especially in the Veneto, where it has become a gastronomic icon.

Baccalà is perfect trattoria food, and many country *trattorie* still carry on the tradition of preparing *baccalà* on Friday. The person who cooks this dish is often the mother or the grandmother, who relies primarily on the taste memory of a food she grew up eating. Both in these trattorie and in homes that still carry on this tradition, soft, flaky *baccalà* is generally served with polenta–soft polenta for *baccalà* cooked in a sauce, fried, roasted, or grilled polenta for sautéed, roasted, or fried *baccalà*.

The two recipes that follow, from the Emilia side of the region, both use *baccalà*, which in this country is easier to find than *stoccafisso*. Pan-Roasted Salt Cod with Fried Polenta was a favorite of my mother. Salt Cod with Shallots and Tomatoes is typical of the city of Modena. Keep in mind that this basic comfort food is best enjoyed in winter.

BUYING, SELECTING, AND SOAKING BACCALÀ

- *Baccalà* can be found in Italian markets and specialty food stores.

- When selecting *baccalà*, look for a piece that is meaty and has a minimum amount of bones or, if you can find them, buy *baccalà* fillets, which are boneless. The flesh should have a nice creamy color, with no yellow or dark parts.

- Soak *baccalà* for at least 2 days to soften it and to remove the salt. Place it in a large bowl, cover it with cold water, cover, and refrigerate, changing the water 3 to 4 times a day.

PAN-ROASTED SALT COD

WITH FRIED POLENTA

Baccalà alla Bolognese con la Polenta Fritta

SERVES 4

½ recipe Polenta (page 206), chilled until firm as instructed on page 207

1½ pounds salt cod, soaked as instructed on page 227

⅓ to ½ cup extra virgin olive oil

1 cup all-purpose flour

1 tablespoon unsalted butter

1 garlic clove, finely minced

1 to 2 tablespoons chopped flat-leaf parsley

1 cup dry white wine

Salt and freshly ground black pepper to taste

Olive oil for frying

½ cup fresh lemon juice

TURN the cold firm polenta out onto a cutting board and cut it into squares or rectangles the size of playing cards. Set aside.

DRAIN the softened cod, pat thoroughly dry with paper towels, and cut into 2- to 3-inch pieces. Remove any bones.

HEAT the oil in a large nonstick skillet over medium-high heat. Dust the cod pieces lightly with flour, on both sides, place in the pan without crowding (if necessary, cook the fish in two batches), and sauté, turning once, until lightly golden on both sides, about 5 minutes. Transfer the fish to a plate.

DISCARD about half of the oil in the pan if necessary and put the skillet back over medium-high heat. Add the butter, garlic, and about half of the parsley and stir quickly once or twice. Add the wine and stir, scraping the bottom of the pan to pick up the browned bits attached to it. When the wine is reduced by approximately half, reduce the heat to low, return the fish to the skillet, cover, and cook at the lowest of simmers, stirring from time to time and adding a bit of water if the fish sticks to the bottom of the pan, until the fish is cooked through, 30 to 40 minutes depending on the thickness. The fish is done when it begins to break into large flakes when stirred with a wooden spoon. Taste and adjust the seasoning.

WHILE the fish is cooking, heat about ½ inch of oil in a large nonstick skillet over medium-high heat. When the oil is nice and hot, carefully lower 3 to 4 pieces of polenta at a time into the hot oil and fry, turning once, until crisp and golden on both sides. Drain on paper towels.

PLACE 1 or 2 slices of fried polenta on each serving plate and place the fish on top. Put the fish pan over medium heat, add the remaining parsley and the lemon juice, and stir quickly. Pour the pan juices over the fish and serve at once.

SALT COD WITH SHALLOTS
AND TOMATOES

Baccalà in Umido

SERVES 4

1½ pounds salt cod, soaked as
directed on page 227

⅓ to ½ cup extra virgin
olive oil

1 large garlic clove,
lightly crushed

⅓ cup finely minced shallots

1 cup dry white wine

1½ cups Homemade Tomato
Sauce (page 22) or canned
Italian plum tomatoes, with
their juice, put through a food
mill to remove the seeds

Freshly ground black pepper
to taste

1 to 2 tablespoons chopped
flat-leaf parsley

DRAIN the softened cod, pat thoroughly dry with paper towels, and cut into 2- to 3-inch pieces. Remove any bones.

HEAT the oil in a large skillet over medium heat. Add the garlic and cook, stirring, until golden brown, then remove and discard it. Add the shallots and cook, stirring, until lightly golden and soft, about 5 minutes. Raise the heat to high and add the wine. When almost all the wine has evaporated, stir in the tomato sauce and season with pepper. As soon as the sauce has come to a boil, add the fish and reduce the heat to very low. Cover the pan and cook at the barest of simmers until the cod is cooked through and begins to break into large flakes when stirred with a wooden spoon, 35 to 40 minutes. Stir and check the consistency of the sauce several times during cooking, adding a bit of water if the sauce reduces too much.

STIR in the parsley, taste, and adjust the seasoning. Serve hot with soft, fried, or grilled polenta or with slices of crusty Italian bread.

BRAISED CATFISH WITH POLENTA

Pesce Gatto in Umido con Polenta

SERVES 4

esce gatto, catfish, was very popular in our house in Bologna, simply because my brother routinely returned from his fishing expeditions with lots of it. I remember once staring at this odd fish, which sported whiskers as long as the ones our cat had, and saying to myself, "I am not going to eat this." But then my mother cleaned it, cooked it in a traditional savory sauce of vegetables, herbs, and tomato, and served it next to golden, soft polenta. And, as usual, I found myself wiping the plate clean.

Today most of the catfish in this country is farm-raised. This preparation is popular on the Emilia side of the region, with each cook putting his or her personal spin on it.

⅓ cup extra virgin olive oil

4 catfish fillets
(6 to 7 ounces each)

Salt to taste

⅓ cup finely minced
yellow onion

¼ cup finely minced celery

¼ cup finely minced carrots

1 tablespoon finely chopped
rosemary

1 small garlic clove,
finely minced

¼ cup red wine vinegar

2 tablespoons double-
concentrated Italian
tomato paste, diluted in
1 cup cold water

Freshly ground black pepper
to taste

1 tablespoon chopped
flat-leaf parsley

½ recipe Polenta (page 206),
kept warm as instructed on
page 207

HEAT the oil in a large skillet over medium-high heat. Season the fish lightly with salt. When the oil is nice and hot, add the fish, without crowding (if necessary, sauté the fish in two batches), and cook, turning once, until lightly golden on both sides, about 4 minutes. With a large metal spatula, transfer the fish to a large plate.

ADD the vegetables to the skillet and cook, stirring, over medium heat until lightly golden and soft, 5 to 6 minutes. Add the rosemary and garlic and stir a few times, then add the vinegar. As soon as almost all of the vinegar has evaporated, 30 to 40 seconds, add the diluted tomato paste. Bring to a gentle boil, season lightly with salt and pepper, and simmer, uncovered, for 4 to 5 minutes.

RETURN the fish to the skillet (at this point, it doesn't matter if the pieces are close together), partially cover the pan, and cook until the fish is opaque all the way through, 6 to 7 minutes.

WITH the metal spatula, transfer the fish to individual warm serving plates. Raise the heat under the skillet and add the parsley. Stir for about a minute, until the sauce has a medium-thick consistency. Taste and adjust the seasoning. Spoon the sauce over the fish and spoon a generous helping of soft polenta next to each fillet.

ROASTED, MARINATED, AND SKEWERED EEL

Spiedini di Anguilla Arrosto

SERVES 4 TO 6

One 2-pound, cleaned eel (head and tail removed)

1 cup extra virgin olive oil

¼ cup red wine vinegar

¼ cup fresh lemon juice

15 to 20 small sage leaves

Salt and freshly ground black pepper to taste

3 ounces thickly sliced pancetta, cut into 2-inch pieces

In the Comacchio and Ferrara area, there is a whole cuisine based on eel. This unusual fish, which has a mild, almost sweet taste and firm flesh, lends itself perfectly to being grilled, roasted, fried, or stewed. In Emilia-Romagna, eel is almost never skinned before cooking it; instead, it is cleaned by rubbing wood ashes over the skin, making it less sticky. If at all possible, try to select a rounder, thicker eel instead of a thinner one, for it will have a larger proportion of flesh to bone. After roasting, the skin can be removed quite easily.

Eel is not common in American fish markets, but many places will order it for you. Look for it in Asian markets, where it will probably be available frozen—when buying it, make sure it does not contain spices of any kind, and use it as soon as it has been defrosted. Most of the eel available here comes already cleaned, with the head and tail removed.

CUT the eel into 2-inch pieces and wash well under cold running water. Dry thoroughly with paper towels.

IN a medium bowl, combine the oil, vinegar, lemon juice, and sage leaves. Season with salt and several grinds of pepper. Stir the eel pieces into the marinade and leave at room temperature for an hour or two.

PREHEAT the oven to 450°F.

THREAD the eel pieces onto metal or wooden skewers, alternating them with the sage leaves and pancetta. Season lightly with salt and pepper and place on a large baking sheet. Brush the fish with some of its marinade and place on the middle rack of the oven. Roast until the eel is golden brown and opaque all the way through, 6 to 8 minutes.

SERVE hot, with soft polenta in winter, or with Fried Zucchini with Vinegar (page 315) in the warmer months.

Calamari

Calamari is the Italian word for squid. This funny-looking cephalopod is very popular in the cooking of Romagna, especially in the many *trattorie* that line the Romagna seacoast. There, small, tender calamari are deep-fried to a crisp succulence. They are also boiled and tossed into salads. They are grilled, braised, stewed–alone or with other seafood–and turned into the glorious fish soups of the region. Calamari can also be stuffed, as in the two recipes that follow and, when properly cooked, can deliver a bundle of flavor.

Calamari come in many sizes. For stuffed squid, I suggest larger calamari, because they will hold the filling more comfortably and be easier to work with. For the seafood salad on page 237, I suggest the smallest calamari available, for they will be more tender.

The secret of tender calamari lies in proper cooking. Cooking calamari properly is really quite simple, once it is understood that to stay tender they need to be cooked either very briefly over high heat or at length over very low heat. Calamari that are fried, boiled, or grilled over high heat will take no longer than a minute or two to be perfect. On the other hand, calamari slowly cooked in a sauce will be at their most tender after 40 to 50 minutes. Anything in between will produce squid that is tough and rubbery.

CLEANING SQUID

Put the squid in a bowl of cold water and soak for about 1 hour; drain. Hold each squid body with one hand and, with the other, pull away the tentacles. Cut the tentacles straight across just above the eyes; discard the head. Squeeze out the small beak at the base of the tentacles. Remove the long cartilage from the squid body. Rinse the body under cold running water, pulling out any matter that remains inside. Still under cold running water, peel away the skin from the body and tentacles (it is OK if some skin remains on the tentacles). Drain and pat dry with paper towels. The squid body can now be cut into ½-inch-wide rings or left whole as a container for stuffing.

Many fish markets now sell squid that is already cleaned. If you prefer, go ahead and buy it cleaned. In that case, rinse it well under cold running water, making sure the bodies are thoroughly cleaned.

BRAISED STUFFED SQUID
WITH TOMATO SAUCE

Calamari Ripieni

SERVES 4

2 pounds whole squid,
with bodies about 6 inches
long, cleaned as directed on
page 252, or 1 pound cleaned
squid, with tentacles

2 tablespoons chopped
flat-leaf parsley

1 garlic clove, finely minced

2 anchovy fillets, rinsed
if packed in salt, finely
chopped

1 tablespoon capers, drained
and finely chopped

⅓ cup freshly grated
Parmigiano-Reggiano

⅓ cup fine dried bread
crumbs

Small pinch of red pepper
flakes, optional

¼ cup extra virgin olive oil,
plus more if needed

Salt to taste

For the sauce

¼ to ⅓ cup extra virgin
olive oil

⅓ cup finely minced
yellow onion

1 tablespoon finely chopped
flat-leaf parsley

1 garlic clove, finely minced

Salt to taste

This is one of the many ways in which the people of Romagna stuff and cook squid. While the stuffing and sauce may take on the stamp of the cook, the method of cooking them, over the gentlest of heat for a prolonged time, is always the same. The result yields squid so tender it can be cut with a fork. This is a great dish to serve next to a few slices of fried or grilled polenta. And, if you have any leftover sauce, use it later over penne or spaghettini.

SET the squid bodies aside. Chop the tentacles very fine by hand or in a food processor and place in a medium bowl. Add the parsley, garlic, anchovies, capers, Parmigiano, bread crumbs, and red pepper, then stir in the oil and season with salt. Mix until thoroughly blended and the mixture has a nice, moist consistency. If too dry, stir in a little more oil.

PLACE the filling in a small pastry bag fitted with a medium round tip and fill each squid body just a little more than half full. (During cooking, the filling will expand, and the bodies will burst if they are filled to capacity.) Close the openings of the bodies with wooden toothpicks.

TO prepare the sauce, in a large skillet that can accommodate the squid in a single layer, heat the oil over medium heat. When the oil is hot, add the onions and cook, stirring, until lightly golden and soft, 5 to 6 minutes. Add the parsley and garlic and stir once or twice, then add the squid. Season lightly with salt. Cook for a minute or two, until the bottom of the squid is chalky white. Turn gently and cook on the other side for a minute or two.

ADD the wine and bring to a boil. Stir gently for about 1 minute, moving the squid around, then add 1 cup of the tomatoes. As soon as the sauce begins to bubble, reduce the heat to very low and cover the pan. Simmer, carefully stirring and turning the squid once or twice, until they are

½ cup dry white wine

1 to 1½ cups canned Italian plum tomatoes, with their juice, put through a food mill to remove the seeds

tender and the sauce has a medium-thick consistency, about 50 minutes. Add the remaining tomatoes if the sauce reduces too much.

REMOVE the toothpicks and place the squid on warm serving plates. Spoon the sauce over and serve hot.

Preparing Ahead: While the dish can be prepared a few hours ahead and reheated gently just before serving, it is really at its most tender best immediately after it has been prepared. However, you can stuff the squid several hours ahead, then, an hour or so before you want to sit down for dinner, simmer it in the sauce until tender.

BRAISED STUFFED SQUID WITH WHITE WINE Omit the sauce ingredients. Stuff the squid as instructed above. In a large skillet that can accommodate the squid in a single layer, sauté ⅓ cup minced shallots in ¼ cup olive oil until soft. Add the squid, season with salt, and cook, turning once, until the squid is chalky white on all sides, 2 to 3 minutes. Add the wine and bring to a fast boil. Cover the pan, reduce the heat to very low, and simmer, stirring occasionally, until the squid is tender and the wine is reduced by about half, 45 to 50 minutes. (If the wine should reduce too much during cooking, add a bit more.) Remove the squid from the pan, remove the toothpicks, and place the squid on a platter. Add some chopped parsley and the juice of ½ lemon to the pan and heat over high heat until the sauce thickens. Pour over the squid and serve immediately.

GRILLED SKEWERS OF
CALAMARI AND SHRIMP

Spiedini di Frutti di Mare

SERVES 4

1 pound whole squid, cleaned as instructed on page 232, or ¾ pound cleaned squid

1½ pounds medium shrimp, peeled and deveined

1 garlic clove, very finely chopped

⅓ cup extra virgin olive oil

¼ cup chopped flat-leaf parsley

⅓ cup fine dried bread crumbs

Salt and freshly ground black pepper to taste

Lemon wedges

This is one of the first dishes I taught when I began my cooking career, because it is simple to prepare and absolutely delicious. This preparation, from Quattro Colonne Trattoria in Rimini, briefly marinates shellfish in flavorful olive oil with bread crumbs, parsley, and garlic before grilling. When the bread begins to char a bit, forming a golden, crisp coating, the cooking is done.

Follow these delicious spiedini *with a salad of ripe tomatoes, basil, and olive oil.*

CUT the squid bodies into 1½-inch-wide rings. Reserve the tentacles for another use. Wash the shrimp under cold running water and pat dry with paper towels.

IN a medium bowl, mix the garlic with the oil, parsley, and bread crumbs. Season with salt and pepper. Add the squid and shrimp and toss to coat well. Cover the bowl and marinate at room temperature for 30 to 40 minutes.

PREHEAT a grill or the broiler. Thread the squid onto 4 metal or wooden skewers, pressing the bread crumb mixture back onto the squid if necessary. Thread the shrimp onto separate skewers, pressing the coating onto the shrimp if necessary. (Because the squid cooks faster than the shrimp, the two need to be skewered separately.)

PLACE the shrimp skewers on the hot grill or on a baking sheet under the broiler and cook until a golden crust forms on one side, about 2 minutes. Turn them over and cook until the other side is golden and crisp, 1 to 2 minutes longer. When you turn the shrimp, place the squid skewers next to them. As soon as one side turns golden, about 1 minute, turn them over to brown the other side. (Do not cook the squid for more than 1 to 2 minutes total, or they will become tough and rubbery.) Serve at once, with lemon wedges.

CLAMS WITH GARLIC AND CHILE PEPPER

Vongole in Padella con Aglio e Peperoncino

SERVES 4

4 pounds littleneck clams or cockles (the smallest you can get), cleaned as instructed on page 162

⅓ to ½ cup extra virgin olive oil

1 garlic clove, finely minced

3 tablespoons chopped flat-leaf parsley

Red pepper flakes to taste

8 slices Italian bread, grilled

Because the small clams of the Adriatic are very flavorful, very little is needed when cooking them. A little oil, a little garlic, and a little pepper is enough to complement the clam's briny juices. Of the many clam varieties found in North America, only a few are appropriate for this preparation, namely, littleneck clams and cockles. The taste of these small clams, even though different from that of their European relatives, will come through loud and clear when cooked in the manner of the Adriatic.

HEAT the oil in a large heavy skillet or casserole over medium heat. Add the garlic, half of the parsley, and the red pepper and stir a few times. As soon as the garlic begins to color, add the clams, stir once or twice, cover the pan, and raise the heat to high. Cook, shaking the pan from time to time, until the clams open. (Some may take a bit longer to open than others; however, if, after several minutes of cooking, any are still firmly shut, discard them.)

WHEN all the clams have opened, add the remaining parsley and shake the pan to distribute it evenly. Ladle the clams and their juices into deep bowls and serve with the grilled bread.

CLAMS WITH TOMATOES, GARLIC, AND CHILE PEPPER
Heat the oil and sauté the garlic, half of the parsley, and the red pepper as instructed above. As soon as the garlic begins to color, add 2 cups canned Italian plum tomatoes with their juices that have been put through a food mill to remove the seeds. Season lightly with salt and cook, uncovered, for 5 to 7 minutes. Add the clams, cover, and cook as instructed above. Just before serving, add the remaining parsley.

SEAFOOD SALAD WITH ARUGULA

Insalata di Frutti di Mare con la Rucola

SERVES 4 AS AN ENTRÉE,
6 AS AN APPETIZER

1 recipe Light Vegetable Broth
(page 217)

¾ pound medium or small
shrimp, shelled, deveined,
and rinsed

½ pound bay scallops,
thoroughly rinsed

1 pound whole squid
(the smallest you can find),
cleaned as directed on
page 232, or ½ pound cleaned
squid with tentacles

1 pound mussels, cleaned and
debearded as instructed on
page 213

1 pound littleneck clams or
cockles (the smallest you can
get), cleaned as instructed on
page 162

½ cup dry white wine or water

1 garlic clove, halved

¼ to ⅓ cup extra virgin
olive oil

Salt and freshly ground black
pepper to taste

3 to 4 tablespoons fresh
lemon juice

1 to 2 ounces arugula
(about 1 small bunch), stems
removed, washed, patted dry,
and coarsely minced

I have never passed up a seafood salad when dining in a seaside restaurant or trattoria. The freshness of the seafood is, of course, of the utmost importance, and so is a light hand when dressing it.

This delightful dish comes from Ristorante Europa in Rimini, where it was served barely lukewarm. The addition of arugula is just enough to give the salad a bit of tartness and color. While the poaching of the fish can be done several hours or a day ahead, the salad is at its best when the freshness of the fish has not been muted by refrigeration.

PUT the vegetable broth in a large saucepan and bring to a fast boil over medium-high heat. Drop in the shrimp and cook for only 30 to 40 seconds. Add the scallops and cook for 30 to 40 seconds, then add the squid and turn off the heat. Let the shellfish sit in the hot broth until the insides are no longer translucent, about 2 minutes. Drain and immediately place the shellfish in a large bowl of ice water to stop the cooking. When cool, drain again and pat dry with paper towels.

CUT the shrimp and scallops into 1-inch pieces. Cut the squid bodies into ½-inch-wide rings, and the tentacles lengthwise in half. Set aside.

MEANWHILE, put the mussels and clams in a large saucepan with the wine, cover the pan, and place over high heat. Cook, shaking the pan from time to time, until the mussels and clams open. Remove them with a slotted spoon to a large bowl as they open. (Some might take a bit longer to open than others; however, if, after 3 to 4 minutes of cooking, any are still firmly shut, discard them.) Remove the meat from the shells and set aside. (Reserve the juices for another preparation if you wish.)

RUB the inside of a salad bowl with the garlic; discard the garlic. Add the mussels, clams, squid, scallops, and shrimp to the bowl. Add 1 tablespoon or so of the oil and toss well to coat (the oil will keep the shellfish moist). Cover the bowl with plastic wrap and chill in the refrigerator for about 30 minutes.

SEASON the seafood with salt and several grinds of pepper and toss with the remaining oil and the lemon juice. Let stand at room temperature for 20 to 30 minutes.

ADD the arugula to the shellfish and toss again. Taste, adjust the seasoning, and serve.

TRICKS OF THE TRADE

Professional cooks would not, and could not, start a dish from scratch at the very last moment. Preparation is the key factor that allows them to cook simple or elaborate dishes to order. Years ago, when I was teaching cooking classes all over the country, my students commented on the ease with which I was cooking and talking to them at the same time. The trick, of course, is the one that everybody in food knows. Do your preparation ahead! Scrub, wash, measure, chop, dice, slice, poach, and shred beforehand, so that at the last minute your dish will come together simply and effortlessly.

POULTRY AND MEAT
Pollame e Carne

While most people in Italy and many others abroad know about the delights of Emilia-Romagna's first courses, such as lasagne alla Bolognese, tortellini in broth, and tagliatelle with meat ragú, not many are aquainted with the equally delectable second courses. The region's *secondi* run a wide gamut and are just as appealing, tempting, and varied as its glorious pasta dishes. They too reflect centuries of the region's history, with the lingering essence of peasant and aristocratic kitchens, which, throughout the years, have blended into the undiluted, comforting deep flavors of *la buona cucina casalinga,* good home cooking.

Until several decades ago, meat in Italy was very expensive, especially beef and veal, and was indeed a luxury for most families. Today, though, while Italians are considerably more affluent and could well afford a thick steak daily, they still opt for humbler types of meats. Rabbit, poultry, and pork are favorites in Emilia-Romagna. These animals, which are still part of the landscape of the region's countryside, are turned into succulent, golden roasts or into long-simmered *cacciatora* preparations. Any good country trattoria or restaurant raises its own small animals or buys them from local farmers. The free-range chickens, fed a corn-rich diet, produce eggs with intense orange yolks, which in turn give home-made pasta its rich, golden color.

When I sat down to decide what types of dishes I wanted for this book and which best represented the second courses of the region, my immediate impulse was to focus on comfort food. I wanted the deep-fried *polpette* (meatballs) my mother made and the pan-roasted sausage. I wanted the traditional *bollito misto* and cotechino sausage, still served steaming hot straight from the steam trolley in a handful of restaurants in Bologna and Modena. I wanted short ribs with potatoes, and a whole golden roasted veal shank just like the one I had many years ago at Trattoria lo Sterlino. I wanted the dense veal stew my Aunt Rina used to make, so I could dip my bread into the sauce and soak up every bit of it. And, yes, I definitely wanted the elegant, deliciously rich *cotoletta alla Bolognese* with white truffles, roasted rabbit with the balsamic vinegar of Modena, and the great mixed grill I had so many times in Romagna. I wanted the flavorful food I knew, not tampered with, unfussy, uncomplicated, and as warmhearted as the people of my region.

And so I set out to follow any lead that would take me to this kind of food. I ordered it in restaurants, *trattorie*, and *hosterie* every chance I had. I ate it in the homes of family and friends, reminiscing with them for hours about the proper way of doing this or that dish, and I ate and ate until my gustatory senses hit overload with the exuberant flavors of *la buona cucina casalinga*. Perhaps I have not discovered anything new (wasn't really trying to), but the fact that I was able to find restaurant and home cooks who still prepare and relish this type of food is perhaps a discovery in itself.

I have, however, left out several delicious dishes because of the lengthy preparations involved, and others because they required hard-to-find ingredients or ingredients made with variety meats that would probably make the average American cook faint. Instead, and hopefully wisely, I have concentrated on dishes whose ingredients are easily available, and which employ simple, straightforward techniques.

Keep in mind as you go through this chapter and, for that matter, through the other chapters in this book, that the regional table has its own distinctive vernacular, its own personal style and language, which is best and most authentically expressed by using the appropriate regional ingredients. It is a simple philosophy that keeps traditional food traditional.

THE KEEPERS OF THE FLAME

I have warm memories of summertime weekend excursions to my Aunt Rina's farm just outside of Bologna. My sister, brother, and I took the bus and got off at the last stop. Then we walked for a couple of miles until we reached Zia Rina's farm, a small, modest farmhouse surrounded by trees that stood all by itself on the flat, fertile land of Emilia. Zia Rina, the oldest of my mother's sisters and the only one who had not elected to leave the farm for the city, was a short, very thin, energetic woman with brusque manners but a large, tender heart. She greeted us with big hugs, then put us immediately to work, feeding the chickens, cleaning the animal barn, or sweeping in front of the farmhouse. We did chores and we played. We climbed trees and ran after the ducks, chickens, and any other animals that came our way. Then, finally, after the sun began to fade and the soft, warm evening changed our moods from boisterous to mellow, we sat down to eat. The food that Zia Rina prepared was made with humble, everyday ingredients. She took whatever was growing on the farm and transformed it into lusty dishes with intense flavors. We soaked pieces of homemade bread in her stew, sopping up every little bit of mouthwatering sauce. We sipped a bit of wine mixed with water, which made us feel very special and very grown-up. On Sunday night, when it was time for us to go back home, Zia Rina filled several bags with fresh eggs, a few freshly slaughtered chickens, some cheese and vegetables, and loaves of her bread to take back to our mother. Then, carrying our precious cargo, we retraced our steps to the bus stop and to the forty-five minute ride back to Bologna, where my mother was waiting for us. The next day, we would sit down in our small kitchen to a dinner that my mother had put together with the ingredients we had brought back from the farm. The setting was different, but the flavors were the same. Of course, my sister, brother, and I didn't realize then that my mother and my aunt were the true keepers of the flame, and that those simple meals would forever linger on our palates and enrich them with the tangible flavors of *la buona cucina casalinga* of Emilia-Romagna.

ROASTED GUINEA HENS AND POTATOES

Faraona Arrosto con Patate

SERVES 4 TO 6

2 guinea hens (2½ to 3 pounds each), quartered, rinsed, and patted dry

3 tablespoons Aglione (page 21)

⅔ cup extra virgin olive oil

2 pounds boiling potatoes

Salt and freshly ground black pepper to taste

*R*abbit, pheasant, or guinea hen rubbed with herbs and garlic and roasted with potatoes is a familiar, much-loved country dish of Emilia-Romagna. My mother, who was of peasant stock and who moved to Bologna with her family as a teenager, used to prepare rabbit, capon, or pheasant in this manner at Christmas. What I remember most were the potatoes that roasted alongside the meat or poultry–crisp on the outside, soft and yielding on the inside, and flavored with the cooking juices and fresh herbs. No other potato ever tasted so good. At Trattoria Vernizzi, located in the flat, fertile Emilia countryside between Parma and Piacenza, these types of dishes never go out of style. The last time I was there, Signor Vernizzi had prepared roasted rabbit and pheasant, which, of course, were served with his splendid roasted potatoes.

This is the type of straightforward dish that needs an assertive touch. Don't be timid with the seasoning. Coat the bird generously with the herb-garlic mixture and season the potatoes liberally with salt, pepper, and oil. Put the pan in a very hot oven and don't touch or fiddle with it until it is time to remove it. The color of the bird, the aroma, and the cooking time indicated in the recipe should be your only guidelines.

PLACE the guinea hens in a large bowl and coat them with the *aglione* and 2 to 3 tablespoons of the oil. Place the guinea hens on a shallow platter, cover, and refrigerate for a few hours to allow the meat to absorb the flavors of the herbs.

PREHEAT the oven to 400°F.

PEEL the potatoes, wash them in several changes of cold water, and pat them thoroughly dry. Place the potatoes in a large bowl, season them generously with salt and pepper, and drizzle with 2 or 3 tablespoons of the oil. Toss well to distribute the seasonings.

PUT the remaining oil in a large roasting pan. Add the guinea hens skin side up and snuggle the potatoes around the pieces. Place the pan on the middle rack of the oven and roast until the hens are golden brown and tender and the potatoes golden and crisp, 40 to 50 minutes. Serve hot with a tablespoon or so of the fragrant, herb-infused pan juices drizzled over each serving.

TWO BIRDS OF A FEATHER

Guinea hen and pheasant are closely related and either can be used in this preparation. These game birds, which today are farm raised and bred for the table, are best suited for roasting and braising. Chicken, although much less interesting in terms of flavor, can be substituted for guinea hen.

ROASTED CAPON

Cappone Arrosto

SERVES 6 TO 8

½ cup extra virgin olive oil

One 7- to 8-pound capon or a
very large plump chicken

2 large sprigs fresh rosemary,
stemmed and finely chopped,
or 1 to 2 tablespoons chopped
dried rosemary

2 garlic cloves, finely minced

Salt and freshly ground black
pepper to taste

Graziella, one of the many sisters of my sister-in-law Emma, lives in a small villa in the hills a few miles outside Bologna. She is a terrific cook and her meals, though simple, are always memorable. When I told her that I was writing a book on our region, she happily and promptly invited me to her house and prepared two absolutely terrific roasts, which she cooked simultaneously and served topped with their own pan juices. The large, plump roasted capon, with its delicate, perfectly cooked, moist white flesh, was my favorite. Serve the capon with any of the roasted potatoes in this book.

PREHEAT the oven to 375°F. Pour two-thirds of the oil into a large roasting pan that can accommodate the capon comfortably.

REMOVE the neck, liver, and gizzards tucked into the bird's cavity and save for another preparation. Wash the capon inside and out under cold running water and pat it thoroughly dry with paper towels.

COMBINE the rosemary, garlic, and the remaining oil in a small bowl and rub it over the capon skin and inside its cavity. Season generously with salt and pepper. Put the capon breast side down in the roasting pan and place on the middle rack of the oven. Roast for 30 to 40 minutes, basting every 20 minutes or so with the pan juices, then lower the oven temperature to 350°F. Carefully turn the capon over and roast, basting occasionally, until the bird has a nice golden brown color and an instant-read thermometer inserted in the thickest part of the thigh reads 170°F (approximately 18 to 20 minutes per pound).

TRANSFER the capon to a cutting board and let it rest for about 10 minutes. Skim off some of the fat from the pan juices. Carve the capon and serve it with some of the pan juices.

Note: Graziella's other roast is Roasted Stuffed Turkey Breast (page 253).

CHICKEN HUNTER-STYLE

Pollo alla Cacciatora

SERVES 4

⅓ cup extra virgin olive oil

2 large garlic cloves,
lightly crushed

1 large, plump chicken
(4 to 5 pounds), cut into
8 serving pieces, thoroughly
washed, and patted dry with
paper towels

Salt and freshly ground black
pepper to taste

½ cup finely minced
yellow onions

½ cup finely minced carrots

½ cup dry white wine

3 cups Homemade Tomato
Sauce (page 22) or canned
Italian plum tomatoes, with
their juice, put through a food
mill to remove the seeds

10 to 12 sage leaves,
finely shredded, or 2 to 3
tablespoons chopped
flat-leaf parsley

Maurizia, who is my nephew Marcello's fiancée, lives on a beautiful farm about twenty miles outside Bologna, near the town of Monteveglio. Maurizia's father, Costantino, who is now retired, is the perfect gentleman farmer. He makes wine from the grapes in the farm's small vignard, *and sausage and prosciutto from the farm's pigs. His wife, Albertina, not to be outdone, prepares splendid yet simple meals, and she bakes large loaves of crusty white bread a few times a week and* tigelle, *small, tile-baked rounds of crisp bread, whenever they have company.*

On a beautiful sunny fall day, my husband and I had dinner at the farm. The menu consisted of local salumi, *pickled vegetables, roasted peppers,* tigelle, *and* pollo alla cacciatora con polenta—*chicken hunter-style with fried polenta. The chicken, as Albertina said, was very simple to make and needed only a bit of attention: "Brown the chicken over high heat. Sauté the vegetables slowly and gently so they can bestow their sweet flavor on the chicken, and use good-quality wine." Maybe it was the pleasure of having dinner outdoors under a large tree, or the warmth and unpretentiousness of the people around me that made the food taste so good.*

HEAT the oil in a large skillet or casserole that can accommodate all the chicken pieces comfortably in a single layer over medium-high heat. Add the garlic cloves and brown them lightly, then discard them. Add the chicken pieces, skin side down, season with salt and pepper, and cook, turning once or twice, until golden on both sides, 10 to 12 minutes. Transfer the chicken to a plate.

REDUCE the heat to medium-low. Add the onions and carrots to the pan and cook, stirring with a wooden spoon, until lightly golden and soft, 6 to 7 minutes.

RETURN the chicken to the pan, raise the heat to high, and add the wine. When the wine is reduced by about half, add the tomato sauce and season lightly with salt. Reduce the heat to low, partially cover the pan, and simmer, stirring from time to time, until the chicken is tender and the sauce has a medium-thick consistency, 40 to 45 minutes. Stir and turn the chicken pieces from time to time, basting them with the sauce; add a little bit of water or broth if the sauce reduces too much during cooking.

A few minutes before serving, add the sage and taste and adjust the seasoning. Serve hot with crusty bread or with grilled, fried, or soft polenta.

THE UBIQUITOUS CACCIATORA

Cacciatora, which means hunter-style, is a dish of chicken, rabbit, lamb, or pheasant that is cooked slowly in a savory sauce. Apparently, this preparation came about when the owner of a simple country trattoria had to improvise a hearty dish to feed a group of hunters who had a considerable appetite. In Italy, there are many versions of *cacciatora*, with every cook claiming only his or hers is authentic.

A *cacciatora* is always and never the same. Ingredients that are always present are onion, wine, and tomatoes, but the dish may also contain pancetta, prosciutto, mushrooms, herbs, garlic, celery, and/or carrots. Soft, creamy polenta or fried crisp polenta slices are the best accompaniment to any *cacciatora* preparation, since it will soak up the dense, rustic sauce beautifully.

PAN-ROASTED CHICKEN WITH

POTATOES AND ROSEMARY

Pollo in Padella con Patate e Rosmarino

SERVES 4

2 tablespoons chopped fresh rosemary or 1 tablespoon chopped dried rosemary

1 garlic clove, finely minced

⅓ cup extra virgin olive oil

1 large, plump chicken (4 to 5 pounds), cut into 8 serving pieces, thoroughly washed, and patted dry with paper towels

Salt and freshly ground black pepper to taste

1 to 1½ cups dry white wine

3 large boiling potatoes (about 1½ pounds), peeled and cut into 1-inch pieces

*Y*ears ago, when ovens were virtually nonexistent in Italian households, most of the cooking was done on the stovetop. I learned how to cook by watching my mother fry, sauté, braise, and pan-roast chickens and other fowl. I soon could identify what she was cooking simply by the odor that emanated from the pot on top of the stove. I could taste the sauces. I could see the changes that occurred as the ingredients in the pot went from their raw state to finished dish. And I learned to love it.

This method of cooking, pan-roasting, is still very popular in Italian households and in country trattorie, because it produces moist, succulent meats. This chicken, which we first tasted at Antica Trattoria Ardegna in the Parma countryside, came to the table gloriously golden and moist, loaded with the flavors of fresh rosemary and garlic. So simple, so appetizing, and so reassuring.

MIX together the rosemary, garlic, and 2 tablespoons of the oil in a large bowl. Add the chicken, season with salt and pepper, and mix well with your hands, making sure to coat each piece of chicken with the savory mixture. Cover the bowl with plastic wrap and refrigerate for a few hours.

HEAT the remaining oil in a large, heavy casserole or deep skillet that can accommodate all the chicken pieces comfortably in a single layer over medium-high heat. When the oil is nice and hot, add the chicken pieces, skin side down, and cook, turning once or twice, until golden on both sides, about 10 minutes. Add 1 cup of the wine and cook, stirring to loosen the browned particles on the bottom of the pot. When the wine is reduced by about half, reduce the heat to medium-low, partially cover the pot, and cook, stirring and turning the chicken from time to time, for about 15 minutes.

ADD the potatoes to the pot and stir them into the pan juices. Partially cover the pot and cook until the chicken and potatoes are tender, 20 to

25 minutes. Stir and baste the chicken with the pan juices from time to time, and add wine if the pan juices reduce too much.

To give a glorious golden color to the chicken and the potatoes, remove the lid and raise the heat to high. Cook, stirring gently and turning the potatoes and chicken a few times, until the pan juices are reduced to a few tablespoons of a thick glazed sauce, the chicken is golden brown, and the potatoes are begining to fall apart. Serve hot.

CHICKEN WITH DRIED MUSHROOMS AND TOMATOES

Pollo con Funghi e Pomodoro

SERVES 4

1 ounce dried porcini
mushrooms, soaked in
2 cups lukewarm water for
20 minutes

1 large, plump chicken
(4 to 5 pounds), cut into 8
serving pieces, thoroughly
washed, and patted dry with
paper towels

2 tablespoons unsalted butter

2 to 3 tablespoons extra virgin
olive oil

Salt and freshly ground black
pepper to taste

1 small garlic clove,
finely minced

1 tablespoon finely
chopped fresh rosemary or
½ teaspoon dried rosemary,
chopped

½ cup dry white wine

1 pound ripe plum tomatoes,
seeded and minced

1 to 2 tablespoons chopped
flat-leaf parsley

In country trattorie, chickens and rabbits are the meats most frequently cooked, because they are easy to raise. Just as for most braised dishes, this benefits from being prepared several hours ahead and reheated gently just before serving.

DRAIN the porcini mushrooms and reserve the soaking water. Rinse the mushrooms well under cold running water and roughly mince them. Strain the soaking water through a few layers of paper towels into a small bowl. Set the porcini and the soaking water aside.

COMBINE the butter and oil in a large heavy casserole or deep skillet that can accommodate all the chicken pieces comfortably in a single layer and place over medium-high heat. When the fat is nice and hot, add the chicken, skin side down, season with salt and pepper, and cook, turning once or twice until golden on both sides, about 10 minutes. Transfer the chicken to a plate.

ADD the porcini, garlic, and rosemary to the pot and stir quickly for a minute or so. Add the wine and stir to loosen the browned particles on the bottom of the pot. When the wine is reduced by about half, add the tomatoes, season lightly with salt, and cook for a few minutes.

RETURN the chicken pieces to the pot and stir them into the sauce. Reduce the heat to low, partially cover the pot, and cook gently until the chicken is very tender, 40 to 45 minutes. Stir and check the sauce from time to time, adding some of the reserved porcini soaking water if it reduces too much.

JUST before serving, stir in the parsley. Taste, adjust the seasoning, and serve.

THE PERILS OF SUCCESS

Many years ago as a cooking teacher I conducted a class at the Cooking School of Marcella Hazan in Bologna. At the end of the week-long cooking session, the whole class, Marcella, her husband, Victor, Giuliano, their son, and I boarded a minibus and headed for a celebration dinner in the small hill town of Stiore, thirty kilometers outside Bologna. Stiore had a few houses, a gas station, and La Perla, the trattoria that was our destination point. At that time La Perla had no more than eight or ten tables and a large bar where the locals met ritually to sip a glass of wine or an espresso, to play cards or shoot pool, and talk about politics, women, and sports. If they were hungry, the small kitchen of La Perla would provide cheeses, prosciutto, *salame,* pickled vegetables, savory bread, and *crescentine,* the delicious deep-fried bread fritters of the region. The food prepared for us that night was wonderful. Tagliatelle with Bolognese meat ragù. Chicken and rabbit *alla cacciatora.* Roasted meats, savory vegetables, and homey sweet ravioli fritters. The wine poured freely. The accordion played for hours and everybody had a marvelous time.

When this book project began, I knew I had to go back to La Perla so I could include it in these pages. And so I went, accompanied by six members of my Italian family. The humble trattoria I had known as La Perla was now a sleek country restaurant. Gone was the large bar and the old patrons. Nobody was playing cards there anymore, since the bar area was now part of the very large dining room.

The young man who hurriedly recited the dishes of the night, and looked about fifteen, was the son of La Perla, the owner of the trattoria. The dishes of the night consisted of three pastas all pretty much standard, three grilled beef dishes, three vegetables, and eggs with fresh white truffle. When I inquired about their famous rabbit *alla cacciatora,* he looked at me and said, "Oh, you must order that one week ahead." When I asked about those great little tortellini in broth his mother used to make, he said: "Well, now we make those only on Sunday because it takes forever to prepare them." As I sat there not knowing what to say anymore, the young man brought over a large platter of the sweet ravioli fritters that used to be so good. And they still were. As I was dipping them into my wine, I looked out at the large, now very full dining room, at the boisterous crowds who seemed so happy to have discovered a hidden gem of a trattoria, and thought about the small, quaint trattoria I had known that served honest, uncontrived food. Perhaps it is true that you can't go home again.

PHEASANT HUNTER-STYLE

WITH PORCINI

Fagiano alla Cacciatora

SERVES 4 TO 6

1 ounce dried porcini
mushrooms, soaked in
2 cups lukewarm water for
20 minutes

2 pheasants (about 3 pounds
each), quartered

⅓ cup extra virgin olive oil

Salt and freshly ground black
pepper to taste

½ cup finely minced
yellow onions

2 to 3 ounces pancetta,
thickly sliced, minced

2 tablespoons chopped
flat-leaf parsley

⅓ cup good red wine vinegar

2 cups canned Italian plum
tomatoes, with their juice, put
through a food mill to remove
the seeds

*raziella, one of my sister-in-law's sisters, and a great regional cook,
is famous within her large family for her cacciatora preparations.
Her husband, Villiam, who is an avid hunter, provides Graziella with a
variety of fowl, and pigeons, pheasants, and quail, as well as rabbits, are
invariably prepared alla cacciatora. Her sauces often have the addition of
wild mushrooms, herbs, pancetta, wine vinegar (which she considers essential to a good cacciatora), and tomatoes. And, to complement the woodsy
richness of her cacciatora, she serves it next to a mound of creamy, soft
polenta and pours a full-bodied local red wine. Just think how good a dish
like this would taste on a cold, rainy night!*

DRAIN the porcini mushrooms and reserve the soaking water. Rinse the
mushrooms well under cold running water and roughly mince them. Line
a strainer with a few layers of paper towels and strain the soaking water
through it into a small bowl. Set the porcini and the soaking water aside.

TRIM away as much fat as possible from the pheasant. Wash thoroughly
under cold running water and pat dry with paper towels.

IN a large deep skillet or casserole that can accommodate all the pheasant pieces in a single layer, heat the oil over medium-high heat. When
the fat is nice and hot, add the pheasant, skin side down, season with salt
and pepper, and cook, turning once or twice, until golden on both sides,
about 10 minutes. Transfer the pheasant to a platter and discard about
half of the fat in the pan.

REDUCE the heat to medium, add the onions, and cook, stirring, until then
begin to soften, 4 to 5 minutes. Add the pancetta and stir for 2 to 3 minutes, then add the porcini, parsley, and vinegar. Stir briefly with a wooden
spoon, scraping up the browned bits on the bottom of the pan. When
almost all the vinegar has evaporated, return the pheasant to the pan,

season with salt and pepper, and stir the pieces briefly, turning and coating them with the savory base.

POUR in the reserved porcini water and the tomatoes. As soon as the sauce comes to a boil, reduce the heat to low, partially cover the pan, and simmer, stirring and basting the meat from time to time, until the pheasant is tender and the sauce has a medium-thick consistency, 40 to 45 minutes. (The dish can be prepared a few hours ahead. In that case, slightly undercook the pheasant, since it will keep cooking in its own hot sauce and during reheating.) Serve hot, with soft, creamy polenta.

ADJUSTING THE SAUCE

If the sauce is a bit thin, transfer the pheasant to a warm serving platter, put the pot over high heat, and cook, stirring, until the sauce has a nice dense consistency. If, on the other hand, the sauce is too thick, add a bit of water or chicken broth and stir briefly over high heat.

SIMPLIFYING AN ALREADY SIMPLE MEAL

To serve this dish with soft polenta, see Polenta: The Almost No Stir Method (page 206), which requires no stirring to speak of. Begin the polenta half an hour or so before you start cooking the pheasant, so that it will be ready just in time.

ROASTED STUFFED TURKEY BREAST

Arrosto di Tacchino Farcito

SERVES 8

For the spinach

1 pound spinach, stems and bruised leaves discarded, or one 10-ounce package frozen spinach, thawed and squeezed dry

Salt

2 tablespoons unsalted butter

2 to 3 tablespoons heavy cream

¼ cup freshly grated Parmigiano-Reggiano

One 4- to 4½-pound boneless turkey breast, butterflied and pounded thin by the butcher

Salt and freshly ground black pepper to taste

10 thin slices mortadella, prosciutto, or baked ham (about ½ pound)

2 tablespoons unsalted butter

2 tablespoons extra virgin olive oil

1 to 2 cups dry white wine

Turkey is popular all year round in Emilia-Romagna. The butcher shops of the region sell turkey cut into pieces.

The breast, generally the most popular part, is sold as a roast, either whole or boned and rolled up, or is cut into thin slices and used for cutlets or scaloppine. The legs are used for braised preparations, and white and dark meat are ground together and turned into ragùs, meatballs, or meat loaves.

Because I am a white meat lover, I find roast turkey breasts irresistible, especially when they are stuffed. I also find them easy to cook and great to prepare for a dinner party. Graziella, the oldest sister of my sister-in-law, Emma, cooked this for me one evening. It came to the table cut into large, thick slices, showing the green spinach and the rosy mortadella. The roast was surrounded by golden, crisp roasted potatoes and sweet-and-sour small onions. It was an absolutely lusty sight.

IF using fresh spinach, wash thoroughly under cold running water, then put 2 cups water, a nice pinch of salt, and the spinach in a large pot and bring to a gentle boil. Cover the pot and cook, stirring a few times, until the spinach is tender, 6 to 8 minutes. Drain the spinach and squeeze out the excess water.

PLACE the spinach on a cutting board and chop very fine.

MELT the butter in a medium skillet over medium heat. When the butter begins to foam, add the spinach, cream, and Parmigiano and season lightly with salt. Stir for a minute or two, until the cheese has melted and the cream and Parmigiano coat the spinach. Transfer to a bowl and let cool.

PREHEAT the oven to 375°F.

PLACE the turkey breast skin side down on a work surface and season with salt and pepper. Cover the turkey with slices of mortadella, leaving a 2-inch border all around. With a tablespoon or a spatula, spread the spinach mixture over the mortadella. Top the spinach with the remaining slices mortadella. Starting from a long side, roll up the turkey breast tightly and tie securely with kitchen string. Season the roast with salt and pepper. (The turkey can be prepared up to this point several hours ahead. Cover with plastic wrap and refrigerate.)

HEAT the butter and oil in a large heavy casserole over medium heat. Add the turkey and cook, turning, until it is golden on all sides, 8 to 10 minutes. Add 1 cup of the wine and bring to a boil. Let the wine bubble for a minute or so, then transfer the casserole to the center rack of the oven. Roast the turkey for about 1 hour, basting it every 20 minutes or so with its pan juices. Add a bit more wine if the sauce in the pan reduces too much. To test the turkey for doneness, pierce it with a long thin knife: if the juices run clear, the turkey is done. Transfer the roast to a cutting board and let it rest for 5 to 10 minutes while you finish the sauce.

SET the pot over high heat and bring the pan juices to a boil. Add a bit more wine or water if needed. Stir quickly with a wooden spoon, scraping the pot to loosen the browned particles on the bottom. When the juices are nicely thickened, turn off the heat.

REMOVE the string, slice the turkey, and serve with a drizzle of the sauce.

Note: To enrich the taste of the pan juices, stir in 3 to 4 tablespoons balsamic vinegar after they have thickened.

TO DIP OR NOT TO DIP?

Nowhere in Emilia-Romagna or, to my knowledge, anywhere in Italy, is balsamic vinegar or olive oil served in little bowls as a condiment for dipping bread. This "Italian custom," which probably started in California, has created some confusion among American restaurant-goers in Italy.

RABBIT HUNTER-STYLE

Coniglio alla Cacciatora

SERVES 4 TO 6

⅓ cup extra virgin olive oil

Two rabbits (about 3 pounds each) cut into 6 serving pieces by the butcher, thoroughly washed, and patted dry with paper towels

Salt and freshly ground black pepper to taste

1 to 2 tablespoons unsalted butter

2 ounces thickly sliced pancetta, finely minced

2 ounces thickly sliced prosciutto, finely minced

5 to 6 sage leaves, minced, or 1 tablespoon chopped flat-leaf parsley

1 garlic clove, finely chopped

1 cup dry white wine

2 cups Homemade Tomato Sauce (page 22) or canned Italian plum tomatoes, with their juices, put through a food mill to remove the seeds

1 cup Chicken Broth (page 73) or canned low-sodium chicken broth

1 tablespoon chopped flat-leaf parsley

The lean white meat of rabbit, when cooked cacciatora, *becomes meltingly tender and succulent. At Trattoria Moretto, on the outskirts of Vignola, this great preparation has the addition of pancetta, prosciutto, fresh sage, and garlic, making it absolutely irresistible.*

Any cacciatora *preparation greatly benefits from pairing it with polenta. It doesn't matter how you serve it, soft, fried, baked, or grilled, polenta is the perfect vehicle to soak up the savory sauce.*

PUT the oil in a large deep skillet or casserole that can accommodate all the rabbit pieces comfortably in a single layer and place over medium-high heat. When the oil is nice and hot, season the rabbit with salt and pepper and add to the pan. Cook, turning once or twice, until golden on both sides, about 10 minutes. Brown the rabbit in two batches if necessary. Transfer the rabbit to a large platter.

DISCARD some of the fat in the skillet and put the pan back over medium heat. Add the butter, pancetta, and prosciutto and stir for a minute or two. Add the sage and garlic and stir for less than a minute. Raise the heat to high and add the wine. Cook, scraping the bottom of the pan with a wooden spoon to loosen the browned bits, until almost all the wine has evaporated.

RETURN the rabbit to the pan (at this point the pieces can be put snugly close together) and add the tomato sauce and broth. As soon as the sauce comes to a boil, reduce the heat to low, partially cover the pan, and simmer, stirring and basting the rabbit pieces occasionally, until the meat is tender and the sauce has a medium-thick consistency, 40 to 50 minutes.

STIR the parsley into the sauce, taste, and adjust the seasoning. Serve hot, with polenta or crusty Italian bread.

RABBIT—SUCCULENCE WITHOUT THE FAT

If you are a rabbit lover, you will be happy to know that the sweet, white lean meat of rabbit is rich in protein, vitamins, and minerals and low in saturated fats.

When cooking rabbit, pay attention to the cooking time. After the initial browning, cook the rabbit over very gentle heat, basting it often with the sauce or pan juices, or its lean meat will dry out. If you are cooking the rabbit a day ahead, under-cook it slightly and let it cool to room temperature, then cover it tightly and refrigerate. Reheat it gently, in a covered pan, adding a bit of broth or water if needed.

THINKING AHEAD

When Italian women cook, they think ahead. Often they make a double recipe of a stewed or braised dish, such as the *cacciatora*, so it can be served again the next day. If only a small amount of meat and sauce are left over, the meat is diced very fine, added to the sauce, and tossed with potato gnocchi, tagliatelle, or penne.

ROASTED RABBIT WITH

BALSAMIC VINEGAR

Coniglio all'Aceto Balsamico

SERVES 4 TO 6

3 tablespoons Aglione (page 21)

2 rabbits (2½ to 3 pounds), cut into 6 serving pieces

3½ cups dry white wine

2 tablespoons unsalted butter

2 tablespoons extra virgin olive oil

Salt and freshly ground black pepper to taste

⅓ cup granulated sugar

⅓ cup balsamic vinegar

*I*n Emilia-Romagna, most of the dishes using balsamic vinegar come from the province of Modena. That is only natural, since it is in and around Modena that this great, aromatic, artisan-made vinegar is produced. There are several versions of roasted rabbit with balsamic vinegar. Some, like this one, which comes from Agriturismo Corte d'Alba in the small town of Monteveglio between Bologna and Modena, marinate the rabbit for several hours before roasting it. Others roast the rabbit, basting it throughout its cooking time with pan juices and a bit of balsamic vinegar, while others add vegetables to the pan, roast them alongside the rabbit, and, at the end, season everything with a few tablespoons of the vinegar. (Balsamic vinegar varies considerably in quality and price; see the discussion on page 10.)

WASH the rabbit in several changes of cold water and pat dry with paper towels. Place the pieces in a large bowl and mix with the *aglione*, rubbing the savory mixture into the meat. Add 3 cups of the wine, cover the bowl with plastic wrap, and refrigerate for 4 to 6 hours.

PREHEAT the oven to 375°F.

REMOVE the rabbit from the marinade, place the pieces on a clean kitchen towel or paper towels, and pat dry.

IN a large casserole that can later accommodate all the rabbit pieces in a single layer, heat the butter and oil together over medium heat. When the butter begins to foam, add the rabbit pieces, without crowding them (you may need to brown them in two batches), and season with salt and pepper. Cook, turning once or twice, until the rabbit is golden on both sides, 6 to 8 minutes. Raise the heat to high, add the remaining ½ cup wine, and stir, moving the rabbit pieces around gently, until almost all the wine has evaporated.

TRANSFER the pot to the center rack of the oven and roast until the rabbit is golden brown and tender, about 30 minutes. Check the rabbit a few times, turning it and basting it with the pan juices to keep it moist. Transfer the rabbit to a large platter and keep warm in the turned-off oven while you finish the sauce.

PUT the pan juices through a fine strainer into a small skillet and place it over medium heat. Remove and discard some of the fat, if necessary. Add the water, sugar, and balsamic vinegar and bring to a gentle boil. Cook, stirring, until the sauce has a medium-thick, glazed consistency. Drizzle the sauce over the rabbit and serve at once.

FOR SUCCULENT ROASTED RABBIT

Again, as in many roasted dishes of the region, the *aglione* adds flavor to the rabbit and the marinade. In this preparation, the rabbit is browned on top of the stove and finished in the oven. The total cooking time, between the browning and the roasting, is 30 to 35 minutes, depending on its weight. Because rabbit meat is very lean, baste it with its pan juices or a bit of wine a few times during cooking.

The rabbit can be put in the marinade in the morning and roasted at dinnertime. Some cut-up potatoes can be added alongside the rabbit and roasted with it.

ROASTED LAMB WITH POTATOES

Agnello Arrosto con Patate

One 5-pound boneless leg of lamb, trimmed of excess fat and cut into 2- to 3-inch pieces

3 tablespoons Aglione (page 21)

1 cup extra virgin olive oil

¼ cup red wine vinegar

Salt and freshly ground black pepper to taste

3 pounds russet potatoes, peeled and cut into 1½-inch pieces

My husband and I are what Italians call due buone forchette, *good eaters. But while I have a saturation point, my husband, who is uncommonly slender for a man who enjoys food so much, seems to be able to eat considerably more than most people. When we set out to research this book, we ate at the homes of family and friends, lingering for hours at the table and tasting as many dishes as we could, and we went to trattorie and restaurants twice a day, often seven days a week. Our lunches generally lasted more than two hours, and our dinners invariably took us to the restaurant's closing time.*

The night we dined at Antica Osteria Ardegna, in Diodolo di Soragna in the countryside around Parma, I could not face another meal. I was tired of so much food, so I ordered only a simple salad and some aged Parmigiano-Reggiano that the owner had recommended. Then the roasted lamb with potatoes that my husband had ordered arrived. The lamb and the potatoes, which were flavored with aglione, *the savory salt-herb mixture used in the region for roasts, were initially cooked separately, then finished together, mixing their flavors and binding them into a most beautiful rustic dish. It was then that I started eating off my husband's plate.*

PUT the lamb in a large bowl, add 2 tablespoons of the *aglione*, ¾ cup of the oil, and the vinegar, and mix well with your hands or a large spoon to coat the lamb thoroughly. Cover the bowl tightly with plastic wrap and refrigerate for several hours, stirring a few times, since the oil will conceal in the bottom of the bowl.

ONE hour before roasting, remove the bowl from the refrigerator to allow the oil to liquefy again, and the meat to come to room temperature.

MEANWHILE, preheat the oven to 450°F.

PLACE the potatoes in a large bowl with the remaining ¼ cup oil and 1 tablespoon *aglione*. Season with salt and pepper and stir well to coat. Put the potatoes in a large roasting pan and place on the middle rack of the oven. Roast until the potatoes have a nice golden color on all sides, about

20 minutes. Remove from the oven and set aside. (The potatoes can be prepared up to this point a few hours ahead.)

PUT a large roasting pan on the center rack of the preheated oven and let it get nice and hot, about 10 minutes. With a large slotted spoon, scoop out the lamb from the marinade and place it in the hot pan, spreading the pieces apart. Roast until the meat turns lightly golden, about 10 to 12 minutes. Add the potatoes and roast for 4 to 6 minutes longer, basting the meat and potatoes once or twice with the pan juices, until the meat is golden brown and crisp on the outside but still pink and juicy inside. Serve hot, with the pan juices.

WINE SERVED IN BOWLS

At Antica Osteria Ardegna, I watched a boisterous group of men eating with joyous abandon and drinking wine from large round soup bowls. Of course, I had to ask our waiter why. It seems that in the Bassa Padana, the often thickly fogged area between Parma and Piacenza, the custom was, many years ago, to serve wine in wide bowls. Apparently the practice originated in the farmland of the region during the long, cold, foggy winter days, when wine was sprinkled over a hot bowl of homemade broth as a way of fortifying it. Field laborers and peasants liked the custom so much that it evolved into drinking only the wine, still in soup bowls. The custom was later adopted by locals.

LAMB STEW MODENA-STYLE

Agnello alla Cacciatora

SERVES 6

For the marinade

1 cup extra virgin olive oil

½ cup red wine vinegar

2 sprigs fresh rosemary, stemmed, or 1 to 2 table-spoons dried rosemary, chopped

Salt and freshly ground black pepper to taste

3 pounds boneless lamb shoulder, trimmed of fat and cut into 2-inch cubes

⅓ cup extra virgin olive oil

½ cup finely minced yellow onions

1 garlic clove, finely minced

1 tablespoon finely chopped fresh rosemary or ½ teaspoon dried rosemary, chopped

1 tablespoon chopped flat-leaf parsley

1 thick slice pancetta (about 2 ounces), very finely minced

Salt and freshly ground black pepper to taste

1 cup dry white wine

3 cups Homemade Tomato Sauce (page 22) or canned Italian plum tomatoes, with their juice, put through a food mill to remove the seeds, plus a bit extra if needed

ancetta, prosciutto, carrot, celery, onion, garlic, parsley, rosemary, sage, thyme, vinegar: these are some of the basic ingredients that, used alone or in conjunction with one another, are the flavor foundation of the ragùs, sauces, stews, and braised dishes of Emilia-Romagna. There are no mysteries in these dishes, and there are no "secret" ingredients. There is only a handful of everyday ingredients that, when properly pre-pared and properly cooked, produce immensely flavorful, appetizing preparations.

This type of stew is fairly standard in the homes of Emilia-Romagna, with each cook adding his or her own personal touch. On occasion, my sister-in-law, Emma, adds some leftover roasted or fried potatoes or cooked beans to the stew during the last few minutes of cooking, which makes it richly dense and absolutely succulent.

To prepare the marinade, combine the oil, vinegar, and rosemary in a large bowl and season with salt and pepper. Add the lamb and toss well to coat. Cover with plastic wrap and marinate for 1 to 1½ hours in the refrigerator.

REMOVE the meat from the marinade and pat it dry with paper towels.

HEAT the oil in a large heavy skillet or casserole over medium-high heat. When the oil is nice and hot, add the lamb, without crowding (brown the lamb in two batches, if necessary), and cook, stirring and turning the meat a few times, until golden brown on all sides, about 10 minutes. With a slotted spoon, transfer the lamb to a large plate.

DISCARD some of the fat in the pan and reduce the heat to medium. Add the onions, garlic, rosemary, parsley, and pancetta and cook, stirring with a wooden spoon, until the mixture has a nice golden color, 4 to 5 minutes. Return the lamb to the pan, season with salt and pepper, and raise the heat to high. Add the wine and cook, stirring and scraping the bottom of the pan to loosen the browned bits, until the wine has almost completely evaporated.

STIR in the tomato sauce. As the sauce begins to bubble, reduce the heat to low, partially cover the pan, and simmer, stirring from time to time, until the sauce has a medium-thick consistency and a deep red color, 1 to 1½ hours. At this point, the meat should be so tender that it can be cut with a fork; if not, add a bit more tomato sauce or water if needed, cover the pan, and cook at the slowest of simmers for 10 to 15 minutes longer.

TASTE, adjust the seasoning, and turn off the heat. Let the stew stand for 10 minutes or so before serving. Serve with slices of grilled or fried polenta or with good crusty bread. (Just as for most stews, this can be prepared a day or two ahead, covered, and refrigerated. Reheat it gently before serving.)

LAMB STEW WITH ROASTED POTATOES While the stew cooks, peel some boiling potatoes, cut them into large chunks, and roast them in a baking pan in a preheated 400°F oven until golden. Add the potatoes to the stew during the last 5 minutes of cooking.

LAMB STEW WITH BEANS Add 1 to 1½ cups cooked borlotti or can-nellini beans to the stew during the last 5 minutes of cooking.

FOR A SMOOTHER SAUCE

When the lamb is cooked, transfer it to a bowl with a slotted spoon. Put the sauce through a food mill or puree it in a food processor and return it to the pan. If the sauce is too thin, reduce it over high heat for a few minutes. Put the lamb back in the sauce and let it stand for 15 to 20 minutes before serving.

BREADED LAMB CHOPS

Costine d'Agnello alla Romagnola

SERVES 4

2 large eggs

Salt

8 single-rib lamb chops, lightly pounded

1½ cups fine dried bread crumbs

½ cup extra virgin olive oil

*T*his typical dish changes slightly from one side of Emilia-Romagna to the other. In Emilia, they coat the chops with a mixture of dried bread crumbs and Parmigiano-Reggiano cheese and pan-fry them in a combination of olive oil and butter. In Romagna, they omit the Parmigiano and fry the chops in only oil.

There are just four ingredients in this dish, and they all should be of the highest quality. Seek out the youngest lamb possible (older lamb has a muttony flavor). Use homemade bread crumbs: let leftover Italian or French bread stand at room temperature for 2 to 3 days, until it is completely dry, then cut it into chunks and grind it to crumbs in your food processor. Use the best extra virgin olive oil you have for frying the chops. And flatten the chops a bit with a meat pounder before pan-frying them, so they will cook faster and will get to the table hot, crunchy, and absolutely succulent.

LIGHTLY beat the eggs in a shallow dish with a pinch of salt. Dip each lamb chop in the eggs, coating the meat and letting the excess egg drip back into the dish. Coat the lamb with the bread crumbs, lightly pressing the crumbs onto the meat with the palms of your hands.

HEAT the oil in a large heavy skillet over medium-high heat. When the oil is nice and hot, add the chops, without crowding (cook in two batches if necessary), and cook until they have a nice golden crust on the bottom, 2 to 3 minutes, then turn and brown the other side, 2 to 3 minutes longer. Transfer the chops to paper towels to drain and pat dry to remove excess fat. Season with salt, place on a warm serving platter, and serve promptly.

Meatballs and Meat Loaves
Polpette e Polpettone

Meatballs and meat loaves were the workhorses of the frugal regional cook, because they could be put together from leftover ingredients—a few pieces of boiled beef, chicken, or veal from a *bollito misto*, a link or two of cooked sausage, a few spoonfuls of veal stew, a few slices of ham.

Every Italian, and certainly every person in Emilia-Romagna, has warm memories of these dishes, memories of mothers and grandmothers mixing the ingredients in a bowl and shaping them into a large loaf or into small meatballs, which in Emilia-Romagna are flattened and look more like patties. Meat loaves and meatballs were generally browned in large cast-iron skillets on top of the stove, and cooked with or without a sauce, depending on the ingredients at hand and the inspiration of the moment.

My mother was a master at making these dishes. In affluent times, she made them with fresh ground veal or pork. Often she added some prosciutto, pancetta, or mortadella for more flavor, then she mixed the meats with eggs and Parmigiano, always adding some bread softened in milk or some ricotta cheese to keep the mixture moist. Fried *polpette* were my favorite. She piled them high on a plate and put it in the center of the table. Sometimes she cooked them with a savory sauce of onion, tomatoes, and peas. In less affluent times, she still made *polpette,* but she used any leftover cooked meats she had, which she chopped very fine. A potato, cooked and mashed, would take the place of the Parmigiano. A bit of milk provided the moisture instead of the eggs. Her ingenuity was the instinctive one of her generation, which often had to make do with little.

As with most other homey dishes, *polpette* and *polpettone* are always and never the same, because their flavors are set not in written recipes but in the imagination and wisdom of the cook.

MY MOTHER'S FRIED MEATBALLS

Polpette Fritte di Mia Mamma

SERVES 6 TO 8

For the polpette

2 slices white bread

1 cup milk

¾ pound ground veal

½ pound Homemade Bolognese Sausage (page 267) or mild Italian pork sausage (containing no fennel seeds, chile pepper, or strong spices), casings removed and chopped

¼ pound sliced mortadella, finely chopped

⅛ teaspoon freshly grated nutmeg

1 cup freshly grated Parmigiano-Reggiano

2 large eggs, lightly beaten

Salt and freshly ground black pepper to taste

2 large eggs

2 cups fine dried bread crumbs

Olive oil for frying

The special craving I have for polpette *is as much emotional as it is gustatory, since it is one of the nurturing dishes of my childhood. Try my mother's* polpette, *then try the variation, in which they are enriched by tomato and bean sauce.*

REMOVE the crusts from the bread and tear it into pieces. Put it in a small bowl, add the milk, and let soak for 5 minutes.

DRAIN the bread and squeeze out as much of the milk as possible. Place the bread in a large bowl and add the veal, sausage, mortadella, nutmeg, Parmigiano, and eggs. Season lightly with salt and pepper and mix until well combined.

TAKE a small amount of the meat mixture and shape it between the palms of your hands into a ball about the size of a very small egg. Place on a plate, then repeat until all the meat is used up.

LIGHTLY beat the eggs in a small bowl. Dip the meatballs in the beaten eggs, coat them evenly with the bread crumbs, and flatten them a little with the palms of your hands. Place the *polpette* in a single layer on a cookie sheet or large platter. (They can be refrigerated, tightly covered with plastic wrap, for several hours.)

HEAT 1 inch of oil in a medium heavy skillet over medium-high heat. As soon as the oil is nice and hot, lower the *polpette*, in batches, into the oil with a slotted spoon, making sure not to crowd the pan. As soon as the *polpette* are golden on one side, 1 to 2 minutes, turn them and brown the other side. Transfer the *polpette* to paper towels to drain. Pile the *polpette* on a warm serving platter and bring to the table.

Note: Fried *polpette* can be served as a casual appetizer, a snack, or a light lunch or dinner. In Emilia-Romagna, they are often served with tender leaves of wild chicory or with Parmigiano-enriched mashed potatoes. Before frying these *polpette*, read the box on page 368.

MEATBALLS WITH BEANS AND TOMATOES

Polpette in Umido con Fagioli

SERVES 8

For the sauce

½ cup dried borlotti beans or pinto beans, picked over, soaked overnight in cold water to cover generously, drained, and rinsed, or 1 cup rinsed and drained canned beans

2 tablespoons unsalted butter

1 tablespoon extra virgin olive oil

½ cup finely minced yellow onions

2 to 3 ounces thinly sliced pancetta, finely diced

1 tablespoon chopped flat-leaf parsley

2½ cups canned Italian plum tomatoes, with their juice, put through a food mill to remove the seeds

½ cup milk

Salt to taste

1 recipe My Mother's Fried Meatballs (page 265), fried as instructed on page 368 and drained on paper towels

ere I take my mother's fried polpette *and simmer them in a savory sauce of pancetta, tomatoes, and beans. This rustic dish is best served on a cold, wintry day next to grilled or soft polenta, or with a nice loaf of crusty Italian bread.*

IF using dried beans, put them in a medium saucepan and cook as instructed on page 82. Drain.

To make the sauce, heat the butter and oil in a large skillet over medium heat. When the butter begins to foam, add the onions, pancetta, and parsley, and cook, stirring, until the onions have a nice golden color, 5 to 6 minutes. Add the tomatoes and milk, season with salt, and bring to a gentle boil. Cook, stirring, for 2 to 3 minutes.

REDUCE the heat to low, add the *polpette* and beans, and partially cover the skillet. Simmer, stirring from time to time, until the sauce has a medium-thick consistency and the *polpette* are meltingly soft, 10 to 15 minutes. Taste and adjust the seasoning. (The dish can be prepared up to 2 days ahead, covered, and refrigerated. Reheat gently in a covered pan.) Serve hot.

MEATBALLS WITH BEANS, TOMATOES, AND SAUSAGE Place 1 pound Homemade Bolognese Sausage (page 267) or mild Italian pork sausage (containing no fennel seeds, chile pepper, or strong spices), prick it in a few places with a fork, and place in a medium skillet. Add 1 cup water and place bring to a boil over high heat. Reduce the heat to medium and cook, turning the sausages a few times, until all the water has evaporated and only the fat released by the sausage is left, 10 to 15 minutes. Raise the heat to high and brown the sausages in their own fat. Add the sausages to the skillet with the *polpette* during the last 5 minutes of cooking.

HOMEMADE BOLOGNESE SAUSAGE

Salsiccia Bolognese

**MAKES 5 POUNDS
(ABOUT 20 LINKS)**

**One 4-pound boneless Boston
butt (pork shoulder roast)**

1 pound pancetta, in 1 piece

2 garlic cloves, finely minced

**1½ teaspoons freshly
grated nutmeg**

Pinch of ground cloves

2 tablespoons salt

**1 tablespoon freshly ground
black pepper**

1½ cups dry white wine

3 ounces hog casings

*ausage has a special place in the cooking of Emilia-Romagna. And
rightly so, since this region produces some of the best pork products
of Italy. And yet, the sausages of the region are almost pristine compared
to those made in other parts of Italy. They never include fennel seeds, chile
pepper, dried herbs, or tomatoes. They are neither sharp nor pungent. But
they are subtly flavorful, since they are made with first-quality pork (often
pork shoulder), pancetta or prosciutto, and seasonings and spices such as
wine, nutmeg, cloves, garlic, salt, and black pepper.*

*Twenty-five years ago, when I began my cooking career, I spent many
days in the kitchen of Bacco, which was then one of the best restaurants
of Bologna. Emilio Volcan, the chef, made sausage once a week, which he
cooked in a multitude of appetizing ways. And I learned then that in making Bolognese sausage, one should strive to achieve a balance of flavors, a
philosophy that in Emilia-Romagna is as important in sausage making
as it is in simple everyday home cooking.*

CUT the pork butt and pancetta into 2-inch chunks, place in a large bowl,
and refrigerate for several hours. (The meat needs to be very cold when
it is put through the grinder so that it will grind easily and won't shred.)

PUT the meat through a meat grinder twice, using the medium holes,
and place in a large bowl. Add all the other sausage ingredients and mix
quickly with your hands until well combined. Cover the bowl with plastic wrap and refrigerate for several hours to allow the flavors to blend
and to chill the meat further.

MEANWHILE, fit the end of the casing over your kitchen faucet, place the
other end in the sink, and run the water through it to clean the inside.
Toss it into a large bowl of cold water to wash the outside of the casing.
Rinse well and soak in cold water until ready to use.

TO make the sausage, fit the casing over the stuffing tube, leaving only a
couple of inches free, and tie the end into a knot. Put the meat mixture
into the "hopper" and begin feeding the meat into the casing; it is impor-

tant that the casing be filled somewhat loosely and that there are no air bubbles. If you stuff the casing too tightly, it will burst as it cooks. If any air bubbles appear, prick them with a needle.

To make the sausage links, sprinkle a large work surface with cold water and lay the sausage on it. With the side of your hand or your fingertips, press down on the sausage every 4 inches or so, separating the meat into links; or pinch the sausage with your fingertips to form the links. As you form the links, twist each sausage link tightly 5 or 6 times in opposite directions so they keep their shape, like candy wrapping twisted in opposite directions.

THE sausages can be refrigerated for a few days or frozen for up to 2 months.

To freeze the sausage, divide it into servings or pounds and place in individual plastic zippered-top bags. Fill each bag with cold water, tightly seal, and freeze. When you defrost the sausages, the melting water will keep the links separate, so they won't stick to each other and break.

PAN-ROASTED SAUSAGE

Salsiccia in Padella

SERVES 4 TO 6

2 pounds Homemade Bolognese Sausage (page 267) or mild Italian pork sausage (containing no fennel seeds, chile pepper, or strong spices)

*S*ausage, water, and a skillet are all you need to transform an excellent ingredient into an excellent dish. In this preparation, which is typical of the region, the sausage is punctured in several places and placed in a skillet with half an inch of water. As the sausage cooks, the water evaporates, allowing the sausage to finish cooking in its own fat, turning plump, golden brown, and immensely appetizing.

PRICK the sausage in a few places with a fork and place in a large skillet. Add about ½ inch water and place over high heat. When the water comes to a boil, reduce the heat to medium and cook, turning the sausage links a few times, until all the water in the pan has evaporated and only the fat released by the sausage is left, about 15 minutes.

RAISE the heat to high and cook, turning the links as needed, until a nice golden brown. Serve hot.

SAUSAGE-MAKING EQUIPMENT

To make sausage, you will need either an electric mixer or meat grinder with a sausage-making attachment. If these are out of reach for you but you have a nice relationship with your butcher, you could ask him to grind the meats and make this special sausage for you. You will probably have to pay him for his services, but I believe that the taste of this sausage is well worth it.

Hog casing can be found in Italian butcher shops or other specialty butcher shops.

FOR THE LOVE OF SAUSAGE

When I was a teenager growing up in Bologna, Sunday's excursions into the countryside with friends had the objective of eating in country trattorie. These trattorie could generally feed a crowd for very little money. We would secure an outside table and feast on large platters of *affettati*–prosciutto, salame, mortadella, and sausage. Sausage made by the owner of the trattoria or by the local butcher tasted better, or so it seemed. Freshly made and grilled, pan-roasted, fried, or cooked on a spit alongside poultry and game, it was utterly irresistible. *Affettati* was generally accompanied by large platters of *crescentine*, the light-as-air, dimpled, savory fried dough of Bologna, or by crisp golden brown slices of polenta, and small bowls of pickled onions, peppers, and artichokes. This was seriously addictive food–bold, tasty, and unsophisticated, but so very good.

During one of my recent trips, my brother and his wife, Emma, took me to Sandoni, a country trattoria that still serves this type of food. It was a hot Sunday afternoon and the trattoria was full of people. We found a small table on the outside patio and proceeded to order all the dishes the trattoria was famous for, including roasted rabbit, and fried savory dough. And we ordered the homemade sausage, lots of it–panfried, grilled, cooked on a spit, stewed with white beans. But we wanted more, so we ordered roasted potatoes, stuffed roasted vegetables, pickled onions, and artichokes. We ate and we drank bubbly local Sangiovese wine. We rested, and then we ate some more–and for a moment, I felt I had been taken back in time. Reality hit that night, when indigestion kept me up till morning. The moral of the story? Sausage, yes, but with moderation!

BAKED MEAT LOAF

Polpettone al Forno

SERVES 4 TO 6

3 to 4 slices Italian bread

1 cup milk

1½ pounds ground pork

½ pound thinly sliced mortadella, very finely chopped

2 tablespoons chopped flat-leaf parsley

1 cup freshly grated Parmigiano-Reggiano

2 extra-large eggs, lightly beaten

Salt and freshly ground black pepper to taste

1 cup fine dried bread crumbs

½ cup extra virgin olive oil

*T*his polpettone, *which comes from Trattoria Sandoni on the outskirts of Bologna, is deliciously soft inside, and crisp and crunchy on the outside. The softness comes from the bread soaked in milk, the crispness from the high cooking temperature. Keep your eye on the* polpettone, *however, especially during the last ten or fifteen minutes of cooking, because it will turn golden brown very quickly.*

PREHEAT the oven to 400°F.

REMOVE the crusts from the bread and tear it into pieces. Place it in a small bowl, add the milk, and let soak for 5 minutes.

DRAIN the bread and squeeze it to remove as much of the milk as possible. Place the bread in a large bowl, add the pork, mortadella, parsley, Parmigiano, and eggs, and season with salt and pepper. Mix well with your hands or a large wooden spoon until thoroughly combined. Put the mixture on a work surface, shape it into a rectangular loaf, and coat lightly on all sides with the bread crumbs.

POUR ⅓ cup of the oil into a large baking dish. With two large metal spatulas, gently transfer the *polpettone* to the baking dish. Drizzle the remaining oil over the *polpettone* and place the dish on the center rack of the oven. Bake, basting the meat occasionally with its pan juices, until the *polpettone* has a nice golden color and a light crust forms on top, about 1 hour. (During the cooking, the *polpettone* will release some of its fat and liquid from the soaked bread, which will not look too appealing; don't worry about it.)

TRANSFER the *polpettone* to a cutting board. Allow the meat to cool and settle a bit for 5 to 10 minutes, then slice it and serve with one of the vegetables suggested in the box on page 274.

POACHED VEAL, MORTADELLA, AND PARMIGIANO LOAF

Polpettone di Vitello Bollito

SERVES 4 TO 6

For the poaching broth

1 medium yellow onion, sliced

2 carrots, sliced into rounds

2 celery stalks, cut into 1-inch pieces

2 sprigs flat-leaf parsley

1½ pounds ground veal

½ pound thickly sliced mortadella, finely chopped

1 cup whole-milk or low-fat ricotta

1 cup freshly grated Parmigiano-Reggiano

¼ teaspoon freshly grated nutmeg

3 medium eggs, lightly beaten

Salt and freshly ground black pepper to taste

⅓ cup fine dried bread crumbs

This unusual polpettone, *a favorite of my niece, Daniela, who is forever trying to cook "healthy" dishes, is poached in an aromatic broth instead of being baked or pan-roasted. It is then cooled, sliced, and served at room temperature. The cooking method produces a compact meat loaf with a light, delicate taste, which looks more like a pâté than a* polpettone. *Serve it with an arugula salad.*

FILL a large pan half full with water. Add the onion, carrots, celery, and parsley and bring to a boil over high heat. Reduce the heat and simmer fairly briskly for about 20 minutes.

MEANWHILE, in a large bowl combine the veal, mortadella, ricotta, Parmigiano, nutmeg, and eggs. Season with salt and pepper and mix with your hands or a large wooden spoon until well combined.

PLACE a large sheet of heavy-duty aluminum foil, approximately 18 by 24 inches, on your work surface (or overlap two sheets of regular foil to make one large one) and sprinkle half of the bread crumbs over it. Put the meat mixture on the foil and shape it into a 2-inch-high loaf. Sprinkle the top with the remaining bread crumbs. Wrap the foil securely around the loaf, making sure that it is tightly sealed.

CAREFULLY place the meat loaf in the simmering broth, reduce the heat to low, cover the pan, and simmer gently for 50 minutes to 1 hour. The broth should stay at a steady simmer, so check it from time to time.

USING two large metal spatulas, transfer the loaf to a cutting board and allow to cool slightly, then remove the foil and cool to room temperature. Slice the loaf and serve.

BRAISED VEAL SHANKS

Ossobuco alla Reggiana

SERVES 4

¼ to ⅓ cup olive oil,
to your taste

4 large 2-inch-thick meaty
veal shanks (from the hind
shank)

1 cup all-purpose flour

Salt and freshly ground black
pepper to taste

3 to 4 tablespoons
unsalted butter

2½ cups finely minced
yellow onions

1 garlic clove, finely minced

1 cup dry Marsala,
such as Florio

2 heaping tablespoons
double-concentrated Italian
tomato paste, diluted in
2½ cups Chicken Broth
(page 73) or canned
low-sodium chicken broth

In Reggio-Emilia, the lovely small town between Parma and Modena where this version of ossobuco comes from, it is served over boiled rice that is tossed briefly with butter and Parmigiano. However, the pairing of the ossobuco with rice is typically Milanese.

Other versions of this dish add carrot and celery to the onions, and some puree the vegetables at the end of cooking. And others use red wine instead of Marsala. I love this one made with just onions, which become sweeter as they cook, and the more aromatic Marsala. Grilled or fried slices of polenta are a fine accompaniment in place of rice.

PREHEAT the oven to 350°F.

HEAT the oil in a large heavy ovenproof pan or casserole over medium-high heat. Dredge the shanks in the flour, shaking off the excess, and slip them into the pan. Season with salt and pepper. Cook, turning once, until a nice golden brown color on both sides, 6 to 8 minutes. Transfer the shanks to a plate.

DISCARD the oil in the pan, add the butter, and place over medium-low heat. As soon as the butter foams, stir in the onions, scraping the bottom of the pan to loosen the flavorful browned bits. Cook the onions, stirring occasionally, until golden and soft, 6 to 7 minutes. Add the garlic and stir until it begins to color, about 1 minute.

RETURN the shanks to the pan, raise the heat to high, and add the Marsala. Cook, stirring and moving the shanks around gently, until the wine is reduced to a thick glaze that coats the onions, about 5 minutes. Add the diluted tomato paste (the broth should come more than halfway up the sides of the shanks but should not submerge them) and bring to a simmer. Cover the pan tightly with aluminum foil and, with a knife, make several slits in the foil to allow the steam to escape.

PLACE the pan on the middle rack of the oven and cook until the meat is very tender and begins to fall away from the bones, 1½ to 2 hours. Baste and turn the shanks a few times during cooking, and add a little more broth if the sauce reduces too much.

PLACE the shanks on individual warm serving plates and check the consistency of the sauce. If it is too thin, put the pan over high heat and cook it briskly until it has a nice thick consistency. Pour the sauce over the shanks and serve with rice or slices of grilled polenta.

COMFORT VEGETABLES

Comfort food should be served with comfort vegetables. Here are some choices:

- Mashed Potatoes with Parmigiano (page 323)

- Oven-Roasted Stuffed Vegetables (page 328)

- Onion and Tomato Stew with Red Wine Vinegar (page 326)

ROASTED VEAL SHANK

Stinco di Vitello Arrosto

SERVES 4

1 whole veal shank
(about 3 pounds)

Salt and freshly ground black
pepper to taste

⅓ cup extra virgin
olive oil

1 garlic clove, finely minced

2 tablespoons finely chopped
fresh rosemary

2 cups dry white wine

1 cup Meat Broth (page 71) or
canned low-sodium
beef broth

1 tablespoon unsalted butter

This is a great company dish because it is simple and straightforward to prepare, and when retrieved from the oven, shining in its golden brown succulence and glazed with the thickened pan juices, it is luscious to look at.

At Trattoria Boni in Bologna it was made with pork shank, not veal. But after several unsuccessful attempts to locate pork shanks here, I decided to try the dish with veal shank. Serve it with Roasted Potatoes (page 324) and Oven-Roasted Stuffed Vegetables (page 328).

PREHEAT the oven to 350°F.

PAT the veal shank dry with paper towels and season generously with salt and pepper.

HEAT the oil in a large heavy ovenproof casserole over medium-high heat. When the oil is nice and hot, add the shank and cook, turning carefully with tongs a few times, until the meat has a nice golden color, 8 to 10 minutes. With a large spoon, remove some of the fat in the pot.

MIX the garlic and rosemary together, add to the pot, and stir quickly once or twice. (The very hot pot will brown the garlic in no time at all.) Add 1 cup of the wine and bring to a fast boil, then turn off the heat.

COVER the casserole tightly with aluminum foil and make a few slits in the foil with a thin knife for steam to escape. Place on the middle rack of the oven and roast the shank for about 2 hours. After 30 minutes or so, baste with ½ cup of the wine, or broth alternatingly. (There should always be some liquid in the pan. If the sauce reduces too much, add more wine or broth.)

REMOVE the foil (pay attention, there will be a burst of steam escaping) and pour in ½ cup more wine or broth. Roast for 10 to 15 minutes longer, uncovered, until the sauce is thick and the meat has a rich golden brown color. Transfer the shank to a carving board, cover with foil, and let it rest for a few minutes while you prepare the sauce.

PUT the pot over high heat. Add the butter and, if needed, a little more wine or broth. As the liquid begins to boil, stir quickly with a wooden spoon to loosen the delicious browned pieces attached to the bottom of the pot, then stir until the pan juices are thick and glazed.

HOLD the shank by the bone with a kitchen towel and carve the meat parallel to the bone into thin slices. Arrange the slices on a warm serving platter, spoon the sauce over, and serve immediately.

ROASTED VEAL SHOULDER

Arrosto di Vitello all'Aglione

SERVES 6

One 3-pound boneless veal shoulder roast, butterflied and pounded thin

3 tablespoons Aglione (page 21)

Salt and freshly ground black pepper to taste

¼ to ⅓ cup extra virgin olive oil

1 cup dry white wine, plus more if needed

2 to 3 tablespoons red wine vinegar

Stuffing is, for the people of Emilia-Romagna, second nature. We stuff more pasta than anyone else in Italy. We also stuff vegetables, fish, meat, and fruit. We do this not because we have nothing else to do, but because we love rich, succulent, flavorful food, and stuffing takes care of that. Just take a nice boneless shoulder of veal, open it up like a giant cutlet, and rub over it a savory mixture of garlic, herbs, and salt. Roll the meat up, tie it, rub more of the flavorful mixture on the outside, and roast it. Simple! Except that the mixture, which on the Emilia side of the region we call aglione, *infuses a great deal of flavor into an otherwise plain roast. Trattoria le Roncole, near Busseto, served this roast at room temperature, next to a lovely Green Bean, Pine Nut, and Mint Salad (page 343).*

PREHEAT the oven to 350°F.

PLACE the veal on a work surface and rub 2 tablespoons of the *aglione* over the meat. Roll up the veal tightly from a long side and tie securely with kitchen string. Rub the remaining 1 tablespoon *aglione* over the outside of the veal and season with salt and pepper.

HEAT the oil in a large ovenproof skillet over medium heat. When the oil is nice and hot, add the veal and cook, turning occasionally, until it is lightly golden on all sides, 10 to 12 minutes. Raise the heat to high, add the wine, and cook, stirring constantly, until the wine is reduced by about half.

PLACE the pan on the middle rack of the oven and roast until the veal has a nice golden brown color and the juices run clear when pierced with a thin knife (160°F on an instant-read thermometer), 1 to 1½ hours. Baste the meat every 15 minutes or so with the pan juices, or with a bit of additional wine. If the juices in the bottom of the pan turn too dark, stir in a bit of water, reduce the oven temperature to 300°F, and cook the roast for 10 to 15 minutes longer. Transfer the veal to a cutting board and let it rest for 5 to 10 minutes before slicing.

MEANWHILE, tilt the pan and spoon off some of the fat. Place the pan over high heat and add the vinegar and about ¼ cup of water. When the pan juices begin to bubble, stir quickly with a wooden spoon to loosen the browned particles attached to the bottom of the pan. Continue to cook until the juices are nice and thick. Slice the roast and spoon with a tablespoon or so of the thickened pan juices over each serving.

VEAL CUTLETS WITH PROSCIUTTO, PARMIGIANO, AND MARSALA

Cotolette di Vitello alla Bolognese

SERVES 4

2 large eggs

Salt

1½ cups fine dried bread crumbs

About ¾ cup freshly grated Parmigiano-Reggiano

Eight ¼ inch-thick, slices veal scaloppine (about 1¼ pounds), lightly pounded

3 tablespoons unsalted butter

2 tablespoons extra virgin olive oil

½ cup dry Marsala

Take a slice of milk-fed veal, coat it with a mixture of bread crumbs and Parmigiano, panfry it in butter, top with a slice of sweet prosciutto di Parma, and sprinkle generously with Parmigiano-Reggiano. This dish, also known as cotoletta alla Petroniana *or* cotoletta all'Emiliana, *appears in several slightly different versions. Some omit the cream and Marsala in the sauce and use broth and a bit of milk. Others prepare it with a little tomato paste diluted in the broth. No matter how it is prepared, the amount of sauce in this dish is kept to a bare minimum, a tablespoon or so per serving. The sauce keeps the meat moist and glazes it ever so slightly.*

This recipe can be done in two stages. (Traditionally, the dish is done completely on top of the stove.) First, panfry the veal, make the sauce, and assemble the cutlets in the baking dish. Then bake the dish just long enough for the cheese to melt. If you serve the cutlets with Oven-Roasted Stuffed Vegetables (page 328), you will have a meal fit for a king.

**½ cup Chicken Broth
(page 73) or canned low-
sodium chicken broth**

¼ cup heavy cream, optional

**8 thin slices (about 6 ounces)
prosciutto**

PREHEAT the oven to 375°F.

LIGHTLY beat the eggs with a pinch of salt in a medium bowl. Mix the bread crumbs with ¼ cup Parmigiano. Dip each veal slice into the beaten eggs, letting the excess drip into the bowl. Coat with the bread crumb mixture, pressing the crumbs onto the meat with the palms of your hands.

HEAT 2 tablespoons of the butter and oil together in a large skillet over medium heat. When the butter foams, slip in the cutlets, without crowding, and cook, turning once, until they have a nice golden color on both sides, about 2 minutes on each side. Transfer the cutlets to paper towels and pat dry to remove any excess fat.

DISCARD the fat in the skillet. Place the skillet over medium-high heat and add the remaining 1 tablespoon butter. As soon as the butter begins to foam, add the Marsala, broth, and the cream, if using. Stir, scraping the pan to loosen the delicious browned particles attached to the bottom, and let the sauce simmer briskly for a minute or two, until it is a medium-thick glaze, then turn off the heat.

GENEROUSLY butter a baking dish that can accommodate the cutlets in a single layer. Put a slice of prosciutto over each one, and sprinkle generously with the remaining Parmigiano. (The dish can be prepared up to this point several hours ahead. Cover with plastic wrap and refrigerate. Remove the dish from the refrigerator 30 minutes before baking.)

REHEAT the sauce briefly and spoon it around the cutlets. Cover the dish with aluminum foil and place it on the middle rack of the oven. Bake until the Parmigiano is melted and coats the top of the cutlets, 5 to 6 minutes. Serve at once, with a tablespoon of sauce spooned over each cutlet. If desired, thinly shave white truffle on top of the melted cheese just before serving.

TURKEY CUTLETS PARMA-STYLE Substitute turkey scaloppine for the veal and dredge and panfry as instructed above.

Arrange the fried cutlets in a single layer in a large skillet. Top each cutlet with a slice of prosciutto and a generous sprinkle of Parmigiano. Melt 1 to 2 tablespoons butter and drizzle it over the cutlets. Pour 1 cup chicken or meat broth into the skillet, cover it with aluminum foil, and simmer until the cheese is melted. (If desired, thinly slice white truffle on top of the melted cheese just before serving.)

VEAL CUTLETS IN TOMATO SAUCE

Cotolette di Vitello al Pomodoro

SERVES 4

2 large eggs

Salt

1½ cups fine dried bread crumbs

⅓ cup freshly grated Parmigiano-Reggiano

Eight ¼-inch-thick slices veal scaloppine (about 1¼ pounds), lightly pounded

2 tablespoons unsalted butter

2 to 3 tablespoons olive oil

For the sauce

¼ cup extra virgin olive oil

⅓ cup finely minced shallots or yellow onion

2 to 3 ounces thinly sliced pancetta, finely minced

2 tablespoons double-concentrated Italian tomato paste, diluted in 2½ cups Chicken Broth (page 73) or canned low-sodium chicken broth

Salt to taste

1 cup fresh peas, blanched in boiling salted water for 2 to 3 minutes, or thawed frozen peas

It is amazing how far a pound or so of veal can go. Here thinly sliced veal is coated with a bread crumb–Parmigiano mixture and fried in butter and oil. The veal cutlets are then added to a sauce of shallots, pancetta, and tomatoes. Occasionally the sauce includes fresh peas, as in this recipe, or reconstituted dried porcini mushrooms.

This dish, which was a favorite of my mother's, will take no longer than twenty minutes to cook, and it has the added bonus that it can be prepared several hours ahead.

LIGHTLY beat the eggs with a pinch of salt in a medium bowl. Mix the bread crumbs with the Parmigiano. Dip each slice of veal into the beaten eggs, letting excess drip back into the bowl, then coat with the bread crumb mixture, lightly pressing the crumbs onto the meat with the palms of your hands.

HEAT the butter and oil together in a large heavy skillet over medium heat. When the butter begins to foam, slip in the cutlets, without crowding (cook in two batches if necessary), and cook, turning once, until golden and crisp on both sides, about 4 minutes total. Transfer the cutlets to paper towels and pat dry to remove any excess fat.

To prepare the sauce, heat the oil in a large skillet over medium heat. Add the shallots and pancetta and cook, stirring, until the shallots are lightly golden and soft, about 5 minutes. Add the diluted tomato paste and season with salt. As soon as the sauce begins to bubble, reduce the heat a bit and cook, uncovered, stirring from time to time, until the sauce has a medium-thick consistency, about 15 minutes.

STIR the peas into the sauce, then add the cutlets and cook for 3 to 4 minutes longer, stirring the sauce and basting the cutlets a few times. Taste, adjust the seasoning, and serve. (The dish can be prepared completely a few hours ahead and gently reheated.)

VEAL CUTLETS WITH DRIED PORCINI MUSHROOMS Soak 1 ounce dried porcini mushrooms in 2 cups lukewarm water for 20 minutes. Drain the porcini and reserve the liquid. Rinse the mushrooms well under cold running water and roughly chop them. Line a strainer with paper towels and strain the soaking liquid into a bowl.

Prepare the cutlets and sauce as instructed above. When the sauce begins to bubble, add the porcini mushrooms and 1 cup of the reserved liquid. Simmer, uncovered, for 15 to 20 minutes. Add the cutlets and cook for 3 to 4 minutes longer. Adjust the seasoning and serve.

WHEN IS A CUTLET A CUTLET?

In Italy, if you take a slice of veal, turkey, beef, fish, or vegetable, dip it in beaten eggs, coat it with bread crumbs, and fry it in butter or oil until crisp, you have a "cutlet." A cutlet is a method of preparing and cooking food that implies a simple, distinctive cooking preparation. The slices of veal you see in butcher shops advertised as "veal cutlets" are just slices of veal. It is only after they have been coated with eggs and bread crumbs and cooked according to the method described above that they become "cutlets."

VEAL STEW WITH POTATOES

Spezzatino di Vitello con Patate

SERVES 4 TO 6

2 tablespoons unsalted butter

2 tablespoons extra virgin olive oil

⅓ cup finely minced yellow onion

¼ cup finely minced carrots

¼ cup finely minced celery

2 pounds boneless veal cross ribs or veal shoulder, trimmed of fat and cut into 2-inch pieces

1 cup all-purpose flour

Salt and freshly ground black pepper to taste

2 tablespoons finely minced fresh rosemary or 1½ teaspoons minced dried rosemary

2 tablespoons finely minced fresh sage or 1½ teaspoons minced dried sage

1 garlic clove, finely minced

½ cup dry white wine

1 cup Homemade Tomato Sauce (page 22) or canned Italian plum tomatoes, with their juice, put through a food mill to remove the seeds

1 cup Chicken Broth (page 73), or canned low-sodium chicken broth

2 large boiling potatoes (about 1 pound), peeled and cut into 1-inch pieces

1 tablespoon chopped flat-leaf parsley

Trattoria lo Sterlino, just a fifteen-minute walk from the center of Bologna, is a homey, no-nonsense place that has been there as long as I can remember. And it is there that my husband and I used to eat when dating as students on a very tight budget. This was one of their comforting stews, which, through the years, I have slightly revised, using potatoes instead of the beans used in the original dish.

HEAT the butter and oil together in a large skillet over medium heat. When the butter foams, add the onion, carrots, and celery and cook, stirring, until the vegetables are lightly golden and soft, 6 to 7 minutes. With a slotted spoon, transfer the vegetables to a bowl, draining the excess oil back into the skillet.

PLACE the veal in a large strainer set over a bowl and sprinkle with the flour, shaking the strainer to coat the veal evenly. Add the veal to the skillet, without crowding (if necessary, brown the veal in a couple of batches), season with salt and pepper, and cook, turning occasionally, until browned on all sides, 7 to 8 minutes. Return the vegetables to the skillet, add the rosemary, sage, and garlic, and stir for about 1 minute. Raise the heat to high and add the wine. Cook, stirring, and scraping the bottom of the pan with a wooden spoon to loosen the flavorful bits attached to the skillet, until the wine is reduced by about half. Stir in the tomato sauce and broth. As soon as the sauce comes to a boil, reduce the heat to low, partially cover the skillet, and simmer, stirring occasionally, for 30 minutes.

ADD the potatoes and stir to distribute them evenly in the skillet. Cover the skillet again and cook, stirring occasionally, until the meat is very tender (you should be able to cut it with a fork) and the potatoes are beginning to break apart in the sauce, 40 to 50 minutes; add a bit more broth or water if the sauce reduces too much.

STIR in the parsley, taste, and adjust the seasoning. Serve piping hot.

VEAL STEW WITH WHITE WINE AND PEAS

Spezzatino di Vitello al Vino Bianco e Piselli

SERVES 4

2 pounds boneless veal cross ribs or veal shoulder, trimmed of fat and cut into 2-inch pieces

½ cup all-purpose flour

2 tablespoons unsalted butter

2 tablespoons extra virgin olive oil

Salt and freshly ground black pepper to taste

2 ounces thinly sliced pancetta, finely chopped

½ cup finely chopped yellow onions

5 to 6 sage leaves, chopped, optional

1 garlic clove, minced

1 cup dry white wine

1½ to 2 cups Chicken Broth (page 73) or canned low-sodium chicken broth

1 cup fresh peas, blanched in boiling salted water for 2 to 3 minutes, or thawed frozen peas

This veal stew is one of my brother's favorites. It can be made with potatoes, carrots, or blanched small onions instead of peas. It can be served next to fluffy mashed potatoes (if there are no potatoes in the stew) or soft, grilled, or fried polenta. It can be prepared a day or two ahead. And it should be served, as my family does, with a red wine such as a Sangiovese di Romagna or a Barbera.

PLACE the veal in a large strainer set over a bowl and sprinkle with the flour, shaking the strainer to coat the veal evenly.

HEAT the butter and oil together in a large heavy skillet over medium-high heat. When the butter begins to foam, add the veal, without crowding (if necessary, brown the veal in a couple of batches), season with salt and pepper, and cook, turning occasionally, until browned on all sides, 7 to 8 minutes. With a slotted spoon, transfer the veal to a dish, draining the excess fat back into the skillet. Discard about half of the fat in the skillet if needed.

ADD the pancetta, onions, sage, and garlic to the pan and stir until the onions turn a pale gold, 3 to 4 minutes. Return the veal to the pan, raise the heat to high, and add the wine. Stir with a wooden spoon, scraping the bottom of the pan to loosen the delicious browned bits, until the wine is reduced by about half. Add 1½ cups broth. As soon as the broth begins to bubble, reduce the heat to low and partially cover the pan. Simmer, stirring occasionally and turning the meat from time to time, until the veal is very tender, 1 to 1½ hours. Add the remaining ½ cup broth if necessary to prevent sticking.

ADD the peas, stir for a few minutes, and turn off the heat. Taste, adjust the seasoning, and serve hot.

FOR A TENDER STEW

- The veal for stew should never be too lean. The most desirable cuts to use are veal cross ribs, shoulder, or shanks.

- Brown the meat over high heat.

- Simmer the stew, covered, at length and very gently, over low heat, with enough liquid in the pan so that the meat stays moist.

- If, at the end of cooking, the sauce is too thin, place the meat on a large platter and keep warm in the oven. Boil the sauce briskly over high heat until it has thickened, then pour it over the veal.

ROASTED STUFFED BREAST OF VEAL

Punta di Vitello Ripiena al Forno

SERVES 6 TO 8

For the filling

2 to 3 tablespoons extra virgin olive oil

1 cup finely minced yellow onions

½ cup finely minced celery

½ cup finely minced carrots

2 tablespoons fine dried bread crumbs

2 tablespoons chopped flat-leaf parsley

1½ cups freshly grated Parmigiano-Reggiano

⅛ teaspoon freshly grated nutmeg

3 large egg yolks, lightly beaten

1 boneless breast of veal (about 4 pounds), with a pocket

Salt and freshly ground black pepper to taste

½ cup extra virgin olive oil

2 garlic cloves, minced

2 tablespoons finely minced rosemary leaves

2 cups dry white wine, plus extra if needed

1 tablespoon unsalted butter

*B*reast of veal, which has a somewhat gelatinous texture and great flavor, has considerable gastronomic importance in the cooking of the Emilia side of the region. A breast of veal, bone in or boneless, can be roasted, poached, or braised. A boneless shoulder can be stuffed with a variety of ingredients, rolled up, and pan-roasted. A pocket can be cut into the meat and filled with a mixture of sautéed vegetables, Parmigiano, nutmeg, and eggs, then the meat can be either roasted or boiled in a flavorful broth. The roasted version, with its golden brown, crisp crust and soft, moist filling, is my favorite.

At Trattoria del Cacciatore in the Parma countryside, the veal was accompanied by deliciously crunchy potatoes that had been roasted with a mixture of garlic and rosemary (see Roasted Potatoes, page 324).

Ask your butcher to trim as much fat from the veal as possible and to make a deep "pocket" in the meat. Make sure that there are no tears in the meat, or the stuffing will escape while cooking. To prepare this dish, you'll need a trussing needle and butcher's twine.

To prepare the filling, heat the oil in a small skillet over medium heat. Add the onions, celery, and carrots and cook, stirring, until golden and soft, about 6 minutes. Scoop up the vegetables with a slotted spoon and place in a medium bowl. Add the bread crumbs, parsley, Parmigiano, nutmeg, and egg yolks and mix well with a wooden spoon until the filling is thoroughly mixed and evenly moistened. (The filling can be prepared a few hours ahead and kept, tightly covered, in the refrigerator.)

PREHEAT the oven to 300°F.

PLACE the filling in the veal pocket, making sure to fill it only two-thirds of the way, and press down gently on the filling. (Too much filling will make the pocket burst.) Using a trussing needle and butcher twine sew the edges of the pocket together so the filling will not escape. Puncture the veal in several places with the needle to allow the steam to escape and to prevent the meat from splitting.

Season the veal on all sides with salt and pepper. Put the oil in a large ovenproof skillet or a roasting pan and place over high heat. When the oil is very hot and beginning to smoke, carefully slip the veal into the pan (the oil will splatter on contact with the cold meat) and cook until the bottom is golden brown, 4 to 5 minutes. Using large tongs, holding the side of the veal where there is no stuffing, turn it to brown the other side and cook for 3 to 4 minutes longer.

Turn off the heat, tilt the pan slightly, and discard about two-thirds of the fat. Add the garlic and rosemary to the pan and stir quickly a few times. (The pan, at this point, is still very hot and the garlic will brown in no time at all even with the heat off.) Add the wine and stir briefly. Cover the pan tightly with aluminum foil and, with a thin knife, make a few slits in the foil to allow steam to escape.

Place on the middle rack of the oven and cook for 1 hour, basting the meat with the pan juices every 15 minutes or so. If the wine reduces too much, add a bit more.

Raise the oven temperature to 350°F and remove the foil. Cook, basting the meat occasionally and adding a bit more wine if needed, until the meat has a deep rich brown color, another 15 to 20 minutes. Transfer the veal to a cutting board and let it rest for 10 minutes.

Meanwhile, put the pan over high heat and add the butter. If the juices in the pan are too thin, boil them briskly, stirring with a wooden spoon to loosen the browned bits attached to the bottom and sides of the pan, until the sauce is reduced to a thick glaze. Slice the meat and serve with a drizzle of the pan juices.

TIPS FOR A PERFECT ROAST

This roast, while not difficult to prepare, requires a bit of attention. The tips below will help you prepare a truly impressive roast.

- Remove, or have the butcher remove, as much fat as possible from the roast without tearing the meat or the pocket.

- Make sure to fill the pocket only two-thirds of the way full with the filling, because the filling will expand during cooking and the meat will shrink.

- Make sure to sew the opening of the pocket tightly closed so the filling will not escape.

- Make sure to puncture the meat after it has been filled and sewn to allow steam to escape, or the meat will split.

- Make sure there is always some liquid in the pan. If the pan juices completely evaporate, the meat will stick to the bottom of the pan and will tear.

- Baste the meat every 15 minutes or so, adding a small amount of wine, broth, or water to the pan as needed, to keep the meat moist.

A HOMEY TOUCH

As the roast cooks, roast some potatoes separately, then, just before serving, toss the crisp potatoes with a few tablespoons of the roast's hot pan juices.

BRAISED PORK SPARERIBS
WITH POTATOES

Costine di Maiale e Patate in Umido

Two 1½-pound racks of pork spareribs, 8 to 9 inches long, cut into single ribs; or baby back ribs

⅓ cup extra virgin olive oil

Salt and freshly ground black pepper to taste

⅔ cup finely minced yellow onions

2 tablespoons finely minced fresh rosemary or 1½ teaspoons crumbled dried rosemary

2 tablespoons minced fresh sage or 1½ teaspoons crumbled dried sage

½ cup dry white wine

Splash of Cognac, optional

3 large boiling potatoes (about 1½ pounds), peeled and cut into 1-inch pieces

2 tablespoons double-concentrated Italian tomato paste, diluted with 3 cups Chicken Broth (page 73) or canned low-sodium chicken broth

Barbara and Ivan are the personable young couple who own Hostaria da Ivan, a little trattoria in the rich farmland of Emilia, about fifteen miles north of Parma. She is in the kitchen and he takes care of the customers. One of the nights we were there, she described this dish in such detail that, even though I was already full, I had to order it. "Signora," she said, "the ribs, which come from our own pigs, are meaty and juicy and when they simmer slowly with the onion, herbs, and potatoes, they practically dissolve in the mouth. Also," she said, "the sauce becomes very thick because the potatoes are cooked until they fall apart in the sauce, thus thickening it. You will love it." And she was absolutely right.

TRIM as much fat as possible from the ribs without having them fall apart. Heat the oil in a large skillet over medium-high heat. When the oil is nice and hot, add as many ribs as can comfortably fit in the skillet without crowding and season with salt and pepper. Cook, turning occasionally, until the ribs are golden brown on all sides, 8 to 9 minutes. With long tongs, transfer the ribs to a plate, then brown the remaining ribs.

DISCARD the excess fat in the skillet, leaving enough to sauté the onions. Reduce the heat to medium, add the onions, and cook, stirring, until lightly golden and soft, 5 to 6 minutes. Add the herbs and stir once or twice, then put the ribs back in the skillet. Raise the heat to high and add the wine and the Cognac, if using. Stir until almost all the wine has evaporated. Add the potatoes and stir for a minute or two, until they are well coated with the savory base. Add the diluted tomato paste and bring to a boil. Reduce the heat to low, partially cover the skillet, and simmer gently until the meat is very tender and the potatoes are beginning to fall apart, about 1 hour.

TASTE and adjust the seasoning. Turn off the heat and let the stew sit for about 10 minutes before serving. (The dish can be prepared several hours or a day ahead, covered, and refrigerated. Reheat gently before serving.)

PORK ROAST WITH

SWEET-AND-SOUR ONIONS

Arrosto di Maiale con Cipolline in Agrodolce

SERVES 6 TO 8

2 to 3 tablespoons Aglione (page 21)

One 4-pound boneless Boston butt (pork shoulder roast), excess fat trimmed, or center-cut double loin pork roast

⅓ cup extra virgin olive oil

1 cup dry white wine

1 recipe Sweet-and-Sour Onions (page 317)

I love rich, succulent pork dishes, and Ristorante Cocchi in Parma, which has been in the same family for several generations, cooks them better than anyone else in the city. There, perfectly cooked slices of pork roast are served with very small sweet-and-sour cipolline *and some of the caramelized onions' sauce.*

RUB the *aglione* all over the pork roast. Place the roast on a large plate, cover with plastic wrap, and refrigerate for a few hours.

PREHEAT the oven to 350°F.

HEAT the olive oil in a large heavy ovenproof pan over medium heat. Add the pork and cook, turning, until the meat has a light golden color on all sides, 8 to 10 minutes.

TRANSFER the pan to the middle rack of the oven. Cook, basting the roast every 15 minutes or so with small additions of the wine and with the pan juices, until it has a rich golden brown color and its juices run clear when pierced with a thin knife, 1½ to 1¾ hours; it should read 160° to 165°F on an instant-read thermometer. Transfer the roast to a cutting board and let it rest for 5 to 10 minutes.

MEANWHILE, reheat the onions over low heat.

SLICE the roast and place on a large warm serving platter. Spoon the onions and their sauce over the roast and serve.

PORK LOIN BRAISED IN MILK

Arrosto di Maiale nel Latte

SERVES 6

1 tablespoon finely chopped
fresh rosemary or 1½
teaspoons chopped dried
rosemary

1 tablespoon finely chopped
fresh sage or 3 to 4 dried sage
leaves, chopped

1 garlic clove, finely minced

Salt and freshly ground black
pepper to taste

One 3- to 3½-pound
center-cut boneless pork
loin roast (see Note)

2 tablespoons unsalted butter

2 tablespoons extra virgin
olive oil

3 to 4 cups whole milk

ork is the quintessential meat in Emilia-Romagna, especially in Bologna, Modena, and Parma, where it is cooked in simple but savory preparations. In Modena, they rub loin of pork with an aromatic mixture of fresh rosemary, sage, and garlic, and braise it slowly in milk. In Bologna, the dish is prepared without the aromatic mixture. Either way, the meat has a light, delicate taste and a rich, golden color, from the cooked-down clusters of browned milk particles.

If your trip to Italy should include Modena, the city of Pavarotti, Ferrari, and great Emilian food, then you must go either to Fini, the best-known, most classic restaurant of Modena, or to Trattoria Bianca, which, for almost fifty years, has served great traditional food, and hope to find, as one of the specials of the day, this outstanding roast. If not, just get in the kitchen and prepare it yourself. This is a dish you will fall in love with.

COMBINE the rosemary, sage, garlic, and salt and pepper in a small bowl and rub it all over the pork. Place the pork on a large plate, cover with plastic wrap, and refrigerate for a few hours.

PLACE a medium heavy pan that will hold the roast somewhat snugly over medium heat and add the butter and oil. When the butter begins to foam, add the pork and cook, turning occasionally, until lightly golden on all sides, 10 to 12 minutes. (Keep your eyes on the butter so it doesn't burn and reduce the heat a bit if needed.)

ADD 1 cup of the milk and stir to loosen the browned bits attached to the bottom of the pan. As soon as the milk comes to a boil, reduce the heat to low, partially cover the pan, and simmer until almost all the milk has evaporated, about 15 minutes. Add 1 more cup milk and continue cooking, basting and turning the meat a few times, until most of the milk has evaporated. Cook the pork in this manner, adding the milk ½ to 1 cup at a time, until it reads 160°F on an instant-read thermometer, about 2 hours. (The pork can be cooked up to this point 1 hour or so ahead. In that case, cook only until it reaches 155°F, because it will keep on cooking as it sits in the hot pan juices.)

Remove the lid and raise the heat to high. If no more milk is left in the pan, add ½ cup or so more. Cook, stirring and scraping the bottom of the pan to release the browned bits and turning the pork once or twice, until most of the milk has evaporated and the meat has a rich, golden brown color. Transfer the pork to a cutting board and let it rest for about 10 minutes while you finish the sauce.

Spoon off some of the fat from the pan. Add ⅓ cup water and stir quickly, over medium heat, scraping the bottom of the pan until only the brown glazed clusters of milk particles remain.

Cut the meat into ½-inch-thick slices and serve topped with a bit of the pan juices.

VARIATION: For the Pork Loin in Milk without the savory herb mixture, first brown the pork in the butter and oil as directed above. When the meat is golden on all sides, add enough milk to come one-third of the way up the sides of the pork and bring to a boil. Partially cover the pan, reduce the heat to low, and simmer, stirring and turning the meat a few times, until the meat reaches 160°F. As the pork cooks, add a bit more milk as needed. When the pork is done, remove the lid, raise the heat to high, and finish the dish as instructed.

AND THE DAY AFTER Any leftover pork can be cut into cubes, tossed with mixed greens or freshly cooked vegetables, and turned into a delicious salad. Some of my favorite vegetables are asparagus tips, peas, white beans, potatoes, broccoli, artichoke hearts, and fresh tomatoes.

Note: Pork loin roast is generally prepared with two center-cut loins tied together, thus making them "double loin roasts." If one loin roast is used instead of the double, the cooking time will obviously be reduced by about half.

Since the pork loin is a lean piece of meat, make sure not to trim away the fat attached to it, because it will add additional flavor.

COTECHINO SAUSAGE WITH
SWEET-AND-SOUR BRAISED CABBAGE

Cotechino con Verza in Agrodolce

SERVES 4

**1 cotechino sausage
(1 to 1½ pounds)**

**1 medium head Savoy cabbage
(1½ to 2 pounds)**

¼ cup extra virgin olive oil

**2 ounces sliced pancetta,
finely chopped**

**½ cup finely chopped
yellow onions**

**Salt and freshly ground black
pepper to taste**

**2 to 3 tablespoons
granulated sugar**

¼ cup strong red wine vinegar

**1 tablespoon unsalted butter,
optional**

his is the type of food that used to be served regularly in homes in Emilia-Romagna, especially during the long winter days when the fog enveloped the region and the need for heartening food was strong. Cotechino would come to the table on a large cutting board, still steaming from the hot broth, often accompanied by bollito misto, *mixed boiled meats. It would be sliced into mouthwatering rounds and served with vegetables such as mashed potatoes, stewed lentils, beans, or cabbage.*

This down-to-earth food is still quite popular in the trattorie of the region, especially in winter. Last fall, when my husband and I dined at Hostaria da Ivan, in Fontanelle di Roccabianca, a small hamlet in the Parma countryside, one of the specials was cotechino with braised sweet-and-sour cabbage; we thought we had died and gone to heaven. Try it, perhaps accompanied with a few slices of grilled or fried polenta.

WITH a fork, prick the skin of the cotechino in several places. Place it in a medium saucepan, cover generously with cold water, and bring to a boil over medium heat. Cover the pan, reduce the heat to medium-low, and simmer for 1 to 1½ hours, depending on the cotechino's weight. Turn off the heat and leave the cotechino in its hot broth for about half an hour or so.

WHILE the cotechino is cooking, remove and discard the tough or bruised outer leaves of the cabbage. Slice the cabbage in half and remove the core. Cut the cabbage into thin strips and set aside.

HEAT the oil in a large skillet over medium heat. Add the pancetta and onions and cook, stirring, until the onions are soft and the pancetta has a rich golden color, 6 to 7 minutes. Add the cabbage and stir for a few minutes. Scoop out about 1 cup of the cotechino cooking liquid and add to the skillet. Partially cover the skillet, reduce the heat to low, and cook, stirring occasionally, until the cabbage is soft and has reduced to about half its original volume, 25 to 30 minutes.

SEASON the cabbage with salt and pepper and stir in the sugar, vinegar, and the butter, if using. Cover the skillet again and cook gently for 10 minutes longer.

REMOVE the lid, raise the heat to high, and stir quickly for a minute or two, until the cabbage has a rich golden color. Taste and adjust the seasoning.

TRANSFER the cotechino to a cutting board and cut into ½-inch-thick slices. Spoon the cabbage onto individual plates, top with the cotechino slices, and serve.

USING LEFTOVER MEATS

Any leftover meat can be chopped fine, mixed with beaten eggs and Parmigiano, and shaped into meatballs (see My Mother's Fried Meatballs, page 265).

The meat can also be sliced, layered on a serving platter, covered with *salsa verde*, and served chilled. But my favorite way is to cut the meat into cubes and turn it into a salad (see Boiled Meats and New Potato Salad, page 338).

BEEF BRAISED IN WINE

Stracotto di Manzo

SERVES 6 TO 8

¼ cup extra virgin olive oil

1 tablespoon unsalted butter

One 4-pound boneless beef chuck or bottom round roast

Salt and freshly ground black pepper to taste

2 cups finely minced yellow onions

2 medium carrots, finely minced

10 black peppercorns, lightly crushed

2 fresh bay leaves or 1 dried bay leaf

Pinch of ground cloves

2 to 3 cups full-bodied red wine

The city of Parma is synonymous with good food. How could it not be, considering that it is the Parma province that some of the best Italian ingredients come from? This is a dish that Ristorante Parizzi, a restaurant that has been in the same family for three generations, shared with me. A large chuck roast is braised very slowly with vegetables and wine until the meat is melt-in-the-mouth tender and the sauce has reduced to a thick, flavorful essence. Serve it with polenta—soft, fried, grilled, baked, it doesn't matter, as long as it is on the plate. This meal also calls for a full-bodied red wine, such as a Barbera.

HEAT the oil and butter together in a large heavy pan over high heat. When nice and hot, add the roast, season with salt and pepper, and cook, turning occasionally, until it is browned on all sides, 8 to 10 minutes. Transfer the roast to a plate.

DISCARD about half of the fat in the pan and put the pan back over medium heat. Add the onions and carrots and cook, stirring occasionally, until lightly golden, 6 to 7 minutes. Add the peppercorns, bay leaves, and cloves, stir a few times, and return the roast to the pan.

RAISE the heat to high and add 2 cups of the wine. As soon as the wine begins to bubble, reduce the heat to low, partially cover the pan, and cook at the gentlest of simmers for 2½ to 3 hours. Stir several times during cooking, turning the meat once or twice and basting it with the wine. Add more wine or some water if the liquid in the pan reduces too much. At the end of the cooking time, the sauce should be medium-thick and reduced to about half its original amount. Transfer the roast to a cutting board and let it rest for 5 to 10 minutes.

IF the sauce is too thin, reduce it over high heat. Taste the sauce and adjust the seasoning.

SLICE the meat and spoon a few tablespoons of the sauce over each serving.

ROASTED STUFFED FILLET OF BEEF

Rosa di Parma

SERVES 6

2 tablespoons finely chopped rosemary

1 garlic clove, finely minced

⅓ cup extra virgin olive oil

One 3-pound beef fillet, butterflied and pounded thin by the butcher

Salt and freshly ground black pepper to taste

¼ pound thinly sliced prosciutto

¼ cup freshly grated Parmigiano-Reggiano

2 tablespoons unsalted butter

½ cup dry Marsala

½ cup Sangiovese di Romagna or other red wine

½ cup Chicken Broth (page 73) or canned low-sodium chicken broth

⅓ cup heavy cream

*L*a Rosa di Parma is a butterflied filet mignon stuffed with prosciutto and Parmigiano and roasted with Sangiovese di Romagna and dry Marsala wine. This elegant, delicious dish, said to have been created by a well-known Parma restaurateur, can be found in many restaurants and trattorie in Emilia-Romagna. I tested this dish first in my restaurant kitchen, and later at home and, on both occasions, the roast disappeared as quickly as it was sliced.

PREHEAT the oven to 400°F.

COMBINE the rosemary, garlic, and 1 tablespoon of the oil in a small bowl.

PLACE the beef on a work surface, cut side up, rub it with 1 tablespoon of the rosemary mixture, and season with salt and pepper. Cover the meat with the slices of prosciutto and sprinkle with the Parmigiano. Starting at a long side, roll up the meat tightly and tie with kitchen string. Rub some of the rosemary mixture all over the roast and season with salt and pepper. (The roast can be prepared up to this point several hours ahead. Cover tightly with plastic wrap and refrigerate. Bring to room temperature before cooking.)

HEAT the butter and the remaining oil together in a large heavy oven-proof casserole over medium-high heat. As soon as the butter begins to foam, add the roast and cook, turning the meat occasionally, until it is lightly browned on all sides, 6 to 8 minutes. Spoon off some of the fat if needed. Add the Marsala and Sangiovese and bring to a boil. Let the wine bubble away gently, stirring with a wooden spoon, until reduced by about half.

TRANSFER the pan to the center rack of the oven and roast the meat for 25 to 30 minutes, turning and basting it with the pan juices and the broth several times during cooking, until it registers 135°F (for medium) on an instant-read thermometer. Transfer the roast to a cutting board, cover it loosely with aluminum foil, and let it rest for about 5 minutes, while you finish the sauce.

PLACE the pan over high heat, add the cream, and bring to a boil. Stir quickly with a wooden spoon, scraping the bottom of the pan to loosen the browned particles attached to it. When the pan juices are nice and thick, taste, adjust the seasoning, and turn off the heat.

REMOVE the string from the roast, slice the meat, and serve with the pan juices.

COOKING A PERFECT ROAST

Here, just as with many other Italian roasts, the meat is given a preliminary searing on top of the stove and finished in the oven. Because, with few exceptions, Italians don't eat beef rare, the roast is removed from the oven when it reads 135°F on an instant-read thermometer. As the roast rests for 5 minutes or so, it continues to cook. By the time the sauce is ready and the roast is sliced, the meat will be moist and lightly pink. (For rare beef, the temperature should read 110–115°F; for medium-rare, 120–125°F; for well-done, 160°F.)

MIXED MEAT GRILL

Grigliata di Carne Mista alla Romagnola

SERVES 4 TO 6

**3 tablespoons Aglione
(page 21)**

½ cup extra virgin olive oil

⅓ cup red wine vinegar

**1 pound pork spareribs
(about 8), cut into
two sections**

**4 links Homemade Bolognese
Sausage (page 267) or mild
Italian pork sausage
(containing no fennel seeds,
chile pepper, or strong spices)**

Four ½-inch-thick pork chops

Four ½-inch-thick lamb chops

**Four ¼-inch-thick slices
pancetta (about 7 ounces)**

Salt to taste

*The technique of grilling has been transformed into art by the people
of Romagna. While the Emiliani sauté, stuff, braise, and roast, the
Romagnoli grill. Anyone who has had the joy of vacationing in one of
Romagna's small coastal towns can recount the delights of a large mixed
meat grill or mixed grill of fish.*

*One of the meats the Romagnoli love to grill more than any other is
castrato. A castrato is a male lamb that has been neutered, kept within a
small space, and fattened. The lack of exercise and the large amount of food
fed to the animal make its meat extremely tender. The fatter the animal,
the more tender the meat. A mixed grill generally also includes plump
sausage, pork chops, spareribs, thickly sliced pancetta, and small lamb
chops. The meats, which are coated with a mixture of rosemary, garlic, salt
and pepper, and olive oil, are constantly brushed as they grill with a mixture of oil and red wine vinegar, which accentuates the individual flavors
of the meats.*

PUT the *aglione* in a small bowl and mix with 3 tablespoons of the oil. In
another small bowl, combine the remaining 5 tablespoons oil with the
vinegar; set aside.

TRIM as much fat as possible from the spareribs without having them
fall apart. Split each sausage lengthwise and open out like a book. Place
the ribs, sausage, pork, lamb, and pancetta in a large bowl, add the *aglione*,
and mix well with your hands, making sure to coat all the meats lightly.
Cover with plastic wrap and refrigerate for a few hours. Remove from
the refrigerator 30 minutes before the meats are to be grilled.

PREHEAT the grill. Begin by putting the meats that will take longest to
cook on the hottest part of the grill, then, after browning them on all
sides, move them to the side of the grill, where the heat is not as intense,
to finish cooking.

Spareribs and Sausage: Put the spareribs on the hottest part of the grill, season them with salt, and brush with the oil-vinegar mixture. Brown the ribs on both sides, 8 to 10 minutes total, then move them to the side of the grill to finish cooking, basting and turning them a few times. Grill them for a total of 13 to 15 minutes. When done, transfer them to a warm large platter, and cover with foil.

Brush the cut sides of the sausages with the oil-vinegar mixture, place cut side down on the hot part of grill, and grill until golden brown, about 5 minutes. Turn and brown the other side, 4 to 5 minutes longer. Transfer to the side of the grill and cook for a few minutes longer, then transfer to the platter with the ribs.

Pork chops and lamb chops: When the ribs and sausage have cooked halfway through, put the chops on the grill. Season with salt, brush with the oil-vinegar mixture, and grill for 3 to 4 minutes on each side, or to the desired degree of doneness. Transfer to the platter.

Pancetta: The pancetta is the last item to go on the grill, since it will become nice and crisp in approximately 5 minutes. Grill it on both sides and add to the platter.

BRING the platter to the table and serve at once.

ORGANIZING YOUR GRILL

Because the variables here are many (grills differ greatly in the amount of heat they generate), the cooking times given for the meats are approximate. Keep your eye on what you are grilling, and cook the meats to the desired doneness. Have the vegetables you are serving already prepared and ready, so you can give your complete attention to the task of grilling.

MIXED BOILED MEATS

Bollito Misto all'Emiliana

SERVES 8 TO 10

1 ripe tomato, halved

2 carrots, cut into pieces

2 celery stalks, cut into pieces

1 medium yellow onion, cut into pieces

A few sprigs flat-leaf parsley

One 3- to 3½-pound boneless beef brisket or chuck roast

One 3-pound veal rump roast

One 7- or 8-pound capon

One 3- to 3½-pound chicken (or half of a 7- or 8-pound capon)

Salt to taste

1 cotechino sausage (1 to 1½ pounds; see page 12)

*B*ollito misto *is one of the great dishes of northern Italy. Until a generation or so ago, it was standard fare in restaurants, trattorie, and homes of Emilia-Romagna. My mother's* bollito misto *was made ritually on Sunday. She got up earlier than usual to assemble all the meats and vegetables in the large stockpot, then simmered them at length until the meats were meltingly tender and the broth had a rich, golden color with an aroma that would instantly make us want to sit down to eat. Everything in that pot would be eaten. The precious broth went into soups and risotto and was used give body and flavor to sauces. The meats were eaten piping hot, served invariably with the traditional* salsa verde *and a red sauce. And the vegetables, deliciously impregnated with the aroma of the broth, were up for grabs.*

Today this magnificent dish can be found only in a handful of trattorie and restaurants on the Emilia side of the region. If you are in Bologna, go to Diana. If in Modena, go to Fini. In Parma, go to Cocchi. There, a waiter will come to your table pushing a steam trolley filled with a large variety of mixed boiled meats, which will be served with an array of traditional condiments and sauces. In the meantime, while you are waiting to go to Italy, gather a group of friends who really enjoy food as much as you do, and make your own bollito misto, *which, you will discover, is much simpler to prepare than you thought.*

MEASURE how much water you need to cook the meats by putting the vegetables, parsley, and all the meats except the cotechino in a very large stockpot and covering them with 3 to 4 inches of cold water. Leave the vegetables in the water, but remove the meats and set them aside.

BRING the water to a gentle simmer and add the beef. After 5 to 10 minutes, skim off the scum that has risen to the surface with a large spoon, then partially cover the pot and simmer gently for 1½ to 2 hours.

ADD the veal and the chicken to the pot. Partially cover and cook at the gentlest of simmers for 1 to 1½ hours longer. Season with salt during the last 10 minutes of cooking. (The meats can be cooked an hour or two ahead; leave them in the broth, covered, and reheat gently just before serving.)

MEANWHILE, bring a medium saucepan of water to a boil. Prick the cotechino in several places with a fork, so it won't burst as it cooks. Add it to the boiling water, reduce the heat to a gentle simmer, partially cover the pan, and cook for 1 to 1½ hours, depending on its size. Leave the cotechino in its liquid until ready to serve. (It can be cooked a few hours ahead and reheated just before serving.)

To serve, slice the meats and sausage and arrange on a large warm serving platter. (Keep any remaining meats you aren't serving right away in the hot broth.) Serve at once, with one or several of the sauces and dishes listed below.

TRADITIONAL SAUCES AND DISHES TO SERVE WITH BOLLITO MISTO

- Piquant Green Sauce with Shallots (page 25)

- Friggione (page 326)

- Mashed Potatoes with Parmigiano (page 323)

STORING LEFTOVER BROTH

Strain the broth and refrigerate it for 2 to 3 days or freeze it. To freeze, pour it into ice cube trays, then divide the frozen cubes among several plastic bags and store in the freezer for up to 3 months, to be used as needed.

BREADED CALF'S LIVER

Cotolette di Fegato

SERVES 4

1 pound calf's liver, cut into
¼-inch-thick slices

2 large eggs

Salt

1 cup all-purpose flour

1½ cups fine dried bread
crumbs

2 to 3 tablespoons
unsalted butter

2 tablespoons extra virgin
olive oil

Lemon wedges

My mother loved variety meats. She adored tripe, sweetbreads, and liver and she cooked them in many ingenious ways. The only way I would eat liver when I was young was when it was breaded and cooked to a brown crisp. Then I would squeeze over enough lemon juice to almost obliterate the liver's taste. What a pity it took me so many years to appreciate it, because fresh calf's liver sliced thin, coated with bread crumbs, and cooked in butter is simply delicious. Serve it with lemon slices or, as they do in Modena, with a few drops of good balsamic vinegar.

REMOVE any membranes from the liver and flatten the slices with a meat pounder.

LIGHTLY beat the eggs with a pinch of salt in a medium bowl. Coat each slice of liver lightly with the flour and dip it into the eggs, letting the excess egg drip back into the bowl. Coat each slice with the bread crumbs, pressing the crumbs onto the meat with the palms of your hands.

IN a large heavy skillet, heat the butter with the oil over medium-high heat. As soon as the butter begins to foam, add the slices without crowding (cook in two batches if necessary), and cook until golden brown and crisp on one side, about 2 minutes. Quickly turn them and brown the other side, about 2 minutes longer. At this point, the liver should be still slightly pink and juicy inside. Transfer to paper towels to drain. Season lightly with salt and serve at once, with lemon wedges.

Note: For the sweetest tasting and most tender dish, the liver should come from a young milk-fed calf. Since milk-fed calf is easier to find in Italy than here, we must do with what we have at hand. Talk to your butcher and ask him to cut the liver into ¼-inch-thick slices, then pound the slices as thin as he can without tearing them. Be gentle when you handle them. Cook the liver only long enough for the bread coating to turn golden brown and crisp, or the liver will be tough.

VEGETABLES
Verdure

Italians have a way with vegetables and prepare them in many exciting ways. Take, for example, humble potatoes. We roast them, panfry them, bake them, and mash them, just as many other countries do, but we also turn them into fritters or croquettes and we use them in a stuffing for pasta and vegetables. We add them to frittatas, risottos, and pasta sauces. We stew them in savory sauces by themselves or add them to meat and fish stews. We make soups, turn them into savory cakes and crisp balls, bake them with butter and Parmigiano, or toss them into a salad. The possibilities are endless, since all cooks prepare them in their own way.

What makes Italians so creative with vegetables? Centuries of traditions and the fact that Italy was, from the beginning, an agricultural society whose people worked and harvested the land, for many, the main source of sustenance.

When my mother came across a good bargain at the produce stand, she always bought a large amount. If tomatoes were on sale, she set aside several pounds to use during the week in different preparations, and used what she had left to make batches of tomato sauce, which she put away for winter use. If she bought fresh peas, she used them in risotto, in stews, in pasta sauces, and in vegetable soups. By taking advantage of the surplus of the season, she saved money and fed us well.

I have memories of cold winters in Bologna, with the city blanketed under several feet of snow. My mother and I would still go to the market to buy our produce. But while we could keep these excursion short and rush back to our warm house, the vendors at the market had to brave horrible weather for hours, and in spite of the fact that they were heavily bundled up, their hands were red and cracked by the cold, their eyes were tearing and their noses were dripping.

The open market of Bologna is where I go as soon as arriving in my city. During a recent visit, while I was checking out a pile of beautifully plump, creamy fennel with long, feathery fronds, I asked an older well-dressed woman, who also was selecting fennel, how she planned to cook it. "I don't know yet," she replied, "I'll decide when I get home."

This attitude, typical of the good home cook who knows that good cooking begins at the market, allows the shopper to select the best ingredients available, then transform them into the dish of her choice. By waiting patiently for seasonal vegetables, instead of opting for something that comes from hundreds of miles away, we are assured of a flavorful dish.

Vegetables in Emilia-Romagna are usually simply prepared, especially when they are served as a side dish to complement, not compete with, the entrée. A small amount of prosciutto, mortadella, Parmigiano, sausage, or balsamic vinegar is often added to a vegetable dish to enhance its taste. Fennel is fennel, but if I boil it, cut it into thin slices, top it with freshly grated Parmigiano, dot it with butter, and bake it until the butter and cheese are melted, I have "Emilianized" the dish. If I boil small onions and toss them with butter, sugar, and balsamic vinegar instead of red wine vinegar, I have again put a regional stamp on the dish. And if I roast a batch of potatoes in the oven and season them with a mixture of herbs and garlic, *aglione*, the flavor of these potatoes will be uncompromisingly regional.

GRATINÉED BRUSSELS SPROUTS
WITH PANCETTA

Cavolini di Bruxelles al Forno

SERVES 6

2 pounds Brussels sprouts

Salt

3 tablespoons unsalted butter

⅓ cup finely minced shallots

2 ounces thickly sliced
pancetta, diced

½ cup freshly grated
Parmigiano-Reggiano

In Emilia-Romagna, it is almost heresy not to add just a touch of pancetta, prosciutto, baked ham, sausage, or any other savory pork product to a vegetable dish, since, as everyone knows quite well, these ingredients add a tremendous wallop of taste even to the simplest or meekest of vegetables. For those who usually turn their noses up at Brussels sprouts, this preparation will change their minds.

TRIM the stem ends of the Brussels sprouts and remove any loose or discolored leaves.

BRING a large saucepan of water to a boil. Add a generous pinch of salt and the sprouts and cook, uncovered over medium heat until the sprouts are tender but still firm to the bite, 8 to 10 minutes. Drain and immediately plunge them into a large bowl of ice water to stop the cooking and set their green color. Drain the sprouts, pat dry with paper towels, and place in a large bowl.

PREHEAT the oven to 350°F.

MELT the butter in a small skillet over medium heat. Add the shallots and cook, stirring a few times, until soft, 4 to 5 minutes. Stir in the pancetta and cook until it just begins to color, 1 to 2 minutes. Pour the contents of the skillet over the sprouts, add about half of the Parmigiano, and season with salt. Mix well to combine.

GENEROUSLY butter a large baking pan, add the sprouts in a single layer if possible and sprinkle the remaining Parmigiano over them. (The dish can be prepared up to this point several hours ahead. Set aside, tightly covered, at room temperature.)

PUT the pan on the middle rack of the oven and bake until the cheese is melted and light golden, 10 to 12 minutes. Serve hot.

FENNEL WITH PROSCIUTTO

AND PARMIGIANO

Finocchi Gratinati con Prosciutto e Parmigiano

SERVES 6

2 large round fennel bulbs (about 2½ pounds)

Salt

16 thin slices prosciutto (about ½ pound)

⅓ to ½ cup freshly grated Parmigiano-Reggiano

2 tablespoons unsalted butter, cubed

Fennel is a delicious, crunchy vegetable that Italians use in many preparations. In Emilia-Romagna, we dip raw fennel into oil and salt, or thinly slice it and turn it into a crisp salad. When it is baked with butter and cheese, fennel becomes sweet and absolutely irresistible. This can be served as a side dish (it is great next to any type of roast), as an antipasto, or as a light lunch entrée.

TRIM off the fennel stalks. Remove any bruised or discolored outer leaves. Trim the base of each fennel bulb and cut it into 6 to 8 wedges, depending on size.

PLACE the wedges in a large skillet, cover them with cold water, and add a nice pinch of salt. Bring the water to a boil over medium heat and cook, uncovered, until the fennel is tender but still a bit firm when pierced with a thin knife, 10 to 12 minutes. With a slotted spoon, transfer the slices to paper towels to drain and cool.

PREHEAT the oven to 375°F. Generously butter a baking dish.

LOOSELY wrap a thin slice of prosciutto (or half the slice if they are large) around each fennel wedge, and arrange them in the prepared baking dish. Sprinkle generously with the Parmigiano and dot with the butter. (The dish can be prepared up to this point several hours ahead or overnight. Cover tightly and refrigerate.)

PLACE the dish on the middle rack of the oven and bake until the cheese is melted and golden, about 10 minutes. Serve hot.

FRIED BUTTERNUT SQUASH

Lucca Fritta

SERVES 6 TO 8

1 small butternut squash (about 2 pounds)

Olive oil for frying

1½ cups all-purpose flour

Salt to taste

PEEL the squash and cut it lengthwise in half. Scoop out the seeds and fibers and discard. Cut the squash across into ⅓-inch-thick slices.

BRING a large pot of water to a boil. Add the squash and cook over medium heat no longer than 2 minutes. Drain and dry thoroughly with paper towels.

POUR about 1 inch of oil into a large heavy skillet and heat over medium-high heat. Spread the flour on a sheet of aluminum foil. Lightly dredge 3 to 4 slices of squash at a time in the flour and slip them gently into the hot oil. Cook, turning the slices once or twice, until golden brown on both sides. Transfer to paper towels to drain and pat dry with paper towels.

WHEN all the squash has been fried, place on a large serving platter, sprinkle lightly with salt, and serve hot.

ROAST SQUASH

Lucca al Forno

SERVES 6 TO 8

1 small butternut squash (about 2 pounds)

3 to 4 tablespoons unsalted butter

⅛ teaspoon freshly grated nutmeg

Salt to taste

2 to 3 ounces sliced prosciutto, diced

1 cup freshly grated Parmigiano-Reggiano

PREHEAT the oven to 400°F. Generously butter a large baking dish.

PEEL the squash and cut it, lengthwise in half. Scoop out the seeds and fibers and discard. Cut the squash across into ⅓-inch-thick slices and arrange them close together in the baking dish.

MELT the butter in a small pan and pour it over the squash. Cover the baking dish tightly with foil, place on the middle rack of the oven and bake for 30 to 40 minutes, or until the squash is tender.

SEASON the squash lightly with salt. Scatter the prosciutto over the squash, sprinkle generously with the Parmigiano, and bake until the cheese is melted and golden brown, about 10 minutes longer.

LET the dish settle for about 5 minutes, then serve while still hot.

THE SQUASH LOVERS OF FERRARA

Even though most of the Emilia-Romagna region loves squash, the people of Ferrara probably consume more squash than anyone else. Winter squash, which comes in a cornucopia of shapes, sizes, and colors, reaches its apotheosis when it is turned into a divine stuffing for pasta such as in Ferrara's famous cappellacci and Bologna and Parma's tortelli, and when it becomes the golden addition to Ferrara's Squash Risotto (page 172).

But in the countryside, where people often grow their own vegetables, squash is also put to humbler use. My aunt Rina used to make a sweet filling of squash and chestnuts for *ravioline*, delicious fried or baked pastry shaped into half-moons. And she used to fry slices of squash in lard (I use olive oil) until they were golden brown and crisp.

Butternut, Delicata, and acorn squash, with their moist, meaty, orange pulp, all work quite well in these dishes.

SAUTÉED EGGPLANT WITH GARLIC AND PARSLEY

Melanzane Trifolate

SERVES 4

2 medium firm eggplant, peeled and cut into 1-inch cubes

Salt

⅓ to ½ cup extra virgin olive oil

1 garlic clove, finely minced

1 to 2 tablespoons chopped, flat-leaf parsley

Freshly ground black pepper to taste

In Italy, vegetables that are trifolati *have been sautéed quickly in oil, garlic, and parsley. Here eggplant is first diced, sprinkled with salt, and allowed to sit for about half an hour so that the salt will draw out the bitter juices. Even though the eggplant is then dried with paper towels, some of the salt will linger–do not season with salt again without first tasting it.*

PLACE the eggplant in a large bowl and sprinkle with salt, tossing so every piece is salted. Let stand at room temperature for about 30 minutes.

DRAIN the eggplant, spread on paper towels, and pat dry with more paper towels.

HEAT the oil in a large heavy skillet over high heat. When the oil is nice and hot, add the eggplant, without crowding (you may need to sauté the eggplant in two batches), and cook, stirring, until lightly golden and soft, 5 to 7 minutes. Add the garlic and parsley, season with pepper, and quickly stir a few times. Taste, adjust the seasoning, and serve.

MUSHROOMS WITH GARLIC AND PARSLEY Remove the stems and wipe the mushrooms clean with a damp towel. Cut into ¼-inch-thick slices. Cook as instructed above.

ZUCCHINI WITH GARLIC AND PARSLEY Trim the ends of the zucchini and cut into ¼-inch-thick slices. Cook as instructed above.

EGGPLANT ALLA PARMIGIANA

Melanzane alla Parmigiana

SERVES 6 TO 8

**4 medium eggplant
(3½ to 4 pounds)**

Salt

Olive oil for frying

1 cup all-purpose flour

2 tablespoons unsalted butter

**2 tablespoons extra virgin
olive oil**

**⅔ cup finely minced
yellow onions**

**1 thick slice mortadella
(about 2 ounces), finely
minced**

**1 thick slice prosciutto (about
2 ounces), finely minced**

**¼ cup double-concentrated
Italian tomato paste, diluted
in 4 cups Chicken Broth
(page 73) or canned
low-sodium chicken broth**

**1 to 1½ cups freshly grated
Parmigiano**

This dish, which in many minor variations is typical of the Emilia side of the region, takes its name from the city of Parma. The famous Neapolitan parmigiana, a distant cousin, covers the eggplant with a spirited tomato sauce and tops it with the superlative local mozzarella. The Parma version enriches the sauce with prosciutto and mortadella and tops it with Parmigiano-Reggiano and butter. In Bologna, where the dish is called alla Bolognese, *diced fresh, tomatoes are used instead of tomato paste.*

PEEL the eggplants and cut lengthwise into ¼-inch-thick slices. Place in a large dish or on a cookie sheet and sprinkle with salt, tossing the slices to salt them evenly. Let stand at room temperature for about 1 hour. (The salt will draw out the eggplant's bitter juices.) Place on paper towels and pat the slices dry with paper towels.

HEAT about 1 inch of oil in a large skillet over medium-high heat. Spread the flour on a sheet of aluminum foil. When the oil is nice and hot, lightly dredge a few slices of eggplant at a time with flour, turning to coat both sides, and lower them into the hot oil. Fry, turning once, until lightly golden on both sides, 2 to 3 minutes, then drain on paper towels. Pat dry with additional paper towels.

WIPE the skillet clean and heat the butter and oil over medium heat. Add the onions and cook, stirring, until lightly golden and soft, about 5 minutes. Add the mortadella and prosciutto and stir for a minute or two, then add the diluted tomato paste and season lightly with salt. Bring the sauce to a boil, then reduce the heat to medium-low and cook, uncovered, stirring from time to time, until the sauce has a medium-thick consistency, 10 to 15 minutes. (Makes about 3½ cups.)

PREHEAT the oven to 350°F. Grease a 12 × 9-inch baking dish with a few tablespoons of butter.

PLACE a layer of one-third of the eggplant, slightly overlapping, in the dish. Spoon one-third of the sauce over the eggplant and sprinkle with one-third of the Parmigiano. Repeat with two more layers each of eggplant, sauce, and cheese. Dot the top with about 2 tablespoons butter.

PLACE the baking dish on the middle rack of the oven and bake until the cheese is melted and golden, about 15 minutes. Remove from the oven and let the dish settle for a few minutes before serving.

PROSCIUTTO AND PARMIGIANO RINDS

These are never discarded in the kitchens of Emilia-Romagna. A small piece of the rinds of prosciutto and Parmigiano added to lentil or bean stews and soups imparts a delicious flavor.

THICK LENTIL STEW

Lenticchie in Umido alla Bolognese

SERVES 8 TO 10

3 tablespoons extra virgin
olive oil

2 tablespoons unsalted butter

½ cup finely minced onions

⅓ cup finely minced carrot

2 ounces sliced pancetta,
finely chopped

1 garlic clove, finely minced

2 tablespoons chopped
flat-leaf parsley

4 to 5 sage leaves, chopped

2 cups (about ¾ pound),
brown or green lentils, picked
over and washed in several
changes of cold water

A small piece of prosciutto
rind (see box, page 309)

1 cup full-bodied red wine

2 cups Meat Broth (page 71) or
canned low-sodium beef
or chicken broth, plus more
if needed

2 cups Homemade Tomato
Sauce (page 22) or canned
Italian plum tomatoes, with
their juice, put through a food
mill to remove the seeds

Salt and freshly ground black
pepper to taste

I can still vividly recall my mother bent over a round earthenware casserole, stirring stewed lentils with a long wooden spoon. The lentils were bubbling rhythmically in the heavy pot, which kept the heat trapped inside and cooked the food evenly, but the aroma of the stew escaped from the pot and lingered in the kitchen, teasing us and whetting our appetites.

On the Emilia side of the region, stewed lentils or stewed beans are traditionally served alongside boiled cotechino or zampone sausages.

HEAT the oil and butter in a large skillet over medium heat. Add the onions, carrot, and pancetta and cook, stirring, until the mixture is lightly golden and the onions and carrot are soft, 8 to 10 minutes. Add the garlic, parsley and sage, and stir for about 1 minute, then add the lentils and the prosciutto rind. Stir until the lentils are well coated, then raise the heat to high and add the wine.

WHEN almost all of the wine has evaporated, add the broth and tomato sauce and season with salt and pepper. As soon as the liquid comes to a boil, reduce the heat to medium-low, partially cover the pot, and cook, stirring from time to time, until the lentils are tender but still a bit firm to the bite, about 50 minutes. The stew should have a nice thick consistency. If it is too liquid, remove the cover, raise the heat to medium-high, and cook until the sauce has thickened; if too thick, add a bit more broth. (The dish can be prepared several hours ahead. Reheat it gently just before serving, and adjust the consistency of the sauce as needed.) Serve hot.

MARINATED ROASTED PEPPERS

Peperoni Arrostiti

SERVES 4

4 large red or yellow bell peppers

Salt and freshly ground black pepper to taste

⅓ cup extra virgin olive oil

Zia Rina, my mother's older sister, was a no-nonsense country cook who spent all her life on a farm. First she worked as a laborer, then, after she married and had two children, she became the proud owner of a small farm. A skinny, wiry woman, she loved to cook but did not like to fuss over the dishes she prepared. These roasted peppers were tossed only with olive oil, salt, and pepper; they stand on their own merit.

ROAST the peppers using one of the methods given in the box below.

CUT the peppers into ¼-inch strips. Place in a bowl, season with salt and a few grinds of pepper, and drizzle with the olive oil. Toss well, cover, and let stand at room temperature for a few hours.

SERVE as a light antipasto, alone or with a few small chunks of Parmigiano, or as a side dish next to any roasted meat.

ROASTING PEPPERS

The oldest Italian technique for roasting peppers is to place them over an open flame. This method, which gives the peppers a slightly smoky taste, is used in most Italian kitchens. Peppers are also delicious when roasted under a broiler or on an outdoor grill. Put the peppers over an open gas flame and roast until partially charred on one side. Turn the peppers with tongs and continue to roast, until the skin is charred all over. Or put the peppers on a broiler pan, place a few inches under the preheated broiler, and broil, turning with tongs until charred and blistered all over. Or put the peppers over a hot outdoor grill fire and grill, turning with tongs, until charred all over. Place the peppers in a plastic bag and secure tightly, or place in a large bowl and cover tightly with foil. Leave the peppers to soften and cool for 30 minutes. Peel off the blistered skin and core and seed the peppers.

BRAISED STUFFED ZUCCHINI

Zucchine Ripiene un Umido

SERVES 4 AS A SIDE
DISH OR APPETIZER

Salt

**4 small zucchini
(about 1 pound)**

For the stuffing

**2 tablespoons extra virgin
olive oil**

¼ pound ground pork

**2 ounces sliced mortadella,
very finely minced**

**⅓ cup freshly grated
Parmigiano-Reggiano**

**1 tablespoon finely chopped
flat-leaf parsley**

Dash of freshly grated nutmeg

1 large egg, lightly beaten

For the sauce

1 tablespoon unsalted butter

**1 tablespoon extra virgin
olive oil**

**½ cup finely minced
yellow onion**

⅓ cup dry white wine

**1 cup Homemade Tomato
Sauce (page 22) or canned
Italian plum tomatoes, with
their juice, put through a food
mill to remove the seeds**

**⅓ cup Chicken Broth
(page 73) or canned
low-sodium chicken broth**

¼ cup milk

Salt to taste

tuffed vegetables are an integral part of la buona cucina casalinga, *good home cooking, but none is perhaps more popular than stuffed zucchini. This placid vegetable becomes beguilingly appetizing when filled with savory ingredients. My sister-in-law, Emma, stuffs her zucchini with a mixture of ground pork, mortadella, nutmeg, and Parmigiano (the same mixture that in and around Bologna is used to make* polpettine, *meatballs). Then she simmers the zucchini slowly in a simple sauce of onion and tomatoes until they are tender and the sauce has thickened. Don't worry if some of the stuffing falls out during cooking; it will enrich the already delicious sauce.*

BRING a medium pot of water to a boil. Add a generous pinch of salt and the zucchini and cook for 2 to 3 minutes. Drain the zucchini and immediately place in a large bowl of ice water to cool and set their green color. Drain and pat dry.

TO prepare the filling, slice off and discard the ends of the zucchini. Cut the zucchini lengthwise in half. With a small melon baller or a small coffee spoon, remove the seeds and center pulp of the zucchini, making sure not to pierce the skin. Put the zucchini cut side down on a clean kitchen cloth to drain.

WITH a large knife, chop the pulp very fine; set aside.

HEAT the oil in a medium skillet over medium heat. Add the pork and cook, stirring to break it up, until it loses its raw color, about 2 minutes. With a slotted spoon, transfer the meat to a bowl.

PUT the skillet over high heat and add the chopped zucchini pulp. Cook, stirring, until the watery juices have evaporated and the pulp turns a pale gold, 3 to 4 minutes. Scoop it out with a slotted spoon and add it to the pork. Add the mortadella, Parmigiano, parsley, nutmeg, and egg and mix well. Using a small coffee spoon or a pastry bag fitted with a large tip, fill the cavities of the zucchini with the pork mixture. Place the zucchini on a large plate and set aside.

To prepare the sauce, heat the butter and oil in a wide skillet over medium heat. When the butter begins to bubble, add the onion and cook, stirring, until lightly golden and soft, 5 to 6 minutes. Raise the heat to high, add the wine, and cook until almost all of it has evaporated.

ADD the tomato sauce, broth, and milk, season lightly with salt, and bring just to a boil. Reduce the heat to low and arrange the zucchini in the pan, placing them snugly together. Partially cover the pan and cook at a gentle simmer, basting the zucchini from time to time with the sauce, until they can easily be pierced with a thin knife, 25 to 30 minutes.

PLACE the zucchini on individual serving plates. Taste the sauce, adjust the seasoning, and spoon over the zucchini. (The dish can be prepared completely a few hours ahead.) Serve hot.

FOR A PERFECT SAUCE CONSISTENCY

If at the end of cooking the sauce is a bit too thin, transfer the zucchini to a large platter and keep warm in a low oven. Put the sauce over high heat and stir until it has reached a medium-thick consistency. If, on the other hand the sauce has thickened too much, add a bit more tomato sauce, broth, or water and stir over high heat until well blended.

BAKED STUFFED ZUCCHINI

Zucchini Ripiene al Forno

SERVES 8 AS A SIDE
DISH, 4 AS AN ENTRÉE

This is a variation of Braised Stuffed Zucchini (page 312), which bakes the zucchini instead of simmering them in the sauce.

**8 small zucchini
(about 2 pounds)**

3 tablespoons extra virgin olive oil

¼ pound ground pork

¼ pound sliced mortadella, very finely minced

½ cup freshly grated Parmigiano-Reggiano

1 tablespoon finely chopped flat-leaf parsley

Dash of freshly grated nutmeg

½ cup Béchamel Sauce (page 28)

Salt to taste

BOIL the zucchini and scoop out their pulp as instructed on page 312. Put the zucchini cut side down on a clean kitchen cloth to drain.

WITH a large knife, chop the pulp very fine; set aside.

PREHEAT the oven to 400°F. Butter a baking dish that can accommodate the zucchini in a single layer.

HEAT the oil in a medium skillet over medium heat. Add the pork and cook, stirring to break up the meat, until it loses its raw color, about 2 minutes. With a slotted spoon, transfer the meat to a bowl.

PUT the skillet back over high heat, add the chopped zucchini pulp, and cook, stirring, until the watery juices have evaporated and the pulp is a light golden color, 3 to 4 minutes. Add to the pork. Add the mortadella, Parmigiano, parsley, nutmeg, and béchamel sauce and mix well to combine. Taste and add salt if needed. (The stuffing can be prepared several hours ahead, covered, and refrigerated.)

USING a small coffee spoon or a pastry bag fitted with a large plain tip, fill the cavities of the zucchini with the pork mixture. Arrange them in the buttered baking dish.

PLACE the dish on the middle rack of the oven and bake until the zucchini have a nice brown color on top and can be easily pierced with a thin knife, about 15 minutes. Serve hot.

FRIED ZUCCHINI WITH VINEGAR

Zucchine Fritte all'Aceto

SERVES 4

1½ pounds zucchini (the smallest you can get), washed, dried, and ends trimmed

Salt

Olive oil for frying

1 cup all-purpose flour

Freshly ground black pepper to taste

2 to 3 tablespoons red wine vinegar

Fried zucchini with vinegar was a favorite of my father, and my mother obligingly prepared it quite often. She selected the smallest zucchini possible, sliced them into thin rounds, and browned them very quickly in hot oil. Just before bringing them to the table, she seasoned them with salt and drizzled them with strong red wine vinegar. Usually they were served as an accompaniment to panfried sausage or mixed boiled meats and cotechino, the famous pork sausage of Bologna and Modena, but occasionally, when we had company, the zucchini would become part of a light antipasto.

CUT the zucchini into ¼-inch-thick rounds and place on a large platter or cookie sheet. Sprinkle with salt and let stand for 30 to 40 minutes so they release some of their excess moisture. Pat dry with paper towels.

HEAT ½ inch of oil in a medium skillet over medium-high heat. When the oil is nice and hot, place a handful of zucchini at a time in a sieve, sprinkle with flour, and shake off the excess. Using a slotted spoon, lower the zucchini into the hot oil, without crowding, and cook, turning once, until golden brown on both sides. Remove from the oil with the slotted spoon and drain on paper towels.

WHEN all the zucchini are cooked, place them in a serving bowl and season with salt and pepper. Sprinkle them with the vinegar while they are still hot and toss gently. Serve warm or at room temperature.

ONIONS FILLED WITH SAUSAGE

Cipolle Ripiene

SERVES 6

4 medium yellow onions, halved crosswise

6 tablespoons extra virgin olive oil

1 link (about ¼ pound) mild Italian sausage (containing no fennel seeds, chile pepper, or other strong spice)

1 cup loosely packed pieces 2-day-old Italian bread (without crusts), cut in 1-inch cubes

½ cup freshly grated Parmigiano-Reggiano

2 tablespoons chopped flat-leaf parsley

1 garlic clove, finely chopped

Salt and freshly ground black pepper to taste

1 large egg, lightly beaten

There are dishes that are intimately associated with la buona cucina casalinga *(good home cooking), dishes that speak a regional dialect, flavors that are strictly related to one area and a certain way of cooking. This is such a dish. My grandmother used to make it, my mother made it, and now my sister prepares it. When I served it to my husband, he said that "it tastes just like the food of Bologna. Wonderful!"*

PUT the onions cut side down in a wide skillet, cover with cold water, and bring to a gentle boil over medium heat. Cook until the onions are barely tender to the touch, 10 to 12 minutes.

HEAT 2 tablespoons of the oil in a medium skillet over medium-high heat. Add the sausage and cook, stirring and breaking up the meat with a wooden spoon, until light golden, 2 to 3 minutes. Scoop out the sausage with a slotted spoon and add to the onions in the bowl.

VERY finely chop the bread by hand or in a food processor and add to the bowl, along with the Parmigiano, parsley, garlic, and remaining oil. Season with salt and pepper. Stir in the egg and mix well to combine.

WITH a slotted spoon, scoop out the onions and place cut side down on paper towels to drain and cool. When they are cool enough to handle, remove the tight inner cores of the onions, chop fine, and place in a bowl.

PREHEAT the oven to 375°F. Generously grease a pan large enough to hold the onions in a single layer.

PLACE some of the stuffing in the onion cavities and arrange them close together in the prepared baking pan. Sprinkle the remaining stuffing over the onions. (The dish can be prepared up to this point several hours ahead and set aside, covered, at room temperature.)

BAKE on the middle rack of the oven until the onions are golden brown and can easily be pierced with a thin knife, 35 to 40 minutes. (If the top of the onions starts to brown too much, cover the pan loosely with foil.) Serve hot or at room temperature.

SWEET-AND-SOUR ONIONS
WITH BALSAMIC VINEGAR

Cipolline in Agrodolce

SERVES 4

2 pounds small white boiling onions

3 tablespoons unsalted butter

1 cup dry white wine, plus more if needed

¼ cup packed dark brown sugar

2 tablespoons red wine vinegar

3 tablespoons good-quality balsamic vinegar (see page 10)

Salt to taste

Tamburini in Bologna, a specialty food store, piles these golden onions on a large deep platter and displays them in its windows next to roasted meats and vegetables. This is a ubiquitous preparation that you eat first with your eyes, because it is so inviting and appetizing looking. Serve these as an antipasto or as a side dish with roasted meat or birds.

To peel the onions, cut an X in the root end of each one. Bring a large pot of water to a boil over high heat, add the onions, and cook for 2 minutes. Drain the onions and drop them into a large bowl of ice water to stop the cooking. Drain again. Peel the onions and remove the dangling "tails." (The onions can be prepared up to this point several hours or a day ahead. Put them in a bowl, between layers of paper towels, cover, and refrigerate until ready to use.)

Melt the butter in a large skillet over medium heat. When the butter begins to foam, add the onions and stir for a minute or two, then add the wine. As soon as the wine comes to a boil, reduce the heat to low, cover the skillet, and simmer gently for 30 to 35 minutes, adding a bit more wine or water if the onions start to stick to the bottom of the skillet. When the onions are tender but still a bit firm to the bite, remove the lid, raise the heat to high, and cook, stirring, until all the liquid has evaporated.

Add the sugar, red wine vinegar, and balsamic and season with salt. Cook, stirring, until the onions are golden and the pan juices reduce to a thick brown glaze that coats the onions. Taste, adjust the seasoning, and serve hot.

PANFRIED PEPPERS WITH BALSAMIC VINEGAR

Peperoni in Padella col Balsamico

SERVES 4 TO 6

6 large red bell peppers

¼ to ⅓ cup extra virgin olive oil

Salt to taste

⅓ cup good-quality balsamic vinegar (see page 10)

A few years ago, while we were having lunch in a small trattoria just outside Modena, the food for the couple sitting next to us arrived. A steam trolley was pulled up to their table and the waiter began removing an array of moist boiled meats, which he sliced and placed on individual plates. Then he proceeded to place an assortment of accompaniments alongside. The one that caught my eye was a medley of strips of dark red peppers with blistered, shiny skin and thick juices obtained by reducing some balsamic vinegar. Naturally I had to order it, and today, this vegetable dish has a place of honor on the menu of my restaurant. Serve this as a side dish or an appetizer.

CUT the peppers lengthwise in half and remove the cores, seeds, and white membranes. Cut into 1-inch strips.

HEAT the oil in a large skillet over medium-high heat. When the oil is very hot and beginning to smoke, add the peppers and cook, stirring from time to time, until lightly charred and soft, 6 to 8 minutes. Pour off the excess oil and raise the heat to high. Season the peppers with salt and stir in the balsamic vinegar. Cook, stirring, until the juices are reduced and thickened and the peppers have a rich brown color and are tender, 3 to 4 minutes. Taste, adjust the seasoning, and serve.

FOR PERFECT PANFRIED PEPPERS

Make sure the oil in the pan is very hot. When you add the peppers, do not crowd the pan, or the peppers won't char properly. If necessary, cook them in two batches; then when all the peppers are cooked, return the first batch to the pan.

SPINACH FRITTERS

Frittelle di Spinaci

MAKES 20 TO 25
FRITTERS
SERVES 10 TO 12

These light, flavorful fritters could be served as a warm antipasto or next to any roasted game or poultry.

½ pound spinach, stems and bruised leaves discarded

Salt

2 large eggs

⅔ cup freshly grated Parmigiano-Reggiano

¼ pound whole-milk ricotta

½ cup all-purpose flour

⅛ teaspoon freshly grated nutmeg

Freshly ground black pepper to taste

2 large egg whites, at room temperature

Olive oil or vegetable oil for deep-frying

WASH the spinach thoroughly under cold running water. Fill a large pot about one-third full with cold water and bring to a boil over medium heat. Add a large pinch of salt and the spinach. Cook, uncovered, stirring a few times, until the spinach is tender, 5 to 7 minutes.

DRAIN the spinach in a colander, cool under cold running water, and squeeze out as much water as you can. Roughly chop the spinach and set aside.

BEAT the eggs with a wooden spoon in a large bowl, or beat in the bowl of an electric mixer fitted with the paddle attachment. Add the Parmigiano, ricotta, flour, spinach, and nutmeg, season lightly with salt and pepper, and mix well.

BEAT the egg whites in a medium bowl until they are thick and smooth and form soft peaks. Do not overbeat. Fold the whites thoroughly into the spinach mixture, cover the bowl, and refrigerate for about 30 minutes.

POUR 2 inches of oil into a heavy medium saucepan and heat over medium-high heat until the oil is very hot (375°F). Drop the spinach batter, ½ tablespoon at a time, without crowding, into the oil. As soon as the fritters are golden on both sides (if the oil is nice and hot, this will happen in no time at all), remove them with a slotted spoon and drain on paper towels. Repeat until all the batter has been used. Sprinkle lightly with salt and serve hot.

CRISP POTATO CAKE

Tortino di Patate

SERVES 8

8 medium boiling potatoes (about 5 pounds)

Salt to taste

4 tablespoons (½ stick) unsalted butter

3 large eggs

¼ pound sliced *prosciutto cotto* (see box) or baked ham, diced

2 tablespoons all-purpose flour

¼ cup chopped flat-leaf parsley

⅛ teaspoon freshly grated nutmeg

1 cup Béchamel Sauce (page 28)

1 cup freshly grated Parmigiano-Reggiano

½ cup fine dried bread crumbs

*P*otato cakes are part of cucina povera, *the cooking of the poor. At one time, these humble preparations were made with a few basic ingredients and whatever leftovers one had in the house. A few potatoes, some cheese, some onion, and perhaps a few slices of cured meats were enough to create a savory cake. Today such dishes have been somewhat embellished by the addition of more extravagant ingredients, but their look remains rustic and their taste delicious.*

PUT the potatoes in a large saucepan and cover them generously with cold water. Bring to a boil over medium heat and cook until the potatoes can easily be pierced with a long thin knife, 25 to 35 minutes. Drain the potatoes and let cool slightly.

PREHEAT the oven to 400°F. Butter a 10-inch springform pan and coat the bottom and sides with the bread crumbs.

AS soon as the potatoes are cool enough to handle, peel them and pass them through a food mill or a potato ricer into a large bowl. (Do not use a food processor to mash the potatoes; it will make them very gummy.) Season with salt.

MELT the butter in a small pan over low heat and add to the potatoes. Beat 2 of the eggs in a small bowl and add to the potatoes, along with the ham, flour, parsley, nutmeg, béchamel, and Parmigiano, and mix thoroughly.

PUT the potato mixture in the prepared pan, shake the pan lightly to distribute it evenly, and smooth the top with a spatula. Beat the remaining egg and brush it over the top of the potatoes. Bake on the middle rack of the oven until the cake has a crisp brown crust on top and a thin knife inserted into the center comes out clean, 30 to 35 minutes. Remove from the oven and let cool for about 15 minutes. Remove the sides of the pan and transfer the potato cake to a serving dish. Serve warm or at room temperature.

PROSCIUTTO COTTO

Prosciutto cotto is cooked ham, and the largest producers in Italy are located in Emilia-Romagna and Lombardy. This large pink ham is made industrially, not artisanally, as prosciutto di Parma is, using the hind legs of pork. The legs are boned and soaked in a brine solution for 20 to 25 days at a steady temperature, until the brine is absorbed by the meat. The legs are then cooked in steam ovens. Once cooked, the prosciutto is hot-pressed to give the meat its characteristic shape.

Prosciutto cotto should have a rosy color and be free of cartilage. It should be moist but not sticky. Sliced *prosciutto cotto* will stay fresh for only a few days. *Prosciutto cotto* can be incorporated in many dishes just as you would use *prosciutto di Parma.*

POTATOES BAKED WITH PARMIGIANO

Patate al Forno col Parmigiano

SERVES 6

6 large boiling potatoes (3 to 3½ pounds)

Small pinch of freshly grated nutmeg

¾ cup milk

Salt to taste

½ cup freshly grated Parmigiano-Reggiano

2 to 3 tablespoons unsalted butter

My sister-in-law, Emma, comes from a large family, with four sisters and four brothers. Once or twice a year, they get together with their respective families to celebrate a birthday or someone's anniversary. They meet at Graziella's house in the countryside just outside Bologna, where children and grandchildren can run freely while the four sisters and Marco, the brother who is a pastry chef, cook the meal. The food they prepare is traditional, rustic, and uncompromisingly tasty. Potatoes baked with Parmigiano is always part of the meal, because they can be prepared ahead and cooked at the last moment.

PUT the potatoes in a large saucepan and cover them generously with cold water. Bring to a boil over medium heat and cook until the potatoes are tender but still a bit firm when pierced with a thin knife, 30 to 35 minutes. Drain the potatoes and let cool slightly.

PREHEAT the oven to 400°F. Generously butter a large baking dish.

As soon as the potatoes are cool enough to handle, peel them, let cool to room temperature, and then cut them into ¼-inch rounds.

LAYER the potato slices in the baking dish, slightly overlapping them. (The potatoes can be prepared ahead to this point, tightly covered, and refrigerated.) Mix the nutmeg with the milk and pour over the potatoes. Season lightly with salt. Sprinkle generously with the Parmigiano and dot with the butter.

PLACE the baking dish on the middle rack of the oven and bake until the cheese is melted and the potatoes are light golden on top, 15 to 20 minutes. Remove from the oven and let cool for a few minutes. Serve warm or at room temperature.

MASHED POTATOES WITH PARMIGIANO

Puré di Patate di Bologna

SERVES 4 TO 6

5 large boiling potatoes (about 3 pounds)

4 to 5 tablespoons unsalted butter

⅓ cup whole milk

½ cup freshly grated Parmigiano-Reggiano

Salt to taste

⅛ teaspoon freshly grated nutmeg

Mashed potatoes in Bologna are made with Parmigiano-Reggiano, sweet butter, and milk. At Trattoria lo Sterlino in Bologna, cream is used instead of milk. Others omit the nutmeg, which they say interferes with the sweet taste of the butter and cheese. I make these mashed potatoes because that is the way my mother made them, and her mother before her. They are luscious, rich, and fluffy.

PUT the potatoes in a large saucepan and cover them generously with cold water. Bring the water to a boil over medium heat and cook until the potatoes are tender when pierced by a thin knife, 35 to 45 minutes. Drain and let cool slightly.

AS soon as the potatoes are cool enough to handle, peel them, pass them through a food mill or a potato ricer into a bowl. (Do not use a food processor, because it will make the potatoes very gummy.)

HEAT the butter and milk in a medium saucepan over medium-low heat. Stir in the mashed potatoes and the Parmigiano. Season with salt. Beat the potatoes with an electric hand beater at medium speed, or a wire whisk or a wooden spoon, until well blended and hot, soft, and fluffy. Stir in the nutmeg and mix well. Taste, adjust the seasoning, and serve hot.

ROASTED POTATOES

Patate Arrosto

SERVES 4

5 large boiling potatoes (about 3 pounds), peeled and cut into 1-inch pieces

Salt and freshly ground black pepper to taste

¼ to ⅓ cup extra virgin olive oil, or more if needed

2 tablespoons finely chopped rosemary

1 tablespoon finely chopped sage

1 garlic clove, finely minced

2 ounces thickly sliced pancetta, diced

*T*hese potatoes, which in Emilia-Romagna are always generously seasoned, often include aglione, *the traditional mixture of rosemary, sage, and garlic, which gives them a burst of flavor.*

At Trattoria del Cacciatore, the potatoes are cooked in two stages. The first roasting is done early in the day. The second, when the savory herb mixture is added, is done just before serving. The results are roasted potatoes that are flavorful and crisp.

PREHEAT the oven to 425°F.

WASH the potatoes under cold running water. Drain and dry thoroughly with a kitchen towel. Place in a large bowl, season generously with salt and pepper, and add the olive oil. Toss well to coat. Spread the potatoes on a large baking sheet or in a baking dish large enough to hold them in a single layer.

ROAST the potatoes on the middle rack of the oven, without stirring them, until they have a nice golden color, 25 to 30 minutes. (The potatoes can be prepared up to this point several hours ahead. Set aside at room temperature, uncovered, until needed.)

IF not making in advance, after 20 minutes or so, reduce the heat to 350°F and finish cooking.

THIRTY minutes or so before you want to serve the potatoes, preheat the oven to 350°F.

PUT the potatoes into a large bowl (or the bowl you used before) and toss them with the rosemary, sage, garlic, and pancetta to coat. Add a bit more oil if needed. Roast until the potatoes and pancetta are golden brown and crisp, 10 to 15 minutes. Taste, adjust the seasoning, and serve hot.

POTATO CROQUETTES

Crochette di Patate

MAKES ABOUT 20
CROQUETTES
SERVES 8 TO 10

1 recipe Mashed Potatoes with Parmigiano (page 323)

1 large egg, lightly beaten

1 tablespoon finely chopped, flat-leaf parsley

1½ cups fine dried bread crumbs

Olive oil or vegetable oil for frying

ew people can resist the sight and aroma of golden, crisp fried food piled high on a platter. At Antica Trattoria Moretto, just outside the town of Vignola, I ate some well-fried dishes. Fried Zucchini Blossoms (page 40) were light and delicate. Thinly sliced Deep-Fried Porcini Mushrooms (page 39) were crunchy. But it was the small, golden, crisp potato croquettes that I could not stop eating. Serve them alongside succulent Pork Loin Braised in Milk (page 289).

COMBINE the mashed potatoes, egg, and parsley in a medium bowl and mix until well blended. Cover the bowl with a kitchen towel and refrigerate until cold.

TO shape the croquettes, pick up 1 heaping tablespoon of the potato mixture at a time and roll it between your palms into an egg shape. When all the croquettes have been shaped, spread the bread crumbs on a sheet of aluminum foil. Coat the croquettes lightly with the crumbs and place them on a large tray lined with parchment or wax paper. The dish can be prepared up to this point a few hours ahead. Refrigerate uncovered.

HEAT about 1 inch of oil in a medium skillet. When the oil is nice and hot, lower a few croquettes at a time into the skillet with a slotted spoon and cook until they are golden brown on all sides, about 2 minutes. Remove with the slotted spoon and place on paper towels to drain.

WHEN all the croquettes are cooked, transfer them to a large serving dish and serve hot.

ONION AND TOMATO STEW
WITH RED WINE VINEGAR

Friggione

SERVES 6 TO 8

⅓ cup extra virgin olive oil, plus more if needed

2 pounds yellow onions, thinly sliced

3 pounds ripe tomatoes, peeled, seeded, and diced (see page 217)

Salt and freshly ground black pepper to taste

A generous splash of strong red wine vinegar

In Bologna, mention friggione *to someone and you will be met with sighs of nostalgic pleasure. Friggione, a stew of onions and tomatoes flavored with a splash of strong red wine vinegar, was standard fare in the homes of Bologna and in the many trattorie of the Emilia region. My mother would make it in a large, black iron pan. She stirred and nurtured it until the onion and tomatoes were completely soft and were turned into a unified colorful, aromatic mixture. Often it included small slices of left-over boiled meats or cotechino, the sausage of the region, or some panfried sausage, which enriched its taste and made it absolutely impossible to resist. Polenta, soft, fried, or roasted, often took its rightful place next to the* friggione. *If the* friggione *was served by itself, the next day the leftovers would be tossed with some pasta or become the side dish to a few fried eggs.* Friggione *is not as fashionable today as it used to be, but places such as Hostaria da Ivan in Roccabianca, Gigina and Boni in Bologna, Da Amerigo in Savigno, and other trattorie still serve it.*

HEAT the oil in a large skillet over medium heat. Add the onions and cook, stirring, until golden and soft, 10 to 15 minutes. Add the tomatoes and season with salt and a generous amount of pepper. Partially cover the skillet, reduce the heat to low, and cook, stirring from time to time, until the onions are meltingly soft, the juices of the tomatoes have thickened, and the *friggione* has a thick, shiny consistency, 40 to 45 minutes. (If you are making *friggione* with tomatoes that are not at their ripest, juiciest stage, add some water to the stew as it cooks if necessary and, perhaps, a bit of additional oil.)

REMOVE the lid and raise the heat to high. Add the vinegar and stir for a minute or two. Taste, adjust the seasoning, and serve hot.

FRIGGIONE WITH ROASTED POTATOES In and around Bologna, roasted potatoes are added to *friggione* during the last 10 minutes of cooking for a hardier, thicker stew.

FRIGGIONE WITH BALSAMIC VINEGAR In Modena and surrounding areas, balsamic vinegar is used instead of red wine vinegar.

FRIGGIONE WITH PEPPERS In the countryside of Piacenza, *friggione* is called *rustisana* and includes sliced bell peppers.

FRIGGIONE WITH MEAT Any leftover boiled, roasted, or grilled meat can be added to *friggione.* Cut the meat into 2-inch pieces, add to the cooked *friggione,* and heat through.

OVEN-ROASTED STUFFED VEGETABLES

Verdure Ripiene al Forno

SERVES 6

3 small Japanese eggplant, ends trimmed and halved lengthwise

Salt

3 medium yellow onions, halved crosswise

3 medium firm but ripe tomatoes, halved and seeded

⅓ cup freshly grated Parmigiano-Reggiano

½ cup fresh bread crumbs

½ cup chopped flat-leaf parsley

2 garlic cloves, finely minced

½ to ⅔ cup extra virgin olive oil

Freshly ground black pepper to taste

3 medium red bell peppers, halved, cored, and seeded

My sister, Carla, loves to cook vegetables and it shows in the fine dishes she prepares for her family. One of my favorites, which she makes for me when I am in Bologna, is a dish that our mother used to make, roasted stuffed vegetables. Onions, bell peppers, eggplant, and tomatoes are filled with the traditional Bolognese mixture of Parmigiano, bread crumbs, parsley, garlic, and extra virgin olive oil. The amount of oil in this dish may seem a bit excessive, but wait until you dip your bread in the oil that has been infused with the juices of the roasted vegetables: you won't be able to stop eating it. Carla serves these hot, alongside roasted meats, or at room temperature as an antipasto.

WITH a tablespoon, scoop out and discard just a bit of the pulp from each eggplant half. Place the eggplant on a large platter and sprinkle generously with salt. Let stand for about 20 minutes to draw out the eggplant's bitter juices, then pat the eggplant dry with paper towels.

MEANWHILE, put the onions in a saucepan and cover with cold water. Bring to a gentle boil over medium heat and cook until the onions are barely tender to the touch, about 10 minutes. Remove the onions with a slotted spoon and place on paper towels to drain and cool.

PLACE the tomatoes cut side down on paper towels to drain.

PREHEAT the oven to 350°F. Lightly grease a large baking pan.

COMBINE the Parmigiano, bread crumbs, parsley, and garlic in a small bowl. Add about ¼ cup of the oil, season with salt and pepper, and mix well to combine. The stuffing should be soft and moist; if necessary, add a bit more oil. Arrange the vegetables in the baking dish. Place some of the stuffing in the cavities of the tomatoes, eggplant, and peppers, and scatter the remainder over the onions. Drizzle with a bit of additional olive oil. (The dish can be prepared up to this point several hours ahead and set aside, covered, at room temperature.)

PLACE the pan on the center rack of the oven and bake until the vegetables are soft and a nice golden color, about 1 hour. Serve hot or at room temperature.

VERSATILE ROASTED VEGETABLES

Leftover stuffed vegetables can be used in a variety of ways:

- Dice them and mix them into beaten eggs for a delicious frittata.

- Dice them, toss in a skillet with a bit of olive oil, and serve over pasta. Or incorporate them into a risotto.

- Make a great vegetable sandwich. The sandwich will be irresistible if you use Bolognese Savory Bread (page 57).

SAVORY SWISS CHARD PIE

Scarpazzone alla Modenese

SERVES 10 TO 12

For the dough

2 cups unbleached all-purpose flour

½ teaspoon salt

14 tablespoons (1¾ sticks) unsalted butter, cut into small pieces

2 large eggs, lightly beaten (if using a food processor, add 1 extra egg)

For the filling

2½ pounds Swiss chard

Salt

1 pound spinach

⅓ cup extra virgin olive oil

½ cup finely minced yellow onions

¼ pound thickly sliced pancetta, minced

1 garlic clove, minced

2 tablespoons chopped flat-leaf parsley

Freshly ground black pepper to taste

5 large eggs

1½ cups freshly grated Parmigiano-Reggiano

2 cups loosely packed pieces 2-day-old Italian bread (crusts removed), very finely chopped

1 large egg, lightly beaten

*T*hree Emilian cities, Modena, Bologna, and Reggio-Emilia, share a savory pie called scarpazzone or erbazzone, and this impressive-looking pie is often prominently displayed in the windows of specialty food stores. Made with sautéed Swiss chard or spinach, scarpazzone generally also includes pancetta or prosciutto, finely minced onion or leeks, and Parmigiano, and, according to the area, it may contain fresh bread crumbs or ricotta. Lard or, as in this recipe, sweet butter makes a flaky and delicious crust. In Romagna, the crust of a similar pie is made with the more rustic bread dough of piadina (page 64). (For the sweet version of this dish, see Sweet Spinach–Almond-Ricotta Pie, page 364.) When I was growing up, occasionally I would find a large wedge of sweet spinach and ricotta pie in my lunch pail. What a treat!

To make the dough by hand, place the flour and salt in a large bowl. Add the butter and, with your fingertips, rub the butter into the flour until the mixture has a fine crumbly consistency. With a fork, stir in the eggs, then mix gently and quickly with your hands just until the dough begins to hold together. Transfer to a lightly floured work surface and shape it into 2 balls, one a little larger than the other. Wrap in plastic wrap and refrigerate for a few hours.

To make the dough with a food processor, place the flour, salt, and butter in a food processor fitted with the metal blade and pulse briefly until the mixture has a fine, crumbly consistency. Add the eggs and pulse very briefly to moisten the dough. Transfer the mixture to a work surface and gather the dough together. Shape into 2 balls, one a little larger than the other. Wrap in plastic wrap and refrigerate for a few hours.

To prepare the filling, remove the Swiss chard stems from the leaves and reserve for another use (see page 332). Wash the leaves in several changes of cold water.

BRING a large pot of water to a boil. Add a generous pinch of salt and the chard and cook for 7 to 10 minutes, or until tender. Drain well and cool under cold running water. Squeeze out the excess water from the chard and finely chop it.

REMOVE and discard the spinach stems. Wash the spinach in several changes of cold water and cook as instructed for the Swiss chard, until the leaves are tender. Drain the spinach, squeeze out the excess water, and finely chop it.

HEAT the oil in a large sauté pan over medium heat. Add the onions and cook, stirring, until lightly golden and soft, about 5 minutes. Add the pancetta and cook, stirring until lightly golden, 2 to 3 minutes. Add the garlic and parsley and stir for about 1 minute, then add the Swiss chard and spinach and season with salt and pepper. Toss the greens for a minute or two, then transfer to a large bowl and let cool.

PREHEAT the oven to 375°F. Butter a 9- or 10-inch springform pan.

IN a medium bowl, beat the eggs with the Parmigiano. Stir in the bread and season with salt and pepper. Add the egg mixture to the Swiss chard and mix well. Taste and adjust the seasoning.

ON a lightly floured work surface, roll out the larger ball of dough into a 14- to 15-inch circle and fit it into the springform pan, letting any excess dough hang over the edges. Spoon the filling into the pan, smoothing the top with a spatula.

ROLL out the remaining dough to a 12-inch circle and place over the filling. Trim off any excess dough, then pinch the edges of the top and bottom doughs together to seal and crimp to make a raised edge. Decorate the raised edge by pressing the tines of a fork into it diagonally all around. Brush the top crust with the beaten egg and prick it in several places with a fork.

PLACE the pie on the middle rack of the oven and bake until the top is golden brown, 40 to 50 minutes. Let the pie cool, then remove the sides of the pan. Serve at room temperature.

SWISS CHARD WITH BUTTER AND PARMIGIANO

Biete al Burro e Parmigiano

SERVES 4

3 pounds Swiss chard

Salt

3 tablespoons unsalted butter

⅓ cup freshly grated Parmigiano-Reggiano

Swiss chard is essential to many traditional pasta fillings of the region. Its leaves are also particularly delicious when sautéed with sweet butter and Parmigiano, as in this recipe, while the broad creamy stalks are best when gratinéed. The mild, creamy taste of this dish pairs well with roasted fish or meats.

REMOVE the stalks from the Swiss chard leaves and reserve for another use. (See below.) Soak the chard leaves in a large bowl of cold water for a few minutes.

PLACE the leaves in a large colander and rinse thoroughly under cold running water, making sure to remove any grit.

PUT the leaves in a large pot, add 2 cups water and a nice pinch of salt, and cook over medium heat until tender, 5 to 6 minutes. Drain well and set aside.

MELT the butter in a large skillet over medium heat. Add the chard, season with salt, and stir for a minute or two, until the chard is thoroughly coated with the butter. Add the Parmigiano and stir for a minute or two longer. Taste, adjust the seasoning, and serve.

SPINACH WITH BUTTER AND PARMIGIANO Spinach can be prepared in the same manner; add just a bit of heavy cream if desired.

GRATINÉED SWISS CHARD STALKS Wash the stalks well and blanch them in boiling salted water for a few minutes. Place them in a buttered baking dish, slightly overlapping, dot with butter, and sprinkle generously with freshly grated Parmigiano-Reggiano. Bake in a preheated 350°F oven until the cheese is melted.

SALADS

Insalate

The most popular salads in Emilia-Romagna are *insalata verde,*
green salad, and *insalata mista,* mixed salad. The latter might
include, in addition to a selection of lettuces, thinly sliced fennel,
radishes, tomatoes, carrots, and other raw vegetables. Both of these salads, which
are traditionally served after the meat or fish course, are meant to cleanse and
refresh the palate at the end of the meal or to prepare it for what follows. A more
casual way of eating salad is to serve it on the same plate with grilled meats or
as a side dish. (This is my brother's favorite combination; he loves the crunchi-
ness of a chilled salad with a bite of well-seasoned warm meat.) The dressing

for these salads is made with extra virgin olive oil, red wine vinegar or balsamic vinegar, and salt. Nothing more except perhaps a bit of pepper.

There are also composed salads, which are made with several ingredients and can be served as an antipasto, a first course, or a second course. Boiled Meats and New Potato Salad can be an entire meal. One of my favorite ways of eating light is to enjoy a bowl of Cooked Vegetable Salad with Prosciutto, a nice chunk of fresh, moist Parmigiano, and a glass of chilled white wine.

When dressing a salad, pay attention to the following: Make sure your greens are washed and thoroughly dried. Season the salad lightly with salt. Drizzle just enough oil over it to coat the greens lightly. Drizzle the vinegar judiciously. You can always add a bit more if needed. Toss the salad thoroughly. Taste and adjust the seasoning to your liking. Serve the salad at once, unless otherwise suggested in the recipe.

Most of these salads are the ones I grew up eating, and when I tested them, it was as if I were revisiting old friends. When you shop for vegetables for salad, adopt the Italian attitude. Go to the market, look for what is in season, and then decide what you will prepare. You will be highly rewarded.

WHITE BEAN, TUNA, AND SWEET ONION SALAD

Insalata di Fagioli, Tonno, e Cipolle

SERVES 6

2 cups dried cannellini beans or white kidney beans, picked over, soaked overnight in cold water to cover generously, drained, and rinsed

1 small red onion, thinly sliced and soaked in a bowl of cold water for about 1 hour

Salt and freshly ground black pepper to taste

⅓ to ½ cup extra virgin olive oil

3 to 4 tablespoons red wine vinegar

Two 7-ounce cans white tuna packed in oil, preferably Italian tuna in olive oil, drained

This is Birrerìa Lamma's famous salad. Although the salad can be found in other regions, I have never found a version as tasty as theirs. As simple as this salad is, it is important not to overcook the beans (and do not be tempted to use canned beans). Use the best extra virgin olive oil you can get. Select a good brand of white tuna packed in olive oil, preferably imported from Italy. Season the salad generously, since beans, like potatoes, need more salt than most other vegetables to come to life. And, as the patrons of the Birrerìa Lamma did, enjoy it with a good glass of cold beer.

COOK the beans as instructed on page 82. Drain them, place them in a large salad bowl, and let cool to room temperature.

DRAIN the onion, spread paper towels, and pat dry.

ADD the onion to the beans and season generously with salt and more lightly with pepper. Stir briefly. Add the tuna, breaking it up into pieces, the oil, and vinegar and toss well. Taste, adjust the seasoning, and serve at room temperature.

BIRRERÌA LAMMA

Until a few years ago, if you had asked anyone in Bologna to direct you to Birrerìa Lamma, you would have received detailed instructions on how to get there, plus advice on dishes that you "absolutely have to try." Lamma, which had been in the same location longer than anybody in Bologna could remember, was well known not only for its food, but also for its selection of national and international beers.

Lamma's large dining room, which dated back to medieval times, was simply appointed with wooden tables and uncomfortable chairs, but the food they served was the best of the Bolognese table. Lamma was always packed, and so was its long, dark counter, where one could order a plate of their famous *lasagne verdi* or *tortellini in brodo,* or just a platter of *affettati misti*, the splendid cured pork products of the region, while sipping a glass of local Lambrusco. The homey food and the trattoria's reasonable prices were what kept customers coming back.

After the Second World War ended, my mother took a part-time job in the kitchen of Lamma to help put food on our table. There, she rolled out large sheets of pasta. She shaped and stuffed the pasta into glorious morsels.

One of Lamma's famous dishes was a rustic salad of large white beans, sweet onion, and white tuna preserved in oil. Generously seasoned, the salad came to the table in a deep bowl accompanied by a large loaf of white bread. In 1960, when my husband and I were dating, Lamma was our favorite trattoria, but often all we could afford was the bean salad. We would sit for hours nursing the salad and a glass of wine, under the disapproving glare of Luigi, one of the oldest waiters, who would have much preferred to turn over the table. At that time, Lamma was crowded with families, laborers, university students, and Americans attending Bologna's prestigious school of medicine, just as my husband was.

Every year during my trips back to Bologna after I married and moved to New York and then Sacramento, I went back to Lamma. Then one day, to my shock, Lamma was gone, and in its place there was a tacky fast-food restaurant. I stood there, looking at a place that for so long had meant so much to so many, and I simply wanted to cry. Then I realized how lucky I was to have been part of a generation that had enjoyed Lamma's food, because in that food there was the essence of the Bolognese table, its tradition, and its culture.

CELERY, PARMIGIANO, AND TOASTED WALNUT SALAD

Insalata di Sedano, Parmigiano, e Noci

2 ounces walnuts (about ¾ cup)

2 large bunches crisp celery

A small chunk of Parmigiano-Reggiano (about 2 ounces)

Salt and freshly ground black pepper to taste

4 to 5 tablespoons extra virgin olive oil

Juice of 1 large lemon

A t the end of a meal, all a salad should impart is freshness and lightness. This salad ended a delicious multicourse meal at Ristorante Cocchi in Parma. Thinly sliced, crisp celery, chunks of pale yellow, aged Parmigiano, and roasted walnuts dressed only with extra virgin olive oil and lemon juice. So simple, yet so delicious.

PREHEAT the oven to 375°F.

SPREAD the walnuts on a baking sheet and toast in the oven until they are lightly golden, 3 to 5 minutes. Cool slightly, then chop them into small pieces.

REMOVE the large outer green stalks of the celery until you reach the white tender celery hearts; save the green stalks for another use. Trim the remaining stalks, wash them well, and dry them. Very thinly slice them and place in a salad bowl.

CHOP the cheese into small pieces (about the size of a chickpea) and add to the celery. Add the walnuts and season with salt and pepper. Add the oil and lemon juice and toss well. Taste, adjust for seasoning, and serve.

BOILED MEATS AND NEW POTATO SALAD

Insalata di Bollito e Patate

SERVES 4 TO 6

9 to 10 new potatoes;
2 large boiling potatoes or
3 medium ones

3 cups cubed Mixed Boiled
Meats (page 298) or roasted
meat or chicken

½ red onion, thinly sliced

1 tablespoon chopped
flat-leaf parsley

Salt and freshly ground black
pepper to taste

⅓ to ½ cup extra virgin
olive oil

In our house in Bologna, boiled meats were mostly prepared on Sunday. The broth of the boiled meats was a soup with some added tagliolini or tortellini. The meats were served as a second course. On Monday, any leftover meats would be turned into a satisfying salad. Of all the salad variations that my mother created, my favorite by far was this one made with potatoes.

PUT the potatoes in a large pot and cover with cold water. Bring to a boil over medium heat and cook, uncovered, until the potatoes can easily be pierced with a thin knife, 25 to 35 minutes. Drain the potatoes and let cool slightly.

PEEL the potatoes when cool and cut them into ¼-inch slices. (Don't worry if some potatoes break into small pieces. The salad will be thickened because of that.) Place the potatoes in a large salad bowl. (The potatoes can be cooked several hours ahead and set aside at room temperature.)

ADD the meat, onion, and parsley to the potatoes. Season generously with salt and pepper and drizzle liberally with olive oil. Toss well, then taste, adjust the seasoning, and serve.

NO VINEGAR, THANK YOU

This salad is seasoned only with extra virgin olive oil and salt and pepper—no vinegar, no herbs. The absence of vinegar gives the potatoes a smoother, creamier consistency. The salad should be served immediately after it has been dressed, or it will dry out somewhat, since the potatoes will absorbed the oil quickly.

For a variation, omit the potatoes and toss the meat with a mixture of tender lettuces, thinly sliced raw fennel, and shredded carrots.

COOKED VEGETABLE SALAD
WITH PROSCIUTTO

Insalata di Verdure con Prosciutto

SERVES 6 TO 8

2 medium red onions,
cut into wedges

Salt and freshly ground black
pepper to taste

2 tablespoons extra virgin
olive oil

1 tablespoon red wine vinegar

1 small head cauliflower
(about 2 pounds)

2 medium boiling potatoes
or 6 to 7 new potatoes

1 large fennel bulb

½ pound string beans,
ends trimmed

2 to 3 ounces thickly sliced
prosciutto, cut into strips

For the dressing

¼ to ⅓ cup extra virgin
olive oil

2 to 3 tablespoons red
wine vinegar

*M*ixed vegetable salads are commonplace throughout Italy. It seems, however, that the people of Emilia-Romagna love this salad more than other Italians, as most restaurants and trattorie serve it regularly. At Le Bistrot, a charming, informal restaurant in the town of Dozza, the vegetables were still slightly warm and were tossed at the table with strips of prosciutto, extra virgin olive oil from Brisighella (the best olive oil of the region), and just a bit of red wine vinegar. A platter of mixed cured meats accompanied the salad for a simple, yet memorable, lunch.

PREHEAT the oven to 400°F.

PLACE the onions in a bowl, season with salt and pepper, and toss with the oil and the vinegar. Spread the onions on a baking sheet and roast on the middle rack of the oven until tender, 20 to 25 minutes. Scoop up the onions with a spatula and place in a large salad bowl.

MEANWHILE, bring a large saucepan of salted water to a boil over medium heat. Remove all the leaves from the cauliflower except the small tender ones and cut an X in the core of the cauliflower. Place it in the boiling water and cook, uncovered, until the core can easily be pierced with a thin knife, 15 to 20 minutes. Drain and place in a large bowl of ice water to stop the cooking; when cool, drain again.

PAT the cauliflower dry with paper towels, separate it into florets, and place them in the salad bowl.

WHILE the cauliflower is cooking, put the potatoes in a saucepan with water to cover and bring to a boil over medium heat. (Don't bring the water to a boil before adding the potatoes, or their skins will burst and they will become waterlogged.) Cook until the potatoes are tender when pierced with a thin knife. (The cooking time will depend on the size and type of the potatoes.) Drain the potatoes and let cool slightly.

As soon as the potatoes are cool enough to handle, peel them. Let cool to room temperature, then cut them into ¼-inch-thick rounds. Add to the salad bowl.

TRIM off the long stalks of the fennel. Remove the thick outer leaves if they are bruised and discolored. Trim the fennel bulb at the base and cut it into ½-inch thick slices. Place the slices in a large skillet, cover them with cold water, and add a pinch of salt. Bring the water to a boil over medium heat and cook, uncovered, until the fennel is tender, about 10 minutes. With a slotted spoon transfer the fennel to paper towels to drain and cool. Cut the fennel into strips and add to the salad bowl.

BRING a medium saucepan of water to a boil over medium heat. Add a generous pinch of salt and the beans and cook, uncovered, until tender but still firm and crisp to the bite. Drain the beans and plunge them into a large bowl of ice water to stop the cooking and retain their green color; when cool, drain again, pat dry with paper towels, and add to the bowl. Chill the vegetables in the refrigerator for about half an hour.

JUST before serving, add the prosciutto to the salad and season it with salt and pepper. Add the olive oil and vinegar and toss well. Taste, adjust the seasoning, and serve.

Preparing Ahead: Don't be put off by the several steps in this recipe. All the vegetables can be cooked several hours or a day ahead. Place them in separate plastic containers or resealable bags and refrigerate them. An hour or two before you want to serve the salad, combine all the vegetables in the salad bowl and leave them at room temperature. Dress the salad just before serving.

EMMA'S SECRET GARDEN

Not everyone in Italy has the good fortune to live in a Tuscan farmhouse with sweeping views of fields or lush hills or a villa overlooking the sea. The majority of Italians, despite what sleek American magazines portray, live in apartment buildings. These people are *il ceto medio*, middle-class working folks. Apartment life, as anyone who has lived in one anywhere can attest, can be a bit confining, especially for Italians, who are for the most part, extroverted and ebullient. Perhaps that is why Italians in large cities and small towns spend so much time congregating at the local café or in the town square.

My brother, Gianni, and his wife, Emma, both retired, own an apartment on the outskirts of Bologna. From two of their large terraces, they have a panoramic view of the luscious hills that surround the city. Pots of geraniums and herbs line the sunny side of their terraces. But Emma's greatest pride is what she calls her "secret garden," a small plot of land just a few miles from their apartment. It is one of the many plots that the city of Bologna assigned to retirees. As we drove to the large beautiful park that houses the fenced-in area of many gardens, Emma steered me toward a small plot of land, and there proudly said, "This is it." She began picking very small, ripe cherry tomatoes and lettuce, which she placed in a basket, while greeting and talking to someone in the next garden. I looked at the thirty or so small gardens around me and saw men and women planting, shredding, pruning, and picking the fruits of their labors. They were sharing tips on how to grow certain vegetables, exchanging recipes, and arguing about sports and politics.

As I listened to the conversations around me, I realized that those vegetable gardens did more than just grow vegetables and lettuce. They were a nurturing ground for people on the threshold of old age who respected nature and benefited from the dignified daily acts of working the small plots. The gardens were, for many, a large outdoor living room, a meeting place, and a home away from home.

Emma turned the cherry tomatoes into a sweet tomato sauce for the pasta, which she topped with aromatic basil from her terrace. The lettuce became a salad that she served next to a large chunk of Parmigiano-Reggiano and another of the local pecorino. Gianni opened a bottle of local Lambrusco, which he had bought, as always, by the case from a local farmer who is an aspiring winemaker. Then we all sat around a table on the terrace, savoring the good food from Emma's secret garden.

RAW ARTICHOKE SALAD
WITH PARMIGIANO

Insalata di Carciofi e Parmigiano

SERVES 4

4 large artichokes, cleaned (see box)

1 large lemon, halved

Salt to taste

¼ cup extra virgin olive oil

¼ pound Parmigiano-Reggiano, cut into thin slivers with a vegetable peeler or small sharp knife

The vegetable and salad offerings in the trattorie and restaurants of Emilia-Romagna leave something to be desired. This might seem strange in such an agriculturally rich region, considering the prominence that vegetables and salads have in home cooking. Occasionally, one finds an exception. Antica Trattoria del Cacciatore, near Bologna, not only serves outstanding food but devotes a considerable part of its menu to vegetables and salads, as shown by this salad and the two that follow.

ONE at a time, remove a wedge of artichoke from the lemon water, dry well with a kitchen towel, and cut it into very thin slices. Place the slices in a salad bowl and squeeze some of the juice from the lemon over it. When all artichokes have been sliced, season with salt and drizzle with the oil. Toss well, taste, and adjust the seasoning.

PLACE the artichokes on individual serving plates, scatter the Parmigiano over them, and serve at once.

CLEANING ARTICHOKES

Fill a large bowl half full with cold water. Squeeze in the juice of 2 halved lemons and drop in the squeezed lemon halves. Remove the outer green leaves of each artichoke by snapping them off at the base. Stop when you get to the pale central cone. Cut off the cone of leaves. Rub a lemon half over the cut part to prevent discoloration. Cut off and discard the stem of the artichoke. Trim off the outer green parts of the artichoke bottom. Cut the bottom into 4 wedges and, with a small knife, remove the fuzzy inner choke. Rub the wedges all over with lemon and drop them in the lemon water. Keep the artichokes in the lemon water until you are ready to use them.

GREEN BEAN, PINE NUT, AND MINT SALAD

Fagiolini in Insalata

SERVES 4

Salt

1½ pounds green beans (the smallest you can find), ends trimmed

½ cup pine nuts

⅓ cup loosely packed shredded mint

¼ to ⅓ cup extra virgin olive oil

Juice of 1 large lemon

PREHEAT the oven to 400°F.

BRING a large saucepan of water to a boil. Add a few large pinches of salt and the beans and cook, uncovered, until the beans are tender but still a bit firm to the bite, 2 to 5 minutes. Drain and immediately drop them into a large bowl of iced water to stop the cooking and to set their green color. Drain well, place in a large salad bowl, and set aside. (The beans can be cooked several hours or a day ahead. Keep them tightly covered in the refrigerator.)

MEANWHILE, place the pine nuts on a baking sheet and toast in the oven until lightly golden.

ADD the pine nuts to the beans, along with the mint. Season with salt, add the olive oil and lemon juice, and toss well. Taste, adjust the seasoning, and serve.

ARUGULA SALAD WITH CRISP PANCETTA AND BALSAMIC VINEGAR

Insalata di Arugola, Pancetta, e Balsamico

SERVES 4 TO 6

3 bunches arugula

¼ to ⅓ cup extra virgin olive oil

3 ounces thickly sliced pancetta, cut into small strips

Salt to taste

3 tablespoons balsamic vinegar

DISCARD any bruised or wilted arugula leaves and remove any large stems. Wash the arugula under cold running water, trying not to crush the tender leaves. Drain, spread the leaves on paper towels, and pat dry with more paper towels. Put the arugula in a salad bowl.

HEAT the oil in a small skillet over medium heat. Add the pancetta and cook until lightly golden. Pour the hot oil and pancetta over the arugula, season lightly with salt, and drizzle with vinegar. Toss well to combine. Taste, adjust the seasoning, and serve.

PINZIMONIO

Assorted vegetables, such as fennel, carrots, celery, red bell peppers, scallions, radishes, artichoke hearts, and/or any other crunchy vegetable

Extra virgin olive oil

Balsamic vinegar

Salt

inzimonio is nothing more than a selection of raw vegetables accompanied by a dish of extra virgin olive oil, salt, and pepper. No garlic, no herbs, no chile pepper. While Italians do not dip bread into a bowl of olive oil, they love to pick from a large assortment of beautiful, crunchy vegetables and dip them into extra virgin olive oil seasoned simply with salt. Many country trattorie bring to the table a pinzimonio *the moment that one sits down. And that is exactly what was put in front of us as we sat down for dinner at Antica Osteria Ardegna in Diodolo di Soragna, in Parma's countryside. A large bowl containing strips of red bell peppers, carrots, celery hearts, fennel, and scallions came accompanied by the olive oil "dip," which was "Emilianized" by the addition of some balsamic vinegar, and which proved to be incredibly appetizing.*

Pinzimonio *can start or end a meal or become a light meal all by itself. The more varied the vegetables, the more satisfying it is going to be.*

CUT the vegetables into 1- to 1½-inch-wide strips. (Keep the strips as long as possible.) Arrange the vegetables attractively in a large glass bowl, as you would arrange a bunch of flowers. If using radishes, arrange them in bunches, with their leafy tops still attached. (The vegetables can be prepared a few hours ahead, covered, and refrigerated. Let them stand at room temperature for an hour or so before serving, since they should never be served cold, just barely chilled.)

TO serve, place the bowl of vegetables on the table. Combine the ingredients for the dressing in a medium bowl, using 3 parts olive oil to 1 part balsamic and seasoning it with salt. Pour the dressing into individual small glass bowls. Place the bowls on individual serving plates and let diners choose their own vegetables.

TAMBURINI

When we were children, my sister and I often accompanied our mother to the medieval open market of Bologna. There, she walked from store to store and from stand to stand, checking out the quality of the ingredients and comparing prices. We followed patiently, often infinitely bored by what seemed to us a long, tedious process. What we were waiting for was for our mother to take us to Tamburini, the most glorious food store of Emilia-Romagna. While she stood in line to buy Tamburini's roasted onions and beets, which she turned into an appetizing salad, my sister and I would get a treat of warm squares of sweet *crema fritta*, fried cream.

Tamburini is, for the people of Bologna, more than a food shop—it is an institution. The window displays are daily and lovingly arranged with just-prepared, inviting dishes. The food lures you in, and once inside, you marvel at the long counter filled to capacity with platters of food. Awaiting customers are marinated vegetables, stuffed vegetables, seafood salads, marinated seafood, sliced roasts, and baked apples and pears, sitting prettily in their thick poaching syrup.

At the far end of the store, a large spit, perpetually in slow motion, roasts rabbits, small chickens, pork loins, and legs of lamb, constantly basted with aromatic branches of juniper berries, rosemary, or sage.

Traditional sausages, such as cotechino and zampone, and large, rosy prosciutti hang from the ceiling. Whole wheels of Parmigiano are prominently displayed on a large table, and the *sfoglina*, pasta maker, is busy rolling out large sheets of pasta by hand.

The store, always jammed with people from all walks of life who buy a lot or a little depending on their pocketbooks, is an ode to the traditional table of the region. Whenever I am in Bologna, I make a ritual visit to Tamburini and can never resist the impulse to buy an array of dishes, which I carry to my brother's house for our evening supper.

ROASTED ONION AND BEET SALAD

Insalata di Cipolle e Barbabietole

SERVES 6

3 medium yellow onions, unpeeled

4 medium red beets

Salt and freshly ground black pepper to taste

¼ to ⅓ cup extra virgin olive oil

2 to 3 tablespoons strong red wine vinegar

Although roasted yellow onions and purple beets are available in Bologna's open market, Tamburini seems to roast them better than anyone else. This is how the store cooks them, and this is how my mother used them in a salad.

PREHEAT the oven to 400°F.

TRIM off and discard the roots of the onions. Place the onions on a large baking sheet.

TRIM off the leafy tops of the beets and cut off their roots. Wash the beets under cold running water, then tightly wrap them, individually or all together, in aluminum foil. Place them on the baking sheet with the onions and place on the middle rack of the oven. Roast until the beets and onions can easily be pierced with a thin knife, 45 minutes to 1 hour. Remove from the oven and allow to cool. (Don't worry if the skins of the onions are deeply charred—the onions will taste even better.)

REMOVE the foil from the beets and peel them. (I hold the beets with a fork and peel them with a small knife, so I won't stain my fingers.) Thinly slice the beets and place in a large salad bowl.

REMOVE and discard the onion skins and slice the onions into thin wedges. Add to the salad bowl. Season generously with salt and several grinds of pepper. Add the oil and vinegar and toss well. Taste, adjust the seasoning, and serve.

CAKES, TARTS, FRITTERS, BISCOTTI, ICE CREAM, AND FRUIT DESSERTS

Dolci

As in other regions of Italy, the desserts of Emilia-Romagna fall into two categories: the elaborate, rich, desserts of the *pasticcerie*, pastry shops, and the simpler, traditional, uncomplicated sweets of the homes. The latter, which are called *dolci casalinghi*, have been made by generations of home cooks and are reserved, just like good china, for weddings, anniversaries, and special holidays. In my family, a rich, buttery jam cake or *zuppa inglese* was enjoyed at Christmas and Easter, while our meals throughout the rest of the year usually ended on a light note with fruit, fresh or baked. Did this mean that we shunned desserts altogether? Of course not.

Often on Sundays, my father would buy *paste miste*, assorted pastries, from our local pastry shop. If company was coming, my mother baked some biscotti or a rice cake, or, if time was short, bought a cake from the bakery. Fritters of any kind were her specialty. Rice, apple, chestnut, and sweet pastry dough fritters often greeted us when we returned from school. She piled them up on a large platter and blanketed them with powdered sugar.

Although after-dinner desserts are not eaten at home on a daily basis, people appease their sweet teeth in the many coffee bars, bakeries, *gelaterie,* and pastry shops, which tempt their customers with dramatic displays of mouthwatering sweets. Sweets are munched on throughout the day, especially by teenagers. Well-dressed matrons sit at fancy cafés enjoying espresso or cappuccino with miniature cookies. Shoppers stop in a *pasticceria* for a refill of espresso and leave with a package of pastries wrapped in colorful paper.

When I am in Bologna, I generally stay at my brother's home. Breakfast is usually nothing more than good, strong espresso. But the moment I hit the *centro* (the center of town), I head toward Zanarini, the century-old café, where I delight in one of the best cappuccinos of the city, and indulge in one, maybe two, of the sublime pastries. And, as I glance around and watch the many people who do balancing acts with an espresso in one hand and a *sfogliatella* or a *cornetto* in the other, I am convinced that for many, this daily indulgence is not only about food, but about the active communal participation of a very pleasant, civilized ritual.

The pastries and sweets in this chapter are what the cooks of Emilia-Romagna once made at home, but today, because of a more hectic lifestyle, are more often than not bought at local bakeries and pastry shops.

And don't forget the fruit, because its versatility is unmatched. When serving an Italian dinner with its progression of small courses, end the meal with fruit. In winter, bake some nice firm pears with good red wine. Reduce the wine to a glaze and pour it over the pears (see page 379). Or bake some apples and coat them with a luscious custard cream (page 361). In spring and summer, when fresh fruit is at its best, look for small, sweet strawberries and toss them with a bit of sugar and a few drops of good balsamic vinegar. Make a fruit salad and dress it with sugar, lemon juice, and fresh mint leaves. Or put a large bowl on the table of fresh ripe fruit.

APPLE CAKE

Torta di Mele

SERVES 8 TO 10

5 Golden Delicious apples
(about 2 pounds)

Grated zest of 1 lemon

Juice of ½ lemon

6 Amaretti di Saronno, finely
crushed (see box, page 352)

2 large eggs

1 cup granulated sugar

1 teaspoon vanilla extract

2 teaspoons baking soda

⅓ cup lukewarm milk

2 large egg whites, at room
temperature

1½ cups all-purpose flour

4 tablespoons (½ stick)
unsalted butter, melted
and cooled

Confectioners' sugar

Every family in Emilia-Romagna makes its own version of apple cake. Sometimes the cake contains nothing more than apples, eggs, and flour. Other times it is enriched with sweet ingredients found in the pantry. Zia Rina, my mother's older sister, prepared an apple cake that was dense with apples and almonds or pine nuts, finely chopped cookies, sugar, eggs, and butter. The following is an adaptation of Zia Rina's cake.

PREHEAT the oven to 350°F. Butter and flour an 8- or 9-inch springform pan.

PEEL, core, and cut the apples into small pieces. Place in a large bowl and toss them with the lemon zest, lemon juice, and crushed amaretti. Set aside.

IN a large bowl, beat the eggs with ¾ cup of the sugar and the vanilla until pale yellow and thick. Gradually beat in the flour. Dissolve the baking soda in the milk and beat the butter and dissolved baking soda into the egg mixture. Fold in the apples. The batter will be quite thick.

IN a medium bowl, beat the egg whites with the remaining ¼ cup sugar until stiff. Fold into the apple mixture. Pour the batter into the prepared pan and shake the pan gently to distribute it evenly.

PLACE the pan on the middle rack of the oven and bake until the top of the cake has a nice golden brown color and the sides begin to come away from the pan, 40 to 50 minutes. Let the cake cool on a rack to room temperature. Remove the sides of the springform pan and serve the cake with a generous sprinkling of confectioners' sugar.

ALMOND CAKE

Torta di Mandorle

SERVES 8 TO 10

1 teaspoon active dry yeast

¾ cup lukewarm milk

2½ cups blanched almonds
(about 10 ounces)

1 cup granulated sugar

5 large eggs, separated,
at room temperature

8 tablespoons (1 stick)
unsalted butter, at room
temperature

2 tablespoons honey

¼ cup almond liqueur or
dark rum

1 cup all-purpose flour

Confectioners' sugar

T is simple, homey almond cake is typical of the mountain areas of Emilia-Romagna, where the beloved nut grows prolifically. A slice of this not-too-sweet cake in the morning with my cappuccino, or at night with a small glass of sweet dessert wine, is one of my favorite treats.

The cake keeps well for several days, wrapped in plastic wrap or stored in an airtight container.

PREHEAT the oven to 350°F. Butter and flour an 8- or 9-inch spring-form pan.

DISSOLVE the yeast in the lukewarm milk, and let proof until foamy.

SPREAD the almonds on a baking sheet and bake until they are lightly toasted, 2 to 3 minutes. Let cool, then place them in a food processor fitted with the metal blade, add 2 tablespoons of the sugar, and pulse until the almonds are very finely chopped but not pulverized. Set aside.

IN a large bowl, beat the egg yolks with ¾ cup of the sugar until pale yellow. Beat in the butter. Add the honey, yeast mixture, liqueur, and almonds and beat to combine. Add the flour in two or three additions, mixing thoroughly.

IN a large bowl, beat the egg whites with the remaining 2 tablespoons sugar until stiff. Gradually fold the whites into the almond mixture. Pour the batter into the prepared pan, shaking the pan to distribute the batter evenly.

PLACE the pan on the middle rack of the preheated oven and bake for about 40 minutes, or until a thin knife inserted in the center of the cake comes out clean.

LET the cake cool for about 10 minutes, then remove the sides of the pan and let the cake cool on a rack completely before serving.

ALMOND-CHOCOLATE CAKE

Dolce di Mandorle e Cioccolata

SERVES 8

2½ cups blanched almonds (about 10 ounces)

2 tablespoons granulated sugar

8 tablespoons (1 stick) unsalted butter, at room temperature

10 ounces granulated sugar

6 extra-large eggs, separated, at room temperature

3 ounces semisweet chocolate, finely grated

2 tablespoons unsweetened cocoa powder

2 tablespoons finely ground espresso beans

¼ cup Kahlúa

2 tablespoons dark rum

Confectioners' sugar or semisweet chocolate curls for decoration

At Antica Trattoria Moretto, just outside the charming small town of Vignola in Emilia, we enjoyed a delicious flourless chocolate cake that was loaded with finely chopped almonds. The cake was dark and rich looking, yet it had a surprisingly light, delicate taste. The owner of the trattoria, Signor Cappi, told me that the cake was his adaptation of torta Barozzi, the most famous cake of Vignola. He graciously shared his recipe with me. Although the cake can be refrigerated, I prefer to serve it at room temperature to ensure that its texture remains light and delicate. If refrigerated, the texture of the cake becomes more compact and dense.

PREHEAT the oven to 350°F.

BUTTER an 8- or 9-inch springform pan. Line the bottom of the pan with a circle of parchment paper or wax paper.

SPREAD the almonds on a baking sheet and bake until they are lightly toasted, about 2 minutes. Let cool, then place in a food processor fitted with the metal blade, add 2 tablespoons of the sugar, and pulse until the almonds are finely chopped but not pulverized. Set aside.

PUT the butter and the remaining sugar in the bowl of an electric mixer and beat at medium speed for 3 to 4 minutes, until light and creamy. Beat in the egg yolks one at a time, beating well after each mixture, then beat in the chocolate, cocoa powder, espresso, Kahlúa, and rum. Turn off the mixer and add the almonds. Turn the mixer on and beat at low speed, stopping and scraping down the sides of the bowl a few times, until well combined, 1 to 2 minutes; do not overbeat, or the batter will be too stiff.

BEAT the egg whites in a large bowl until stiff peaks form. Transfer the batter to a wide bowl, and fold in the egg whites in two additions. Scrape the batter into the prepared pan and shake the pan gently to distribute the batter evenly.

PLACE the pan on the middle rack of the oven and bake until the top is golden brown and a thin knife inserted in the center of the cake comes out clean, 40 to 45 minutes. Set the cake pan on a rack and let cool for 15 to 20 minutes, then remove the sides of the pan and let cool completely.

PLACE a large round platter over the cake and invert the cake onto the platter. Lift off the bottom of the pan and gently peel off the parchment paper. Just before serving, decorate the cake with a dusting of confectioners' sugar or with curls of semisweet chocolate.

AMARETTI

Amaretti di Saronno are Italian almond cookies that taste like no other. They are used as a component in many desserts. Amaretti can be found in Italian and specialty food markets, sold in small or large red tins. The cookies are wrapped by the pair in colorful paper and can be kept for months.

To crush amaretti, remove the paper and place the cookies between two sheets of plastic wrap. Crush with a rolling pin, rolling the pin back and forth.

RICE CAKE

Torta di Riso

4 cups milk

⅔ cup granulated sugar

Grated zest of 1 lemon

1 cup Arborio rice

2 to 3 tablespoons fine dried bread crumbs

3 Amaretti di Saronno (see box, page 352)

¾ cup blanched almonds

3 large eggs

2 tablespoons amaretto or dark rum

2 large egg whites, at room temperature

Confectioners' sugar

One of the treats my mother prepared for us was a bowl of hot, creamy rice that had been slowly cooked in milk and sugar. Later I realized that this humble bowl of rice was the base of Bologna's most beloved cakes, torta di Riso; *at Easter, every family baked or bought one. The recipe for this cake comes from Trattoria Boni in Bologna. There, the cake is pricked with a fork and sprinkled with almond liqueur or rum.*

COMBINE the milk with ½ cup sugar and the lemon zest in a saucepan and bring to a boil over medium heat. Add the rice, reduce the heat, and simmer, uncovered, stirring, until the rice is tender and the milk has been absorbed, about 40 minutes. During the last few minutes of cooking, stir the rice constantly. The rice should have the consistency of a thick porridge. Transfer the rice to a large bowl and cool to room temperature.

PREHEAT the oven to 375°F. Butter an 8- or 9-inch baking pan. Sprinkle the bread crumbs over the bottom and sides of the pan, then turn the pan upside down and shake out the excess crumbs.

PUT the amaretti and almonds in a food processor fitted with the metal blade and chop them very fine, but do not pulverize them. Beat the eggs in a large bowl until thick and pale yellow. Add the chopped amaretti and almonds and the liqueur and mix well. Gradually mix in the cooled rice.

IN a medium bowl, beat the egg whites with the remaining sugar until stiff. Fold the whites into the rice mixture. Pour the batter into the prepared pan and shake the pan lightly to distribute it evenly.

PLACE the pan on the middle rack of the oven and bake until the top of the cake is golden brown and a thin knife inserted in the center comes out clean, 30 to 40 minutes. Let cool on a rack to room temperature. (The cake can be prepared up to a day ahead. Let cool, cover, and refrigerate. Bring to room temperature before serving.)

REMOVE the cake from the pan and place on a round serving plate. Sprinkle with confectioners' sugar and serve.

HONEY-WALNUT-RAISIN PIE

Spongata

SERVES 8

For the dough

2 cups unbleached
all-purpose flour

¼ cup granulated sugar

Pinch of salt

8 tablespoons (1 stick)
unsalted butter, at room
temperature if mixing by
hand, chilled and cut into
small pieces if using a food
processor

1 large egg, lightly beaten

⅓ to ½ cup cold milk

For the filling

½ cup raisins, soaked
in lukewarm water for
20 minutes

3 tablespoon fine dried
bread crumbs

2 cups (about 9 ounces)
walnuts

¾ cup pine nuts

⅓ cup very finely diced
candied citron

1 teaspoon grated lemon zest

⅛ teaspoon freshly
grated nutmeg

1 teaspoon ground cinnamon

¾ to 1 cup honey

3 to 4 tablespoons dark rum

alled spongata *in and around Parma and Piacenza and* La Bonissima *in and around Bologna and Modena, this is a pie that is filled with a delectable mixture of chopped walnuts, raisins, honey, candied citron, rum, and spices. A traditional Christmas pie whose dense, sweet consistency and crumbly, buttery crust is not unlike that of baklava, it has many variations. This one comes from Hostaria da Ivan in Fontanelle di Roccabianca, a small hamlet in the countryside between Parma and Piacenza. Serve with a glass of sparkling or dessert wine.* Spongata *keeps well for several days at room temperature.*

To prepare the dough, combine the flour, sugar, and salt in a medium bowl, add the butter, and mix with your fingertips until crumbly. Add the egg and milk and mix until a soft dough forms. (Or combine the flour, sugar, and salt in a food processor, add the chilled butter, and pulse until crumbly. Add the egg and milk and pulse until the dough is loosely gathered around the blade. Divide the dough into 2 parts, one a little larger than the other, and shape into 2 balls. Wrap in plastic wrap and refrigerate for an hour or two.

MEANWHILE, prepare the filling: Drain the raisins, pat dry with paper towels, and set aside. Place the bread crumbs in a small skillet and stir over medium heat until lightly golden, 15 to 20 seconds. Transfer to a small bowl.

PUT the walnuts, pine nuts, and bread crumbs in a food processor fitted with the metal blade and pulse into very small, granular pieces. Transfer to a medium bowl, add the citron, raisins, lemon zest, nutmeg, and cinnamon and mix well.

COMBINE the honey and rum in the top part of a double boiler (or in a heatproof medium bowl) and place over simmering water. When the honey is warm and a bit runny, pour it over the walnut mixture and stir well to combine. Cover the bowl and set aside for an hour or two. (The filling can be prepared several hours ahead and refrigerated. Bring to room temperature before using.)

1 large egg, lightly beaten

1 tablespoon granulated sugar

Confectioners' sugar

PREHEAT the oven to 375°F. Butter a 14-inch pizza pan.

ON a lightly floured surface, roll out the smaller ball of dough to a 12-inch circle. Place the dough on the pizza pan. Spread the filling over the dough in a small mound, leaving a 2-inch border all around.

ROLL out the remaining dough and lay it over the filling. Press the edges of the bottom and top dough together and fold them over to form a 1-inch border. Press the tines of a fork all around the border to seal and to form a decorative edge. (If the fork sticks to the soft dough, dip it into flour.) Brush the dough with the beaten egg, sprinkle with the granulated sugar, and prick it with a fork in several places to allow the steam to escape.

PLACE on the middle rack of the oven and bake for 25 to 30 minutes, or until the crust is golden brown. Let cool completely.

DUST the top of the pie generously with confectioners' sugar and serve.

CHRISTMAS JAM CAKE

Pinza Natalizia

SERVES 8 TO 10

For the filling

½ cup golden raisins, soaked in 1 cup good-quality red wine for several hours

¾ cup good-quality plum preserves

¾ cup good-quality sour cherry preserves or other thick, tart jam

½ cup pine nuts

Grated zest of 1 lemon

For the dough

2 large eggs

½ cup granulated sugar

2 teaspoons baking soda

½ cup lukewarm milk

2 cups all-purpose flour

8 tablespoons (1 stick) unsalted butter, melted and cooled slightly

1 large egg, lightly beaten

¼ to ⅓ cup granulated sugar

At Christmastime, the people of the hill towns and farmland in the province of Bologna make this enriched version of pinza *and fill it with two types of jam, pine nuts, raisins, and lemon zest. Make the cake in the morning and leave it at room temperature until serving time. Or, prepare it a day or two ahead and refrigerate tightly wrapped.*

To prepare the filling, drain the raisins and pat dry with paper towels. Place the raisins in a bowl with the jams, pine nuts, and lemon zest and mix thoroughly. Cover the bowl and refrigerate until ready to use. (The filling can be prepared several hours ahead.)

Preheat the oven to 350°F. Butter and flour a large baking sheet.

To prepare the dough, beat the eggs and sugar in a large bowl until thick and pale yellow. Dissolve the baking soda in the lukewarm milk.

Mound the flour on a large wooden board or other work surface. With your fingertips, make a round well in the center of the flour. Place the egg mixture, the milk, and butter in the well. Stir the ingredients briefly with a fork, then draw the flour, starting with the inside walls of the well, into the mixture, until all the flour has been incorporated and you have a soft, rough, moist dough. Sprinkle the dough with a bit of flour if it sticks too much to the board and to your hands.

Lightly flour the work surface, flatten the dough with your hands, and dust with a bit of flour. Roll the dough out into a 10 × 12-inch rectangle. Spread the filling in a 3-inch-wide band lengthwise down the center of the dough. Fold the long sides of the dough over the filling, slightly overlapping them, and lightly press the seam with a fork to seal. Seal the ends of the cake by pressing them with a fork.

With two large metal spatulas, transfer the cake to the prepared baking sheet. Brush with the beaten egg and sprinkle with the sugar. Bake on the middle rack of the oven for 40 to 50 minutes, or until the cake has a nice golden brown color. Let cool on a rack to room temperature and serve.

JAM TART

Crostata di Marmellata

SERVES 8

For the dough

1¾ cups unbleached
all-purpose flour

½ cup granulated sugar

1½ teaspoons baking powder

Grated zest of 1 lemon

12 tablespoons (1½ sticks)
unsalted butter, chilled and
cut into small pieces

2 large eggs, lightly beaten

3 Amaretti di Saronno
(see box, page 352)

3 cups high-quality thick
plum or fig jam, or other
slightly tart jam

1 large egg, lightly beaten

*O*ne of the most popular desserts of the region is jam tart. A simple dessert to make, but its success relies heavily on the quality of the jam used. Look for thick, dense plum or fig jams imported from Italy or France, because they are considerably less sweet than those made in this country. This dish comes from Villa Gaidello, a popular guest farm located in the countryside around the small town of Castelfranco in the province of Modena, where owner Paola Bini and her staff prepare dishes rooted in local traditions.

To make the dough by hand, combine the flour, sugar, baking powder, and lemon zest in a large bowl. Add the butter and, with your fingertips, rub the butter into the flour until the mixture has a fine crumbly consistency. Stir in the eggs with a fork, then mix gently with your hands until the dough begins to come together.

To make the dough in a food processor, place the flour, baking powder, sugar, and lemon zest in a food processor and pulse a few times to combine. Add the butter and pulse briefly until the mixture has a fine crumbly consistency. Add the eggs and pulse very briefly to moisten the ingredients evenly.

TRANSFER the dough to a work surface and shape into a ball. Wrap in plastic wrap and refrigerate for a few hours. (Before rolling out the dough, see the tips on page 363.)

PREHEAT the oven to 375°F. Butter a 9-inch fluted tart pan with a removable bottom.

PUT the amaretti between two slices of plastic wrap and roll back and forth with a rolling pin until they are finely crushed, or finely chop them in a food processor.

CUT off about one-third of the dough, wrap it, and put it back in the refrigerator. On a lightly floured work surface, roll out the larger ball of dough into a 12-inch circle. Place in the tart pan and press the dough gently and evenly into the pan. Remove any overhanging dough by rolling the rolling pin over the top of the pan.

SPRINKLE the amaretti crumbs over the bottom of the tart shell. Spoon the jam into the shell, smoothing the top with a spatula.

ROLL out the smaller ball of dough. With a scalloped pastry wheel, cut it into eight ¼-inch-wide strips. Arrange the strips on top of the tart to make a lattice. Brush the dough with the beaten egg.

PLACE the tart on the middle rack of the oven and bake until the pastry is golden brown, 20 to 25 minutes. Let the tart cool for about 10 minutes, then carefully remove the tart ring. Cool the tart completely before serving.

EMMA'S PASTRY RING

Ciambella

SERVES 8 TO 10

For the ciambella

3 large eggs

¾ cup granulated sugar

2 teaspoons baking soda

⅓ cup lukewarm milk

10 tablespoons (1⅓ sticks) unsalted butter, melted and cooled slightly

3½ cups all-purpose flour

2 teaspoons honey

Grated zest of 1 lemon

Ciambella *is as homey and unassuming as it is delicious. This Bolognese pastry ring is simple to make at home, but it is nevertheless a staple in bread and pastry shops. As always, the variations on this theme, while subtle, are many.*

This is the cake that nurtured my sister, brother, and me from infancy to young adulthood. In the morning before school, we dunked it in caffe-latte *(espresso diluted with lots of hot milk). In the afternoon, we snacked on a large wedge. And at the end of a festive dinner, we occasionally joined our father in dipping a slice of* ciambella *into a bit of Lambrusco, and today both my sister, Carla, and my sister-in-law, Emma, carry on the tradition. Emma adds a few teaspoons of honey to her* ciambella, *which, she says, gives the dough a rich, golden color, and then tops the cake with slivers of almonds.*

1 large egg, lightly beaten

⅓ to ½ cup sliced blanched almonds

¼ cup granulated sugar

PREHEAT the oven 400°F. Butter and flour a large baking sheet.

BEAT the eggs and the sugar in a large bowl until pale yellow and thick. Dissolve the baking soda in the lukewarm milk.

MOUND the flour on a large wooden board or other work surface. With your fingertips, make a round well in the center of the flour. Place the egg mixture, the milk, butter, honey, and lemon zest in the well. Stir the ingredients briefly with a fork, then, with the fork, draw the flour, starting from the inside walls of the well, into the mixture. When all the flour has been incorporated, scrape off and discard the bits and pieces attached to the working board, and shape the dough quickly into a ball. Sprinkle the dough very lightly with flour if it sticks too much to the board and to your hands. Flour your hands lightly and shape the dough into a long roll about 2 inches thick.

PLACE the roll on the prepared baking sheet and pinch the ends together to make a ring. Brush the ring with the beaten egg. With a thin sharp knife, make a few diagonal slashes in the top of the dough. Scatter the almonds into the slashes and over the top of the cake, and sprinkle with the sugar.

BAKE on the middle rack of the oven for 25 to 30 minutes, or until the cake has a golden brown color and a long thin knife inserted in the center comes out clean. Let the cake cool to room temperature before serving.

FOR A PERFECT CIAMBELLA

- Shape the dough quickly and lightly into a ball, just as you would any pastry dough, but do not refrigerate it.

- As it bakes, the cake will rise to about twice its original height.

- The texture will be somewhat firm and dense on the inside and a bit crumbly on the outside. Cool completely before slicing it.

- *Ciambella* tastes better several hours or a day after it has been made. Wrap it in foil and keep at room temperature.

FOR THE LOVE OF PASTRIES

Half a block from our apartment building in Bologna, there was a pastry store that had an incredible display of luscious pastries and cakes in its windows. On Sunday after mass, our entire family would go to the store to buy *paste miste*, assorted pastries, as a special treat for our Sunday meal. Occasionally we children were permitted to go there alone to buy a bag of candies. During one of these visits, on one side of the long marble counter, a large silver tray displayed an array of pastries, with a sign next to it that said, *"Assaggio."* Try. My brother, who was around twelve and is the oldest of the three of us, assured us that the sign meant that we could taste the pastries before buying them. So we selected our pastries carefully and began eating them slowly and nonchalantly, but devouring as many as we could, until the owner, who knew us, began to doubt our ability to pay for them. He escorted us back to our house, where he was promptly reimbursed by our very angry mother.

CUSTARD CREAM AND RICOTTA TART

Crostata di Crema e Ricotta

SERVES 8

For the dough

1¾ cups unbleached all-purpose flour

½ cup granulated sugar

1½ teaspoons baking powder

Grated zest of 1 lemon

12 tablespoons (1½ sticks) unsalted butter, chilled and cut into small pieces

2 large eggs, lightly beaten

For the custard cream

1½ cups milk

Grated zest of ½ lemon

4 large egg yolks

½ cup granulated sugar

⅓ cup all-purpose flour

1 pound whole-milk ricotta

Confectioners' sugar

*I*talian custard cream, crema pasticcera, *is one of the basic elements of many Italian desserts. In Emilia-Romagna, it is essential to* zuppa Inglese, crema fritta, *and many of the tarts, cakes, and baked fruit dishes. My sister, Carla, who loves to bake, makes a tart with a rich, buttery crust and fills it with a voluptuous fluffy mixture of custard cream and ricotta cheese. I love this tart so much that I put it on my restaurant menu.*

To make the dough by hand, combine the flour, sugar, baking powder, and lemon zest in a large bowl. Add the butter and, with your fingertips, rub the butter into the flour until the mixture has a fine crumbly consistency. Stir in the egg yolks with a fork, then mix gently with your hands until the dough begins to come together.

To make the dough in a food processor, place the flour, sugar, baking powder, and lemon zest in a food processor and pulse a few times to combine. Add the butter and pulse briefly until the mixture has a fine crumbly consistency. Add the eggs and pulse a few times to moisten the ingredients evenly.

TRANSFER the dough to a work surface and shape into a ball. Wrap the dough in plastic wrap and refrigerate for a few hours.

To prepare the custard cream, combine the milk and lemon zest in a small saucepan and bring to just under a boil. Remove from the heat.

BEAT the egg yolks and sugar in a large stainless-steel bowl, using an electric hand mixer, or in the bowl of an electric mixer, using the balloon whisk, until pale yellow and thick. Beat in the flour a little at a time. Add the hot milk in a thin stream, beating on low speed.

LEAVE the mixture in the bowl or transfer to the top part of a double boiler and set over simmering water. Stir constantly and thoroughly with a rubber spatula until the cream begins to thicken, about 10 minutes.

Once the cream thickens, switch to a wire whisk, and continue to stir constantly, reaching all the way to the bottom of the bowl, until the cream is thick and easily coats a spoon, 6 to 8 minutes longer. Remove from the heat, and place a sheet of plastic wrap directly on the cream to prevent a skin from forming. Refrigerate until cold.

PREHEAT the oven to 375°F. Butter a 9- or 10-inch fluted tart pan with a removable bottom.

PUT the ricotta in a large bowl. Gently but thoroughly fold in the custard cream; set aside.

CUT off about one-third of the dough, wrap it, and put it back in the refrigerator. On a lightly floured work surface, roll out the larger ball of dough into a 13-inch circle. Place in the tart pan and press the dough gently and evenly into the pan. Trim the edges of the dough with scissors, leaving a ½-inch overhang.

POUR the cream-ricotta mixture into the shell and smooth the top with a spatula.

ROLL out the smaller ball of dough. With a scalloped pastry wheel, cut it into eight ¼-inch-wide strips. Arrange the strips on top of the tart to make a lattice. Fold the overhanging dough over the strips to secure them and to form a border, then press the border with the tines of a fork to seal the ends and make a decorative rim. Brush the dough with the beaten egg.

PLACE the tart on the middle rack of the oven and bake until the top has a golden brown color, 20 to 25 minutes. Let the tart cool for about 10 minutes, then carefully remove the tart ring.

WHEN the tart is completely cool, dust with confectioners' sugar and serve.

TIPS

- This rich buttery dough must be quite cold before it is rolled out.

- Sprinkle the work surface with flour, and sprinkle some flour on the dough as you roll it out. Work quickly, or the butter will warm up and the dough will become too soft and will tear. If that should occur, though, do not worry. Simply patch up the torn parts with scraps of dough.

- The dough can also be rolled out in the following manner: Place a large piece of plastic wrap on a work surface and dust it generously with flour. Place the dough on the plastic, sprinkle it with flour, and roll it out. Holding the plastic wrap, invert the circle of dough into the tart pan. Carefully peel off the plastic and fit the dough into the pan.

- The custard cream can be cooked directly over the heat, and in that case, it will be done in about half the time. However, you will need to stir it constantly and adjust the heat from time to time to prevent the eggs from curdling. The double-boiler method, while longer, will ensure a smooth, silky, lump-free custard.

SWEET SPINACH-ALMOND-RICOTTA PIE

Erbazzone Dolce all' Emiliana

SERVES 10 TO 12

For the dough

2 cups unbleached all-purpose flour

½ cup granulated sugar

2 teaspoons baking powder

Grated zest of 1 lemon

14 tablespoons (1¾ sticks) unsalted butter, chilled and cut into small pieces

2 large eggs, lightly beaten (if using a food processor, add 1 extra egg)

For the filling

2 pounds fresh spinach or 1½ 10-ounce packages frozen spinach

Salt

¾ cup raisins, soaked in lukewarm water for 20 minutes

3 large eggs

1 cup granulated sugar

¼ cup dark rum

Grated zest of 1 lemon

1 cup blanched almonds, finely chopped

1 pound whole-milk ricotta

2 large egg whites, at room temperature

1 large egg, lightly beaten

Confectioners' sugar

his impressive-looking pie is the sweet version of the classic scar-pazzone of Modena and Reggio-Emilia. Here, spinach, ricotta, sugar, lemon zest, raisins, almonds, rum, and eggs are combined into a wonderfully unusual, complex filling, which is enclosed into a rich pastry crust.

Make sure to chill the pastry dough well before rolling it out. If it tears as you roll it out or place it in the tart pan, simply patch it with scraps of dough.

To make the dough by hand, combine the flour, sugar, baking powder, and lemon zest in a large bowl. Add the butter and, with your fingertips, rub the butter into the flour until the mixture has a fine crumbly consistency. Stir in the eggs with a fork, then mix gently with your hands until the dough begins to come together.

To make the dough with a food processor, place the flour, sugar, baking powder, and lemon zest in a food processor and pulse a few times to combine. Add the butter and pulse briefly until the mixture has a fine crumbly consistency. Add the eggs and pulse very briefly to moisten the ingredients evenly.

TRANSFER the dough to a work surface and shape into 2 balls, one a little larger that the other. Wrap them in plastic wrap and refrigerate for a few hours.

PREHEAT the oven to 375°F. Butter a 9- or 10-inch springform pan.

TO prepare the filling, if using fresh spinach, remove and discard the stems. Wash the spinach in several changes of cold water. Bring a large pot half full with water to a boil. Add a generous pinch of salt and the spinach and cook until the spinach is tender, 3 to 5 minutes. Drain and cool under cold running water. Squeeze out the excess water from the spinach and chop it fine.

Drain the raisins and pat dry with paper towels.

Beat the eggs with ¾ cup of the sugar in a large bowl. Add the rum, lemon zest, almonds, ricotta, and raisins and mix well with a wooden spoon or a rubber spatula. Add the spinach and mix well.

In a medium bowl, beat the egg whites with the remaining ¼ cup sugar until stiff. Fold the whites into the spinach mixture.

On a lightly floured work surface, roll out the larger ball of dough into a 15-inch circle and fit it into the prepared pan. Spoon the filling into the pan, smoothing the top with a spatula.

Roll out the remaining dough to a 12-inch circle and place over the filling. Trim off any excess dough, then pinch the edges of the top and bottom dough together and roll the dough over to make a raised edge. Decorate the raised edge by pressing the ribs of a fork into it diagonally all around. Brush the top with the beaten egg and prick the dough in several places with a fork.

Place the pie on the middle rack of the oven and bake until the top has a nice golden brown color, 40 to 50 minutes. Let the pie cool on a rack. Remove the sides of the pan, sprinkle the top with confectioners' sugar, and serve at room temperature.

MY MOTHER'S PASTRY FRITTERS

Sfrappole della Mamma

SERVES 8

2 cups all-purpose flour

4 tablespoons (½ stick) unsalted butter, at room temperature if making the dough by hand, chilled and cut into small pieces if using a food processor

¼ cup granulated sugar

Grated zest of 1 lemon

2 large eggs

¼ cup sweet Marsala or white wine

Vegetable oil for deep-frying

Confectioners' sugar

To make these, my mother rolled out a large sheet of sweet golden dough, stretching it with the long rolling pin, until it was very thin, almost transparent. She quickly cut the dough into long ribbons, tied it into large knots, and dropped into the black iron pot used only for frying. What emerged were the puffed-up, golden, crisp fritters that my brother, sister, and I loved so much. At that point, we took over the job. We piled the fritters high on a platter, sprinkled them liberally with powdered sugar, and ate them as fast as we could. To me, nothing else ever tasted that good, and nothing was ever more fun to prepare. I sometimes prepared these fritters for my daughters, Carla and Paola, when they came home from school with a friend or two in tow. And yes, they too made the fritters disappear in no time at all.

To make the dough by hand, put the flour in a medium bowl, add the butter and, with your fingertips, mix until the butter is in very tiny pieces. Add the sugar, lemon zest, eggs, and wine and mix until a smooth, soft dough forms.

To make the dough with a food processor, place the flour in a food processor fitted with the metal blade, add the butter, and pulse until the mixture is crumbly. Add the sugar, lemon zest, eggs, and wine and pulse until the dough is loosely gathered around the blade. Remove the dough from the bowl and knead briefly until smooth and soft.

Lɪɢʜᴛʟʏ flour the dough, wrap in plastic wrap, and refrigerate for about 1 hour.

Oɴ a lightly floured wooden board or other work surface, roll out the dough ⅛ inch thick. (The dough should be quite thin, or the fritters will be chewy.) Using a pastry wheel or sharp knife, cut the dough into strips, about ¾ inch wide and 10 to 12 inches long. Tie the strips into loose knots and place them on a lightly floured cookie sheet.

POUR 2 inches of oil into a large deep skillet or saucepan and heat over medium-high heat until 360°F hot but not smoking. (Test the temperature by dropping in a small scrap of the dough; if the oil sizzles immediately around the dough, it is ready.) Lower 2 to 3 pastry knots into the hot oil and fry until golden on the first side, then turn with metal tongs and fry the other side. Do not let them turn too dark; lower the heat a bit if the oil is is too hot. Drain on paper towels and fry the remaining pastry.

PILE the fritters on a large platter, sprinkle generously with confectioners' sugar, and serve hot or at room temperature. These keep well at room temperature, uncovered, for several days.

THE PASTRY FRITTERS OF CARNIVAL

Carnival in Italy is a time of jubilation. And it is when eating excesses are tolerated, because Lent is just around the corner, when abstinence or moderation are mandatory. The Bolognese *sfrappole* are always made at Carnival, but one can also find large platters of *sfrappole* in most Bolognese homes at Christmas, New Year's, Easter, or other holidays. Pastry fritters are popular in other Italian regions as well, where they take on different shapes and names.

PERFECT DEEP-FRYING

Follow these few simple rules, and fried desserts will turn out greaseless every time.

- Choose a deep heavy pan that conducts heat evenly, such as a cast-iron one. Make sure the pan is larger than the burner you are using, so in case of spillage, the oil will not fall on the lit burner.

- Use an oil that has a high smoking point, such as "pure" olive oil or peanut oil. Extra virgin olive oil is not suitable for deep-frying.

- Put a generous amount of clean oil in the pan and let it get nice and hot over medium-high heat. Test the temperature of the oil on a deep-frying thermometer: it should read 365° to 370 °F. If you do not have a thermometer, just drop a cube of bread into the oil. If the oil sizzles immediately around the bread and the bread turns golden in less than a minute, the oil is ready.

- Do not crowd the pan, or the temperature of the oil will drop and your food will be greasy instead of crisp.

- Do not let the oil get to the smoking point, or it will need to be discarded. Adjust the heat as needed.

- Add the food to the pan, turn it, and remove it using the proper tools. Long tongs or slotted spoons are fine.

- Drain fried food well on paper towels or on a wire rack that is set over a sheet of parchment paper or a baking sheet.

- If cooking in batches, work fast and keep the fried food warm in a low oven while you finish the frying.

- Remove and discard any batter or food particles that float in the oil so they won't burn.

APPLE FRITTERS

Frittelle di Mele

SERVES 4 TO 6

For the batter

2 large eggs

⅓ cup granulated sugar

⅔ cup milk

2 tablespoons dark rum

1 tablespoon baking soda

Grated zest of 1 lemon

1 cup all-purpose flour

4 Golden Delicious apples

Olive oil or vegetable oil for deep-frying

Confectioners' sugar

Rounds of crunchy apples, dipped into a sweet creamy batter and deep-fried, are absolutely heavenly. There is something so homey and so reassuring about sweet fritters. There was a time when many country trattorie offered this dessert. The fritters would come to the table piled high on a platter dusted with powdered sugar, and they were often served with a glass of sweet local wine. Apple fritters were also very popular in the homes of Emilia-Romagna, and were often a Sunday treat.

To prepare the batter, put the eggs in a medium bowl, add the sugar, and beat with a wire whisk until thoroughly blended. Add the milk, rum, baking soda, and lemon zest and beat well to blend. Gradually add the flour, mixing well with the whisk to prevent lumps, until the batter is thick and smooth; it should coat and cling to a slice of apple. Cover the bowl and let the batter stand at room temperature for about 1 hour.

Peel and core the apples. Cut them into ¼-inch-thick rounds and pat dry with paper towels.

Pour 2 inches of oil into a deep medium skillet and place over high heat. When the oil is very hot (it is ready when a bit of batter dropped into the oil turns golden right away), dip a few slices of apple at a time into the batter and lower them into the oil. When the first side is golden brown, turn them gently and fry the other side. Remove the fritters with tongs or slotted spoon and place on paper towels to drain. Repeat until all the slices are fried.

Arrange the fritters on a serving plate, sprinkle generously with confectioners' sugar, and serve hot.

CHESTNUT-RICOTTA FRITTERS

Frittelle di Castagne e Ricotta

SERVES 4 TO 6

2 large eggs

⅓ cup granulated sugar

1 teaspoon vanilla extract

1 teaspoon baking soda

½ pound whole-milk ricotta
(about 1 cup)

¼ cup chestnut flour
(available in Italian and
specialty markets and health
food stores)

¼ cup all-purpose flour

Olive oil or vegetable oil for
deep-frying

Confectioners' sugar

I often prepared ricotta fritters as a treat for my daughters and their friends when they returned home from school. I made the batter for the fritters only with ricotta cheese, sugar, and eggs. I allowed it to sit for several hours so it could thicken, then, as soon as I heard the school bus stop in front of our house, I would begin dropping the batter into the hot oil and in no time at all I had a plate filled with golden, puffed-up fritters.

This version of the fritters, which uses chestnut flour instead of white flour, is the way my friend Mara, who lives in the mountain town of Poretta Terme, makes them. They are simply delicious. If necessary, you can substitute all-purpose flour for the chestnut flour, and they will still be good.

IN a large bowl, using a wooden spoon or an electric hand mixer, beat the eggs with the sugar until pale yellow and thick. Add the vanilla, baking soda, and ricotta and beat until well incorporated. Add the flour a little at a time, folding it in, or mixing on low speed, until thoroughly incorporated. Cover the bowl and let the batter stand at room temperature for about 1 hour.

POUR 2 inches of oil into a medium heavy saucepan and heat over medium-high heat. When the oil is very hot (it is ready when a bit of batter dropped into the oil turns golden brown right away), drop the batter by the tablespoonful without crowding, into the hot oil. Turn as needed. When the fritters are golden on both sides (1 to 2 minutes), remove them with a slotted spoon and drain on paper towels. Repeat until all the batter has been used.

PLACE the fritters on a serving platter, dust with confectioners' sugar, and serve hot.

NONNA'S CHESTNUT FRITTERS

Frittelle di Castagne

SERVES 4 TO 6

⅓ cup golden raisins

1 cup sweet Marsala

2 large egg whites

Pinch of salt

1 cup chestnut flour
(available in Italian and
specialty markets and
health food stores)

1 teaspoon baking soda

¼ cup granulated sugar

⅓ to ½ cup milk

1 tablespoon extra virgin
olive oil

Olive oil or vegetable oil for
deep-frying

Confectioners' sugar

Nonna Fiorina, my sister-in-law Emma's grandmother, died when she was ninety-nine years old. She was as beautiful as a painting. Her hair, as white as snow, was held back by a colorful scarf, and she was always immaculately, though modestly, dressed, with a long apron perennially wrapped around her body. Nonna Fiorina loved three things. She loved to watch television. She loved President Kennedy, so much so that when he died she put one of his photos next to her statue of the Virgin Mary. And she loved to cook. Even when she grew older and feeble, she insisted on preparing, with the aid of Emma or other adult grandchildren, her favorite chestnut fritters. This is how she made them.

SOAK the raisins in the Marsala until soft, about 30 minutes. Drain and pat dry with paper towels.

IN a medium bowl, beat the egg whites with the salt until soft peaks form.

COMBINE the flour, baking soda, and granulated sugar in a medium bowl. With a wire whisk, slowly beat in enough milk so you have a thick batter. (The batter should have a sour cream-like consistency.) Stir in the oil, then fold in the raisins and the egg whites. Cover and let the batter stand at room temperature for about 1 hour.

POUR 2 inches of oil into a deep medium saucepan. When the oil is very hot (it is ready when a bit of batter dropped into it turns golden right away), drop the batter a tablespoonful at a time, without crowding, into the oil. When the fritters are golden on both sides, 1 to 2 minutes, remove them with a slotted spoon and drain on paper towels. Repeat until all batter has been used.

PLACE the fritters on a serving platter, dust with confectioners' sugar, and serve hot.

FRIED CUSTARD CREAM

Crema Fritta di Bologna

SERVES 6 TO 8

For the custard cream

2 cups whole milk

4 large eggs

½ cup granulated sugar

Grated zest of 1 lemon

¾ cup all-purpose flour

2 to 3 cups fine dried bread crumbs

2 large eggs

About 2½ cups vegetable oil or olive oil for deep-frying

Confectioners' sugar

*O*ne of Bologna's signature dishes is *fritte misto alla Bolognese, which fries morsels of tender lamb, veal, cheese, vegetables, and sweet custard cream and combines them into a glorious entree. The fried custard cream, with its crunchy, golden exterior and its hot creamy filling, is unforgettable, served with deep fried meats or alone. When I am in Bologna and yearn for fried custard cream I go to Boni and Gigina because they make exceptional renditions of this traditional dessert.*

To prepare the custard cream, in a medium saucepan, bring the milk to just below a boil. Remove from the heat.

Beat the eggs, sugar, and lemon zest in a large stainless steel bowl with a hand mixer or in a bowl of an electric mixer fitted with the balloon whisk, until pale yellow and thick. Beat in the flour a little at a time. Add the hot milk in a thin stream, beating on low speed.

LEAVE the mixture in the bowl or transfer to the top part of a double boiler and set over a couple of inches of simmering water. Cook, stirring constantly and thoroughly with a rubber spatula, scraping the sides of the bowl, until the cream begins to thicken, about 10 minutes; make sure the water is kept at a low simmer. Once the cream begins to thicken, switch to a wire whisk and stir constantly, reaching all the way to the bottom of the bowl, until it is thick and easily coats a spoon, 6 to 8 minutes longer. Remove from the heat.

MOISTEN a cookie sheet with a bit of cold water and spread the cooked cream evenly ½ inch thick. Let cool to room temperature, then cover with plastic wrap and refrigerate for several hours, or overnight (or, to speed things up, freeze the cream for an hour or two.)

LINE a baking sheet with parchment or wax paper, and sprinkle some of the bread crumbs over the baking sheet. Lightly beat the eggs in a shallow bowl.

CUT the chilled cream into 1½- to 2-inch squares. A few at a time, coat the pieces in the bread crumbs, dip them into the beaten eggs, and coat again with bread crumbs. Place the breaded squares on the prepared baking sheet. The cream can be fried immediately, or it can be refrigerated, uncovered, for several hours.

POUR 1 inch of oil into a deep medium skillet and place over medium-high heat. When the oil is very hot but not smoking, lower a few squares of cream at a time into the oil with a slotted spoon and fry until the first side of the cream is nice and golden, about 1 minute. Turn the pieces and brown the other side. Remove from the oil with the slotted spoon and place on paper towels to drain.

WHEN all the pieces have been fried, arrange them on a serving platter, dust them liberally with confectioners' sugar, and serve nice and hot.

TIPS FOR MAKING DELICIOUS
FRIED CREAM EFFORTLESSLY

More than twenty-five years ago, when I began my culinary career as a cooking teacher, I prepared this delicious custard cream quite often in my classes. At that time, I would beat everything by hand, which took more time and energy. Now that I own a restaurant, I have learned a few tricks that allow me to whip up large batches of custard cream without much effort.

- Use a stand mixer or hand-held electric mixer.

- Pour the hot milk *slowly* into the eggs so it won't cook and curdle them.

- Keep your eyes on the cream as it cooks. To keep it smooth and lump-free, the cream should thicken gradually. Make sure the water is simmering very gently; if it is too hot, it will curdle the eggs.

- If you need to rest your arm as you cook the cream, remove the pan from the heat for a minute or so.

- To test the cream, drop a tablespoon of cream onto a plate. If it stays in a nice little mound and does not spread all over the plate, it has reached the right consistency; if not, cook it a bit longer.

- Be sure the cream is very cold before you cut it, or it won't hold its shape. If the knife sticks to it as you cut it, put the pan in the freezer for an hour or two to firm it up.

- After the cream squares have been breaded, they can be fried right away or refrigerated for several hours. Refrigerating them will make it easier to fry them.

BAKED SWEET TORTELLI

Tortelli Dolci

MAKES ABOUT 25
TORTELLI

For the filling

**1 cup good-quality plum
preserve or sour cherry
preserves**

**2 Amaretti di Saronno, finely
crushed (see box, page 352)**

Grated zest of 1 lemon

For the dough

2 large eggs

⅓ cup granulated sugar

1 teaspoon baking soda

¼ cup lukewarm milk

2½ cups all-purpose flour

**6 tablespoons (¾ stick)
unsalted butter, melted and
cooled slightly**

1 large egg, lightly beaten

Confectioners' sugar

*T*he Emilia side of the region is known for its incomparable stuffed
pasta dishes. But, as if stuffing pasta were not enough, the Emiliani
also take great delight in stuffing meats, vegetables, and desserts. Sweet
tortelli, *as they are called in Parma, or* raviole, *as they are called in Bologna, are filled, half moon-shaped morsels made with a sweet dough. The
dough is thinly rolled and cut into 3- to 4-inch rounds. A bit of filling, including thick tart jam, chestnut puree, amaretti cookies, ricotta, and/or finely
chopped almonds or walnuts, is spooned into the center of the rounds.
Each one is folded and sealed, and then the tortelli are baked or fried,
depending on the local custom.*

*When I see a platter piled high with golden, crisp tortelli, blanketed
with powdered sugar, a rush of warm, happy memories embrace me. My
mother in the kitchen, with an apron wrapped around her body, rolling
out the dough for tortelli, stuffing and sealing them. The lush aroma of the
tortelli as they are baking, and finally the piling of the tortelli on a large
platter. This is happy, unpretentious food that one does not ever tire of.*

*If you should find yourself in Parma, go to Ristorante Cocchi and at
the end of the meal, ask for sweet tortelli. If you should find yourself in
Bologna, go to Ristorante Rodrigo and ask for sweet ravioli. You'll be glad
you did.*

To prepare the filling, put the jam, crushed amaretti, and lemon zest in a
small bowl and mix well. Cover and refrigerate until ready to use.

Preheat the oven to 350°F. Lightly butter a large baking sheet and line
it with parchment paper (the butter will keep the paper in place).

To prepare the dough, beat the eggs with the sugar in a large bowl until
pale yellow and creamy. Dissolve the baking soda in the lukewarm milk.

Mound the flour on a large wooden board or other work surface. With
your fingertips, make a round well in the center of the flour. Place the egg
mixture, the milk, and butter in the well. Stir the ingredients briefly with
a fork, then draw the flour, starting with the inside walls of the well, into

the mixture until all the flour has been incorporated and the dough comes together into a soft, rough, moist mass. Sprinkle the dough with a bit of flour if it sticks too much to the board and to your hands, but do not knead it.

LIGHTLY flour the work surface, flatten the dough with your hands, and dust it with a bit of flour. Roll out the dough to pie thickness, dusting it with a bit more flour if needed. With a round cookie cutter or a large glass, cut the dough into 3- to 4-inch circles. Place 1 heaping teaspoon of the jam mixture in the center of each circle of dough, fold each circle in half over the filling, and press the edges firmly to seal. Press the tines of a fork around the edges to seal the dough firmly and decorate it.

ARRANGE the tortelli on the prepared baking sheet, brush them lightly with the beaten egg, and place on the middle rack of the oven. Bake until they have a golden brown color, 15 to 20 minutes. Let cool, then sprinkle with confectioners' sugar and serve.

CORNMEAL COOKIES

Gialletti

MAKES 30 TO 35
COOKIES

2 large eggs

1 cup granulated sugar

1½ cups finely ground
yellow cornmeal

1 cup unbleached
all-purpose flour

12 tablespoons (1½ sticks)
unsalted butter, melted and
cooled slightly

Grated zest of 1 lemon

Confectioners' sugar

*G*ialletti, *or* zalet, *as they are called in the Bolognese dialect, are corn-meal cookies typical of Emilia-Romagna and of the neighboring Veneto. A dough of cornmeal and flour, butter, eggs, and sugar produces fragrant, crunchy cookies with a pronounced corn taste. Some bakers add pine nuts and softened raisins to the dough. Serve a few of these cookies as an accompaniment to Pears Baked in Lambrusco (page 379).*

BEAT the eggs with the sugar in a medium bowl until well blended.

COMBINE the cornmeal and flour and mound the mixture on a large wooden board or other work surface. With your fingertips, make a round well in the center of the mixture. Place the egg mixture, the melted butter, and lemon zest in the well. With a fork, stir the ingredients briefly, then draw the flour, starting with the inside walls of the well, into the egg mixture. When all the flour has been incorporated, shape the dough quickly into a ball (do not knead it), wrap it in plastic wrap, and refrigerate for at least 1 hour, or longer.

PREHEAT the oven to 350°F. Lightly butter a large baking sheet and line it with parchment paper (the butter will keep the paper in place).

PULL off small pieces of dough about the size of a walnut, roll them into balls, and flatten them with the palms of your hands into ¼-inch-thick rounds. Place on the prepared baking sheet, about ½ inch apart, and bake on the middle rack of the oven until they have a rich golden color, 8 to 10 minutes.

LET the cookies cool on a rack to room temperature. With a spatula, transfer them to a large serving plate, sprinkle with confectioners' sugar, and serve. (They will keep well for several days stored in a cookie jar or a tin.)

Three Fruit Desserts

Italians don't eat dessert at the end of a meal on a daily basis. But fruit, they can't live without. Fresh fruit is often baked, poached, or marinated in wine or balsamic vinegar. It is amazing how delicious a baked pear can be when it has been basted with good wine, and how appetizing it looks when it emerges from the oven lusciously golden brown with a shining, wrinkled skin. And it is amazing how inviting a baked apple can be when a creamy custard is poured over it.

The three recipes that follow are homey, unfussy desserts that require no special presentation.

BAKED APPLES WITH CUSTARD CREAM AND AMARETTI

Mele al Forno con Crema Pasticcera e Amaretti

SERVES 4

PREHEAT the oven to 375 F. Generously butter a large baking pan.

For the apples
4 tart firm apples, cored
1 cup dry white wine
⅓ cup granulated sugar

For the custard cream
1½ cups whole milk
Grated zest of 1 lemon
4 large egg yolks
½ cup granulated sugar
⅓ cup all-purpose flour

8 Amaretti di Saronno
(see box, page 352)

TO prepare the apples, put them in the buttered pan, add the wine, and sprinkle with the sugar. Place the dish on the middle rack of the oven and bake, basting the apples from time to time, until they are tender, 40 to 50 minutes. Transfer to a serving platter.

MEANWHILE, prepare the Custard Cream, following the instructions on page 361, using the proportions given here.

PLACE the amaretti between two sheets of plastic wrap and finely crush them with a rolling pin; do not pulverize them to a powder.

SPOON the custard cream over the apples and sprinkle with the crushed amaretti. Serve warm or at room temperature.

STRAWBERRIES WITH BALSAMIC VINEGAR

Fragole al Balsamico

SERVES 6

PUT the strawberries into a large bowl and toss with the sugar. Cover the bowl with plastic wrap and refrigerate for about 30 minutes.

2 pints ripe strawberries, rinsed, hulled, and halved or quartered if large

¼ to ⅓ cup granulated sugar

Balsamic vinegar
(see page 10) to taste

SPRINKLE the strawberries with balsamic vinegar, toss gently, and serve in chilled glasses.

STRAWBERRIES WITH WINE Combine the strawberries with the sugar and about 2 cups of fruity red wine or sweet Marsala. Toss well, cover, and marinate for about 1 hour.

PEARS BAKED IN LAMBRUSCO

Pere al Forno col Lambrusco

SERVES 6

6 Bosc pears with stems

Lambrusco or any medium-dry red wine such as a Californian Sangiovese

⅔ cup granulated sugar

PREHEAT the oven to 375°F.

CUT a thin slice off the bottom of each pear. Place the pears in a baking pan that holds them snugly. Add enough wine to come about 1½ inches up the sides of the pears and sprinkle the pears with ⅓ cup of the sugar.

PUT the baking dish on the middle rack of the oven and bake, basting the pears from time to time, until they are tender and their skin is nicely wrinkled, about 1 hour. (If the tops of the pears become dark, reduce the heat a bit.) Transfer the pears to a large serving dish and cool.

TRANSFER the wine in the baking dish to a small saucepan; set aside.

JUST before serving the pears, bring the wine to a fast boil. Add the remaining ⅓ cup sugar and cook, stirring from time to time, until reduced to a thick syrupy consistency. Spoon the sauce over the pears and serve.

Note: Lambrusco is a dry sparkling wine typical of the Emilia-Romagna region. American Lambrusco is slightly sweeter than its Italian counterpart but either can be used in this dish.

ZUPPA INGLESE

SERVES 8 TO 10

For the cake

4 large eggs, separated, at room temperature

½ cup plus 2 tablespoons granulated sugar

Grated zest of 1 lemon

¾ cup cake flour

For the custard cream

3 cups whole milk

Grated zest of 1 lemon

8 large egg yolks

⅔ cup granulated sugar

½ cup all-purpose flour

2 ounces semisweet chocolate, finely chopped, or chocolate chips

1 cup heavy cream

¼ cup each dark rum and cherry liqueur or Grand Marnier

Grated semisweet chocolate or chocolate curls for decoration, optional

*Z*uppa inglese *is one of the most popular desserts of Italy. The word* zuppa *(soup) refers to the pudding-like preparation, which is eaten with a spoon like a soup.*

In Emilia-Romagna, this luscious dessert can be made with sponge cake, as it is here, or with ladyfingers. It may have the addition of sour cherry jam. One or several types of liqueur can be added. It may be made with thick, rich yellow custard cream or layered with a combination of plain and chocolate custard cream.

Zuppa inglese was, in my family, served only on special occasions, such as Christmas, New Year's, and special birthdays or anniversaries. It is the very first dessert I made, when as a young bride I followed my American husband to New York, and many years later, I taught it in my cooking classes. In spite of the several steps in this recipe, zuppa inglese *is quite simple to make. If you don't have time to make the sponge cake use a good-quality store-bought one. This dessert can be prepared a day ahead.*

To prepare the cake, preheat the oven to 350°F. Butter an 8- or 9-inch round cake pan and line the bottom with a round of waxed or parchment paper.

Put the egg yolks, ½ cup of the sugar, and the lemon zest in a large bowl, and beat with an electric mixer at medium speed until the mixture is thick and pale yellow and forms a ribbon when the beaters are lifted, 5 to 6 minutes. Set aside.

In another large bowl, beat the egg whites with the remaining 2 tablespoons sugar until soft peaks form. With a large spatula, fold about one-quarter of the egg whites into the yolk mixture to lighten it. Fold in the remaining whites.

Sift about one-third of the cake flour over the eggs, folding it in quickly with a large rubber spatula. Fold in the remaining flour in two or three batches.

Pour the batter into the prepared cake pan, then shake the pan lightly to distribute the batter evenly. Place the pan on the middle rack of the oven and bake until the top of the cake has a nice golden brown color and the cake begins to come away from the sides of the pan, 25 to 30 minutes. Remove from the oven and let cool on a rack for a few minutes.

Loosen the sides of the cake from the pan with a small knife, then invert it onto a rack. Peel off the paper and let cool to room temperature. (The cake can be made a few days ahead and refrigerated tightly wrapped.)

To prepare the custard cream, combine the milk and lemon zest in a small saucepan and bring to just under a boil. Remove from the heat.

Beat the egg yolks and sugar in a large stainless steel bowl with a hand-held mixer or in the bowl of an electric mixer fitted with the balloon whisk, until pale yellow and thick. Beat in the flour a little at a time. Add the hot milk in a thin stream, beating on low speed.

Leave the mixture in the bowl or transfer to the top part of a double boiler and set over simmering water. Cook, stirring constantly with a rubber spatula, until the cream begins to thicken, about 10 minutes. Once the cream starts to thicken, switch to a wire whisk and stir constantly, reaching all the way to the bottom of the bowl, until the cream is thick and easily coats a spoon, 6 to 8 minutes longer. Remove from the heat.

Scoop out about one-third of the cream, place in another bowl, and immediately add the chopped chocolate. Stir until the chocolate is melted. (The finer the chocolate is chopped, the faster it will melt.) Place a sheet of plastic wrap directly on the surface of each batch of cream to prevent a skin from forming and refrigerate until cool.

Beat the heavy cream in a bowl until thick. Fold one-third of the cream into the chocolate custard. Fold the remaining cream into the plain custard.

To assemble the dessert, cut the cake into ¼-inch-thick slices. Line the bottom of a deep serving dish or a 2-quart glass bowl with slices of cake. Brush the cake generously with the rum mixture and cover with half the plain custard cream. Top with another layer of cake, brush with rum, and cover with the chocolate cream. Add last layer of cake, brush with the remaining rum mixture, and top with the remaining plain custard cream. Cover with plastic wrap and refrigerate for several hours, or overnight.

BEFORE serving, decorate the cake with grated chocolate or chocolate curls if desired. Spoon the chilled *zuppa* into individual serving bowls.

MASCARPONE-ZABAGLIONE MOUSSE

Coppa di Mascarpone e Zabaglione

SERVES 6

For the zabaglione

6 large eggs

½ cup granulated sugar

Grated zest of 1 lemon

½ cup dark rum

1 pound mascarpone cheese

4 Amaretti di Saronno, very finely crushed (see box, page 352), or grated semisweet chocolate, for decoration

My first experience with a rich, fluffy mousse was at the house of one of my father's sisters. Zia Maria had just returned from a vacation to Paris, where she had fallen in love with a decadent chocolate mousse. My first bite of mousse left me mesmerized. I loved it, and couldn't understand why no one in our family had ever prepared it before. But that was then—today's Italian cooks can whip up some outstanding mousses. These desserts are now quite common in many restaurants and fancy trattorie of the region.

This recipe comes from Trattoria del Cacciatore in the small hamlet of Frassinara, in the Parma countryside. There, the zabaglione is prepared not with the usual rum, but with nocino, *a local liquor made with green walnuts that have been steeped for weeks in a mixture of alcohol, cloves, and cinnamon.*

To prepare the zabaglione, put the eggs, sugar, and lemon zest in the bowl of an electric mixer and beat at medium speed for about 1 minute, until well blended. Turn the machine to high speed and beat until the mixture is pale yellow and has tripled in volume.

TRANSFER the mixture to a large heatproof bowl, or the top of a double boiler and set it over a few inches of simmering water. (Do not let the water boil, or it will scramble and curdle the eggs.) Slowly add the rum, beating energetically with a large wire whisk, and continue to whisk until the eggs have doubled in volume and the mixture is hot to the touch, about 10 minutes. Place the bowl over a larger bowl half-filled with ice and whisk for a few minutes to cool.

PUT the mascarpone in the bowl of the electric mixer, fitted with the paddle attachment, add about half of the zabaglione, and beat at medium speed just to combine. Beat in the remaining zabaglione. Do not overbeat.

SPOON the mousse into dessert glasses. Cover the glasses with plastic wrap and refrigerate for several hours, or overnight. Just before serving, sprinkle the chopped amaretti or grated chocolate over the mousse.

Gelato

Few would not agree that Italian ice cream is tempting, inviting, and positively irresistible. *Gelato,* as it is called in Italian, dates from Roman times. It is firmly entrenched in the habits and culture of Italy. We love gelato. We pursue it in a never-ending quest to find the absolute best.

Italians rarely make gelato at home, because it is much more fun to walk to the nearby *gelatería,* choose from a large number of flavors, and enjoy it at an outdoor caffé while watching the world go by.

Gelato is lighter than American ice cream. It has a denser, softer texture and a fresh, not-too-sweet taste. Gelato is also considerably lower in butterfat, since more milk is used than cream. In Italy, gelato flavors are limited only by one's imagination.

After a delicious long lunch at Da Ivan, a well known trattoria in the small town of Roccabianca in the countryside of Parma, we asked Ivan about his gelato. He suggested we try the gelatis of Bar Centrale just down the road. There the choices were so many that we sat at a table and slowly and methodically began tasting as may as we could. Emanuela, the owner and gelato maker, shared the following gelati recipes with me.

Making gelato is quite simple, since there are so many reliable ice cream machines available. Of the several gelati here, perhaps my favorites of all are the strawberry, because it looks and tastes like a soft mound of strawberries, and the wildly decadent chocolate gelato with preserved cherries. Before making your first batch, read the following tips, which will guide you through the making of Italian gelato.

TIPS FOR MAKING GELATI

- Buy fresh, unbruised fruit, fresh eggs, whole milk, fresh nuts, and the best-quality chocolate you can afford.

- Don't use low-fat substitutes, or the taste of your gelato will be substantially altered.

- Wash all equipment thoroughly in hot soapy water to get rid of any residual odors.

- If using fruit, wash it in cold water.

- Always chill the gelato mixture before putting it in the ice cream machine.

- Ideally gelato should be served immediately after it has been made, when it is at its softest, most voluptuous. If you must freeze it, place it in an airtight container, and freeze it only for a few hours. (If you must freeze it longer, let gelato soften in the refrigerator for 30 minutes to 1 hour before serving.)

- Homemade gelato will soften faster than commercial ice cream, so serve it in slightly chilled glasses or bowls.

RICH CUSTARD GELATO

Gelato di Crema

MAKES ABOUT 1 QUART

3 cups whole milk

8 large egg yolks

¾ cup granulated sugar

Diana Restaurant in Bologna has long been regarded as a bastion of traditional Bolognese cooking. The gelato di crema, *which has been on the restaurant's menu ever since I can remember, is timeless—and delicious.*

PUT the milk in a medium saucepan and bring to just below a boil over medium heat; do not let it boil. Turn off the heat.

MEANWHILE, put the egg yolks and sugar in a bowl and beat with a wire whisk or an electric hand beater until pale yellow and thick. Gradually pour the hot milk into the beaten yolks in a thin stream, stirring constantly with a wire whisk.

RETURN the mixture to the saucepan and place over medium-low heat. Cook, stirring constantly, until the custard thickens and coats the back of a spoon, 5 to 6 minutes. Do not let the custard boil, or it will curdle.

STRAIN the custard through a fine-mesh sieve into a clean metal bowl. Set the bowl over a larger bowl of ice water and cool completely. Cover the bowl and chill in the refrigerator until cold. (The custard mixture can be kept in the refrigerator for a day or two.)

FREEZE the mixture in an ice cream freezer according to manufacturer's instructions. Serve immediately, or transfer to a tightly sealed container and freeze for a day or two.

CUSTARD COOKED IN A DOUBLE BOILER This is a safer, if longer, method of cooking the custard, since there is less chance of curdling the eggs. Heat the milk. Beat the eggs with the sugar in the top of a double boiler or a heatproof bowl and add the milk as instructed above. Place over a few inches of slowly simmering water (do not let the water boil), and cook, stirring constantly, until the custard thickens and coats the back of a spoon, 15 to 20 minutes. Strain the custard and proceed as instructed above.

CHOCOLATE GELATO WITH
PRESERVED CHERRIES

Gelato di Cioccolata e Amarene

MAKES ABOUT 5 CUPS

½ cup unsweetened
cocoa powder

4 ounces good-quality
bittersweet chocolate,
coarsely chopped

1 recipe Rich Custard
Gelato (page 385), strained
and still hot

1 cup amarena (see box),
drained and minced

The venerable and fashionable Zanarini Caffé in Bologna has always been the place to see and be seen. Sitting down at a table on a sunny afternoon and slowly savoring a rich, creamy gelato while taking in the beautifully dressed people who stroll by restores one's faith in la dolce vita. Zanarini's gelati, which come in a kaleidoscope of flavors and colors, are made on the premises and are not to be missed. I had one of my first gelati at Zanarini. My sister, brother, and I, all dressed up in our best Sunday outfits, sat at one of the tables with our parents. When the waiter put in front of me a huge dish of gelato, I wondered how I could possibly finish it all. This is one of Zanarini's gelati, which combines egg custard, chocolate, and preserved cherries in a voluptuous, creamy gelato.

ADD the cocoa powder and chocolate to the hot custard and stir until the chocolate is thoroughly melted and the mixture is smooth. (If the custard is not warm enough to melt the chocolate, place the bowl over a pan of slowly simmering water and stir until the chocolate is melted.)

SET the bowl over a larger bowl of ice and cool completely. Cover the bowl and chill in the refrigerator until cold.

FREEZE the mixture in an ice cream freezer according to the manufacturer's instructions. Put the gelato in a chilled bowl and fold in the cherries. Serve immediately, or transfer to a tightly sealed container and freeze for a day or two.

STRAWBERRY GELATO

Gelato di Fragola

MAKES ABOUT 3½ CUPS

1 pound ripe strawberries,
rinsed, hulled, and halved

¾ cup granulated sugar

2 tablespoons fresh
lemon juice

1 cup whole milk

⅓ cup cold heavy cream

PUT the strawberries, sugar, and lemon juice in a food processor fitted with the metal blade and process until smooth. Add the milk and cream and process until well combined. Transfer the mixture to a bowl and refrigerate until cold.

FREEZE the mixture in an ice cream freezer according to the manufacturer's instructions. Serve immediately, or transfer to a tightly sealed container and freeze for a day or two.

MIXED BERRY GELATO Substitute 3 cups of mixed fresh berries of your choice for the strawberries.

AMARENA

Amarena, or amarene, are Italian cherries preserved in heavy syrup that come from Vignola, a small town between Bologna and Modena. When they are fresh, the cherries are dark red, plump, and absolutely delicious. I remember summer excursions with friends to Vignola, riding on the back of speeding motor scooters, anticipating the joy of eating cherries. We would climb fences, pick cherries, and eat them while sitting under the great cherry-laden trees until someone found us and chased us away.

Amarena in heavy syrup are very popular in Italy and are often incorporated into desserts or ice cream. Fabbri, the most famous brand of imported amarene, can be found here in specialty food markets and Italian food stores.

ALMOND-ZABAGLIONE GELATO

Gelato di Mandorle e Zabaglione

MAKES ABOUT 1 QUART

1½ cups (about 6½ ounces) blanched whole almonds

3 cups whole milk

For the zabaglione

8 large egg yolks

½ cup granulated sugar

½ cup amaretto

PREHEAT the oven to 350°F.

SPREAD the almonds on a baking sheet and toast them in the oven for a couple of minutes. Place the almonds in a food processor fitted with the metal blade and chop them very fine, but do not pulverize them.

PUT the almonds in a medium saucepan, add the milk, and bring to just under a boil over medium heat, stirring a few times. Remove from the heat and let cool completely.

PLACE a large sieve over a bowl and strain the milk, pressing on the almonds with a wooden spoon to release as much liquid as possible. Discard the solids, cover the bowl tightly, and refrigerate for about 1 hour.

TO prepare the zabaglione, in a large stainless steel bowl, beat the egg yolks and sugar together with a hand-held electric mixer or a large wire whisk until thick and pale yellow.

LEAVE the mixture in the bowl or transfer to the top part of a double boiler and set over a few inches of simmering water (do not let the water simmer briskly or it will curdle the eggs). Slowly add the amaretto, beating energetically with a large wire whisk. Cook, whisking constantly, until the mixture has doubled in volume and is soft and hot to the touch, 5 to 6 minutes.

PLACE the bowl over a larger bowl half-filled with ice and whisk until cool. Cover tightly and chill in the refrigerator for about 1 hour.

GRADUALLY add the almond milk to the zabaglione, whisking until well incorporated. Freeze the mixture in an ice cream freezer according to the manufacturer's instructions. Serve immediately, or transfer to a tightly sealed container and freeze for a day or two.

THE WINES OF
EMILIA-ROMAGNA

No book on the cuisine of Emilia-Romagna would be complete
without at least a brief mention of its wines. Just as the food of
Emilia-Romagna has unique characteristics, so do its wines.

The typical wines of Emilia-Romagna are perhaps less well known to American readers than the Super Tuscans or the big Barolos of Piemonte. But the
wines of the region are so well in harmony with the cuisine that they shouldn't
be overlooked.

Emilia-Romagna can be divided roughly into four distinct wine areas: the hills to the south and west of Piacenza and Parma, where Barbera and Bonarda predominate, no doubt influenced by the neighboring region of Lombardia; the land of Lambrusco, the provinces of Reggio nell'Emilia and Modena; the hills to the south and west of Bologna; and the vast wine-producing area of Romagna, where Sangiovese di Romagna is king and Albana di Romagna is queen.

It is a truism that wine preferences are as regional as cuisine. In many Italian restaurants and trattorie, the local wines, *vino della zona*, are often the only ones served. Emilians are quite proud of the slightly sweet, and often bubbly, effervescent wines that go so well with the rich cuisine. In Romagna, still white and red wines dominate the scene. I give a few broad suggestions for enjoying the wines of Emilia-Romagna, recognizing that the wines may not be as readily available in the United States as other Italian wines. These wines are beginning to receive their due recognition, and are ideal partners for the food of Emilia-Romagna. The list of wines and wine producers that follows is meant only to serve as a starting point.

White Wines

Albana di Romagna comes in four types: dry (*secco*); semi-sweet (*amabile*); sweet (*dolce*); and *passito*, made from semi-dried grapes. This is the only wine with Denominazione di Origine Controllata e Garantita (DOCG) status in Emilia-Romagna. The dry variety goes particularly well with vegetable risottos or pastas with fresh vegetables. In Romagna, this wine is often served with *passatelli in brodo*, the traditional soup of meat broth and Parmigiano–bread crumb strands and, of course, with many fish dishes. Some prefer to serve the *amabile* version during meals. The sweet and *passito* versions are clearly dessert wines. Serving *ciambella*, the traditional cake of the region, with Albana di Romagna Passito, is a favorite among Romagnoli.

Trebbiano di Romagna is the everyday white of the region, a light, dry, unobtrusive wine with hints of flowers and fruit. It also comes in a sparkling, or *frizzante*, variety, and it may be served instead of Albana di Romagna.

Pignoletto is made from the grapes of the same name, particularly in hilly vineyards surrounding Bologna, Colli Bolognesi. It may be *amabile, secco*, or *frizzante*. It is a pleasant wine with hints of fruit and crisp acidity, and it is often served with sliced cured meats (*affettati*) or with boiled and poached fish with delicate sauces.

Ortrugo, made from the Ortrugo grape, is most typical of the Colli Piacentini. It may be still (*tranquillo*) or *frizzante.* It is a delicate wine, and the still variety is well suited to light antipasti, egg dishes, and fresh cheeses.

Chardonnay, Sauvignon, and Pinot Bianco, varieties well known to readers in the United States, are prevalent in the Colli Bolognesi. The wines are fruity and have good varietal character, with little or no oak aging.

Red Wines

Sangiovese di Romagna, the banner red wine of the region, is produced in regular, "Superior," and "Reserve" versions. It is a hearty red that goes well with most pasta and meat dishes of the region. Some producers are now blending Sangiovese di Romagna with Cabernet Sauvignon with outstanding results. Sangiovese is the most popular and versatile dry red wine in Emilia-Romagna.

Gutturnio, a blend of Barbera and Bonarda from the Colli Piacentini, is made as both a still wine and *frizzante.* It is smooth and generally best drunk when young.

Barbera, a hearty, tasty red wine best exemplified in the Colli Bolognesi, is often blended with other red wines. Barbera goes well with hearty pasta dishes and most meats.

Lambrusco is the popular sparkling wine of the region. There are four DOC appellations: Lambrusco di Sorbara, Lambrusco Grasparossa di Castelvetro, Lambrusco Reggiano, and Lambrusco di Santa Croce. All are dry, *frizzante,* and nicely scented with violets, and are suitable for many of the typical dishes of Emilia cuisine, especially hearty grilled dishes.

Cabernet Sauvignon and Merlot are especially popular in the Colli Bolognesi. As with Chardonnay and Sauvignon, these Italian wines have good varietal character with little or no oak aging.

Dessert/Sweet Wines

Albana di Romagna—the *dolce* and *passito* versions are outstanding.

Cagnina di Romagna, a softly sweet red wine made from Cagnina grapes, a relative of the Refosco grapes found in Friuli.

Malvasia *Frizzante* and *dolce* versions are found in the Colli di Parma.

Some Wine Producers from Emilia-Romagna

Francesco Bellei

Cantine Romagnole

Castelluccio

Cavacchioli

Umberto Cesari

Fattoria Paradiso

Fattoria Zerbina

La Stoppa

Romagnoli

Vallona

Vini Pregiati Celli

WHERE TO EAT IN EMILIA-ROMAGNA

The following is a list of suggested restaurants, trattorie, and *osterie* (wine bars that serve food) scattered throughout Emilia-Romagna. Some are elegant, expensive establishments that provide great food and service. Others are simpler, casual places that serve the traditional, homey food of the area. This selection includes my personal favorites and does not represent a complete regional coverage.

Piacenza

Antica Osteria del Teatro
Via Verdi 16
0523-323-777

Near Piacenza

La Fiaschetteria
Besenzone (PC)
0523-830-444

Faccini
Locauda San Antonio 10
Castell'Arquato(PC)
0523-896-340

Parma

Ristorante Parizzi
Via Repubblica 71
0521-285-952

Ristorante Cocchi
Via Gramsci 16a
0521-981-990

Angiol d'Or
Vicolo Scutellari 1
0521-282-632

Antica Cereria
Borgo R. Tanzi 5
0521-207-387

Near Parma

Ristorante Villa Maria Luigia
Via D. Galaverna 28
Collecchio (PR)
0521-805-489

Da Ivan
Via Villa 73
Fontanelle (PR)
0521-820-113

Antica Osteria Ardegna
Via Maestra 6
Diodolo di Soragna (PR)
0524-599-337

Trattoria Le Roncole
Via della Processione 179
Busseto (PR)
0524-930-015

Modena

Osteria Giusti
Vicolo Squallore 46
059-222-533

Osteria la Francescana
Via Stella 22
059-210-118

Ristorante Fini
Piazzetta San Francesco
059-223-314

Near Modena

Lancellotti
Via A. Grandi 120
Soliera (MO)
059-567-406

Osteria di Rubbiara
Via Risaia 2
Nonantola (MO)
059-549-019

Villa Gaidello Club
Via Gaidello 18
Castelfranco Emilia (MO)
059-926-806

Antica Trattoria Moretto
Via Frignanese 237
Vignola (MO)
059-772-785

Ferrara

**Trattoria il Testamento
del Porco**
Via O. Putinati 24
0532-760-460

Quel Fantastico Giovedi
Via Castelnuovo 9
0532-760-570

Ai Tri Scalin
Via Darsena 50
0532-207-544

Bologna

Ristorante Rodrigo
Via della Zecca 2
051-220-445

Ristorante Diana
Via Indipendenza 24
051-228-162

Da Sandro al Navile
Via Sostegno 15
051-634-3100

**Antica Trattoria del
Cacciatore**
Via Caduti di Casteldebole
25
051-564-203

Bitone
Via Emilia Levante 111
051-546-110

Trattoria Gianni
Via Clavature 18
051-229-434

**Antica Trattoria del
Pontelungo**
Via Emilia-Ponente 307
051-382-996

Trattoria Gigina
Via Stendhal 1
051-322-132

Ristorante Cesari
Via de Carbonesi 8
051-237-710

Al Pappagallo
Piazza Mercanzia 3
051-232-807

Franco Rossi
Via Goito 3
051-238-818

Battibecco
Via Battibecco 4/D
051-263-579

Near Bologna

Buriani
Pieve di Cento (BO)
051-975-177

Dolce e Salato
Piazza L. Calori
San Pietro in Casale (BO)
051-811-111

Da Amerigo
Via Marconi 16
Savigno (BO)
051-670-8326

Imola

San Domenico
Via Sacchi 1
0542-29-000

Osteria del Vicolo Nuovo
Via Codronchi 6
0542-32-552

Ravenna

**Saporetti, Trattoria al
Pescatore**
Via N. Zen 13
Marina di Ravenna
0544-530-298

Capannetti
Vicolo Capannetti 21
0544-66-681

Near Ravenna

Gigiolé
Piazza Carducci 5
Brisighella (RA)
0546-81-209

Near Forli

Ristorante la Frasca
Via Matteotti 34
Castrocaro Terme (FO)
0543-767-471

Paola Teverini
Piazza Dante 2
Bagno di Romagna (FO)
0543-911-260

Cesenatico

La Buca
Corso Garibaldi 41
0547-82-474

Ristorante da Pippo
Via G. Bruno 7
0547-80-378

Gambero Rosso
Molo di Levante
0547-81-260

Rimini

Trattoria 4 Colonne
Via Ortigara 65
0541-51-252

Osteria de Borg
Via Forzieri 12
0541-56-074

Lo Squero
Lungomare Tintori
0541-27-676

Riccione

Azzurra
Piazzale Azzarita 2
0541-648-604

Osteria di Carloni
Via Lodi 13
0541-649-802

INDEX

bread:
  dipping of, 255
  enriching of soup with, 92
  and lentil soup, 86–87
  soup, 89
bread crumbs, dried, 203
breaded lamb chops, 263
bread gnocchi, with bean and
    mushroom sauce, 201–3
breads, savory, 55–68
  Bolognese, 57–58
  flatbread of the "bread sisters" of
    Bologna, 61
  fried flatbread fritters, 59–60
  griddle bread turnovers, 67–68
  "little muffins" with pesto, 62–63
  Romagna's flat griddle bread, 64–65
broiled mussels, 46
broths, 70–71
  anolini in, 77–78
  capon, *see* capon broth
  fish, 178
  freezing of, 73, 299
  meat, 71
  vegetable, 169
  vegetable, light, 217
  see also soups
Brussels sprouts, gratinéed, with
    pancetta, 303
butter, 11–12
  anolini with sage and, 78
  gnocchi with asparagus tips, ham
    and, 195
  risotto with prosciutto, Parmigiano
    and, 167
  Swiss chard with Parmigiano and,
    332

cabbage:
  and rice soup, 90
  risotto with, 173–74
  risotto with sausage and, 174
  sweet-and-sour braised, cotechino
    sausage with, 291–92
Cabernet Sauvignon, 391
cacciatora, see hunter-style
Cagnina di Romagna, 392
cakes:
  almond, 350
  almond-chocolate, 351–52
  apple, 349
  Christmas jam, 356
  crisp potato, 320
  rice, 353
calamari, *see* squid
calf's liver, breaded, 300
cannelloni, 99
  with meat stuffing, 118–20
  topped with Bolognese ragù, 120

capers, sautéed halibut with olives,
    tomatoes and, 214
capon, roasted, 244
capon broth, 72–73
  tortellini in, 74–75
catfish, braised, with polenta, 230
celery, Parmigiano, and toasted
    walnut salad, 337
Chardonnay, 391
cherries, preserved, chocolate gelato
    with, 386
chestnut:
  flour tagliatelle with pancetta and
    sage, 130–31
  fritters, Nonna's, 371
  -ricotta fritters, 370
chicken:
  with dried mushrooms and
    tomatoes, 249
  hunter-style, 245–46
  pan-roasted, with potatoes and
    rosemary, 247–48
chickpea(s):
  cooking of extra, 92
  soup with rosemary, 91
chile pepper:
  clams with garlic and, 236
  clams with tomatoes, garlic and,
    236
  risotto with clams and, 182–83
chocolate:
  -almond cake, 351–52
  gelato with preserved cherries, 386
Christmas jam cake, 356
ciambella, see pastry ring
clams:
  cleaning of, 160
  with garlic and chile pepper, 236
  risotto with chile pepper and,
    182–83
  risotto with tomatoes and, 180–81
  sauce, white, spaghettini with, 159
  spaghettini with tomatoes and, 160
  with tomatoes, garlic, and chile
    pepper, 236
cooked vegetable salad with
    prosciutto, 339–40
cornmeal cookies, 376–77
cotechino sausage, 13
  with sweet-and-sour braised
    cabbage, 291–92
cream:
  pappardelle with sausage,
    mushrooms and, 138–39
  rigatoni with sausage, peas,
    tomatoes and, 157
  -tomato sauce, potato gnocchi with,
    191
crisp potato cake, 320
croquettes, potato, 325

culatello, 18
custard cream:
  baked apples with amaretti and, 378
  fried, 372–74
  and ricotta tart, 361–63
cutlets, 280
  turkey, Parma-style, 278
  veal, in tomato sauce, 279–80
  veal, with prosciutto, Parmigiano,
    and Marsala, 277–78

deep-fried porcini mushrooms, 39
deep-frying, tips for, 368
desserts, 347–88
dessert/sweet wines, 392

eel, roasted, marinated, and
    skewered, 231
egg and Parmesan strands,
    soup of, 76
eggplant:
  alla parmigiana, 308–9
  sautéed, with garlic and parsley,
    307
Emilia-Romagna, 1–8
Emma's pastry ring, 358–59

fennel with prosciutto and
    Parmigiano, 304
fillet of sole with white wine, 224
fish:
  broth, 178
  mixed grill of, 220
  pan-roasted, with pancetta and
    potatoes, 222
  soup, 212–13
  see also specific fish
flatbread
  of the "bread sisters" of Bologna, 61
  fritters, fried, 59–60
  Romagna's flat griddle bread, 64–65
flavor foundations, 20
freezing:
  of broth, 73, 299
  of stuffed pasta, 78
fresh herbs, risotto with, 168
fried:
  asparagus, 35
  butternut squash, 305
  custard cream, 372–74
  deep-, porcini mushrooms, 39
  deep-frying, tips for, 368
  flatbread fritters, 59–60
  polenta with pancetta, sage, and
    vinegar, 54
  polenta with prosciutto, porcini,
    and Marsala, 53

AAX 4491